Teaching Shakespeare
into the
Twenty-First Century

Teaching Shakespeare

INTO THE TWENTY-FIRST
CENTURY

Edited by

Ronald E. Salomone
Ohio University–Chillicothe

James E. Davis
Ohio University–Athens

Ohio University Press
Athens

Ohio University Press, Athens, Ohio 45701
© 1997 by Ronald E. Salomone and James E. Davis
Printed in the United States of America
All rights reserved

Ohio University Press books
are printed on acid-free paper

01 00 99 98   5 4 3 2

Library of Congress Cataloging-in-Publication Data

Teaching Shakespeare into the twenty-first century /
  edited by Ronald E. Salomone, James E. Davis
      p.   cm.
    ISBN 0-8214-1203-5 (pbk. : alk. paper)
    1. Shakespeare, William, 1554-1616—Study and
teaching. 2. Drama—Study and teaching. I. Salomone,
Ronald, E., 1945-   . II. Davis, James E., 1934-   .
PR2987.T364   1997
822.3′3—dc21   97-23373
                                        CIP

for
Ann and Hazel

Contents

IV. Beyond Traditional Settings and Approaches

V. Beyond the Text

VI. *Into the Future*

Preface

*A*s each year passes, Shakespeare's popularity grows. More and more books; more and more media versions! And the challenges of teaching Shakespeare increase also. From the tentative and puzzling introduction of a Shakespeare play in middle school (or even elementary), through generating a receptive attitude during Shakespeare's slot on the undergraduate English survey syllabus, teachers and students confront this situation daily in classrooms across the country. School boards and curriculum committees, possibly without even knowing exactly why, encourage a major unit on Shakespeare at the secondary level at the same time that they might compress modern British and American fiction and poetry into a single unit. College English departments, too, design full term courses on Shakespeare's comedies or tragedies while they list a single course in "American Literature since the Civil War."

Why all this emphasis on Shakespeare and teaching Shakespeare's works? For one thing, it is difficult to believe that any other writer better understood human behavior. He not only was a master at portraying evil but showed human beings capable of integrity and grace as well. Of all the world's writers, none has received more attention than Shakespeare. Only the Bible is available in more languages. No other writer has had a larger body of critical works generated about his writings. His plays are performed every day somewhere and in almost all of the world's languages.

Recently, in "A Critical History of *Hamlet*," Susanne L. Wofford observed that "we have determined for Shakespeare a central, shaping and defining role in our culture: in an important sense, it is felt that a person is less fully civilized, less fully instructed in what Western culture values if she or he has not encountered the writings of Shakespeare" (*Hamlet* [Boston: St. Martin's Press, 1994], 182). Throughout the centuries, it seems that people have felt and still feel that Shakespeare speaks with power and relevance.

But if we try to picture in our mind a typical Shakespeare class today, contradictory images appear. Ordinarily, it is at least a 300- or 400-level college course (if not graduate) and devoted to the tragedies, the comedies, or the histories. It is taught by one of the English department's "Shakespeareans." The students, for the most part, are English majors who have already discovered their own special interest in the Bard or are fulfilling major requirements. At this level, the students probably are not experimenting with elective possibilities. They have already struggled with Shakespeare's language, worked through several of the plays, and maybe taken their first steps toward becoming part of the "Shakespeare establishment." Almost certainly, the instructors, dealing with their specialty, try to keep themselves abreast of the endless stream of scholarly interpretations and re-interpretations and delight in bringing these illuminations to their classes. Indeed, the overwhelming majority of publications—countless articles on every conceivable facet of Shakespeareana (more than enough, truthfully, to fill libraries)—target just these uppermost tiers of academic effort.

Unfortunately, the scenario we have just described has precious little to do with most students' encounters with Shakespeare or with the general public's perception of Shakespeare's importance to Western culture.

Consider, instead, the following settings; they are far more common. The students are thirteen or fourteen years old. The teacher holds elementary certification, took a few required English surveys, and for two weeks must introduce the students to *Romeo and Juliet,* their first Shakespeare play. Imagine the disquietude on the part of the teacher and the negativity on the part of the student ("It's in that old English, isn't it?"). Picture that same student two years later, in high school. The play might be *Macbeth* or *King Lear* and the class "college prep," but it will probably have over thirty students. And the teacher, secondary certified with maybe a "concentration in language arts," might have as many as six other classes each day. Or, finally, think of the college freshman in an "Intro to Lit" survey that offers *Othello* along with fifteen short stories, forty-five poems, and another play or two by Miller or Ibsen.

It is for these teachers and these students that we have prepared the present volume. *Teaching Shakespeare into the Twenty-First Century* is a collection of success stories, thirty-two essays written by middle school, high school, and college teachers. In these essays, our teacher-authors record their best attempts at bringing Shakespeare and the student together in the "classroom" of today and tomorrow.

An additional consideration is that the classroom itself is undergoing change at a pace that both frustrates and bewilders the teacher. Interestingly, our collection of essays and the six sections into which they are organized reflect much larger currents evolving in the world of education. In Ohio, for example, the Board of Regents recently distributed an outline that highlights some of these trends in today's schools. The Board recognized noteworthy transitions—from lecture method to inquiry-based learning, from transmission of factual information to discovery of new knowledge, from isolated class to students connected electronically to the outer world, from teacher as transmitter of knowledge to teacher as facilitator and guide, from student as passive recipient of information to student actively engaged in learning, and so on.

The pattern of *Teaching Shakespeare into the Twenty-First Century* parallels these trends. We start off with the traditional arrangement—the text in class. But even here, as we begin with an essay on the basic question of writing assignments, the discussion encourages student involvement, performance teaching, and "that peak of creative educational achievement, the moment when Shakespeare and the class are as one" (Styan). Section 2 focuses exclusively on performance and includes a discussion of the sonnets and work with theater professionals. Section 3 examines some current directions in literary theory. Section 4 initiates the move "beyond traditional settings," while Section 5 carries the reader "beyond the text" (media, film, animation). And, finally, Section 6 contemplates the future, specifically, the impact of the computer.

Our selections, as anyone can see, have not been limited to a single critical approach. On the contrary, we have attempted to gather a generous collection of the latest ideas and suggestions for teachers. The selected essays cover the most contemporary of issues (matters of race and gender), of critical theories (feminist and new-historicist commentary), and of classroom approaches (interdisciplinary, whole language, and team teaching). They explore the value of festivals, workshops, animation, videotapes, and film versions of the plays. The concluding section investigates futuristic trends (email exchanges between American and foreign students, virtual classrooms, laserdiscs, and CD-ROM) and their possible place in the study of Shakespeare.

The goal in teaching Shakespeare should be to teach in a manner that encourages students to return to his work again and again on their own, either through reading, attending performances, or in cyberspace. Toward that aim, we have talked to literally hundreds of teachers who struggle each term with the challenge of bringing Shakespeare alive for their students. Repeatedly we heard of their desire for an up-to-date and accessible work devoted to the teaching of Shakespeare from middle school through the early undergraduate years. And our goal, quite simply, has been to provide them with a useful, "friendly," and forward-looking resource as they teach Shakespeare into the twenty-first century.

Acknowledgments

We wish to express our gratitude to professors Richard Whinery and Jan Schmittauer, Dean Delbert Meyer, and the members of the OU-C Faculty Development Committee for all their support. And we especially wish to thank our research assistant, Brenda Mackin, for her exceptional work. She helped us throughout the entire project, and her contributions were consistently excellent.

I

The Classroom: Language and Writing

CHAPTER I

The Writing Assignment
The Basic Question

J. L. STYAN

Northwestern University
Evanston, Illinois

The first section of this book gathers some of the more traditional approaches to the teaching of Shakespeare in today's classrooms. But even within the traditional we find a distinct freshness. In the first chapter, Styan focuses on the difficulty of generating effective writing assignments; yet throughout his essay, he returns again and again to ideas that have become synonymous with his name, for example, "Performance teaching aims . . . to turn a dead classroom into a seeing and hearing place, a living theater." Specifically, Styan wishes "to ensure that the written exercise on Shakespeare is not arid, does not destroy what is alive, but is an appropriate extension of the creative act of performance," and to that end he offers a simple suggestion for writing assignments that will promote close reading, encourage visualization of performance activities, and call for critical judgments by the students.

Those who teach Shakespeare as performance must naturally feel uneasy about any written paper assigned in the course. In performance teaching, the peak of creative educational achievement—the moment when Shakespeare and the class are as one—arrives when the thinking and analyzing have been done and all the elements of the drama have come together in the synthesis of *performance,* tested on an audience of peers. A written exercise in these circumstances threatens to be an anticlimax, a betrayal of principle, a descent from Everest.

We know that writing can have the virtues that have always been argued for it, those of the individual intelligence taking stock of what it knows, thinks, and feels, under the very special circumstances of solitude and reflection. Our question can hardly be one for an exam, where the formal circumstances must inhibit reflection, if nothing else, and I would not wish to return to some of the horrors of the past, when Shakespeare's grammatical irregularities and philological foibles were set up for learned annotation, or when Dr. A. C. Bradley's treacherous questions of spurious theater were raised: what would Cordelia have done in Desdemona's place? Where was Hamlet at the time of his father's death? What had Iago and Napoleon in common? Speaking for an earlier generation, Ivor Brown said he was "wearied almost to revolt by this examination business of commenting and annotating"— hour after hour he had "examined significances, contrasted characters, explained allusions" until he was "almost beyond the hope of therapy" (*Shakespeare,* 1949).

The challenge is to ensure that the written exercise on Shakespeare is not arid, does not destroy what is alive, but is an appropriate extension of the creative act of performance, whether in classwork or in the theater itself. We must ask, then, what are the purposes of teaching Shakespeare in the first place, and the abiding principle is to know that his drama lies in the *experience* of it, and that any "meaning" can be found only there. It is also crucial to remind oneself that the words on the page are to be seen as signals for actors to pass on, refined and amplified, as new signals to their audience. Performance teaching aims therefore to recognize some of those signals in class and to turn a lifeless classroom into a seeing and hearing place, a living theater. Student participation ranges from the reading of parts with students *seated* in their places, an aural experience at best, to one with the students *standing* in front of the class, the aural experience merging with the visual, and the presence of the audience, however modest, beginning to make its contribution.

It may be that a written exercise can never approach in impact even a simple reading, but if what is written is organized as an assessment of each textual signal and stage moment, of what the spectator can see, hear, and understand, it may share some of the sophistication of the play performed. Granville Barker once advocated that the proper training of drama students should have them work out all the details of performance in rehearsal short of actual performance—something like the torture of Tantalus. The solution, first satisfied through the senses and to a great extent what a beginning student of Shakespeare can manage, is to seek a unity in what the words convey to the eyes and ears.

It is true that in Shakespeare the nose has its appointed tasks. If in *The Merry Wives of Windsor* Master Fenton "smells April and May" and Falstaff in his buck-basket is smothered with "stinking clothes that fretted in their own grease," the spectator's sense of smell has full employment. By proxy the sense of touch is also amply catered for. In *King Lear,* "Be your tears wet?" Lear asks of Cordelia, and as he touches her cheek to find out, so do we all. In *Othello,* "Cold, cold, my girl?" the Moor asks of his dead bride and his caress persuades us that she is. In *The Winter's Tale,* of course, Leontes may not touch Hermione the statue because her paint is still wet, although the audience has a pretty shrewd idea that the touch of her skin will betray her long before Leontes cries, "Oh, she's warm!" As for the sense of taste, Shakespeare supplies a cornucopia: lips come in all suggestive colors and flavors—"cherry lips," "ruby lips," "coral lips," "scarlet lips," "two lips, indifferent red" (for Olivia), "two blushing pilgrims" (for Juliet), most of them ripe and tempting, although Thisbe thinks, disconcertingly, that Pyramus has "lily lips."

It may be admitted, however, that the great bulk of textual signals are visual and aural, and should be less elusive. Nevertheless, an audience is not to *hear words*; rather, it will hear them as signals, as voices and the sounds they make—their tones and inflections, their pace and their song, or the silence they leave. Nor does an audience *see characters*; rather, it sees bodies, what the actors are wearing and what they look like—fat, thin, tall, short, making gestures, pulling faces, standing still, moving apart, all alone or in a group. So the stage creates a mood, builds tension, creates a relationship, fills out a situation, passes into realism or ritual, seduces or attacks its audience, works for a response, tries for a laugh, secures the spectator's participation, stops his breath.

All the time the audience at a performance is excessively busy, piecing together in its imagination the thousand fragments that bombard it from the stage, making guesses and choices and decisions about what will happen next, whether a character means what it says, whether what it does is psychologically probable, whether morally justified. From the make-believe of the stage an audience constructs an edifice of the mind to which there need be virtually no limit. It is to this fictional world of the imagination that performance helps to contribute, and to which by hook or by crook any written assignment to do with the play ought to contribute.

This lengthy preliminary is to justify the simplicity of the basic question behind any written assignment on a Shakespeare play, which, given a specific scene or incident in the play, is:

What does the audience see, hear, and think?

This is the question, or variants of it, which over the years has seemed to bring a maximum reward. It goes immediately to the heart of the matter, requires a reading of the text in close detail, a reconstruction of the theater event possibly in its own medium, as well as something of a value judgment on the action. It covers the writing, the performance, and the reaction. It fits all plays, all scenes, all speeches, of all lengths. It is capable of being answered to any depth and in one page or twenty. Under scrutiny, it grows and grows. It challenges the doctoral candidate as well as the freshman. It is wonderfully simple, yet formidably complicated, and it is likely that the teacher will learn as much from the assignment as the student. It may be feared or revered, loved or hated, but it is likely to be all of these at the same time. And, for the record, it need never be repeated, nor ever abused by plagiarism. The commonest problem with it is not wondering what to write, but what to leave out and when to stop.

It may be possible to show how the question works, first by choosing a single, very well-known line from *Julius Caesar,* and then by chewing on an extended piece of twenty lines from *King Lear.* The single line is from Antony's speech over the body of Caesar:

"Friends, Romans, countrymen, lend me your ears." (3.2.75)

Let us follow the thought-train. What do we *see*? We see immediately that there is more than one actor involved. How many then? More than two, many more, if the oratorical voice is to seem warranted. Could Antony manage with just two, with the audience substituting for the Roman citizenry—commonly done in the good name of audience participation? Hardly: when later the crowd calls for blood ("seek, burn, fire, kill, slay!"), the audience is not in a position to share the passions of the citizens if it is first to perceive how Antony is manipulating them. So the stage calls for more than two: let us settle for four, which happens to be exactly the number named by Shakespeare himself.

An address to four or more people implies a physical relationship, that of a speaker facing but separated from his listeners, standing not sitting, perhaps elevated by a step or a stool. A certain dramatic separation also marks a dramatic relationship between the speaker and his auditors, here a suspicious attitude towards the speaker, as previously signalled by such comments as these:

—Stay ho! and let us hear Mark Antony. (64)
—'Twere best he speak no harm of Brutus here! (70)
—Peace! let us hear what Antony can say. (73)

"Stay ho!" suggests that some are walking away; "'Twere best . . ." is threatening; "Peace!" suggests that some are muttering doubtfully among themselves.

The ears are inseparable from the eyes. What do we *hear*? We recognize the careful widening of reference in "Friends, Romans, countrymen," with each sound stronger and longer and more to the point, and so we are prompted to make a gentle beginning in the analysis of dramatic verse. The line also confirms that Antony is having trouble getting attention: it is heavily stopped and he must increasingly pause and raise his voice so that the second half of the sentence ("lend me your ears") will seem at odds with the mood of the citizens with whom Brutus has just been reasoning. In this way the audience listens to what Antony is saying, while his whole line teaches him *how to speak it*. He says he wants their ears, beseeching them to listen, but also implying that he does not want their hearts, and his office appears to be the simple one of the chief mourner: "I come to bury Caesar, not to praise him." It is, of course, the deceptive beginning of his stratagem to take advantage of Brutus's honest and innocent offer, for we soon learn that he means the opposite of what he says. That part of the question which requires the student to assess what the audience *thinks* also requires him to envision the rest of the scene.

For a slightly longer instance, I have turned the pages of *King Lear* at random. I am drawn to this play because for some years after Lamb's "On the Tragedies of Shakespeare" (1811) it was widely considered to be too big for the stage. The notorious statement is,

> It may seem a paradox, but I cannot help being of the opinion that the plays of Shakespeare are less calculated for performance on a stage than those of almost any other dramatist whatsoever.

He was thinking of Shakespeare's "absolute mastery over the heart and soul of man" set against the actor's "low tricks upon the eye and ear," and he concluded that "The Lear of Shakespeare cannot be acted"—probably having seen at that time only Nahum Tate's distorted version. This line of argument was shared by Hazlitt and confirmed nearly a century later by A. C. Bradley in his influential *Shakespearean Tragedy* (1904), in which he wrote, "The stage is the test of strictly dramatic quality, and *King Lear* is too huge for the stage" (247). I am reminded of a killer question set in 1954 for a senior level exam in the U.K.:

> What we see upon the stage is body and bodily action; what we are conscious of in reading is almost exclusively the mind and its movements. The best plays, then, are better when read than when seen acted. Discuss.

Truly a question that Dr. Bradley might have been pleased to ask fifty years before.

Nevertheless, there are simple answers to such a question. One might be that Shakespeare certainly wrote *King Lear* for performance and his company did in fact perform it.

Indeed, it is difficult to think of another play in which the spectator's eyes and ears are more fully engaged from the first act to the last, all in order that the play should work on the stage, and with such particular, such a physical, text, our exercise could well be used as proof that this play *is more* "calculated for performance on a stage" than any other.

The book opens at the moment in the play—not the most wonderful—when the King and his Knights have returned to Goneril's house from hunting, and Oswald, her steward, having rudely ignored the King a moment before, re-enters to put on his air of "weary negligence" a second time:

> *Lear.* O! you, sir, you, come you hither sir. Who am I, sir?
> *Oswald.* My Lady's father.
> *Lear.* "My Lady's father!" my Lord's knave: you whoreson dog! you slave! you cur!
> *Oswald.* I am none of these, my Lord; I beseech your pardon.
> *Lear.* Do you Bandy looks with me, you rascal? [*Striking him.*]
> *Oswald.* I'll not be strucken, my Lord.
> *Kent.* Nor tripp'd neither, you base foot-ball player. [*Tripping up his heels.*]
> *Lear.* Thank thee, fellow; thou serv'st me, and I'll love thee.
> *Kent.* Come, sir, arise, away! I'll teach you differences: away, away! If you will measure your lubber's length again, tarry; but away! Go to; have you wisdom? [*Exit Oswald.*] So.
> *Lear.* Now, my friendly knave, I thank thee: there's earnest of thy service. [*Gives Kent money. Enter fool.*]
> *Fool.* Let me hire him too: here's my coxcomb. [*Offers Kent his cap.*]

> (1.4.82–100. From the Arden edn., ed. Kenneth Muir, 1952.)

Directors have every incentive to make this scene of the return from the hunt into something spectacular and have done so, but this kind of production is not our business here. In fact the scene is written to make one or two quite simple dramatic points: first to tell the story and demonstrate the new relationship between Goneril and the King, and then, more importantly perhaps, to contrast the ways of two servants and establish the ironic image of three "fools."

First, Lear's overweening self-importance, unchanged from the earlier scene in which he divided his kingdom, has in the eyes of the audience already been undermined. The same offstage hunting horns that alerted the audience to his arrival and entrance also forewarned Goneril, and in 1.3 she prepared the scene by instructing Oswald to say that she was sick and to put on "what weary negligence you please." The stage is therefore alive with the possibilities of what is to come when father clashes with daughter. However, set against this portentous prospect is a balancing direct address in verse from Kent, who in conspiracy with the house announces his disguise as a servant and with some wit gives the audience some confidence that all is not yet lost. In this way, the scene of the brawling knights will be seen in a doubly ironic light.

Our extract focuses on Oswald's second entrance in the scene. His first ("You, you, sirrah, where's my daughter?" — "So please you" and exit) had theatrically pointed up the servant's insult to the King by his quick and haughty departure, and its appalling lese-majesty. His now anticipated re-entrance carries an immediate reaction from everyone on the stage. It is likely that the on-stage audience of Knights sees him as a fop: at 2.2.55 Kent offers him the scornful aspersion, "A tailor made thee," and although this is a proverbial slur it seems likely that Oswald was dressed like a tailor's dummy with a voice to match, set in complete contrast with the rugged, muddy horsemen around him. Now he indeed has an on-stage audience that makes him look like an ostentatious dandy.

However, the Knights have a vital role: they represent the living symbol of the King's "authority," of which Kent had been speaking a moment before. To the question, "Who am I, sir?" Oswald's impertinent response, "My Lady's father," therefore, will receive from the Knights a gasp of amazement that seems to echo the audience's own sense of outrage.

This is the appropriate moment to take a closer look at the business Shakespeare has called for to mark the insult to the King and the manner in which it is repaid. None of the stage directions in the Arden text, except for *"Enter Steward"* and *"Enter Fool,"* are in the Folio, whose text is probably nearer to that used in Shakespeare's Globe Theatre, and it might be illuminating to the class if this bit of text were reprinted without the stage directions in order to give students a sense of the way the lines accurately depict the business Shakespeare intended. Or if in their writing they were invited to indicate the evidence for which subsequent editors decided on their own stage directions, they might agree with something like the following:

— Oswald's "I'll not be strucken, my Lord" (90) prompted Nicholas Rowe first to insert *"Striking him"* in 1709.
— Kent's "Nor tripp'd neither" (91) next urged him to add *"Tripping up his heels."*
— Kent's "Go to; have you wisdom?" (97) prompted Lewis Theobald to insert *"Exit Oswald"* in 1733.
— Lear's "there's earnest of thy service" (99) was the occasion for Edward Capell's *"Gives Kent money"* in his edition of 1768.
— The Fool's "here's my coxcomb" (100) suggested *"Offers Kent his cap"* to Rowe again.

Yet none of these editorial stage directions, which have been repeated in almost every edition of the play since the eighteenth century, is in itself adequate to describe what the actor does, to convey the attitude of the character, or to suggest the dramatic intention behind the business. Further discussion might arrive at more subtle conclusions:

— Long before the King strikes Oswald, he is told to *"enter"* so that everyone may see and watch him and the King well before Lear explodes in his rush of angry words. Using a different lineation and punctuation, the Folio here has, "Oh you Sir, you, come you hither Sir?," but even reading the Arden line aloud with its grammatically correct punctuation will reveal the rising emphasis of the three "you"s and the three "sir"s, vocally building up to the blow. The Knights may laugh, but, dangerously nevertheless, the King has shown himself as human and vulnerable.

— With a quick reaction Kent makes his contribution to the scene when he trips Oswald up, and the audience on and off the stage is shown the loyal and the disloyal servants as a pair. But Shakespeare has Kent *say* that he is tripping the man up because Oswald is also being instructed to turn his back a second time and walk away, this insulting movement and gesture being more important, indeed more essential, than the fact that he falls flat on his face.

— Kent's "Go to; have you wisdom?," spoken as Oswald struggles to his feet amid the roar of approval from the Knights, certainly encourages his "*exit,*" but it also suggests his hesitation and their threat of further violence. Perhaps Kent has also given Oswald an extra push to see him on his way, but it also shows Kent joining Lear in demeaning himself, while Goneril, the primary cause, remains untouched.

— The King certainly gives Kent a purse of money, but it is as if he had bought his loyalty, and once again we see the aggrieved father become the comfortable, self-satisfied man of the opening court scene in which he divided his kingdom with such assurance. However, this time the tyrant seems weaker, humiliated, disarmed, hollow. He wears the face of another man, one whose story has not ended, but is just beginning.

— The Fool makes his incongruous first entrance (his presence in the court scene would have been a distraction), and he enters dancing and dressed in his irreverent motley at precisely the moment of the King's maximum susceptibility. The flippancy of his words, the antic manner of his movement and the impertinence of his gesture aptly provide a satirical comment on what has passed. The editors have all jumped to the conclusion that his line "Let me hire him too: here's my coxcomb" implies that he offers his cap to Kent (which also requires them to alter the Folio text from Lear's "Why my boy?" to Kent's "Why, Fool" at line 103). However, an outrageous ambiguity is just what the incident calls for. The fool's coxcomb belongs to the Fool, is refused by Kent, but could as well be worn by the King: three great fools together.

The Knights may laugh and roar their misplaced approval, but the audience does not laugh. It sees the impropriety of the King's blow to a servant: Lear has been dishonored and now he dishonors himself. It sees Kent's ill-considered follow-up, and it does not laugh with the Knights. It knows that Oswald represents Goneril's wishes and that his pettiness stands for something much more insidious. Although she is unseen at this moment, her evil presence is all about. The Fool's impudent entrance with his coxcomb makes a visual comment and offers a fool's wisdom, a prophetic image of folly to remain in the mind until the storm breaks on the heath. The audience has already found a sympathy with the King it did not have before, but, because of the Fool, one that is guarded. Shakespeare has achieved his customary balance in the scene's tragic vision and our indeterminate response.

This incident, like a hundred others in the play, is one that the sedentary student can to some extent bring to life by writing about it, and the "See—Hear—Think" equation may be as near as an instructor can get to encourage the student to direct the scene in his head without actors and without an audience. In this kind of written exercise, length does not determine the achievement, but perception does. The short extract from a key scene is only a sample of the rest, of course, but it should prove that the student could read the rest of the play with equally close attention to what matters in the theater and the real values of the play. More importantly, after a few assignments like this, the class will be confirmed in the habit of reading a Shakespeare who is more lively, stimulating, and profound, the joy we know him to be.

CHAPTER 2

Paraphrasing Shakespeare

WILLIAM T. LISTON

Ball State University
Muncie, Indiana

According to Liston, the difficulties in understanding and enjoying Shakespeare derive not just from major changes in language since the 1600s, but also from the fact that contemporary students are not very skilled at close reading nor very familiar with grammatical constructions once learned in foreign language classes. His recommendation is a daily paraphrase, a practice he has been following for several years and one that offers a range of pedagogical benefits.

Traditionally, Shakespeare's language has been thought of as a barrier to the understanding and enjoyment of his plays. And of course it is, but it's not an insurmountable barrier, as anyone who has ever seen Shakespeare performed by a good company knows. Good actors and directors know what the words mean and how to deliver them.

And the fault is not Shakespeare's that the language has changed since his day. But it has not changed nearly so much as students new to Shakespeare think. What has changed, I think, is that contemporary students, though they are sensitive to contemporary styles of talking (I'm like, . . . ," "I didn't miss *that* many classes") are frequently not skilled in reading carefully, nor in hearing voices from the printed page. Nor are they familiar with many grammatical constructions that students of an earlier age would know through the study of a foreign language.

In my classes I have resorted to two different techniques, or exercises, to enable students to master the language, and thereby enable them to understand and enjoy the plays, and to enjoy themselves.

My goal in teaching Shakespeare (or anything else, for that matter) is not to cover certain plays, or even to cover a certain number of plays, though I am certainly disheartened every term by what I do not cover. My goal above all is to enable the students to read and understand any of the plays, at least at the level of what the characters are saying, on their own. Matters of historical fact and of Elizabethan customs are something else, and can be learned from introductions and notes, and, of course, from class discussions.

One of these techniques is to have small groups of students—four or five—dramatize somewhere between a dozen and a hundred lines to bring out some important element in the play: for instance, the revelation of character and of self-knowledge in the last forty lines or so of the opening scene of *King Lear,* as and after Cordelia says farewell to her sisters. Having two different groups dramatize the same segment brings out differing interpretations and forces thought about how to make sense of the lines. This very effective practice I owe to an NEH workshop on Shakespeare in Performance at the Folger Institute in the summer of 1981, directed by Homer Swander and Audrey Stanley.

The exercise that I want to concentrate on here, though, is the daily paraphrase. At the beginning of each class period, I distribute a passage of about five to ten lines from the play under study, and give the students five to ten minutes to complete the passage—whatever is necessary. I have been following this practice for several years now, with, on the whole, good results. Among the values of this procedure is the fact that I can never really anticipate the difficulties students will have. I try to pick passages that are reasonable to do in the time, that use constructions common in Shakespeare, and that are important to the plot of the play. I never deliberately use a passage that is tricky or misleading.

For instance, here is a passage that everyone will recognize, as I present it to the students, with the lines to be paraphrased triple-spaced so that they can write interlinearly.

Shakespeare   Name _____

W T Liston   Mac. 1.5.16

Please paraphrase rather slavishly the following lines; that is, re-write the lines in your own words, but from the same point of view as the speaker. Lady Macbeth speaks:

                    Yet do I fear thy nature,

        It is too full o' th' milk of human kindness

        To catch to nearest way. Thou wouldst be great,

        Art not without ambition, but without

        The illness should attend it. What thou wouldst

        highly,

        That wouldst thou holily; wouldst not play false,

        And yet wouldst wrongly win.[1]

From the headnote, I realize that this paraphrase is one that I have used in the first couple of days of a course. What I discovered very quickly, when I first tried this sort of exercise, is that many students do not know what a paraphrase is. Even with explicit instructions, many students will summarize the passage ("Lady Macbeth is telling Macbeth that . . . "). Just after the paraphrase exercise on a given day, I have a couple of students read good paraphrases from the preceding class, and I comment on particularly difficult passages or constructions. Only after several days of this sort of modeling and of practice does everyone understand just what a paraphrase is, and what it is intended to do. All this is time-consuming, of course, but it is time well spent.

Though we are all familiar with this very important passage and we all know what it means, it is nevertheless a fairly difficult passage to paraphrase, to my surprise.

It is unlikely that anyone relatively new to the study of Shakespeare will know that *human kindness* is better understood as (and might be better spelled as) *humankind-ness*. The point—that Lady Macbeth thinks Macbeth too human, or too humane—is important, but it is the sort of thing that can be cleared up in a minute. Much more difficult, and a much greater justification for doing this paraphrase, is what I have discovered about the verbs, and that problem is more difficult to treat.

The last five lines of the passage turn on contrasts, signified by *wouldst* and, once, *should*. What I have found repeatedly is that students do not perceive the rather obvious contrasts, and do not understand the optative (or the subjunctive). Generally speaking, in this and most other passages involving an optative or a subjunctive, the students convert the verbs to indicatives.

The same problem reveals itself in Hamlet's address to the Ghost (1.4.39). I omit the heading for this and all subsequent examples.

"Look, my lord, it comes," says Horatio as the Ghost enters. Please paraphrase rather slavishly Hamlet's address to the Ghost.

> Angels and ministers of grace defend us!
> Be thou a spirit of health or goblin damn'd
> Bring with thee airs from heaven, or blasts from hell,
> Be thy intents wicked, or charitable,
> Thou com'st in such a questionable shape
> That I will speak to thee.

Again we have a series of contrasts, and again we are in the subjunctive. Invariably, a great many students convert much of the passage to the indicative: *are defending us, You bring, You are, Your intents are.*[2] In doing so they miss the point, Hamlet's uncertainty. Obviously worthy of comment here is Hamlet's use of the familiar *thou* throughout, and the implications of that usage.

And, speaking of pronouns, another problem that paraphrasing can isolate for clarification is the use of pronouns with respect to their referents. For an example I go to *Macbeth* again, the scene (2.1.23 ff.) in which Banquo's wariness in committing himself to Macbeth's counsel confirms Macbeth's fear that Banquo may not be his ally. Because of the heavy reliance of both Macbeth and Banquo on pronouns whose references are oblique at best (they know what they are talking about, and both are wary not to be specific), I provide more context than usual in setting up the exercise.

Macbeth and Banquo have just spoken of the witches and of the prophecies the witches have made. Macbeth is now turning to another subject.

> *Macb.* Yet when we can entreat an hour to serve,
> We would spend it in some words upon that business,
> If you would grant the time.
> *Banq.*   At your kind'st leisure.

Please paraphrase rather slavishly the continuation of the conversation, making clear the referents of the pronouns in bold type; that is, make clear what Macbeth and Banquo are talking about. *Hint:* Macbeth is referring to one thing with his *it;* Banquo is referring to something else with his *none* and *it.* Also be sure to make clear what Banquo means in his opening clause—*So I lose none,* etc.

> *Macb.* If you shall cleave to my consent, when 'tis
> **It** shall make honor for you.
> *Banq.*   So I lose **none**
> In seeking to augment **it,** but still keep
> My bosom franchis'd and allegiance clear,
> I shall be counsell'd.

The *So I lose* construction, which poses no problem to an experienced reader of Shakespeare, often gives difficulty to students, as I have found on earlier versions of this exercise in which I neglected to point it out; and it is a construction that occurs repeatedly in Shakespeare.

Another scene in *Hamlet* illustrates other constructions frequently used, and frequently troublesome, in Shakespeare.

Gertrude informs Claudius that Hamlet has just killed "The unseen good old man." Please paraphrase rather slavishly Claudius's comment on the act. Be especially sure to make clear what Claudius means by "It had been **so** with us" (14); **answer'd** (17); and "It will be **laid** to us" (18).

> O heavy deed!
> It had been so with us had we been there.   14
> His liberty is full of threats to all,
> To you yourself, to us, to every one.
> Alas, how shall this bloody deed be answer'd?   17
> It will be laid to us, whose providence   18
> Should have kept short, restrain'd, and out of haunt
> This mad young man.

If I remember correctly, my specific directions at the end of the headnote derive from unsatisfactory performance on a version of the exercise without those instructions. In addition to what I have suggested there, other problems are related to the royal *we.* Not every student will pick that up; and, of course, there is Claudius's alienation from Gertrude implied in his separation of *you yourself* from *us*.

Comedy presents problems equal to those in tragedy. The language is essentially the same, but in fact Shakespearean comedy is often more difficult for students to understand because of the playfulness with language. The problems (and rewards) in reading *Much Ado About Nothing* are typical. The exercise I use for *Ado* 1.1.12 ff. alerts the students to the linguistic problems immediately.

> In the opening scene of *Much Ado About Nothing,* Leonato says that "I find here [probably in a message that has been handed him] that Don Pedro hath bestow'd much honor on a young Florentine call'd Claudio." Please paraphrase the Messenger's comment in answer to this statement. Note that it is in prose. The wordplay in it is typical of *Ado*. Be sure that you understand to whom all the pronouns refer; and you might find it necessary to strip the 'poetry'—the images—out of the passage.
>
>> Much deserv'd on his part, and equally rememb'red by Don
>> Pedro. He hath borne himself beyond the promise of his age,
>> doing in the figure of a lamb the feats of a lion. He hath indeed
>> better bett'red expectation than you must expect of me to tell
>> you how.

Among other things, this exercise demonstrates that the difficulties in reading Shakespeare are not restricted to verse. This prose passage is every bit as imaginative and figurative as poetry. The second sentence concludes with an alliterative contrast imaginatively reporting Claudio's manly deeds despite his boyish appearance. The third plays off parts of speech against each other to make its point: the verb *bett'red* modified by the adverb *better;* the noun *expectation* echoed by the verb *expect*.

I suppose I should provide what I would consider a reasonable paraphrase of the passage. One must hold oneself to the same standards one requires of others.

> Claudio deserved the honor, and Don Pedro bestowed the degree of honor on him that he earned. Claudio has conducted himself beyond what one would expect of so young a person, doing despite his boyish appearance the deeds of a mature soldier. Claudio has indeed exceeded what anyone could have expected of him, by so much in fact that you can't expect me to be able to do him justice in the telling.

Another example from *Much Ado About Nothing* illustrates the value of being alert to parallel sentence structure to understand the meaning of extended clauses. The example is from the gulling of Beatrice (3.1.59 ff.).

> During the gulling of Beatrice, Ursley says that it were best that Beatrice not know of Benedick's love for her, "lest she'll make sport at it." *Hint: Note that the*

parallel sentence structure established in If fair-fac'd *continues after the ellipsis.* Please paraphrase rather slavishly Hero's reply:

> Why, you speak truth. I never yet saw man,
> How wise, how noble, young, how rarely featur'd
> But she would spell him backward. If fair-fac'd,
> She would swear the gentleman should be her sister;
>
> .   .   .   .
>
> If speaking, why a vane blown with all winds;
> If silent, why a block moved with none.

The passage presents several problems beyond the parallel sentence structure. Hero's second sentence (also built on parallel construction) would require in contemporary English something like an added *no matter*; i.e., "I never yet saw any man, no matter how wise," etc. And of course *spell him backward* is likely to give trouble, but I should think that from context a good reader would intuit that it means something like "say just the opposite about him." At the risk of overkill, I would paraphrase the last few clauses thus:

If he were good-looking, she would say that the man looked like a girl; if he talked, she would say that he jabbered about anything that blew into his head; if he were not talkative, she would say that he was just like a block of wood, insensitive to anything in the air around him.

One more example from *Much Ado About Nothing,* demonstrating more of the same, and, like the others, concerned with something at least moderately important in the movement of the plot. And, like the others, it requires an extended setting of context if it is not to be a test (or quiz) on close reading.

As the group assembles for the wedding of Claudio and Hero in the final scene of *Much Ado About Nothing,* Benedick tells Leonato that Beatrice has looked on him with an "eye of favor" and "I do with an eye of love requite her." Leonato replies:

> The sight whereof I think you had from me,
> From Claudio, and the Prince. But what's your will?

Please paraphrase Benedick's answer, being especially clear to distinguish the various senses of *will* that Benedick plays with.

> Your answer, sir, is enigmatical,
> But for my will, my will is your good will
> May stand with ours, this day to be conjoin'd
> In the state of honorable marriage
> In which, good friar, I shall desire your help.

Enigmatical is likely to give trouble, but that problem can be taken care of in discussion (and certainly should have been faced by the reader with a dictionary or a footnote, a worthy lesson in itself).

Though I have concentrated on the value of these exercises in facing the problems of Shakespeare's language for a modern reader, they have several other pedagogical values.

For one thing, they put some pressure on the student to be prepared for class. Though I do not intend them to be reading checks, obviously they reward the prepared student and are likely to penalize the unprepared student. No harm in that.

And they put a premium not only on attending class, but in arriving on time. I distribute the exercise exactly at the beginning of the class period, and after the first one has been handed in, I do not allow latecomers to take the paraphrase.

The grading, on a scale of 1 to 10, and recording do not take much time. At the end of the term, I have a record (which I keep in the computer) of 30-40 exercises, with a possible perfect score of 300+ points. I discard three or four of the lowest scores before totaling the scores. Where *ab* or *lt* appears in the record rather than a numerical score, a student has little leeway to have a 4 or 5 dropped.

With respect to grading, one of the great values, for the students, of the physical evidence of the daily grade on a piece of paper is that they cannot lie to themselves. A person repeatedly getting Cs cannot realistically say "I'm doing OK, probably getting a 'B.'"

In many ways, the greatest pedagogical benefit is to me as teacher. Though in my teaching I repeatedly ask "Any questions? Is there anything you don't understand?" I do not get nearly so many questions as I would like. What these paraphrases alert me to is what the students don't understand that I, with years of familiarity with Shakespeare and his language, take for granted. In the hundred or so of these that I have used, there is hardly a one that has not surprised me with some usage or construction that I thought everyone knew. I suppose that most of us know by now that many people misunderstand what Juliet means when she laments "O Romeo, Romeo, *wherefore* art thou Romeo?" And after all, *wherefore* is an archaic word. But how many would anticipate a problem with Portia's assertion to Shylock that mercy "*becomes* / The throned monarch better than his crown"?

In short, even *wherefore* isn't "Old English." And little else in Shakespeare's language is really inaccessible to a student who is immersed in the language daily.

Notes

1. Citation throughout is to *The Riverside Shakespeare,* ed. G. Blakemore Evans (Boston: Houghton Mifflin, 1974).

2. In "Changing What We Sing," *The State of the Language,* ed. Christopher Ricks and Leonard Michaels (Berkeley: University of California Press, 1990 [315-40]), an article deploring the new hymnal that "emanates from the First Congregational Church, Amherst, Massachusetts," Margaret A. Doody points out that "All imperatives (including those of the 'let us' variety) have been changed into calm statements of fact" (319). Her example is the changing of "O worship the King" to "We worship thee, God."

CHAPTER 3

Role-Playing

Julius Caesar

MARY T. CHRISTEL AND CHRISTINE HECKEL-OLIVER
Adlai E. Stevenson High School
Lincolnshire, Illinois

Christel and Heckel-Oliver base their work in the realm of the traditional and then move beyond it. Through their strategy of role-playing and journal writing, they have designed a series of assignments that encourage students to do research, critical thinking, creative and expository writing, and performance. By linking the journal entries to events in Julius Caesar, *the authors give their students "the opportunity to synthesize the research material and the character dossier with their understanding of the play itself."*

"My name is Marcus Valius."

"My name is Alexander Lepidus."

"I am Darius, head chef for the noble Julius Caesar."

So what then is in a name. What is its power? What are its secrets? What is its history? How can the creation of names and voices and histories enhance the teaching of literature? Of Shakespeare's *Julius Caesar*?

This year we used role-playing and journal writing for prereading activities as well as carrying them through the analysis of *Julius Caesar*. We have used this strategy in the past to teach Dickens's *A Tale of Two Cities* and Erich Maria Remarque's *All Quiet on the Western Front* and found that it enhanced the level of comprehension and engagement a student brings to the text. This assignment requires students to employ a variety of skills from research and critical thinking to creative writing and performing or visual arts depending on the choices that a teacher makes in enhancing the basic concept of creating a character.

With *Julius Caesar,* it involved assigning students to investigate the lives and attitudes of people living in Rome at the time the tragedy takes place. Students were not assigned characters from the play; instead they were assigned roles that represent the variety of people living outside the immediate world of the play, but people whose lives would be impacted by the death of Caesar. Roles might have been assigned once students began reading the play; however, a preliminary investigation of the Roman world and their roles set the stage for understanding the historical and cultural context of the tragedy. It also reinforced the material covered earlier in the year in a World History course.

We drew from the following list of possible roles:

Senator #1	the senator's wife #1
Senator #2	the senator's wife #2
spoiled son of a senator	rebellious daughter of the senator
nurse (probably Greek)	tribune
Professor of Rhetoric	teacher (magister)
counsel/lawyer	librarian (librarii)
publisher (bibliopolae)	Stoic preacher
poet	soldier
goldsmith	sailor
Tyrian trader	astrologer
merchant	Arab spice merchant
scribe for the Senate	supervisor of the public baths
augurer for Julius Caesar	tanner
wrestler	physician
village Rustic (farmer?)	provincial from Gaul
waiter (ministratores)	barber
matron	charioteer
chambermaid	slave
dancer	chef
shoemaker	financiers
dressmaker	silk merchant
butcher/wife of the butcher	candlestick maker
widow	mime
street musician	sculptor
falconer	praetor (judge)
gladiator	architect
fishwife (piscatrix)/fishmonger	merchant of marbles (marmorarius)
clothing merchant (sagarius)	carpenter/wife of the carpenter
druggist (apothecary)	high priest/priestess for the Temple of Isis
tire-woman (ornatrix)	hairdresser/make-up artist
tavern-keeper	wife of the tavern-keeper
paedagogus ("slave who served as a tutor, guardian, and the servant of the child")	

This list was developed with help from *Daily Life in Ancient Rome* by Jerome Carcopino. Some roles are patricians, some plebeians, and some emigrants or visiting dignitaries. Students used library research, their vivid imagination, and the text of *Julius Caesar* to create a voice for one of these, to give each an identity, a name, a place in history. As the roles were assigned by the teacher or selected by the students, all students were encouraged to jot down their classmates' names next to the roles. This facilitated working in small groups based on social class and/or occupation and lent the opportunity for some students to create relationships between characters. After all, the senator needs a new toga once in a while and he must also hire musicians for his great banquets. The charioteer must make purchases in the market and the barber was often hired to let blood.

When students were initially turned loose in the library with their characters in mind, the following questions helped them create a dossier for their characters that focused on basic elements of family, education, attitudes, daily routine, and social position:

What is your character's role? What name will you use?

When and where were you born?

What is your social status? Patrician, plebeian, emigrant, visitor, slave?

Describe your parents.

What is or was your father's occupation?

Describe your siblings and your relationship with them.

What kind of education did you have? What is your favorite childhood memory?

What is the most frightening thing that has ever happened to you?

What is your most treasured possession? Explain its values.

If you could change one thing about your life, what would it be? Why would you make the change?

Describe your clothing. Your shoes? headgear? satchel?

At this time in your life, what is a typical day like for you?

List any other pertinent details about your character not covered here.

This information provided the foundation for journals that each student created for an individual character that blended the research with impressions and interpretations of the events that unfold in *Julius Caesar*. At this stage of the project, students kept a bibliography of sources for the preliminary information and answers to the dossier questions. Keeping a bibliography helped students go back to key sources for additional historical information that enhanced the authenticity of the journals.

The most critical aspect of this project as a writing activity was the importance of creating the appropriate voice for the character. Using a series of journal entries tied to the events of the play gave students the opportunity to synthesize the research material and the character dossier with their understanding of the play itself. Some students needed to consider carefully how to produce the voice of a character who is not very well-educated or articulate. Depending on how comfortable a teacher feels about this level of creativity, students who must depict characters of little education or sophistication may need to selectively write in a substandard manner. All characters must write journals, at least two pages in length, responding to the following list of dates and events:

The first entry. Use this first entry to create your character. Flesh out the role, providing family and work details as well as a reaction to the world of Rome in 46 B.C.

The second entry. It is the feast of Lupercalia (and the opening of the play). Write a journal entry describing and reacting to the day's events (Caesar's procession, the tribune's removal of the decorations, the appearance of the soothsayer, Antony's running in the ritual, etc.) What events did your character attend? What did he/she see? What rumors did he/she hear?

The third entry. March 15. The Ides. React to the day's events. Make specific reference to the speeches in the forum. Does your character take a side? Whose? Is he or she fickle?

The fourth entry. Choose a day in the month following the assassination and describe the chaos of Rome.

The fifth entry. You have an encounter with your arch enemy. (This encounter will be with someone in class. You will create a script and deliver the lines in front of the class). In your journal you will describe the enemy, the encounter, the insults, and the outcome. Examine Act IV, Scene 1 for models of insults.

The sixth entry. Years have passed (you decide how many). Provide some sort of closure for your character.

The journals can be submitted on notebook paper as any assignment could, but this creative experience can be further enhanced by requiring students to prepare a journal that physically reflects both the historical period and their characters' occupation and social status. Perhaps a journal is so seditious that it must be hidden. Where would a duplicitous charioteer or a rebellious senator's daughter hide theirs? An illiterate character could prepare his/her journal entries on an audio tape and house that tape in something characteristic of his/her work. Obviously adding this dimension to the assignment allows for the exploration of visual arts to communicate an understanding of the historical period and the character.

This type of character development activity can also lead to various kinds of creative drama or improvisation in the classroom as well. Certainly after reading the speeches in the forum, students can assume their roles and discuss the events. One class proposed a party for April 21, the celebration of the founding of Rome, a detail they discovered in their research. Intrigues and liaisons could be developed providing more fodder for their journal writing. The later scripts between enemies developed in the fifth entry should be shared after Act IV as well. Students can use their roles to create improvisations based on the events depicted in the play. It is suggested that teachers assume a role to be fully integrated into a small group script or a full class improvisation. This strategy allows the teacher to adopt naturally the role of gatekeeper or facilitator for the event depicted.

This assignment would be evaluated at the end of the *Julius Caesar* unit. Teachers who feel uncomfortable evaluating creative responses in place of expository or analytical essays need only keep in mind as they read the journals that the major objective for the project is to read the play closely and carefully in order to apply the events of the play to the development of a character who would have lived through those events. If the entries are richly and specifically composed using details from the research, the dossier, and the play itself, then the students can create a clear and consistent voice for a character in much the same way a student can express his/her opinion on a standard arguable thesis.

The standards by which a student was measured included the following: a clear strong voice; strong connections to the text; credible weaving of historical details from the class research; completion of six journals; mechanics; and appropriate "presentation." The first three were, of course, weighted more heavily. Following are some excerpts from this year's responses:

A clear strong voice. The Priestess from the temple of Isis discovered in her research that the cult in Rome at the time of Caesar was re-emerging in popularity because of Cleopatra. She, like Calpurnia, dreams of Caesar's death and she must decide whether or not to warn the dictator. Her voice and her connections to the text dominated her entries.

> I dreamt of Caesar dying, of people screaming. I dreamt that someone died! I heard the panic and the crowd rushing me away. Again and again I saw the person standing next to me reaching out for my hand as the crowd tore me away. I dreamt I was being dragged by the mob to fall next to Caesar's dead corpse. I saw those hollowed eyes, I smelled the blood stain, and my mouth being pushed into it tasted it too. Suddenly everything spun around, earth, water, fire and air became one and they all smelled, and looked and tasted of blood. The primeval soup was being contaminated.
> "No!"
> I woke up in a cold sweat, and was very relieved to find that the so-called blood was only sweat. The people outside were shouting about something. The fish smell reeked through the window. I vaguely heard the tribunes denounce the mob for their worship of Caesar and call them stones, and then I felt the pain. It was localized behind my eyes in between my temples, and it was horrid! It felt like fireants crawled into my brain and bit. "Isis help me," I whispered and reached over for the wine. After an eternity it seemed, the pain abated to a dull ache. I wasn't sure how long I lay there on the floor, but when I got up I had made up my mind to know everything I could about Caesar, and see whether it would be wise to inform him of his untimely demise. I was certain of it. Caesar would die on the Ides of March and likely I wouldn't warn him or he would not listen. There was little that could be done to prevent his death.

Strong connections to the text. A grain merchant from Alexandria chose a letter for his six entries. He wrote to a business partner about Caesar's death.

> Dear Icculus,
> Such a tragedy as has occurred today is the greatest of all human history. The effects, both immediate and long term, will be felt by all forever in great sadness of what could have been but will never be. As you probably heard before and shall for years to come, today was the Ides of March, the most fateful day mankind has ever seen. Today great Caesar was slain. Today is a day of grieving.
> As I am a lowly grain merchant in the eternal universe of Rome, I know not everything. I do know that his fate was sealed by the likes of his dearest friends.

Brutus, Cassius, Cinna, and others have been implicated. I know not their motives. . . . Possibly to your disfavor, I was forced to close shop and hear out the great men of Rome. Brutus spoke first and gave a short convincing speech of how Caesar had to be stopped before his ambition could destroy Rome. This is the same ambition that has made Rome the greatest and largest Empire in history. At first, many, myself included, were swayed by his entrancing speech. Antony spoke next and showed us the true path. Brutus's reasons were poor and in no way sufficient to demand the death of Caesar. He read us Caesar's will and showed us all that Caesar had done for us and all that he could do if he could have had the opportunity to continue his rule. He was clear and straight forward in expressing his sincere love and respect for Caesar . . . .

Credible weaving of historical details from the class research. The chef included a review of the delicacies he served to Caesar at a recent banquet:

The appetizers were boiled tree fungi with peppered fish-fat sauce and jellyfish with eggs. The main course included boiled ostrich with sweet sauce, roast parrot, dormice stuffed with pork and pine kernels, and flamingo boiled with dates. Some of the dessert items were fricassee of roses with pastry and stoned dates stuffed with nuts and pine kernels, fried in honey.

Presentation. Most of the journals arrived singed or stained with tea or coffee to achieve the element of aging. One student had accidentally spilled soy sauce on her paper and when she liked the effect, she spilled some more. A few arrived with cover sheets from some professor or archaeologist who had unearthed the journals and translated them. Many arrived in cloth bags that somehow revealed the role. An architect's arrived with some antique measuring instruments and the Tyrian trader's dye covered her box. The supervisor of the public bath enclosed his in a jar of oil. He graciously provided a reading copy of his journals so that the oil-submerged sheets could remain intact. Since he did not explain the word "Mazola," we assumed his writing, like Shakespeare's, contained anachronisms.

The journals were an opportunity for students to play to their strengths and interests as well. The poet worked on a poem entitled "The Ides of March" throughout her entries. She created a strong connection to text as well.

I only dared to venture out in the early afternoon, when the sun's warming rays seemed to calm the city. For a short time, everything was silent. It was then I saw him. He lay in the center of the road, with his arms bent unnaturally. His one leg was missing, and the other was bleeding heavily. As I walked towards the body, I heard myself cry out. Suddenly, I no longer was there. It was as if I was looking down upon myself from the heavens above. There I stood, crying, screaming. Only then I realized that the man my tears were covering was my friend Cinna. A fellow poet like myself, he once longed for the day that success would govern his life. And now he was dead.

Other students created strange liaisons and plots. Affairs and intrigues dominated. The senator's wife sought the arms of the supervisor of the baths; the librarian was imprisoned for his treatment of Caesar's scrolls; the soldier and the sailor wrote to each other celebrating their various feats. All these made great material for the argument.

One result which surprised us was the attention to language. A list of Shakespearean insults had been distributed for use during the scripting of the battle of words with one's enemies. While most students used the list, the abler ones realized that they needed to be specific, they needed to insult the candles made by the candlestick maker or attack the honor of the senator's wife or the heritage of the merchant's family. Thus one insult to a chef was that he was "not fit to cater to the swine which he prepares."

Students even realized that the metaphor they used needed to be appropriate for the character and for the times. "My father's frail voice wavered like a toga on a windy day" wrote Isis and in another section, she said, "I remember very little of my mother, but I clearly remember her standing in front of a roaring fire with a kitchen utensil clenched in her fist like a sword readied to strike upon anything that came in its destructive way." The grain merchant wrote that "Government without Caesar is like the night without the moon, thus not just any new system will work." It was also the grain merchant's philosophy that "Rome, aside from obvious small things, is much like Alexandria. Regardless of location, people are people, and that is what I've learned most from my travels."

So what then is in a name? It can be a strong voice, a history, a linking of words with Shakespeare. Students who are invited to enter the world of the play in such a specific and creative fashion cannot help but experience the tragedy of Caesar with greater interest and enthusiasm. The more students know about the Roman world the better they can understand the play as well as the character they create, which becomes their personal link to the play.

References

Carcopino, Jerome. 1940. *Daily Life in Ancient Rome*. New Haven: Yale University Press.

CHAPTER 4

Writing Down,
Speaking Up,
Acting Out,
and Clowning Around
in the Shakespeare Classroom

JAMES R. ANDREAS
Clemson University
Clemson, South Carolina

The emphasis in Andreas's discussion is on wordplay and vulgarity in the plays, specifically that they do not simply afford "comic relief" but rather articulate "a philosophic purpose and thematic structure." He focuses his comments on Dogberry, Much Ado About Nothing, *and what we call clowning around, and demonstrates how "the scenes they [the clowns and fools] domesticate and equivocate represent the hooks to catch and secure the students' interest, engagement, and even affection."*

Next to Bottom and Falstaff, Dogberry, that hilarious forerunner of the Keystone Cops and Inspector Clouseau, sticks in memory as one of the funniest of Shakespeare's comic heroes. And hero he is in *Much Ado About Nothing* because, as the villain Borachio exclaims when he is "comprehended" by the watch, "What your wisdoms could not discover, these shallow fools have brought to light" (5.1.213–14). Dogberry and his watch "dissolve," as he might say, the treachery of Don John and his henchmen in the play. Dogberry may well be "*writ down* an ass" by the court and the critics, but he nevertheless "*speaks up*" and "brings to light" through the levity of malaprop the treachery that legal systems, at least according to Machiavelli, are probably designed more to foster and conceal than to deter and reveal. The defense of the watch against Machiavellian manipulation by their "betters" may not seem so strange to students, for they too must rely on their naiveté, their faith in their fellow human beings, and, most of all, their verbal gift for malaprop and verbal variation on the norms of the law to adapt and survive in a world where they will often find themselves "writ down an ass"—especially when final grades are assigned.

The vectors represented in my title—writing *down*, speaking *up*, acting *out*, and clowning *around*—have social, ethical, and pedagogical correlatives. The play is "written down" when it is "set in print," but it is vocalized when actors and student performers "speak up," and it is fully dramatized when the gestures implied in the lines are "acted out," that is, as David Bevington has so brilliantly demonstrated, are given body and motion through performance. Education, that leading of students out of and beyond themselves and their cultures, has not been a purely visual matter, a matter simply of "seeing," since Walter Ong and Marshall McLuhan revealed the limitations of the eye back in the sixties. But there is more to the matter than pedagogy. Traditionally, writing as a technology represents the access of the privileged, patronized by the privileged, to information that is privileged. In *Romeo and Juliet, A Midsummer Night's Dream, Much Ado About Nothing,* and almost every other play Shakespeare wrote, there is a running commentary on the condescension, the arrogance, indeed on what Elspeth Stuckey has called "the violence and the tyranny" of *literacy.* By contrast, the plays are rife with examples of "clowning around," the flexibility and adaptability of living speech, which Dante called the "vulgar tongue" from the Latin *vulgus,* meaning of the folk. Although "comparisons are odorous," Dogberry represents those powers of "speaking up" and "clowning around" that work benignly but persistently against the regulative powers of "writing down."

Samuel Taylor Coleridge's utter contempt for the popular, clownish, vulgar element in Shakespeare's plays has for most of this century gone all but unchallenged, particularly in the international school curriculum where most of the world encounters the plays for the first and the only time. In attempting to prove that *Macbeth* is Shakespeare's most successfully *pure* tragedy, unblemished by vulgar dependence on jokes, puns, pranks, and other disruptive elements in the text, Coleridge attributes the base comic scenes in all the plays to oral interpolation by unruly clowns in Shakespeare's acting company. In some notes toward a lecture on *Macbeth* Coleridge writes: "Excepting the disgusting passage of the Porter, which I dare pledge myself to demonstrate an interpolation of the actors, I do not remember in *Macbeth* a single pun or play on words." In defense of Coleridge, he goes on to explain that even Shakespeare's verbal barbarisms and vulgarities could be justified on a higher philosophic plane. Coleridge writes:

> I defer my answer to this thousand times repeated charge against Shakespeare to a more fit opportunity, and merely mention the fact [of *Macbeth's*] freedom from puns as justifying a candid doubt at least whether even in these figures of speech and fanciful modifications of language Shakespeare may not have followed rules and principles that merit and stand the test of philosophic examination (188).

As far as I can tell, Coleridge never undertook such a project, which actually sets the agenda for my paper.

The function of the wordplay and vulgarity in these plays, the "speaking up," "acting out," and "clowning around" of my title, is not simply to afford "comic relief" from the tragic intensity of all the plays that either *begin* in tragic circumstance or *end* in tragic outcome. Rather, farce, pun, malaprop, and prank often articulate a philosophic purpose and thematic structure that pose generic and existential alternatives to the tragic paradigms of judgment, punishment, pain, exile, and death. The obscenity of the Porter and the malaprops of Dogberry more often represent an enduring *belief* in the good faith and sound judgment of the unwashed than they do "relief" from the tragic complications worked up for them by their social betters.

H. L. Mencken once quipped that "Shakespeare made [all] his heroes foreigners and his clowns Englishmen" (147). He did so for good reason. Truth often can be perceived only from the historical, geographic, or cultural margin, from a healthy distance off-center in a given civilization, from the view, in short, of foreigners, but also of clowns and tramps like Bottom, Dogberry, or closer to our own time, Charlie Chaplin. The clowns in Shakespeare's plays are us, as Germaine Greer argued so persuasively at the Tokyo meeting of the International Shakespeare Society in the Summer of 1991. They are the students, the working people, the theater-goers themselves, who wander onstage almost accidentally from time to time to disrupt the dramatic illusion and dis- or re-orient characters engaged onstage in the portrayal of cultures, classes, and eras that simply do not represent or engage their own best interests. They localize and contemporize the fable retold dramatically, giving the airy shapes and concerns of theoretical enterprise a name—often a vulgar, offensive one at that. Such "clowning around" and wordplay represent not so much a diversion from given dramatic contexts as an alternative paradigm for interaction and behavior, a paradigm to be duplicated in the classroom where students "speak up" about the themes of the play, or "act out" their meanings, or better yet, parody and travesty what they don't understand or appreciate about the behavior of their own "superiors." The wordplay of the clowns also does not depend so much on "invented" vocabulary—neologisms or barbarism, for instance—as it does on "reinvented" or reinvigorated terminology. Tired but dangerous legal, political, and religious cliches are cathartically cleansed of the interdiction they have come to represent in malaprops and in "malaproverbs." Shakespeare's servant-clowns represent the group, the collective, the *vulgus* from which we get the pejorative adjective *vulgar,* but also the noun *folk.*

Following Coleridge's admonition about clowning, the Porter's scene is often deleted as gratuitous "comic relief" in the textbooks used in secondary schools. If it is retained, the sexual innuendo is muted. First and foremost, the "knocking" at the door is a preeminently aural moment that echoes throughout the scene. The Porter as a "commoner" introduces equivocation into a play about tragic resolve. Like the African-American trickster figure Esu of Gates's *The Signifying Monkey,* he represents the ambivalence that Macbeth and his queen would characterize as "infirm of purpose" just at the moment when the murder of their king, patron, and guest is upon them (2.2.49). Lady Macbeth believes a "little water clears us of this deed," as she hears the knocking and commends her husband for his "constancy" in attending to the deed of murdering her guest and benefactor (63–65). But even Macbeth equivocates a bit here. He wishes the knocking would undo this horrid murder just as the Porter wobbles onstage. "Wake Duncan with thy knocking! I would thou couldst" (2.2.71–72). The Porter speaks directly to the audience and to students, like all of Shakespeare's talking clowns. He is the doorkeeper and the frame-breaker. This is the pivotal scene that my students appreciate in the "speaking up" and "acting out" not simply because it relieves tragic tension, but because it offers us a human alternative to certain tragic outcomes in the ambivalence of open alternatives, in a value system that has the flexibility to swerve from the tragic path, to discharge tragic stress, to up the odds for survival, and even to guarantee escape from fixed outcomes. The Porter liminalizes this horrific scene, underscores blessed inconsequence and "equivocation," and restores the audience to its sense of everyday norms measured against which the terrors of those in charge seem horridly preposterous—all by clowning around.

The mythological resonance works beautifully in this scene and is introduced by the Porter himself. He knows he is a figure in the Pantheon of border-crossers and tricksters. He compares himself to a "porter of Hell Gate" (2.3.2), and swears by the name of "Belzebub," or "th'other devil's name," which he obviously has forgotten, much like our students do when they drink of the river Lethe. The Porter is, of course, the old devil Vice, the vicar, the leader of the opposition, the fool to Macbeth's Prince and Lady Macbeth's queen, and, like Blake's Milton, "of the devil's party." Throughout the scene he is cussing out his superiors and anybody who would dare to disturb the easy sleep he enjoys that is beyond the reach of the Macbeths.

At this moment of premature peripety, the Porter introduces a riddle with a sexual innuendo that plays off the ominous political prophecy of the witches. Macduff is his straight man, appropriately so as Macduff is also of Macbeth's own "denatured" stripe. The Clown always seeks out and plays his or her gags off the most straitlaced, "linear" thinkers among available superiors. He tells Macduff that "drink, sir, is a great provoker of three things":

> Marry, sir, nose-painting, sleep, and urine. Lechery, sir,
> it provokes, and unprovokes; it provokes the desire, but it
> takes away the performance. Therefore, much drink may be
> said to be an equivocator with lechery: it makes him, and it
> mars him; it sets him on, and it takes him off; it persuades
> him, and disheartens him; makes him stand to, and not stand
> to; in conclusion, equivocates him in a sleep, and, giving
> him the lie, leaves him.
>
> (2.3.28–36)

The Porter reintroduces sexuality in the play after Lady Macbeth has called for her "unsexing." He also introduces the festive ambiance that was supposed to be in effect during Duncan's visit to Macbeth's castle. And finally, his discussion of the effect of alcohol on the libido, that it makes a "man stand to," but "not stand to," and "equivocates him in a sleep," offers comic, erotic contrast with the violent, deadly deed of Macbeth, the king who unfortunately did "stand to"—adamantly—and who, with his queen, will nevermore "equivocate in a sleep." The Porter goes on to admit too that "drink gave him the lie," but that he was "too strong for him [drink]" and "made a shift to cast him" (37–41). The language here is not simply providing "relief" from tragic tension; it offers an alternative to tragic violence. Like so many of Shakespeare's clowns, the Porter here would modulate and shift dramatic gears to comedy. He is a pivotal figure in the wrong context, a genre-shifter in the wrong play. He represents faith in comic *belief*, not simply comic *relief*. The Porter, like the Nurse in *Romeo and Juliet*, is able to make comic capital from tragic events, because he can "make a shift," or "come about" to a jest, in this case, from murder itself to the festive sense that Duncan and Macduff were expecting in their visit to Macbeth's castle.

We could, of course, talk about any number of such scenes students relish, such as the opening of *Julius Caesar,* when the Cobbler tries to mollify the angry tribune Murellus by claiming he is "a mender of bad soles" and he could "mend" Murellus too, or the peripety of *Titus Andronicus* where the Clown enters as the "messenger of the gods," homophonically confusing Jupiter with "gibbet-maker" just as Titus has sent his arrows of complaint *Ad Jovem* and *Ad Appolinem*. Or we might mention the most famous example of comic *belief* of all, the exchange of the gravediggers and Hamlet when the Prince resurrects the fool Yorick and experiences the ultimate metaphysical moment of the play and perhaps of all literature. However, one of Shakespeare's most prolonged expressions of vulgar sublimity and the leap of comic faith surfaces nowhere so brilliantly as it does in the activities of Dogberry and his watch in *Much Ado About Nothing*. Dogberry's and Verges' malaprops have a linguistic and thematic method to their madness. Students adore the good humor of these puns, which are worthy of a Joyce. And these are puns with a "point." They make "palpable hits" in the play, just as we say "touché" when we feel the prick of a good joke at our expense. The malaprops concentrate the thematic and ethical energy of the play for students the way jokes do, according to Freud's theory of the compression of humor expressed in the arc of laughter. Dogberry appropriates the terminology of the law, "moiders" it, and reappropriates it for comic and cosmic purposes. Ethically speaking, as the pivotal comic character he "shifts" or converts the invidious lies of intrigue and slander to the energy of laughter and love.

The watch enters the scene immediately after their "superiors" have done their worst, after Don John and his henchmen have conspired to discredit Hero and break up her marriage to Claudio. They walk onstage discussing the character of the "good and true" person. Verge delivers the first malaprop, converting "condemnation" or "damnation" to "salvation."

Dogberry. Are you good men and true?
Verges. Yea, or else it were pity but they should suffer
salvation, body and soul.

(3.3.1–3)

These clowns are pivotal characters, like the Nurse, the Porter, Bottom, etc., who modulate dramatic mood, thematic structure, and ethical direction all by reappropriating the language of the law and of their social "betters," and refashioning it through malaprop and metaphor. They are thus lightning rods for student attention and vectors for comedic/religious conviction. In deciding to appoint the constable, Dogberry "anoints" the most "desartless" man, George Seacole, because, significantly, he "can read and write." Men of desert become "desertless" and "heartless" because they can "write" people down "an ass" in this malaprop which "equivocates," that is compresses two meanings into a single verbal vessel. When Seacole is given the assignment as constable, Dogberry warns against the vanity of literacy: "and for your writing and reading, let that appear when there is no need of such vanity. You are thought to be the most senseless and fit man for the constable of the watch" (20–23).

What follows is the most brilliant deconstruction of legal procedure and the injustice that can derive from it that we will see until the Marx Brothers' *Duck Soup*. Instead of "apprehending vagrants," Dogberry charges the constable with "*comprehending* all vagrom men" (25). With more malaprops from the bottom up, Dogberry equivocates, switching the verbal polarities of the word "apprehend," cleansing it of its legalistic, punitive associations and charging it with renewed sensitivity and compassion. The watch should "comprehend," that is *understand* the vagrant, and then let him go about his business. If the vagrant "will not *stand?*" — there is that word "stand" again, a word we would translate as "freeze" — "Why then, take no note of him, but let him go, and presently call the rest of the watch together, and thank God you are rid of a knave" (25–30). Resonating with the title, "take no note of him" may well mean, do not "write him down an ass." Do not use writing against him vainly.

After condoning sleep during the watch, recalling our groggy Porter, Dogberry explains how the drunks are to be rounded up for the night in Mayberry. If they will not oblige, "Why then, let them alone till they are sober," when they will not be "the men you took them for" and there will consequently be no need for arrest (45–48). If the watch should meet a thief, they should not "meddle" with or "lay hands on . . . such kind of men," because "they that touch pitch will be defiled" (51–60). A thief is no problem because he will "show himself what he is, and steal out of your company." Dogberry always pursues and recommends the "merciful" and the "peaceable way." "I would not hang a dog by my will, much more a man who hath any honesty in him" (63–64). If a child wails at night, let the "child wake her [the Nurse] with crying," "for the ewe that will not hear her lamb when it baes will never answer a calf when he bleats" (65–72) in other words, a constable when he shouts. In hilarious language that is remarkably scriptural and pastoral, Dogberry pacifies the police, recommends independent decisions for people, and assumes there is honesty in every person, even the thief. The students find all of this funny because it rings "true," particularly in a world where people are indeed brutally beaten from time to time, like Rodney King was for all to see, by the police.

Dogberry admits one exception to his sense of "mercy." Since the constable is to "present the Prince's person," if he should meet the Prince himself, he "should stay him," but "not without the Prince be willing." The metaphysical logic here is troubling and dazzling. The Prince, who is certainly above the law in our own country, as the recent spate of presidential and gubernatorial pardons at election time has demonstrated once again, may nevertheless be arrested, presumably because he is the executive and the representative of the law and must adhere to its dictates even more conscientiously than his subjects. However, even the free will of a Prince may not be abrogated. "Marry, not without the Prince be willing; for indeed the watch ought to offend no man, and it is an offense to stay a man against his will" (79–82). Dogberry's final charge is to assign the watch the premises of Prince Leonato where they will indeed spy their betters conspiring against each other to discredit the honesty and fidelity of Hero. Even Hero's father and fiancé will, in the presence of the community and God, make this innocent woman "stand to" and discredit her on the basis of calculated "hearsay."

The comic trial of Borachio and Conrade begins when Dogberry convenes the "whole dissembly" and identifies the "malefactors" as himself and his colleague: "Marry, that am I and my partner" (4.2.4), again comically taking responsibility for the dissembling all around him. Upon hearing that Borachio had received a thousand ducats for wrongfully accusing

Hero, Dogberry exclaims: "O villain! thou wilt be condemn'd into everlasting redemption for this" (56–57) and insists that he be "opinion'd" (67) for his crime. As they are being led away, the indignant defendant calls Dogberry an "ass," which is where we came in. Dogberry's flustered response brings the house down in performance, for both the effect and the ethic here is high comedy.

> Dost thou not suspect my place? Dost thou not suspect my
> years? O that he were here to write me down an ass! But,
> masters, remember that I am an ass; though it be not written
> down, yet forget not that I am an ass. No, thou villain,
> thou art full of piety, as shall be proved upon thee by good
> witness. I am a wise fellow; and, which is more, an officer;
> and, which is more, a householder; and, which, is more, as
> pretty a piece of flesh as any Messina; and one that
> knows the law, go to; and a rich fellow enough, go to; and
> a fellow that hath had losses; and one that hath two gowns,
> and every thing handsome about him. Bring him away. O that
> I had been writ down an ass!
>
> (74–87)

The humor and absurdity of the situation turns on Dogberry's determination to have everything "writ down," as it should be in a court of law. As a clown, he instinctively "suspects" that the function of writing *down* is ultimately to make everybody an *ass* in the eyes and in the hands of the law. The malaprops continue to crackle: Conrade does not "suspect" Dogberry's place or station, but as a "varlot," Conrade is "full of piety." But the real humor in the situation is that Dogberry *wants* to be "writ down an ass," meaning that he wants it recorded in memory that he has been called an ass—orally—by Conrade. Once again Dogberry assumes the role as comic, almost sacrificial victim. In the crucible of his misplaced metaphors and awkward malaprops he alchemically transforms the dross of legally sanctioned villainy—what Simone Weil called the *gravity* of the law—into the comic flight of *grace* in speaking *up* and acting *out* the perceptions and the aspirations of the *vulgus*. He is truly, as are all his sisters and brothers in motley, the irrepressible *vox populi*.

 In the late twentieth century we are rediscovering what Shakespeare understood implicitly in the late sixteenth century: "speaking up" and "acting out"—what we call "clowning around"—are much more lively and entertaining ways to communicate than simply "writing down." The difference between reading and attending a Shakespeare play is the difference between reading a sex manual and having sex. The most oral, the most unruly, the most vulgar, and unpredictable—that is, unable to be scripted—of Shakespeare's characters is his army of clowns and fools. It is no wonder that Hamlet focuses our attention on the lips of Yorick as he recalls his jibes and antics. To the clowns is given the task of scrambling the fixed, inflexible meanings of their superiors, which they receive aurally and reconstitute orally in reconceiving the world. The scenes they domesticate and equivocate represent the hooks to catch and secure the students' interest, engagement, and affection.

These are the scenes they should read, speak up about, act out, and clown around about, not necessarily in that order. These are the scenes they might themselves vary and rewrite, in other words, appropriate. Northrup Frye, C. L. Barber, and Mikhail Bakhtin have recovered for us the technical terminology that was lost with the disappearance of the second book of Aristotle's *Poetics,* which dealt with comedy. Thanks to them we can now candidly discuss festival, bawdy, carnival, slapstick, farce, in other words all the joys of so-called "vulgar entertainment." Thanks to them, we should be losing once again our theoretical and pedagogical "fear of laughing" in the classroom and the academy.

References

Bakhtin, M. M. 1968. *Rabelais and His World*. Trans. Helene Iswolsky. Cambridge, Mass.: MIT Press.

Barber, C. L. 1959. *Shakespeare's Festive Comedy*. Princeton: Princeton University Press.

Coleridge, Samuel Taylor. 1959. *Coleridge's Writings on Shakespeare*. Ed. Terence Hawkes. New York: Capricorn Books.

Freud, Sigmund. 1963. *Jokes and Their Relation to the Unconscious*. Trans. James Strachey. New York: Norton.

Frye, Northrup. 1949. "The Argument of Comedy." In *English Institute Essays 1948,* ed. D. A. Robertson, Jr., 58–73. New York: Columbia University Press.

Gates, Henry Louis. 1988. *The Signifying Monkey: A Theory of African-American Literary Criticism*. New York and Oxford University Press.

Mencken, H. L. 1955. *The Vintage Mencken*. Ed. Alistaire Cooke. New York: Vintage Books.

McLuhan, Marshall. 1962. *The Gutenberg Galaxy: The Making of Typographic Man*. Toronto: University of Toronto Press.

Ong, Walter J. 1982. *Orality and Literacy: The Technologizing of the Word*. London: Methuen.

Shakespeare, William. 1974. Ed. G. Blakemore Evans. *The Riverside Shakespeare*. Boston: Houghton Mifflin.

Stuckey, Elspeth. 1991. *The Violence of Literacy*. Heinemann/Boynton Cook.

II

Performance In and Out of Class

CHAPTER 5

Shakespeare in Production

MARY Z. MAHER

University of Arizona
Tucson, Arizona

Although Maher designed her performance-oriented "Shakespeare in Production"
course for graduate students, many of her thoughts and suggestions are equally
appropriate for the undergraduate classroom. In her discussion, Maher investigates
a central question— "What are the limits of interpretation in Shakespeare
production?"—which for her is the single "idea [that] unified the course in terms
of making Shakespeare's text central to the discussion." Throughout, she offers
excellent advice on the possibilities and limitations of performance criticism and on
outside readings that might accompany the viewings of stage/video/film productions
of the plays.

There is one mandate that performance criticism has expounded with insistence: a given playtext has options in the performance of it. What performance criticism is less clear about is the articulation of criteria for judging performed texts. Performances are often judged against abstract aesthetic values such as unity, balance, and coherence. Yet, how do we come to terms with the concrete reality of an acting choice, a carefully selected costume, or a serious editing job on Shakespeare's original text?

I decided to investigate this problem by developing a graduate course about Shakespeare in production, considering stage productions, films, and video versions of the plays as produced entities with "production values." The film camera and the video camera (and their subsequent effects on the production) were not discounted but were included as strategies of production along with acting and interpretation, directing, costume design, lighting, sound and music, and scene design.

When I taught the course (I have done so in both theater departments and English departments), I drew between twelve and twenty graduate students from theater, English, and Communications. These populations included current or future teachers in secondary education, community college, and college situations. This was a plus: the more variety in "majors," the richer the class discussion. I had some very teacherly principles I wanted to inculcate.

There are a great variety of productions of Shakespeare available on video: stage productions transferred to video by installing cameras in the theater space and recording the production as it was presented to the public; productions that originated as stage productions and were video-recorded for archival reasons; productions (such as the BBC

"Shakespeare Plays" television series) scripted for television from the outset; productions originally filmed as a movie and later transferred to video; and many more. The genesis of any given video (the most used resource in today's classrooms) should be known by the person who uses it in class because that production may have had a prior existence in another medium, i.e., onstage or on film.

A film shown in class needs an appropriate and thorough introduction; it needs to be placed in its proper historical and social context. Overworked teachers often elect to show the latest, most acclaimed version of a film if it has the requisite Hollywood "glitz," a reputation earned from the result of an extensive public-relations campaign by the producers. There are considerations beyond checking out whether or not middle school students can tolerate suggestive language or nudity. Most important of all, there are a great many tools available to help teachers in deciding which films to use: advanced students and future teachers need to be introduced to these resources.

Finally, our students are televisually saturated beyond what we present to them in school. They need background and training in "reading" media materials, especially in terms of performance. It is important to understand how stage, film, and video operate, including such processes as determining focus, framing actors in scenes, the applications of individual film and television shots. Production values can link up with language in determinate ways: costumes can reinforce text; set designs can convey context; acting choices can help with meaning; music can create and heighten emotion. If we equip students with critical skills about the way that media shape their reality, we have gone a long way toward showing how thought control is one of the ends of technology. Students need training in discriminating and in judging media just as much as they need to learn how to write.

These weighty considerations tell us to be circumspect in selecting Shakespearean films. Is there a way to turn potential danger zones into positive learning experiences? Could these ideas be channeled into constructive goals and objectives in the teaching of Shakespeare through performance? Such notions ran through my head as I shaped my course. Eventually, I came up with the following broad-based descriptors:

1. The topic of the course was Shakespeare in production and that included stage, television, and film. Students would receive (sometimes through guest lectures) a general introduction to the aesthetics and mechanics of all three production modes.

2. The central question was "What are the limits of interpretation in Shakespearean production?" This idea unified the course in terms of making Shakespeare's text central to the discussion.

3. Students would be able, through outside readings and through viewing the films, to gain vital information about the social background and historical context of a given production. They would be required to research context.

4. Although Shakespeare's text was the essential measuring stick, we would also explore close-to-text versions, adaptations, mutations, and spin-offs, as well as downright perversions of Shakespeare's plays. In so doing, we would attempt to forge a common vocabulary of terms for our discoveries.

There was a great deal of homework in the course. In addition to the outside readings, some films had to be viewed at college-library media centers, some checked out from video rental stores and seen at home, and a few seen in "popcorn groups" in my living room so that we could avoid copyright problems. I emphasized that students should never make judgments about an entire film based on seeing only segments of it.

There were outside readings from books and journals that addressed ideological and textual issues in each production, exemplified solid pieces of criticism, and provided historical background. For these, I leaned heavily on hallmark books about Shakespeare on film and television, including Roger Manvell's *Shakespeare and the Film,* Anthony Davies's *Filming Shakespeare's Plays,* Susan Willis's *The BBC Plays: Making the Televised Canon,* Jack Jorgens's *Shakespeare on Film,* and James C. Bulman and H. R. Coursen's *Shakespeare on Television. Shakespeare on Film Newsletter* (now included in *Shakespeare Bulletin*) was one of the best resources for current articles on film and video because it carried extensive reviews of modern stage productions. Also, *Literature and Film Quarterly* often devoted an entire issue to Shakespeare on film and video. Two other resources which orient students to filmography and videography where Ken Rothwell and Annabelle Melzer's essential reference, *Shakespeare on Screen,* and Jo McMurtry's *Shakespeare Films in the Classroom: A Descriptive Guide.* I included a short bibliography of "production resources," such as Samuel L. Leiter's *Shakespeare around the Globe: A Guide to Notable Postwar Revivals,* primarily for research about stage productions of Shakespeare.

Each student gave a fifteen-minute "oral presentation" on a subject that I assigned. That saved me occasional lecture preparation and also took advantage of students' special interests. For example, one graduate student had an expertise in stage combat, so I set him to work comparing the fight scenes in film and video versions of *Hamlet* with Shakespeare's script. Another student was very interested in the double texts of *King Lear,* which dovetailed nicely with one of my units and also emphasized the background and breadth of knowledge a director needs to have in directing a Shakespearean text. Finally, each student had to write a major ten-to-fifteen-page "ready for publication" paper, which s/he presented "conference-style" during the last three weeks of the course. I encouraged a great many "comparison-contrast" papers, especially for novices in stage and media criticism.

The introductory units in the first two weeks of the course were designed to stimulate discussion. A good chunk of the grade was given for strong involvement in class discussion, and non-participants would be disadvantaged. I told students that one did not always have to answer a question directly but could "feed into" an answer (offer a bit of information that drew the group closer to conclusions) or pose an important question.

In the first unit, I attempted to articulate some basic questions that would repeat themselves throughout the semester. What exactly was a "production concept" or a "production design"? How was this different from stage to video to film? How did the "auteur" idea of film-making directly conflict with restrictions a stage director had to follow? Did the stage director have limits on his/her artistic vision? What were these? Did these go beyond the aesthetic to the practical—to budgetary and box-office considerations, theater space and size, the limits or choices in casting?

By the very nature of the course, many issues remained unresolvable. I had to deal (especially in "reading" acting interpretations) with the thorny issue of *taste*. I tried at all times to push beyond "I really like it" or "I hated her in it" responses to why did you like or approve or sanction this or that performance option? On what evidence in the film/video/stage production did you base your arguments? This method not only forced participants to state their criteria for judging but often introduced new stimuli and got us back on an active—as opposed to dead-ended—discussion track.

We explored the guideline of "relevance" as it began to be articulated by Peter Hall as he took over management of the Royal Shakespeare Company in the 1950s. How important was it that production should speak to our century or our culture? Was relevance inherent in Shakespearean texts or did the director need to insert it or emphasize it? Can a director stage *all* the "themes" present in a given Shakespearean play? Does any one Shakespeare play simply not speak to a modern audience, say, *Troilus and Cressida*? Why or why not? Are certain plays appropriate for only advanced students or only beginning students? Are certain plays not "audience fodder"? What kind of experience has the Royal Shakespeare Company had with relevance? Does this well-known company lead in establishing taste in Shakespearean production? What kind of influence does the system of Shakespearean festivals in the United States (some fifty-odd organizations) have? Do film directors "automatically" make a film relevant? How so? What different pressures do television and film directors respond to? How does the "star system" affect film and television?

Finally, we had a brief brush with an ornery problem: cutting and editing a Shakespearean text for production. How does cutting the play change the shape of the work of art that Shakespeare wrote? On a smaller scale, how does the gentle (or not-so-gentle) editing of a particular role (say, the Fool, in *King Lear*) change the shape of that role? Does the actor still "use" the lines that were cut from the text in order to shape his/her characterization for performance? What does a director do with a play like *Hamlet,* which runs (stage-time) up to four hours uncut? What criteria should a director use to eliminate lines (or business) from this well-known tragedy?

The first contentious topic we encountered was the discussion of who became *auteur* once we accepted some of these premises. I opened this discussion via a 1982 article from *Saturday Review,* which lamented bizarre stage productions and decried far-out film versions. The arguments needed a thorough airing, yet most teachers opt for retaining as much of Shakespeare's language as possible. The BBC "Shakespeare Plays" productions, even though they varied in quality throughout the series, provided a rough standard for using full texts.

Another major issue was the "if it works, use it" criterion often adopted in theater companies to sell tickets. Theater students particularly are susceptible to the "you gotta have a gimmick" school of producing Shakespeare, and I wanted to re-introduce the ideal of allowing and trusting a text to speak for itself.

After these initial questions emerged, I began to saturate the class with versions of *The Tragedy of Hamlet, Prince of Denmark*. I used Derek Jacobi's 1980 BBC *Hamlet* (directed by Rodney Bennett); Kevin Kline's PBS 1990 *Hamlet* (directed by Kirk Browning); and Laurence Olivier's 1948 *Hamlet*. Questions came up about Zeffirelli's *Hamlet* with Mel Gibson, so I included that version as part of the discussion, but it was not required viewing. These productions provided a look at *Hamlet* across time as well as a range of acting styles and media treatments. Jacobi's production was originally scripted for television; Kline's was a theater production at the New York Shakespeare Festival in the Public Theatre, which was later adapted for public television; Olivier's was, from the outset, a film. All three actors had played the role onstage during their careers—Jacobi did a two-year world tour prior to playing it on television; Olivier acted a version in 1938 at the Old Vic; Kline performed it with the New York Shakespeare Festival in 1985. Both Kline and Olivier had directed themselves in the role. Here were no novices. The Olivier film in particular had been much discussed by film historians and critics.

I began discussion of the *Hamlet*s by reiterating the differences between the media of stage, film, and television. I provided readings which described each production and also gave vital information about how and why Shakespeare's text had been edited to create the finished product, constantly homing in on questions of what might have been lost and what might have been gained in the text-editing process.

The *Hamlet* unit served as an appropriate beginning because everyone knew the play and some students had studied it more than once as undergraduates. Secondly, it offered opportunity to begin talking about *performance criticism,* what it is and what it isn't, what its possible boundaries might enclose. Students interested in performance should learn the terminologies, discover its foundations in historical criticism, and understand how it applies to each medium.

Everyone believes herself/himself to be an expert on the subject of acting and no one believes that a critic needs training in that field before s/he offers an opinion about a performance. Here was the ideal opportunity for a thorough discussion of acting, acting styles and fashions, acting choices, the interpretation of individual lines, the mitigating quality of cut and included lines, the "reading" of body language (gesture, facial expression, and movement), and how these might have been selected or supervised by a director or a cameraman. Film and video have one major advantage over stage productions: repeatability. Films and videos can be paused, fast-forwarded, frame-freezed, rewound, and even tape-recorded. One can transcribe and annotate from film and video. Thus, one can research from them; one can "prove points," one can argue from them. Also, ephemeral acting terms such as "being in the moment," "being vulnerable," and "good listening and reacting" can be examined as *concretes* and not just as suggestive descriptions. In technological media, the instructor can educate about what the visual field is, what it is communicating, how, and why (the BBC *King Lear* is especially good for this). Production values—not only acting, but color, framing, costumes, lighting, music, editing—can be demonstrated, not just glossed over with an "I didn't care for that."

There was one major problem with the course, which I was acutely aware of but never fully resolved: there are few archival recordings of theater pieces available for the classroom. The Canadian Stratford Shakespeare Festival recorded some in the 1980s and the rough and grainy and immediate 1964 *Hamlet* with Richard Burton (directed by Gielgud) is finally becoming available. Students still need to study theater reviews and the rare traces of theatrical documentation—promptbooks, costume plates, programs—often bare shadows of the original production. They are often frustrated by this necessity.

The unit after *Hamlet* was *The Tragedy of Macbeth*. The assigned viewings were the 1982 BBC *Macbeth* with Nicol Williamson (directed by Jack Gold) and the 1979 Trevor Nunn version of *Macbeth* with Ian McKellen and Judi Dench. To begin the unit, I brought an unnamed video to class and asked students to remain open-minded and simply to watch. I then showed *Men of Respect,* a 1990 production directed by William Reilly with John Turturro in the title role. The production concept of this creative work featured the plot of *Macbeth* performed with a Mafia motif set in a large eastern city (in colloquial language) by characters whose names reflect Shakespeare's, e.g., Mikey Battaglia (Macbeth) and Cordero (the Thane of Cawdor). Early on, the chief or don enacts a blood ceremony in bestowing a heroic title on the man who had committed brutal slaughter in the shoot-out which opens the film. Soon, students began to catch on to my ruse, and urged me to show more because it was fun to anticipate how the film would depict the witches' scene, or Banquo's ghost, and so on. Although we were still dealing with similar issues to those in the *Hamlet* unit—what are the interpretive possibilities in the main role, how does production shape or demand certain interpretations in Macbeth and in other characters—this unit was really the first thorough plunge into versions, perversions, and major surgeries on a Shakespearean playtext. The shaping questions of this discussion were—when were we dealing with a version of Shakespeare's play and when were we dealing with a complete re-writing of the text? How did the creators communicate this? What were the benefits of a "new version" (I showed a few minutes of Kurosawa's 1957 *Throne of Blood* and Orson Welles's 1949 *Macbeth* to emphasize the point)? What new aesthetic criteria came into play in order to judge the "new" artwork? When I first tackled this subject, the discussion became diffuse and uncontrollable. Later, I discovered that Ken Rothwell had written a very helpful paper for a film seminar at the annual Shakespeare Association of America meeting. He had adapted two useful terms, describing films and videos as "closed" and "open." The "closed" film/videos (which are exemplified by most of the BBC "The Shakespeare Plays" series) are those which circumscribe discussion because the video-recording itself retains most of Shakespeare's dialogue, stays close to the author's original "intention," and thus permits limited interpretation. "Open" films are those which might be described as less constructionist and more far-ranging and post-modern in their sensibilities and certainly permitted free association and discussion in terms of treatment and messages.

The next unit focused on the question, "Is Shakespeare still our contemporary?" In it, I dealt with selected scenes that illustrated feminist issues in the 1981 *Troilus and Cressida* (BBC version), the 1979 *Measure for Measure* (BBC version), and the 1966 *The Taming of the Shrew* (directed by Zeffirelli, with Richard Burton and Elizabeth Taylor). Twentieth-century feminist criticism had generated new or radically changed views of the roles of women in particular plays, which certainly invited re-interpretation of traditional roles. For example, Cressida was seen as a courtesan and coquette in most of the critical literature of the early twentieth century; now that modern culture had more experience of love relationships in a war context, critics demanded a more nuanced and complex character conception for her.

The unit which followed featured *The Tragedy of King Lear*. It began with a student report about the double text in *King Lear,* which emphasized that even Shakespeare, in variant quarto and folio texts, can provide a director with differing blueprints for the actualization of the play. The 1982 BBC *King Lear* (directed by Jonathan Miller with Michael Hordern) and Laurence Olivier's 1983 *King Lear* were shown against Peter Brook's 1971 film of *King Lear,* providing examples of artistically sophisticated versions based on the "same" play. The first was textually complete and used a Jacobean production design with all-black costumes and sets. Brook's *Lear,* on the other hand, was a heavily excised version of Shakespeare's text set in a dim and bleak countryside and employed a surreal, Bergmanesque style of cinematography. All of the roles were severely edited, yet the film was a triumph of mood and atmosphere. (The film also had its genesis in a prior stage production).

The final unit compared two outstanding versions of a history play, Laurence Olivier's 1944 *Henry V* and Kenneth Branagh's 1989 *Henry V.* Both were directed by the actors who played the title role. Both were reactions to historical events: the first film was commissioned by the British Foreign Office to shore up the blitzed and beleaguered British population during World War II, and the second was a response to the British invasion of the Falklands. Two unique rhetorical purposes determined the flavor of each film, the reasons for editing, and the tone and tenor of the *mise-en-scène.* Technological advances made one film appear deceptively naive and the other seem more modern and hard-edged.

The ready-for-publication papers that emanated from these units were a triumph of each student's invention and my intervention. Students were not permitted to proceed into a final paper without an office conference, most often spent narrowing each topic to something manageable. At this point, I could call into play all those other fine journal articles that had to be left out of the class reading list.

The final papers explored a number of critical points of view. A list of titles will demonstrate the variety:

— A feminist analysis of Cressida in Jonathan Miller's *Troilus and Cressida*
— A chart and comparison of the cuts made in Olivier's *Henry V* and Branagh's *Henry V*
— "Ciphers to this great accompt": the Chorus in Branagh's *Henry V* and Brechtian alienation in film
— A comparison and discussion of the battle scenes in Olivier's *Henry V* with those in Branagh's *Henry V*
— Text versus the fight choreographer in Hamlet's duel with Laertes: Kevin Kline, Derek Jacobi, and Laurence Olivier
— The design concept in Miller's *King Lear:* Gothic horror or Jacobean sophistication
— How cutting Ophelia's lines shaped her video image: a look at Ophelia in the BBC *Hamlet*
— Images of Christ as a visual metaphor in Jonathan Miller's *King Lear*
— Mel Gibson as Hamlet: lethal weapon or Elizabethan duelist?
— Lady Macbeth as sexual tyrant in the BBC version of *Macbeth*
— Hippies at work in Peter Hall's 1969 *Midsummer Night's Dream*: a social analysis of the costumes (or lack of)
— Bottom's Up: the use of physical comedy by Benny Hill and Mickey Rooney in *A Midsummer Night's Dream*

This course raised a number of pedagogical questions. First and foremost, was it licit to move so flexibly between the mediums of stage, film, and television? Was the preparation I provided at the outset sufficient to justify this ease of movement? Should I have eliminated stage productions altogether? Electronic media are not the same as the "live presence" of the actor and have far different selection techniques for determining what the audience saw; a filmed or video-taped version of a live performance was certainly not the same perceiver-experience as being in a theater audience. Since performance is a product of its historical/cultural context, how does the film/video/stage version reflect that?

The major dilemma—*not enough time*—was never solved. Having students watch films out of class was fairly successful. If copyrights were available on more videos, resources could all be located conveniently in one viewing location.

The final question, however, was the most haunting. Although students continued to have opinions about what they saw, the issue of taste was never resolved. I pushed forward: What is taste, exactly? What is it composed of? Who defines it? How does it get established? Can we measure it? What is bad taste? Here, I would console myself with the idea that a college course is a work in progress.

After the course was over, two young actors-in-training came to my office to tell me that after class, while putting on makeup for the production they were performing in on campus, they sat side-by-side at the dressing tables, still arguing about issues raised in class. Their story was remarkably reassuring.

References

Gilman, Richard. 1982. "Directors vs. Playwrights." *Saturday Review of Literature* (April): 30–35.

CHAPTER 6

Teaching the Sonnets with Performance Techniques

ROBERT B. PIERCE
Oberlin College
Oberlin, Ohio

Pierce tells what happened when he adapted performance techniques to the teaching of Shakespeare's sonnets. On the surface, the sonnet might seem less suited to such methods than the plays. But Pierce argues that the sonnets encourage the student to imagine a dramatic setting, are poetically rich, have an emotional center that may be close to the reader's experience, and are brief enough to be convenient for class treatment. He details the line-by-line performance exercises he uses to sharpen students' attention to sounds, to the rhythm of iambic pentameter, and to the interconnectedness of rhythm, meaning, and interpretation.

*P*ractically all teachers of Shakespeare believe in reading aloud in class, having students walk through scenes, using the actual bodies and voices of the students as ways of exploring and coming to understand the dramatic richness of Shakespeare's language. In recent years I have found myself devoting more and more class time to this approach and also devising more systematic techniques for exploiting its values. In particular I have adapted techniques exploited by some of the Royal Shakespeare actors during visits to the Oberlin College campus, techniques also revealed in the videotapes marketed by Films for the Humanities.[1]

These techniques are invaluable for teaching scenes from the plays, but I have also used them more and more to teach Shakespeare's sonnets, which I frequently include in the first half of our chronologically arranged two-semester sequence of the plays and which I often teach in other courses, including an introductory poetry course. The sonnets might seem less suited to such methods than the plays, but I am convinced otherwise, and it is significant that they are used as a favorite exercise for acting classes. By exploring some of Shakespeare's sonnets through performance, a student can learn a great deal about the creation of a dramatic voice by language and rhythm, about the value of trying to imagine a dramatic setting and audience, and about how to read poetry with real understanding.

The sonnets provide all sorts of opportunities for such exploration. They are of course poetically rich, and many of them have great intricacy and difficulty of meaning—it is often hard to arrive at a sentence-by-sentence paraphrase of even the most direct sonnet, for example. At the same time most of them have an emotional center that is close to the reader's experience and so immediately recognizable—"I really enjoy being in love with you"; "please don't scorn my love, even though I deserve being scorned." Thus they demand close analysis while not being forbiddingly impervious to a first reading. They are intensely dramatic, and they play in complex ways with sound and rhythm. They are also short enough to be convenient for handling in a class, and often a teacher can even ask students to memorize one of them.

I shall illustrate the possibilities of the pedagogical approach by describing how I might teach Sonnet 90, though my discussion will be somewhat hampered by the limitations of print. On the page I cannot directly represent much of what I would do, which depends on my direct interaction with the student, what I can hear in his or her voice and can suggest with my own.

> Then hate me when thou wilt; if ever, now;
> Now, while the world is bent my deeds to cross,
> Join with the spite of fortune, make me bow,
> And do not drop in for an after-loss.
> Ah, do not, when my heart hath 'scaped this sorrow,
> Come in the rearward of a conquered woe;
> Give not a windy night a rainy morrow,
> To linger out a purposed overthrow.
> If thou wilt leave me, do not leave me last,
> When other petty griefs have done their spite,
> But in the onset come; so shall I taste
> At first the very worst of fortune's might,
> And other strains of woe, which now seem woe,
> Compared with loss of thee will not seem so.[2]

I approach the study of the sonnets in a Shakespeare or poetry class by using several workshop exercises in order to prepare the group for the kind of attention I want them to pay. Having them stand in a circle, I lead them in a couple of relaxation and breathing techniques and then some exercises with sounds and individual words. To begin the latter, I suggest that the most important word in Shakespeare is "O" and that we late-twentieth-century Americans tend to underplay it because we are typically less rhetorical and emotionally flamboyant than the Elizabethans seem to have been. With an exhortation to cut loose, I instruct the class as a group to imitate me in unison as I say the "O" sound in various (sustained and more or less hammy) patterns. My object in this exercise is to attune their ears to effects of meaning and feeling in sound and also to release their inhibitions so that they will be uninhibited with their own voices when we actually get to the poems.

I then invite the class to repeat a few individual words and phrases from the sonnet after me, paying special attention to fully articulating the sounds. I urge them to relish the sounds in themselves, actually tasting the d's and s's and a's or whatever. For Sonnet 90 I might select "hate," "rearward," and "purposed overthrow." In this exercise my object is to sharpen their attention to sound, to generalize their experience from "o" to the other sounds, and to prepare them to notice some specific sound effects in the sonnet to be worked on.

After that I work on the rhythm of iambic pentameter by having the class repeat nonsense syllables after me, first a perfectly regular deeduh, deeduh, deeduh, deeduh, deeduh, and then variously irregular lines, ending with an actual pattern from one of the lines in the sonnet. Thus I might end the series of nonsense-syllable lines with dee duh duh duh duh dee dee duh dee duh. Then I give them the actual line "And do not drop in for an after-loss," delivering it in that same rhythm. I use this method rather than formal scansion to teach the basic rhythms of iambic pentameter because it seems to me to work better for those who do not already have a pretty good sense of how metrical rhythm works: it is easier for a student to hear the rhythm of a line than to see its abstract pattern in scanned notation. Again the object of these preliminary exercises is to get students ready to hear metrical effects and to try for them in their own voices reading aloud.

I then have the class, still standing in a circle, read the sonnet (or two or three, depending on class size); each person takes one line, beginning with me and going all the way around the circle. The first time through I ask only that each person pick up his or her line immediately and quickly from the previous person. (I actually stop and begin reading again if someone comes in late or misses his or her place completely. My object is to begin to establish a class feeling of joint responsibility for recreating the poem.) I then explain that we are going to work toward an oral reading of the sonnet, with the goal of our sounding as though there were a single person reading it aloud as effectively as possible.

Next I go around the circle very slowly line by line, allowing each person to comment and ask questions about his or her line, by way of deciding how to read the line. I point out that each person has freedom to decide on the reading for that line but that the choices will be affected by how the previous readers choose to do their lines. I offer comments and ask questions myself, and I invite the rest of the class to participate, but I emphasize that each person is the final judge for his or her line. This process consumes most of the class time and is the heart of the exercise.

I begin with myself so as to set up some of the kinds of topics for discussion. Thus I note that a line can be given several different rhythms, and I suggest that one way of exploring the different possibilities is to choose one word as a climax for the line. I illustrate by giving three different oral readings of my own line, "Then hate me when thou wilt; if ever, now," giving the greatest stress to "hate," then to "thou," and then to "wilt." Afterwards I ask how the line is different in my three versions. I am careful to say "different" and to steer discussion away from deciding which one of the three readings is right, though I may comment that some choices are almost certainly wrong, like accenting "me" or "if" in the line. My emphasis here is on encouraging students to explore a range of possibilities for their lines, even though they must eventually settle on just one for actual performance.

At this point I discuss the need to give an oral marking to the end of my line in some way, so as to indicate the poetic structure while also setting up the syntactic and emotional relation of my line to the next. Thus I might explore how to express the force of the semi-colon after "now" as an end-of-line marker while still preparing for the immediate echo of the word at the beginning of line 2.

I then look at various poetic elements in the line, treating them as indicators for how to speak the line. I might comment on the Then-now antithesis at the two ends of the line, the t-alliteration in the two verbs hate-wilt, and the preponderance of time adverbs and monosyllables in the language. In all this discussion I keep the focus on how I am going to deliver the line and on what happens to the effect of the line based on the choices I make: thus I might in a sample reading orally underline the t-sounds in "hate" and "wilt" and ask what that does. After allowing the class to comment on ideas that strike them about my line, to ask questions, and to offer suggestions, I give a reading of the line as I have decided to do it.

While we go around the circle line by line, I am careful to give the individual student control over his or her line, even at the cost of putting up with some confusions and of not getting to some valuable points. I do allow myself some gentle guiding, especially through drawing attention to poetic elements like an image, a pun, a bit of sound play. Also I clear up puzzles where specialist knowledge might help—does the student know what "bent" means in line 2? I urge students to overplay rather than underplay and to give oral emphasis to the formal elements and artifice, vocally underlining antitheses, enjoying the sounds of words, bringing out repetitions, visualizing images as they say them. Thus I might ask the student in charge of line 3 to visualize "make me bow"—or even to enact being bowed down—and then to comment on what the image expresses.

If the class is not too large and if I am lucky, I can get around to everybody in a fifty-minute class. When necessary I simply stop before getting to everyone; of course people have been surreptitiously looking ahead to their own lines and working on them anyway. I always end the class with their actual performance of the sonnet or sonnets. (The students invariably end up performing the poems very well, by the way, though of course some students get the hang of oral performance better than others.) I find this technique of line-by-line performance invaluable right at the beginning of the semester because it can get the students to pay close attention to nuances of language, it can encourage exploratory discussion over dogmatic positions, and above all it can show them how to cultivate their understanding and responsiveness through oral performance.

Another technique that I use early in the semester is to have each student memorize a sonnet and come in to perform it for me individually in my office. The prospect of doing that does strike terror in student hearts, and a few freeze up when they come in, despite all my efforts to reassure them. Sometimes as a last resort I allow a panicked student to switch to reading the sonnet from a text, a compromise which still allows for doing much of what I want to do. When I think they have not really tried to memorize the sonnet, however, I send them away to come back later. (I have warned everyone in advance that it is wise to do the memorizing sooner than the day before coming in to perform, so that the words have time to get set in the memory.) The main value of the memorizing is, of course, to get the student thoroughly familiar with the poem and used to speaking its words aloud in various ways.

One can ask many of the same questions with this technique as with the previous one, but it also lends itself to attention to other aspects of the poem, and it allows one to help the individual student work with a whole poem, not just one line. When the student has recited the poem for me, I usually ask first of all whether he or she envisages saying those words in some specific situation: whether for example as the speaker of Sonnet 90 he or she is directly speaking to the other person, or perhaps writing a letter, or whatever. Some students will not have thought of the poem in that way, while others will have a specific situation worked out in some detail. I usually try to flesh out the situation that the student chooses: How would you be feeling as you say the first four lines? How would you be wanting the listener to respond? Can you invent some previous event that explains your saying "Then" at the beginning of the poem?

Frequently after this exploration I ask the student to imagine a different dramatic situation—for example, being in the other person's presence, if the previously imagined situation was writing a letter. (I find that students often prefer the letter-writing situation as their first instinct, perhaps because they think of the poet himself actually sitting down to write the poem, or perhaps because they are inclined to avoid the intensity of a face-to-face encounter.) I let the student speak a few lines in the new situation, and then I ask how saying it that way feels different; I emphasize the *feels* in my question in order to be sure that the student looks at the human reality of the situation rather than veering off to discuss abstract meaning.

Often I have the two of us imagine two or three such dramatic situations for the poem. One little drama that I enjoy using with some of the more sophisticated students I set up as follows: imagine that you are a great poet and that you have gone to a poets' convention. There is a contest to choose the best poet, a contest in which each poet is given a first line and told to improvise a sonnet. You are given the first line, "Then hate me when thou wilt; if ever, now," and in response you improvise Sonnet 90 (i.e., whichever sonnet the student has memorized). Now say the sonnet under those circumstances. I always point out that this situation certainly never crossed Shakespeare's mind, whatever might be said about any of the other dramatic situations we have imagined, but that it gets at something really present in the poem; that is, Shakespeare's sonnet participates in the game of sonnet-writing and demonstrates the virtuoso skill of being able to bring off the poem's meaning and feeling within the confines of the form. The poem is an artistic showpiece as well as a "sincere" exploration of feeling. And of course all sorts of elements in the oral performance take on very different significance in this dramatic situation. A pause in this performance means: I am reaching for the perfect word; or perhaps a word for the rhyme won't come to my mind; or I know what I'm going to say, but I'll tantalize you my listeners for a split second. The neatness of the closing couplet performed in this situation says in effect: you see—I did it! I got everything into my poem perfectly despite the apparent casualness of my language. I really am a master poet who can sound perfectly sincere while bringing off a virtuoso-piece.

There are all sorts of ways to respond valuably to details in the students' performances and so to teach much about Shakespeare and Shakespearean poetry. I listen for places where the student hesitates or stumbles over the words. If he or she finds "'scaped this sorrow" a tongue-twister, I suggest that Shakespeare wants the reader to slow down over pronouncing the words and in doing so to look at them carefully. Thus the tongue-twister is a sort of stage direction to the performer. In particular the reader should ask whether there is a way of saying the words that makes them easier to pronounce. If the student is baffled, I might suggest or demonstrate accenting "this"—"'scaped *this* sorrow." The result of that delivery is that an aura of implication, something like "all this immediate grief, not to mention a lot of additional unspecified trouble that has me in such a self-pitying mood" hovers around the word. It is striking how often the hard-to-pronounce passage is an emotional crux of the poem. (In this specific phrase I myself take Shakespeare to be gesturing with "this" toward an undefined melancholy, like that of Antonio and then Portia when they first come onstage in *The Merchant of Venice*.) Almost any tongue-twister in a sonnet offers a place for that kind of close attention and experimentation.

Memory slips can also be useful opportunities for exploration. Students often lose their place and forget how to go on when they get to a point of emotional transition or a structural division—the break between two quatrains, for example. When I ask what places they tend to stumble over, having the two of us look at those points of the poem allows me to ask how the shifts and divisions of the sonnet are marked; and the student can explore the divisions and markers as rhetorical opportunities, not just traps for the memory. Students also lose their place when they don't understand a passage and so have been trying to memorize nonsense. If a student stumbles over lines 2–4, having the two of us sort carefully through the syntax can lead to a sudden leap of understanding, along with the discovery that sentences in poetry do usually make sense.

This process of working through a memorized sonnet helps any student to find how much that he or she has not noticed is going on even in a poem that the student already knows well, having committed it to memory. The difficulty—one I don't always solve—is how to help the student out of impasses while allowing the reading itself to be the main source of discovery, so that the student finds how much can be discovered by listening closely to his or her own voice exploring the words on the printed page. For the professor working with an individual student on a memorized poem, the model of the golf pro or athletic coach is especially valuable: you cheer the student on; you suggest a trick here, a modification there; you toss in a bit of knowledge or a rule of thumb. Meanwhile the student is doing the actual job of swinging the club and hitting the ball: arriving at a performance of the poem that is also an understanding of it.

The methods and approaches of this technique can of course be used less intensively, more mingled with others, in more typical classroom discussions and even in lectures. I usually have a Shakespeare sonnet read aloud to begin a discussion of it, and as often as I possibly can I have the discussion end with the sonnet performed by me or one of my students. My justification for the performance of the poem at the end is the principle that a poem should be put back together after it is disassembled. Of course I also urge students to read the sonnet again later, so that they may discover how the experience of a poem can be altered and renewed by having analyzed it closely in the past.

When we are arguing about the meaning of a passage, I often ask the disputants to read it aloud so that they can try to express their own interpretations in their voices. I suggest that being able to do so strengthens the case for their interpretation, while not being able to do so is an argument against it. In reading poems aloud, techniques to produce what the Russian formalists called estrangement can be useful to get freshness of response: having a poem read as fast as possible (ask the student to do it as fast as he or she can, and then say, "Now, read it even faster"), having it read very slowly, having a poem with a male speaker read by a woman, etc. Even the most arbitrarily imposed differences of performance have a way of bringing out unnoticed aspects of the sonnet.

This approach through performance should be as articulate as possible: one should always talk about the insights that the oral performance enables. But at the same time it is important to recall that our voices say more than we can articulate in other words, through critical commentary. The insight in a moving performance of a line may be perfectly real even though it cannot be expressed in an article. But then maybe electronic publishing will eventually allow us critics to do part of our arguing with our voices. At any rate, I am convinced that, in the classroom and in one-on-one encounters of teacher and student, oral performance combined with analytical exploration of the performance is one of the most valuable tools for studying Shakespeare's sonnets or indeed almost any poem. A teacher who loves to read, listen to, and talk about poems can devise scores of techniques for incorporating this approach into the process of educating readers of Shakespeare.

Notes

1. There are two separate series: a two-cassette set, *Preparing to Perform Shakespeare* and *Speaking Shakespearean Verse,* and a nine-cassette set with the general title *Playing Shakespeare,* Films for the Humanities, Inc., Box 2053, Princeton, NJ 08540. Though both are valuable, the former is enough to illustrate many of the most valuable techniques. I have also drawn on ideas from colleagues and friends in both English and Theater.

2. *The Sonnets,* ed. William Burto, rev. ed. (New York: Signet, 1988), p. 130.

CHAPTER 7

Using Playgrounding to Teach *Hamlet*

FRANCES L. HELPHINSTINE
Morehead State University
Morehead, Kentucky

Inspired by England's St. George Theatre, Helphinstine has adapted to her own classes elements of its program for visiting schoolchildren. Through an elaborate sports analogy, she explains the ways she brings her students to a fresh awareness of all facets of the theater experience. Then, limiting her discussion to Hamlet, *she describes the small group activities she uses to focus on staging clues and set design and how she gets each group to block the action and search the text for additional lighting, costume, and prop clues. She concludes with some suggestions for post-performance evaluations.*

For ten or more years, Ken Davis (now at Indiana University–Purdue University at Indianapolis) and I took busloads of both traditional and non-traditional students to Stratford, Ontario, to see productions of Shakespearean, as well as other, plays. In the early years, we noticed that those who had studied any one of the plays in school were frequently disappointed that the Stratford production ran counter to "the" classroom interpretation. We also noticed that those who had seen film versions of Shakespeare had little sense of how the preponderant emphasis on visual images, which one after another displace the predecessor, makes the film so time-bound and earth-bound in comparison to the stage. We realized two things: First, our students had very limited understanding of the theater experience. Second, the classroom frequently ignores the theatrical vantage point, which looks for "producible interpretations." Inspired by visits to England's St. George Theatre, Ken and I adapted elements from their program, in which schoolchildren are brought in, permitted to explore costumes and props departments, handed scripts, and asked to read lines in response to various directions, much like actors in real rehearsals.

Ken created classroom materials that promoted understanding of how all components of the theater interact, which he tested on succeeding groups and eventually published in *Rehearsing the Audience: Ways to Develop Student Perceptions of Theatre.* In my introduction to literature classes, I found that students with no theater experience grow in their abilities to imagine how scenes might work on stage and how the audience feeds that performance just by engaging in Ken's classroom playgrounding activities. I follow informal strategies for introducing the reading of any play with specific performance study techniques for *Hamlet.*

I begin the drama unit by talking about how a play is more than a "thing" or a piece of literature. A play is an "event." Even young children can quickly brainstorm terms that label "things" versus terms that label "events." We then discuss some of the traits of the specific events which they have named. With no coaching, students comment about spectator or audience responses to the performers in the event as well as the performer's response to spectator behavior, which is the primary transaction that also takes place in the theater.

In addition, students note that audience members also talk among themselves or combine to cheer what they are viewing. When I ask what that audience interaction is in response to, students describe an event as a story taking place: one of the ways that an audience enjoys a play, too.

Returning to one of the examples of events that the students have listed in our opening brainstorming, I ask, "What are the chances for the story of that specific event to end as the audience would like?" Teaching in Kentucky, I find that students often list UK basketball as an event. With no coaching, they soon describe the performance of their favorite player. I can then note that a second way that an audience enjoys a play is as a performance of a story.

Soon students recognize that live performance is theatrical. To read about a game does not equal seeing it. We are then ready to explore the next issue: "What makes a good audience?" Continuing with their UK basketball example, we discuss the effects of good cheerleaders; of unruly behavior in the stands; of a dull, miserable crowd; of fans holding their breath during every important shot, etc. By working with their answers, I can soon draw parallels for the theater audience: the more the theater audience gives alert attention to the performance, the more the audience receives from it. If, in watching a play, we breathe with the actors, riding over the top of the climaxes with them, holding our breath in suspense, or exploding in laughter, the actors on stage notice this just as our favorite star on the basketball floor seems to play better when we the crowd support him/her. An ideal theater audience is like ideal fans for a sporting event: we sit on the edge of the chair—giving undivided attention to the stage.

We then discuss activities that precede the basketball player's performance during the game. Students may speak of increasing knowledge of how the next opponents play by watching films, devising strategies to prevent the opponents from getting in the three-point corner, and other specifics. I then use the general knowledge that the students have of basketball as *event* to explain how the theater event works. For example, training films forecasting what is likely to happen in a specific game compare with the script a playwright prepares for a theater performance. In the arena, the fans know the typical plot lines of what makes their team a winner or a loser so well that, during any game, they soon recognize how the "performance" of a specific player is likely to make that game/story end. In the theater, too, the actors start with the script, but the performance of each, just as that of each player on a sports team, affects how the audience judges the whole event. Conversely, fan responses affect players' performances just as the response of the audience affects the actor on stage.

Following this introduction to play as event, with interaction between players and spectators, I have the class explore its role as audience more deeply. I ask questions such as "What is primary?" "Feeling or Thinking?" "Which is more influential?" Following through with the UK basketball example, students indicate that some fans will be as analytical as their favorite sports writer. Others will be emotional, loyal fans. I intersperse questions such as "Does the sports story affect what the spectator expects?" "Does the fan have knowledge of what to look for?" "Does the response of other fans sitting around you or those for the opposing team affect your response?" The class answers soon approach John Styan's view that "the spectator interprets and so contributes to and finally becomes the [event], whose image is all and only in his mind" (Styan 4). This principle parallels the variety of effects experienced by theater spectators.

Then I am ready to address how a theater audience *shares expectations* by asking pre-performance questions such as "What do I feel?" and "What do I expect?" I then address how an audience *shares knowledge* with questions such as "What might I look for?" and "How might I understand the event?" Whether sports or theater spectators, the audience shares expectations and knowledge. Then with *Hamlet,* we discuss what the students expect the play to be like. Here, I encounter some of the usual "feeling" statements such as "I hate Shakespeare" or the jubilant note "I won't need to read the play. I saw the Mel Gibson film." By continuing to draw parallels with our earlier discussion of basketball as event, I label their expectations as "feeling statements." I then guide students to share knowledge of *Hamlet* by asking: "What might I look for?" "How might I understand it?"

Continuing my analogies with basketball as event, I ask the class "Why do spectators return again and again to see the same team play?" "Is the game as exciting if we can predict who will win from the beginning?" "If so, explain why," etc. Soon their answers lead to another insight that is helpful when viewing any event: An open mind is part of what makes attendance enjoyable. Continuing the basketball analogy, we discuss what spectators do following a game. We compare the activities of those who were present at the performance and those who only saw a television "live" broadcast or heard a radio account. The class observes that those present at the arena frequently go for a meal afterwards at which they analyze how the performance of key players or the behavior of coaches or referees affected the outcome and discuss the behavior of other fans or anything else that captured their attention at the arena. Those listening to the game on radio hear replay of the most exciting moments or analysis of how the performance of key players affected the game, or player and coach responses from the locker room. Groups of listeners may have follow-up conversations similar to those of spectators at the arena. In each case, the class recognizes that what is meaningful for the spectator comes to the forefront.

Perspective comes into play as we address questions such as "Is sitting at home and listening to the game as exciting as being at the arena?" or "What does being at the arena offer that causes fans to pay ticket prices?" From their answers, I continue the analogy: Reading a play is like listening to an event from the privacy of one's home. Our imaginations have to provide what the script does not.

The class is then ready to do the same preliminary activities that can also be used to enhance their knowledge of plays for attending a live performance or imagining one. Building on the introductory discussion of "event," I return to the point that audience pleasure comes partly from knowledge. One essential piece of knowledge for enjoying *Hamlet* is plot frame. Background information on Shakespeare's life and times also affects audience response. I include the Renaissance philosophical ideal of order that linked all existence together in a "great chain of being" from God at the top, through humanity at the midpoint, to the basest matter at the bottom. This foundation fed a Renaissance growth in geographic and scientific explorations, in classical and popular learning, and in middle-class prosperity. I provide the sketch only so I can raise questions such as "What is the role of 'order' in *Hamlet*?" "In what ways, if any, is *Hamlet* a conflict between the forces of order and disorder?" "What, if anything, does *Hamlet* say about correspondences between the natural, human, and supernatural worlds?" "In what ways, if any, does *Hamlet* reflect a sense of growth in exploration, learning, or prosperity?" "In what ways is *Hamlet* out-of-date, and in what ways is it modern?" After the class unit, this last question may be addressed in a number of ways, including analysis of how the recent movie versions have altered the script.

I also discuss how the plot structure of a comedy differs from that of a tragedy. In Renaissance comedy, the plot moves from problem to solution, giving the main character life, freedom, and community. The character, "life-sized" or smaller, establishes personal identity, has reunion with loved ones, and establishes a new order. In Renaissance tragedy, by contrast, the plot has downward movement. The main character, "larger-than-life," faces provocation and revenge that leads to isolation, confinement, and death. The main character loses established identity, becomes separated from loved ones, and the order of the society dissolves because of a mistake made. As the students work through *Hamlet*, they may be asked to trace the events that lead to Hamlet's separation from loved ones.

Because "celebrities" and sequels to their movies dominate modern culture, I include background information on earlier versions of *Hamlet*, such as that of Belleforest, which did not contain Ophelia and her family, Fortinbras and his revenge, and the ghost. (I ask the class to note what considerations they add to Shakespeare's play). I add that *Hamlet* was probably based on an earlier work, the *Ur-Hamlet*, now lost. Among scholars, Hamlet is a celebrity. More books have been written about the Prince of Denmark than about any other person, real or imaginary, except Jesus and Shakespeare.

If we are going to stay in the classroom for the whole unit, I encourage my students to see the dramatic action while they read the words of the literary text. I have them work in small groups of five. First, each group is directed to discover all the possible staging clues in the text. They may begin by pretending to manage the television camera, just as for a sporting event, by focusing on the visual aspects of the play, small segment by succeeding small segment. Each group sets the stage for the opening scene by focusing on the first thirteen lines of the play.

Each group becomes set designers, and, therefore, needs to briefly explore acting space on stage designs as varied as the stage with three walls and a curtain or the thrust stage, with its different levels, shown in most textbooks. As each group studies stage directions, each discovers that a "platform before the castle at Elsinore" is needed. I ask the class to then work with the most popular current Shakespearean theater design, a one-level stage that extends into the audience, with spectators sitting on three sides. Each group then discusses how it can convey levels by assigning playing spaces on different segments of the stage. Each group then reads the dialogue to see whether the set must include detailed scenery or mere "suggestion scenery," a practice introduced by Tyrone Guthrie with his relatively bare stage.

Each group then blocks the action as each draws a floor plan to show where the actors will move within that space. Essentials include that Francisco stands guard at a post on the platform. Bernardo comes in at an entry and moves to the post area where Francisco stands guarding the castle. Francisco then moves to exit through that entry.

Groups then search the dialogue for clues used by lighting, costume, and set designers. Since Bernardo does not know who stands watch, but Francisco, on hearing his voice, calls him Bernardo, the groups conclude that the twelve o'clock must refer to midnight and that it must be dark. One who stands guard probably wears a uniform and needs a weapon as a prop. "'Tis bitter cold" suggests that gloves or other protective features be added to the costume.

After each group has set the scene, the class discusses how the performance space may influence their delivery of lines. For example, having audience on three sides requires the actor to slowly turn, if sitting, or move, if standing, in a circle, so that at different moments everyone in the house can see his eyes and the expression on his face. The movements must be carefully planned and executed very slowly and smoothly.

Each student group then begins to create the play by using their voices, their bodies, and the words and rhythms of the poetry to tell the story. They read the dialogue between Francisco and Bernardo, gathering delivery clues from the punctuation and the subject matter. As each of the classroom student groups has designated members read lines, others in the group suggest changes in pace, gestures or other body language to convey what the character is feeling (e.g., "the bitter cold" or "I am sick at heart"). The readers experiment with the effects of slowing the rhythm at different points in the dialogue to underscore different lines or phrases. As they explore, they recognize that change in delivery style influences character and plot. Furthermore, this pedagogical approach encourages even the most reticent student to contribute to class discussion because it emphasizes multiplicity of interpretations rather than a single correct one.

Following a short designated time frame assigned for these student preparations, each group rehearses the opening lines for the whole class. Prompters and/or the page of script are necessary. The whole class then discusses which script clues are evident in each performance.

Then, I ask the groups to continue with lines 14–39 to introduce the next two characters to the action: Horatio and Marcellus. Each group is to continue making notes for set design, blocking (making the floor plan) the movement of actors, lighting, costuming, and stage properties. Before long, several students wonder whether it is something that the now departed Francisco has seen during his watch that has elicited his comment "I am sick at heart." The intrigue builds as Marcellus asks "What, has this thing appeared again to-night?" and adds clues that "this dreaded sight," "we have two nights seen." Although Horatio labels the report "but our fantasy," Bernardo is asked to repeat details of the previous appearances. Expectancy dominates, for he describes the present time of evening. The ghost reappears.

The importance of story comes to the forefront. With difficulty, I now get the groups to record dialogue clues to set needs: a star, a bell to ring out the hour, etc. I can hardly get them to practice delivery of lines. Curiosity dominates as the students rush into the next segment from directions "[Enter Ghost]" through line 51. I ask them to bring the performance along with the story line. I ask "Should the ghost be imaginary or acted out and why?"

Horatio says, "What art thou, . . . / Together with that fair and warlike form / In which the majesty of buried Denmark / Did sometimes march?" (1.1.46–49). Of course, some groups take these lines literally and want the dead father to appear. Others stick with Horatio's earlier stance that a ghost must be merely "our fantasy" and direct the speaking characters to address an empty spot on the stage. As they discuss ways to represent the ghost, they find that some popular movie representations of ghosts are not performable. They think of popular sound effects that might suggest a ghost. Again, we pause and have each group share its "performance" of the presence of the ghost as the whole class asks questions and makes suggestions for gestures, special lighting, and other dramatic effects.

Each group then works through the rest of scene 1 to learn what it is that the men are standing watch (guard) for. The appearance of the ghost is so powerful that few are interested in learning that young Fortinbras has a desire to reclaim lands that the dead King Hamlet took from his father in war. They are more interested in why the ghost of dead King Hamlet has appeared. The students share the curiosity of the men, who, standing guard at Elsinore castle, are unable to get the ghost to respond. When Horatio suggests that the young Hamlet may be able to get it to speak, the class is eager to meet Hamlet.

The class is now ready to focus on how particular scenes fit into the structure of the play as a whole and interweave character, theme, and previous action to present a coherent and theatrically powerful moment. Approaching the play from this theatrical vantage point highlights the contradictions in the play. Students begin to offer interpretative possibilities for production choices that can be handled in a variety of ways. Gradually, they learn to fit the segments together for what would be "producible interpretations" of the play.

Because most units do not permit time for the students to work with the total play, I focus on scenes in the play that paradoxically embrace contradictions, making one interpretation founded on lines within the script no more valid than another. Writers have addressed three such issues for centuries: "Why does Hamlet delay?" "Is Hamlet insane or only pretending to be?" and "Should Hamlet dominate the action throughout or should memorable supporting characters receive balanced attention?"

First, "Why does Hamlet delay?" Is it to be sure that the ghost is telling the truth? (3.2.163–265). Is it his fear that the ghost is evil? (1.2.255–258; 1.5.1–111). Is it because he is a weak intellectual, incapable of action? (2.2.500–559). Is it because he envies Claudius for fulfilling Hamlet's own Oedipal fantasies? (1.2.133–158, 180–184; 3.4.89–217). Is it because he wishes to establish Claudius's guilt beyond doubt? (2.2.487–559; 3.2.65–77). Is it because he wants to be sure Claudius is damned? (3.3.73–99). The role of Hamlet has been played each of these ways. I ask separate groups to work with scenes that fit one of the questions. Each group is asked to identify which character traits, speeches, images, and scenes a director needs to emphasize to encourage the audience to see Hamlet's delay in just one of these ways. I also make the class aware that in some stage productions Hamlet does not delay at all.

Second, each group may be required to describe how the lines in one of the key scenes where Hamlet's sanity is in question must be played to support their interpretation. "Does Hamlet only pretend madness?" (1.5.163–190; 2.2.215–291). "Does Hamlet collapse into madness at any stage?" (2.1.74–120). "What suspicions develop?" (2.2.34–57; 3.1.156–183; 3.3.1–26). "How does Hamlet verify or disprove those suspicions?" (5.2.198–305). "How does

Hamlet's behavior in each case contrast with that of some other character? (e.g., Ophelia: 4.5.21–92). Such contrasts lead to a third issue. Do supporting characters paint a picture of Hamlet's world or provide a contrasting perspective on an issue over which Hamlet broods? Groups then work through the dramatic possibilities for Claudius (3.3.37–73), Polonius (1.2.55–87), Ophelia (4.5.39–73), Laertes (4.5.111–148), the ghost (1.5.137–190), or the gravedigger (5.1.101–188).

After each classroom group has performed its answer to one of the most debated questions about *Hamlet,* the class is ready for typical post-performance evaluations that include both shared perceptions and shared feelings. The class answers questions such as "What did I experience?" and "How did I understand it?" We then compare how we felt before the workshop with how we feel afterwards. We discuss how working with *Hamlet* has changed us. We discuss why we have responded as we have to some of the features of the play. We are aware that we have experienced *Hamlet* as an event. As Louise Rosenblatt (1978) describes it:

> [Each of us] brings to the [performance] [his/her] past experience and present personality. Under the magnetism of the ordered symbols of the [performance], [he/she] marshals [his/her] resources and crystallizes out from the stuff of memory, thought, and feeling a new order, a new experience, which [he/she] sees as the [play]. (12).

References

Davis, Ken. 1988. *Rehearsing the Audience: Ways to Develop Student Perceptions of Theatre.* Urbana, Ill.:ERIC Clearinghouse on Reading and Communication Skills and National Council of Teachers of English.

Rosenblatt, Louise M. 1978. *The Reader, the Text, the Poem: The Transactional Theory of the Literary Work.* Carbondale: Southern Illinois University Press.

Shakespeare, William. 1992. *Hamlet.* In *The Norton Anthology of World Masterpieces.* 6th ed., 2014–110. New York: W. W. Norton.

Styan, John. 1963. *The Elements of Drama.* Cambridge: Cambridge University Press.

CHAPTER 8

Professional Theater People and English Teachers
Working Together to Teach Shakespeare

MICHAEL FLACHMANN
California State University
Bakersfield, California

For the past twelve years, Flachmann has spent his summers as company dramaturg at the Utah Shakespearean Festival. In this chapter, he explores the differences between the worlds of English teachers and theater professionals and asserts that "both disciplines, English and theater, can learn a great deal from each other." He then identifies seven primary areas in which English teachers and theater professionals diverge in their approach to Shakespeare's plays, and he demonstrates how in each case the English teacher might gain something by considering the approach and method of the theater professional.

I like to describe myself as "an English teacher who went bad." After beginning my career with a fairly traditional B.A., M.A., and Ph.D. in English literature and a decade's experience teaching Shakespeare at the university level, I made a delightful but unexpected detour fifteen years ago into the seductive excitement of professional theater, where I've been moonlighting during the summers as a dramaturg—a scholar who helps actors, directors, and designers understand and investigate the scripts of plays. I've served as company dramaturg at the Utah Shakespeare Festival for the past twelve seasons, where I've been a member of the artistic teams for over forty different productions; I've also been dramaturg and/or textual consultant for shows at the Oregon Shakespearean Festival, the La Jolla Playhouse, the Arizona Shakespearean Festival, the Southwest Shakespeare Company, California Institute of the Arts, and several other west coast theaters. Because of this rather schizophrenic oscillation between the two parallel worlds of English teachers and theater professionals, I've come to believe over the years that these two groups of people instinctively *think* about Shakespeare in entirely different manners.

In fact, I'm continually amazed at the stunningly contradictory ways in which theater professionals and English teachers approach a wide range of problems relating to Shakespeare's plays. Academic cross-pollination is always useful in our profession, but nowhere is this collaboration as important and necessary as it is in the instruction of Shakespeare in English courses, where many teachers still routinely approach his plays as "literature" rather than as "theater." I feel strongly that both disciplines, English and theater, can learn a great deal from each other; but since the target audience for this book is principally English teachers, I'd like to concentrate on ways in which this group can profit from emulating the traditional methods used by their colleagues in professional theater. Specifically, I have isolated seven primary areas in which I feel English teachers and theater professionals approach the plays in widely divergent ways.

Solving Problems

Most theater people naturally look for the problems in a script first, then decide how they are going to work them out; English teachers more frequently identify for their students the common larger themes and images of the play—what is *known,* rather than what is *unknown*— and avoid problem areas if these troublesome theatrical moments do not fit within one or more of the major themes they have classified. Thus, the English teachers' natural and commendable impulse to clarify the play for their students is often at odds with the organic complexity and richness of interpretation available in Shakespeare's scripts. By trying too hard to "solve" the play in their classrooms, English teachers will sometimes rob their students of the delicious ambiguity and paradox that reside in these brilliant theatrical documents. As the innovative modern director Peter Sellars explained in a recent *Time* magazine interview, "When I direct Shakespeare, the first thing I do is go to the text for cuts. I go through to find the passages that are real heavy, that really are not needed, places where language has become obscure, the places where there is a bizarre detour. And then I take those moments, those elements, and I make them the centerpiece, the core of the production" (31 Oct. 1994, 78).

As this quotation illustrates, most theater people realize in a manner that English teachers generally do not that the real excitement and reward of working with a Shakespearean script lies in locating and solving the important cruxes which define it as a unique and challenging work of art. Through our interaction with the script, we become theatrical detectives combing through the evidence of the text for hidden clues that will help us understand and appreciate its deeper mysteries. In *Macbeth,* for instance, who is the third murderer? Why does Lady Macbeth speak so formally (or is it informally?) in her opening soliloquy in 1.5? Why doesn't Macduff stay home to protect his wife and children? Why does Macbeth actually see the ghost of Banquo, yet he only *imagines* he sees the "dagger of the mind" in 2.1? And finally, why is the Malcolm-Macduff discussion in 4.3 so long and tedious? What did Shakespeare intend for us to discover in this scene about Scotland's future king? Once difficult questions such as these are analyzed and answered in the rehearsal hall, then the production can proceed with confidence. The same is true in the classroom, I believe, where the process of beginning with problems to be solved can often yield more satisfying results than our tried and true "English" method of making certain our students understand the larger, more comprehensible issues of a play before we move on to increasingly cryptic and challenging concerns.

Working Inside-out and Outside-in

Similarly, while English teachers begin their units on Shakespeare with such important but peripheral topics as Shakespeare's life, the Globe Theatre, or a history of the Renaissance, theater people will invariably go directly to the script to determine what it means to them before they read anyone else's opinion about the play or the world that produced it. I call this English approach working from the "outside-in" since the pedagogical method clearly implies that Shakespeare's plays are so hopelessly complex that the students won't begin to understand them unless they are given an immense amount of background material before they actually pick up the script and start reading it. This reinforces the students' latent fears that Shakespeare is too difficult for them, which can often begin the unit on a remarkably sour note. If the actors' approach of working "inside-out" were used more frequently in English classrooms, students would begin by reading the script and then naturally develop questions about the peripheral areas, which could be answered by their teachers when these queries occur in the normal process of reading the play rather than in an awkward clump at the beginning of the unit. Instead of our starting a classroom discussion on *Hamlet,* for example, with a lengthy canned lecture about melancholia or Danish history or Renaissance ghost lore, what would happen if the students simply began by reading the script? What would they discover in the opening lines that might spark their curiosity and provide occasion for some helpful background information from the teacher? First of all, some smart cookie is bound to inquire why the wrong guard is issuing the challenge. Francisco is on the watch, and Bernardo comes to relieve him. Why, then, does Bernardo ask "Who's there?" Francisco, as the official guard on duty, should interrogate the newcomer. Furthermore, what hints can we find about the country we are in? The century? And what were the duties of guards in that place and time? Why are these soldiers on guard anyway? What has happened in the kingdom to make everyone so frightened? Why is the password "Long live the king"? Has the current king already lived a long time? Or is he relatively new to the throne? Why is Francisco "bitter cold"? What season are we in? And why is he "sick at heart"? More important, what kind of play begins with so many vivid images of fear, cold, and sickness? Beginning inside the play like this helps our students take immediate "ownership" of the script; as a result, their questions will seem to guide the discussion (and our subsequent lectures) toward answers they require to make sense out of this wonderful Shakespearean puzzle. The alternative method, which most of us have followed in the classroom for years, is to structure the introduction to the play around *our own* questions, which makes *us* the sole custodians of knowledge and reduces the students to passive recipients of seemingly useless and arcane information that has little relevance to their own complex twentieth-century lives.

Rehearsing

Although actors routinely perfect their understanding of Shakespeare by repeating their lines aloud through rehearsal, most English students are seldom encouraged to perform speeches out loud in class, much less to "act out" entire sections of the play before the rest of their classmates. Even as they read the play at home, preparing for future classroom discussions, English students seem most content envisioning the play in the quiet theater of their minds, rather than in the rough give-and-take rehearsal with other intelligent human beings that creates all legitimate productions of Shakespeare's plays. The word "rehearse" means, of course, to "rehear": to say the lines over and over trying out in the process different inflections, various metrical patterns, and diverse interpretations that confer meaning upon the dull, lifeless words imprisoned on the page. Classrooms devoid of such theatrical collaboration will seldom shimmer with the excitement of discovery that so often accompanies the theatrical rehearsal process. By "performing" the verse out loud, actors as well as students are able to make Shakespeare's words their *own,* thereby entering into a partnership with the play in which both the script and the reader's voice are necessary to bring the Bard's highly textured and evocative language to life.

In Antony's famous "Friends, Romans, countrymen" monologue in 3.2 of *Julius Caesar,* for instance, we might experiment in the classroom with one student playing Antony, while the rest of the class takes the part of the crowd. Then, through the dynamics of rehearsal, we can ask the students whether the crowd is silent or noisy when Antony begins to speak. If they are noisy, why is this so? Who or what has incited them? And at what point does Antony quiet them down? A major clue is that his speech starts out with a single stressed syllable, followed sequentially by a trochee, a dactyl, a spondee, and finally a regular iamb (´ ´˘ ´˘˘ ´´ ˘´). This predominance of initial stressed syllables in each foot clearly implies that Antony is attempting to be heard over a number of other voices. In order to experiment with this concept, have the crowd become silent and loud at different parts of the monologue, then see how this alternation between rapt attention and verbal agreement helps confer meaning upon Antony's great speech. At which precise moments in his address will Antony pause? And why does he do so? Does he move from one part of the stage to another? If so, why? Will a pause in one section of the monologue be as effective as a pause somewhere else? Exactly when does he produce the will? And when should he display Caesar's bloody body to the angry crowd? Adventuring in the classroom with such rehearsal techniques can help clarify for even our most recalcitrant students the principal dramatic options in a scene, thereby inviting them to understand in a visceral, right-brained manner the fact that plays achieve their most complete and satisfying expression when they are performed live on stage and that the same black words floating softly on the pristine white page can bring forth a substantial number of viable interpretive choices. Best of all, our students will eventually claim the play as "theirs" by performing selected scenes in this fashion. Through the rehearsal process, they will put their own unique stamp on the material, which allows them to become one with its mystery and brilliance and enables them to understand through intuition valuable truths that may still lie beyond their intellectual grasp.

Finding Objectives

In order to research and develop the characters they play, actors are continually in the process of searching for "objectives": What does this character want? And what is he willing to do to get it? English teachers and their students, on the contrary, seem more often involved in finding the thematic parallels between various characters, along with the predominant motifs and images which yoke together the entire play. That is, we English teachers move immediately toward abstraction and symbolic representation, while our theatrical counterparts look instinctively for the humanity of the characters they will portray. If Iago is depicted in the English classroom, for example, as a descendant of the medieval vices and a personification of pure, motiveless evil, his more "human" counterpart on stage is simply a very clever, angry man obsessed with effecting horrible revenge on Othello and Desdemona. His objective may be *to ruin* Othello and Desdemona, *to convert* others to his sordid view of the world, or *to dignify* his own trivial existence in the play. But he will always have a single, specific, and very "actable" dramatic objective which humanizes and particularizes his unique character. In short, an actor can't "play" a personification; he can't act out a literary symbol. As a result, our laudable desire in the classroom to simplify the script for our students and identify its symbolic significance can sometimes rob it of its most important, enduring, and fascinating element: the vibrant humanity of the characters.

One extremely effective way of isolating and responding to character objectives in an English classroom is through a teaching technique called "psychodrama," in which students are asked to impersonate various characters from a play. If your class is studying *Romeo and Juliet,* for instance, ask your students to move their chairs into a huge circle in the center of the room, and then select a young woman to sit in the center of the circle and pretend that she is Juliet. Encourage the students on the outside of the circle to ask about her life in Verona: Are you happy? Do you love your parents? How do you feel about this Romeo fellow you've just met? You may have to begin the process with a few easy questions, but most students will immediately warm to the opportunity of interviewing an actual character from the play. Instruct the girl playing Juliet not to worry too obsessively about basing her answers directly on the script; the technique will work much better if she simply reaches inside her own psyche and responds as if she had actually *become* Juliet. Once you've got the process going, the real fun begins. Keep Juliet where she is, then bring into the circle another student who will play the part of her mother. Have them speak directly to each other in character, responding not only to what they say to each other, but also to the new questions and comments from the students on the outside of the circle. Then bring in Lord Capulet, then Romeo, the Friar, etc. If your unit includes other plays by Shakespeare, you might even want to create wildly imaginative psychodramas in which Hamlet, Othello, and Macbeth visit with each other in your classroom. Whatever configuration of characters you choose, this technique of psychodrama will consistently demonstrate for your students one of the single most important truths of Shakespearean study: All these characters live within ourselves, and all we have to do to understand them is find the very "human" objectives which motivate their actions and mark their kinship with us as vivid, unique individuals in this world. Like the quest for the Holy Grail, the search to understand Shakespeare's characters truly begins and ends inside ourselves.

Making Choices

As the preceding explanation of psychodrama implies, actors and other theater personnel are continually in the process of making definitive choices: this accent or that one, this color dress or that color, this reading of a line or that one. English teachers, on the other hand, generally seem most comfortable when the interpretation of plays is left open to individual student opinion. One of the great joys, in fact, of studying plays simply as literature is that we can allow many different interpretations of a scene, a character, or a line to exist in our heads simultaneously without being required to make choices among them. Unfortunately, theater artists don't have such luxuries. While the English approach is admirable in that it validates many different student beliefs about important moments in a script, it overlooks the crucial and highly "theatrical" manner in which specific choices are always able to crystallize and energize student opinion on critical issues in a play.

One productive way English teachers can encourage their students to make such theatrical choices within the classroom is through the process of staging scenes, during which the student actors can have a great deal of fun attempting various line readings, blocking configurations, and character portrayals; the teachers can then poll their student audiences about which specific interpretations they liked best. As a result, students will often instinctively begin to understand and identify with scenes in which they have recently made an emotional investment by choosing from among the various artistic options presented by their classmates. In *Othello,* for example, how important is it for Desdemona to be played by a relatively young actress, perhaps sixteen or seventeen years old? How would the play change for you and your students if she were played by a twenty-eight-year-old actress? Which would you prefer? Why? Often a brief viewing of two different videotapes highlighting the same scene or character in a play will help define for your students the entirely distinct responses such an age difference will make. By the same token, how "native" should the character of Othello be? How "tribal" are his costumes and behavior? If he is played closer to a Moor than an African, how will this theatrical choice influence audience response toward the rest of the production? Similarly, how "Jewish" is Shylock in *The Merchant of Venice*? Is he exotically different from the Venetian Christians, or is he more merchant than Semite?

By "playing" and then evaluating these and other important dramatic options in your classroom, you can help your students discover that each individual artistic choice will reverberate into the rest of the script in ways that will either be pleasing or irritating to them as interpreters of the production. In fact, their individual responses to these choices will eventually define the play for them, because the script will therefore exist most meaningfully not on paper but in their minds as a sequential collection of theatrical images that they have seen and heard and reacted to based upon their own developing standards of taste and artistic sensibility. And isn't that eventually what a Shakespeare unit ought to do: Give our students some sense of their *own* interpretation of these brilliant plays? Otherwise, why are we teaching these scripts in our classrooms?

Experimentation

While English teachers seem, as a whole, slavishly devoted to the spelling, punctuation, and stage directions embodied in the scripts chosen for their classroom use, most actors, directors, and designers understand that these "accidentals" of a Shakespearean text are not meant to be taken as gospel truth. In fact, they beg the alert reader for experimentation—particularly the stage directions, which were not written by Shakespeare but by modern literary scholars who, in editing the play, have simply recorded their best opinions about what was happening on stage during a number of important theatrical moments.

Obsessive reverence for these non-Shakespearean elements of the play can stifle creative responses to the scripts on the page and on the stage. Since Shakespeare did not oversee the publication of his plays, and since all decisions about spelling and punctuation in twentieth-century texts are made by modern editors (some of whom have never set foot inside a theater), English teachers and their students would do well to emulate the actors' well-founded contempt for such textual decisions that have little legitimate claim to Shakespearean authority. Does Hamlet say, for example, "O, that this too too *sullied, solid,* or *sallied* flesh . . ."? And what difference would each of these words make in the meaning of his well-known soliloquy? In his "To be, or not to be" speech, what punctuation follows the second "be"? A colon? A comma? Or a question mark? How would each of these textual accidentals change the reading and interpretation of the line? The plays are, of course, rife with similarly crucial orthographic options, and a brief look at the early quarto and folio editions, where such variant readings reside, will often liberate us from the tyranny of textual choices made by modern editors masquerading as William Shakespeare.

One enjoyable classroom exercise that encourages students to experiment with such variants in punctuation is for the teacher to type up a speech or part of a scene omitting all the commas, semicolons, colons, periods, and question marks contained in the text. The students are then asked to fill in the punctuation where they believe it ought to go. Another good assignment is to tell your students they need to cut, say, fifty lines out of a particular scene because the running time of your hypothetical production is too long. Ask them which fifty lines they would cut and why. Similarly, have them play with changes in the stage directions found in your classroom script. In 3.1 of *Hamlet,* for example, at what point does the prince discover that Claudius and Polonius are eavesdropping on his conversation with Ophelia? If he learns of their presence early in the scene, how will this knowledge influence the rest of his dialogue with Ophelia? And what if he finds out later in the scene? Have your students stage the scene three or four times, with the discovery located at different points in the script each time. The classroom discussions resulting from such experimentation with word choice, punctuation, stage directions, and potential cuts will not only focus attention on the play you are studying, but will also help sensitize your students to the fact that these scripts invite enormously satisfying creative responses from attentive readers and viewers. One of the great joys of dealing with Shakespeare's plays is that nothing is engraved in stone: Everything is open to interpretation.

Script Theory

Finally, actors, directors, and designers understand, in a way that English teachers and their students seldom do, that Shakespeare's plays are not literary documents meant to be analyzed solely within the sterile confines of a high school or college classroom, but instead are "scripts" intended for production. Even the language that English teachers traditionally employ in reference to these two wildly different entities—the printed text of a play and its eventual performance on stage—deliberately blur the crucial distinction between the two. Most English teachers use the same word, in fact, to designate both extremes of the same continuum. We say, "Have you read the play?" and "Have you seen the play?," thereby perpetuating a semantic confusion which deliberately distorts the two genres and implies through the semiotics of names, that the reading of a play is just as fulfilling as seeing it performed on stage. In essence, the two experiences must be identical since we use the same word to denote each of them.

By homogenizing within their students' minds these two distinct experiences—reading a play and watching a production—English teachers have perverted the traditional artistic reason playscripts exist, which is to be produced before paying spectators within the ritualistic, nurturing environment of a theater. Actors know exactly what to do with scripts: They perform them! When we import these "plays" into the study or the classroom, however, we often lose sight of the primal, instinctive, and authentic purpose behind them and must, instead, begin to invent other, more artificial reasons why the study of Shakespeare, like artistic broccoli, is good for us: so we can perform well on SAT and ACT exams; so we can appreciate "literature"; so we can think and act like civilized human beings. All of these sophisticated and valid arguments seem pale indeed, however, when contrasted with the high-energy, gut-wrenching, joyful, intense, pressure-filled experience of wrestling with a play so you can perform it on stage. Theater people encounter this feeling daily, while English teachers and their students rarely, if ever, experience it. The closer we can get to this excitement in our classrooms through teaching the plays as "theater" rather than as "literature," however, the more we can recreate for our students the unbelievable thrill of seeing a vibrant, satisfying, and well-crafted production of one of Shakespeare's scripts. In fact, no higher purpose exists in our lives as English teachers than to provide our students with this complete and authentic experience whenever they read the plays.

In the final analysis, if we want to "mend" the way we teach Shakespeare in our English classrooms, we have to be willing to *think* about his scripts through these new and innovative interdisciplinary methods. If some of the techniques you currently use to teach the plays work well for you and your students, please don't abandon them totally. You may, though, want to supplement your normal pedagogical methods with some of the approaches traditionally used by our colleagues in the world of theater—particularly if your students react to the prospect of reading *Julius Caesar* or *Macbeth* as if they were about to undergo a root canal. After all, theater people have been studying, watching, and producing Shakespeare's plays for nearly four hundred years—much longer than we English teachers have been teaching them! Perhaps, if we're willing to revolutionize the way we think, we can learn a few tricks from them about teaching these magnificent scripts.

CHAPTER 9

Mirrors, Sculptures, Machines and Masks

Theater Improvisation Games

MARGO A. FIGGINS

University of Virginia
Charlottesville, Virginia

In this final chapter of the performance section, Figgins presents her thoughts about the value of improvisational theater games. She details three basic improvisation exercises—mirrors, sculptures, and machines—and then combines the exercises with the study of Much Ado About Nothing, *a practice that she believes frees the student from the more daunting performance technique of playing the role of a Shakespearean character. Act by act, she offers suggestions for adapting the individual exercises to specific elements in the text.*

When I registered for a three-day pre-conference workshop in improvisational theater at the 1969 convention of the National Council of Teachers of English (NCTE), I had been teaching English for only a few years. Still a novice, I had been at it long enough to know that something was missing; further, that even if I perfected what I was doing, whatever was missing would still be missing. I would continue to have students who didn't like English, and I would always be a convenient target for whatever angered or disappointed them. So when Robert Alexander, Director of The Living Stage Theatre Company, introduced his improvisation workshop with the following words, he had my full attention:

> If you have someone who doesn't want to learn, it's because they're afraid they're not going to be successful at it, and they don't want to be there. They don't like you, themselves, or the world they live in. You can't force feed information to someone who's in a state of contraction. You've got to get them in a state of expansion. The way to do that is to create the conditions for their success. And the way to do that is to create an improvisational workshop where everything is not only relevant to their lives, but also where they cannot be wrong as they explore, discover and communicate what's on their minds and in their hearts. (Alexander 1969)

The three days that grew out of those opening words marked a fundamental turning point in my approach to teaching. By their end, I had learned how to turn the air around me into molasses, howl like a screech owl, turn the line "My problem is that the mangos are never ripe enough" into an entire monologue, twist myself into the shape of a pretzel, and order scrambled eggs in gibberish. I returned home "in a state of expansion."

The next ten years in my classroom looked very different. With students up and out of their seats, enacting lines in an Emily Dickinson poem—one day cautiously straddling a row of chairs that were planks they had to walk, another day huddled onto my desk and rowing it through Eden without map or compass, and, after that, wading together, jeans rolled knee high, in a pool of grief marked by chalk lines at the middle of the room—the class became all action. Using improvisational theater games, my students crossed the literary threshold into other worlds less familiar, even strange. Once there, they could more readily explore the dramatic situations they found there and, in the process, explore meaning in their own lives as well. Since that time, I have come to see all learning as improvisation.

In *Peripheral Visions* (1994), Mary Catherine Bateson makes a strong case for improvisation as one of the most important life skills for living in a rapidly changing and interdependent world where novelty is the rule, not the exception. Successful encounters with the unfamiliar depend upon one's ability to see out of the corner of the eye where essential clues lie and to use them to survive the vertigo caused by such moments. I was made newly aware of this on my recent odyssey to Sappho's birthplace on the island of Lesbos, where I found myself with not a word of Greek in my vocabulary nor an alphabetic letter in common with anyone around me. Abruptly immersed in the ambiguity of cultural differences, I found myself improvising my way from one moment to the next. The ambiguity inherent in such challenges to long-held patterns and values is something one may never be fully prepared for; however, as Bateson asserts, one may respond more effectively if one "can claim a history of improvisation" (6). This, she suggests, is tomorrow's challenge: "Instead of passing on hallowed certainties and maintaining the status quo, [parents and teachers] must make childhood an open-ended introduction to a process of continual change . . ." (8).

I share Bateson's premise that "ambiguity is the warp of life, not something to be eliminated," and that improvisation is key to coping with its inevitable tensions. Further, there are real pleasures to be found in using improvisational theater strategies in the classroom. They can provide an exciting connection for students to those worlds presented in literature, many of which appear bewildering to them. Shakespearean texts are among those which teachers find hardest to bridge, distanced as they are in language and time, obstacles further complicated by the fact that students find more immediacy and allure in the multimedia texts which dominate their own culture.

I will describe three basic exercises with which to begin work in improvisation: Mirrors, Sculptures, and Machines. Building on these initial exercises, I will illustrate their application within the context of *Much Ado About Nothing*. The purpose of such work is two-fold: first, students will use improvisation to gain access to and greater ease with Shakespearean texts; second, and more implicit in the process, students will be learning ways to respond in unfamiliar and unpredictable contexts and to more consciously construct their experience.

Three Basic Improvisation Exercises

These improvisational exercises can best be done with the desks pushed back against the walls. At the very least, there should be enough space in some part of the room so that students' movement can be unimpeded. I suggest introducing these exercises as theater games used by professional actors and actresses to sharpen their mental concentration and train their bodies to move with precision in much the same way that athletes train. Let them know that, after having practiced these basic exercises, they will be using them to interpret and perform both plays and poetry and that, in order for the group to get to that point, it is important that they take the work seriously and follow your coaching in the same way they would follow the directions of a basketball, gymnastics, or voice coach.

The main ingredient of the coaching process is what Viola Spolin (1963) calls the *point of concentration* (POC). Giving the exercise its primary focal point, its function is to keep the student's mind occupied with solving the acting problem. For example, if students are throwing an imaginary ball to each other, the POC would be to "keep your eye on the ball at all times." Each of the following exercises has a POC, and you will want to coach students to return to it whenever you observe distraction. Another aspect of coaching, demonstration, is crucial. You must be prepared to participate in whatever way may be necessary, e.g., as a student's partner or modeling response to an exercise.

The first few times you try these exercises, you can expect a certain degree of noise, most often due to students' self-consciousness in trying something new. You will need to focus and re-focus their attention as a way of coaching them through their discomfort. Proceed in small steps and provide multiple opportunities to practice any one exercise over a period of days and weeks. As you and your students gain confidence with the exercises, expand upon them. Your students are quite likely to see variations that you do not; be willing to work with their ideas.

Mirrors
(Point of Concentration: To reflect another person's movement)

Begin with everyone standing. Tell students that you are going to call out various movements like **climb**, and you want them to make each movement you call out **in slow motion**. Make it clear that this exercise is **non-verbal** and that you want them to try it first with their eyes closed and standing in one spot. In this way, they won't have to worry about others watching them nor will they hurt themselves. I suggest that you demonstrate a climbing motion first. Then, when they are still, with eyes closed, call out the following movements, one at a time, with enough time in between each word for students to respond fully to the prompt (15–20 seconds): **fly** (pause) **dance** (pause) **salute** (pause) **hitchhike**. (Your coaching phrases will be: Do the motions with your feet in one place! Eyes closed! Don't forget—slow motion! Slow it way down, as though the air were molasses!) Playing slow instrumental music in the background helps to deepen concentration and discourage talking.

Following this warm-up, ask students to find a partner, number themselves 1 and 2, face each other, and stand at arm's length. Explain to them that #1 is the person looking in the mirror; #2 is the mirror whose job it is to reflect that person's image. Tell them that now you are going to call out those same five movements again and, as they move—still in slow motion but now with their eyes open—the mirror will reflect their movement as precisely as possible; further, that they should continue the movement until you call out the next movement, at which time they should make the transition into it as fluidly as possible. (Your coaching phrases may be: Keep it slow so that the other person can follow you! No noise;

this is non-verbal! Maintain eye contact! Mirror exactly what you see!) Then ask students to change roles and repeat the exercise. Once students are handling the exercise well, try a different set of motions (e.g., **tiptoe, twist, knock, peek**); you might also involve students in brainstorming a list of movements that can be done standing in one place, with them choosing from that list the ones they want to mirror.

Sculptures
(Point of Concentration: To express a theme word or concept physically)

An effective non-verbal warm-up to sculptures is to instruct everyone to begin moving about in the playing area naturally, as though they were in a crowded shopping mall and trying to walk around without bumping into others. Once they are in motion, weaving in and out, tell them that you will occasionally call out the word *"Freeze!"*, at which time they should stop on a dime in whatever position the word catches them. When they seem comfortable with this freeze-frame technique, tell them that you will begin calling out different words in place of **freeze** and that, whenever they hear one, they are to strike a position which captures and reflects that word in some way. For example, you might call out the word **sports**; one person may strike the position of a football player about to hike the ball while another stands with a bat ready for the next pitch. Students should hold their positions (ten seconds) until you say *"Move!"* at which time they resume movement until you call out the next word. It is important to keep the pace lively and the spirit spontaneous. You might alternate words which signify concrete images with more abstract concepts, e.g., **animal, boredom, fireworks, fear.**

Having participated in this warm-up activity, students will be more comfortable with the sculpture exercise. Dividing the group in half, direct each group to opposite sides of the playing space. Explain to students that this time, as you call out words, they will be creating a multidimensional sculpture that includes everyone in their group. Beginning with one of the two groups, call out a theme word (e.g., **winner**) and ask someone to begin building the sculpture by coming to the center of the playing space and striking a position that in some way communicates that concept. Once begun, your job is to coach the remaining students in the group to add on to the sculpture; one at a time, they link themselves to someone else, giving the sculpture a new dimension while not disturbing others' positions, i.e., striking a position that is lower or higher than another's or contracting the body in contrast to another's expansion. In other words, coach them into filling the space in interesting ways. Once the first group has created their sculpture of "winner," the second group might then create its opposite—**loser**—repeating the same process. Other evocative combinations are **war/peace, schoolday/weekend, adults/teenagers, conformity/individuality, freedom/enslavement.** (Your coaching phrases may be: Freeze in position; don't move a muscle! Now *feel* that word in every muscle! Keep your eyes focused on one spot; don't let them wander! Support your own weight! Sharpen your position!) As sculptures are completed, you can invite the observing group to look at it from different angles as one might a sculpture in a museum. Ask students to imagine that they themselves are its sculptor and to suggest changes that might strengthen the sculpture's representation of the theme word, e.g., the placement of a hand, the focus of someone's eyes, the way in which one person connects to another. Then reverse the groups and repeat the exercise.

When students are working comfortably with non-verbal sculptures, you can experiment with a variation involving sound. Following the preceding process to form the sculpture, suggest to students that their part of the sculpture has a mechanism for sound in it and that when you say "*Go!*" everyone makes a sound that suggests the theme. If the theme is **pain**, that sound might be a scream, a moan, or actual words like "Ouch!" or "That hurts!" Once the various sounds have been voiced simultaneously, you can alter the exercise so that each individual sound is heard. To do this, when the sculpture is in place, tell students to make their sound only when you tap them on the shoulder. This creates some interesting possibilities. Once you have heard each person's sound, you can orchestrate the sounds in interesting sequences, alternating among one person's moan, someone else's words, and yet another person's expletive, resulting in an impromptu script which tells a kind of story through the sounds, depending upon the order in which they are voiced.

Machines

(Point of Concentration: To create a repetitive machine-like sound and motion)

As with previous exercises, a full-group warm-up encourages greater participation. With students spread out in the playing area, ask them to close their eyes and imagine themselves in an automobile factory; what are some of the machine sounds they might hear? How would those machine sounds differ from those in a carpenter's shop? Or from those in a hospital emergency room? In each instance, ask students to make some of the machine sounds typical of each setting. Then, with their eyes still closed, ask students to imagine themselves part of a machine which manufactures bad weather; what sound does their part of the machine make? Direct them to make that sound when you say "*Go!*" and to continue the sound until you call "*Freeze!*" Practice this several times until everyone is participating. Next, ask them to imagine the movement of the part that makes that sound. Be ready to demonstrate a mechanical, repetitive movement to accompany your own sound for the bad-weather machine. Then, altogether, everyone joins in with their sound and movement. The next step is to assemble the parts of the machine. To do this, everyone moves to the edges of the playing space, someone becomes the first part in the bad-weather machine and, one by one, others add their sound and movement. As with sculptures, each person's movement should be in some way joined to that of another but without impeding it. As students are watching for the best place to add on, coach them into altering their sound and movement in whatever way will add more variety and interest to the machine's overall effect. The object is to invent an amazing machine whose individual parts move in complex rhythms together. (Your coaching phrases may be: I can't hear everyone's different noise! Work off of each other's movements! Make sure you are connected to some other part in the machine! Keep your rhythm consistent!)

Following this full-group machine, you can divide the groups into two teams that take turns spontaneously creating machine types that you call out, e.g., a spaghetti machine, a gossip machine, one that makes fortune cookies. The possibilities are endless; don't be afraid to be fanciful.

Combining Improvisation and *Much Ado About Nothing*

While simply practicing these exercises and their variations accomplishes numerous language arts objectives, these exercises are also effective in exploring the meaning of various texts. Because students generally love participating in these theater games but typically care much less about Shakespeare, I have found improvisational exercises and Shakespearean texts to be an excellent combination: students' enthusiasm for improvisation transforms their resistance to Shakespeare into positive energy which can result in students feeling more interested and invested in their reading.

Against the background of the preceding exercises, I will illustrate the implementation of these basic exercises within the context of *Much Ado About Nothing* to suggest how they can enliven the study of Shakespeare. Whatever the text you select, the process of applying these exercises is the same: identify theme words, central tensions, and key motifs; then couple them with one or more of the three improvisational exercises. Approaching Shakespearean plays in this way frees students from the more typical but often daunting theatrical approach of playing the part of a Shakespearean character. That these exercises can involve *all* students is another distinct advantage. No longer limited by the number of reading parts available, there need be no students left on the sidelines.

As a general approach, I recommend prefacing students' reading of any one act with one or more improvisational activities that anticipate narrative tensions and highlight themes and motifs. Sometimes full-group participation may be most appropriate; at other times, you may find it more effective if fewer students develop any one improvisation. These decisions will depend upon your instructional purposes. I would encourage you to structure the work so that *all* students have participated in at least one or two improvisational activities related to each act. In any case, the basic format holds: you will need to identify a point of concentration (POC) for each exercise and provide the necessary side-coaching. (Note: In the following summaries provided for each act, theme words, central tensions, and key motifs appear in bold type; selected illustrations for their use follow.)

> *Act 1*: A messenger arrives in Messina with a letter for Leonato bearing news of the prince Don Pedro who is arriving with his victorious army. Claudio and Benedick, the prince's good **friends**, and Don John, Don Pedro's **jealous** bastard brother and self-described **villain**, are among those accompanying the prince. The very sight of **Hero**, Leonato's daughter, renews Claudio's **love** for her; in contrast, Beatrice and Benedick resume their characteristic **warring**, her taunts deepening his resolve never to be tempted by **marriage**. Don Pedro offers to woo Hero on Claudio's behalf at the masked ball that same night. Hearing of Don Pedro's plan, Don John embarks upon his own plan of **deceit** to turn Claudio against Don Pedro. Information gained by **eavesdropping** leads both Leonato and Claudio to believe it is Don Pedro who wants Hero's hand.

Improvisation to Preface Act 1 Reading

Because **eavesdropping** is a key motif upon which much of the plot turns, and students will recognize it as a familiar way by which information travels, it offers an effective and playful point of departure. Begin by asking students what they understand the word to mean, why one might eavesdrop on others, what some of the situations are in which they or their friends are most likely to eavesdrop (e.g., lunchroom or locker room conversations, parental talk behind closed doors, a telephone call), and what typically happens with information obtained this way (e.g., gossip, which gives an opportunity to refer back to the gossip-making machine created earlier). Then invite students to create a sculpture on the theme of eavesdropping. A variation: You might pass a piece of overheard information through the sculpture (in the spirit of the familiar "telephone game") to demonstrate what can happen as a result of information obtained this way.

Another introductory activity is a mirror exercise involving the concept of villain. Referring to students' earlier work with the concept of a friendship, ask students to consider how **villain** contrasts with **friend**. Who are some contemporary villains (e.g., the Joker in *Batman,* the World Trade Center bombers)? Are there any "local villains" (e.g., community drug dealers, the neighborhood bully)? Then direct students to pair up for a mirror exercise in which they create a physical image of a villain; reversing their roles, repeat the exercise and coach the second of the pair into another physical interpretation of the word. A variation: Freeze students in their mirror image of **villain** and instruct the mirror to transform the image, slowly remaking the image into one of **friend**. Before moving on, ask students to talk about what it felt like physically to be villains, and how their bodies felt differently in the image of friend.

These introductory activities prepare students for their reading of the first act by focusing on one of the central conflicts first introduced (Don John's jealousy of Claudio, who is favored by John's brother Don Pedro) and a key motif (eavesdropping) that advances the plot. Building on this introduction, students can speculate about the relationship between eavesdropping and the play's title.

Improvisation during Act 1 Reading

There are numerous occasions in Act 1 for improvisational interludes. In 1.1, students might create a sculpture of **fencing**, and then consider how Benedick and Beatrice's talk is like a fencing match. A variation: A sculpture with sound involving two people who, in the roles of Beatrice and Benedick, exchange lines and, with each verbal jab, alter their fencing positions. (You might look for someone in a local theater or athletic group to demonstrate various fencing moves.) The first scene also introduces through Claudio and Hero the theme of **love**, which exists against a background of war and Beatrice and Benedick's continual verbal warring. Students might search out the vocabulary attached to "love" and "war" in the various scenes and then create two contrasting machines which incorporate those words. This also provides an initial occasion for observing differences in men's talk and women's talk.

Finally, as a concluding activity, students can create a sculpture which summarizes Act 1 events. To do this, students assume the different character roles in the first act and, through their position in the sculpture, portray their relationship to other characters as Act 1 ends. For instance while Beatrice and Benedick are joined in fencing positions, Claudio and Don Pedro might be the center of others' attention, as Don John stands on the sidelines scowling, and so forth. A variation: From their character positions in the sculpture, each person voices a key line from Act 1 which best identifies the character. This particular sculpture variation can be repeated at the end of each act as a way of dramatizing how the various characters and their relationships change over the course of the play.

> *Act 2*: The various struggles for **power** and **position** intensify. Beatrice speaks disparagingly of **marriage** and continues her **war** with Benedick, exchanging verbal insults like **fencing** jabs. At the dance, Don Pedro's entourage enters wearing **masks** and the various plots of **deception** advance. Benedick, thinking himself disguised, is once again bested by Beatrice; Claudio is wounded by what he believes is Don Pedro's **betrayal**. Benedick, coming to the defense of Claudio's **honor**, is assured by Don Pedro that he has kept his promise and Claudio and Hero are betrothed, despite Don John's scheme. Benedick exits, smarting from Beatrice's persistent mocking. With the **wedding** set for a week ahead, Don Pedro proposes entertainment for the interim—**plotting** Beatrice and Benedick's fall into love. As Beatrice and Benedick's **friends** execute their plan, Don John conceives a more deadly plan to destroy Claudio and Hero's future.

Improvisation to Preface Act 2 Reading

A variation of the mirror exercise effectively anticipates a dominant motif in Act 2—the mask. In this warm-up, students first work individually. Explain that they are going to pretend that their face is a mask made of plaster. Closing their eyes, they are to begin very slowly bending and twisting the muscles in their face until the plaster breaks to reveal another mask beneath it. Then they must twist and contort their face to break that one, revealing yet another. Each new mask will have its own distinct expression. Next, in partners, have students mirror each other's masks. Coaching them, suggest different types of masks: **angel, monster, shyness, confusion** and, tying this activity to Act 1, **villain**. A variation: As any one new mask emerges, students make the sound that expresses the feeling associated with that mask.

This exercise creates a context for students to consider how masks function in their own lives. What situations require masks? What are the different masks that they wear? Why do they need their masks? What, if anything, is able to crack their masks? Using this discussion as a bridge into the reading of Act 2, where the mask becomes a tool of deceit, suggest that students look not only at how masks function literally in the first scene, but at how characters mask their true feelings from others. If time allows, students can choose the character who at this point interests them most, imagine the mask that might best suit them, and then make that mask, which then can be actually used in subsequent improvisations. (You might invite the art teacher or a local artist to conduct a mask-making workshop for this purpose).

Improvisation during Act 2 Reading

In 2.1, Beatrice describes her ideal man and, in 2.3, Benedick lists the virtues he requires in a wife. Dividing the group by gender, the males' task is to create a sculpture which reflects the attributes of Beatrice's ideal man, while the females portray those of Benedick's virtuous woman. A variation: Students create sculptures reflecting their own ideal man or woman;

or, switching modes, the females create a machine which produces the ideal man and the males, the ideal female. This provides an occasion for discussing the difference between appearance and reality, a theme that will become increasingly important. Moving in yet another but related direction, you might use the description of Beatrice in Scene 1 as a bad-tempered cow with short horns to initiate the creation of animal metaphors for the characters. This could result in an animal sculpture to which sounds could be added and with them, undoubtedly, a certain amount of hilarity. Animal metaphors could also form the basis for the masks of the different characters.

To conclude, assuming character masks have been created, students could develop a sculpture in which they both portray the change in the characters' relationships since Act 1 and don their masks to voice one or more hidden thoughts of that character and, in so doing, begin to dramatize characters' inner realities as well as their outward appearances.

> *Act 3:* As the playful conspiracy to join Beatrice and Benedick proceeds, Don John enters with a more deadly **deception**, further confusing **appearance** and **reality**. He discloses Hero's **infidelity** to Claudio and Don Pedro and takes them to witness her faithless rendezvous with Borachio. Charged with the night **watch** by Dogberry, the Master Constable, the deputies **eavesdrop** on Borachio and Conrade's drunken conversation and discover the villainous deed against Claudio and Hero. By Act 3's end, both Beatrice and Benedick are determined to return the other's affection.

Improvisation to Preface Act 3 Reading

In this scene Beatrice and Benedick's disposition toward each other shifts dramatically. Until now, they have been mistress and master of the insult; now they must find the words to compliment. Engaging students in machine-building exercises that first produce insults (and here a word about appropriate limits may be desirable), and then compliments, will prepare students for these character changes. Prior to this activity, ask students to consider how they experience insults and compliments differently. Is an insult the same as a "put-down"? Barring profanity, what are some of the things people say to purposely put another person down? Why do people do this? Why do Beatrice and Benedick behave in this way toward each other? Such questions create the terms for students to recognize words as weapons. Considering the compliment, students might discuss the kinds of comments that, in contrast, make them feel good about themselves. Once the two machines have been performed, invite students to consider which machine struck them as more powerful and why. If they conclude the insult machine, they might consider why insults linger in the memory while compliments tend to fade.

Improvisation during Act 3 Reading

The centerpiece of Act 3 is Don John's deception of Claudio involving Borachio's tryst with Margaret, who is made to appear as Hero. To explore this distortion of reality, after reading Scene 2 students can divide into as many as six groups, each group selecting one of six characters on which to focus: Hero, Claudio, Don John, Leonato, Beatrice, or Benedick. Suggest to students that they create the dream they imagine that character having the night before

Claudio and Hero's wedding and that, as an extra challenge, they must find a way to employ *at least two* of the three improvisation techniques in their enactment of the dream. Following their portrayals, students can consider the connection between dream and reality: To what extent are dreams real? How might dreams influence one's actions? What actions might have been provoked by those dreamt by their character? Can dreams deceive? How does one know the difference between dream and reality? In what way is Don John's deception of Claudio like a bad dream? In Claudio's position, what action would they have taken?

The appearance of Dogberry provides comic balance to the darker side of this act. Dogberry's humorously muddled speech may, in fact, reflect the way Shakespeare often sounds to the students' ears. Here is an opportunity for students themselves to have fun with language in the spirit of Dogberry's mangled tongue. After focusing on those sections of Dogberry's speech and decoding them at least enough to see more clearly the ways in which he misuses words and confuses syntax, have students create a machine that mangles the English language. This can result in a good-spirited parody of Shakespearean language.

At the end of Act 3, I recommend another sculpture once again reflecting the shift in relationships among the various characters. Once the tableau is formed, it can become the focal point of both a summarizing and predictive discussion, e.g., how has Don John's position in the sculpture changed? How do Claudio and Don Pedro see Don John differently? To conclude, invite students to create a second sculpture reflecting how they think these relationships will have changed by the next act. Having anticipated Act 4 in this way makes it possible to proceed directly to the reading.

Act 4: As Friar Francis begins the wedding ceremony, Claudio publicly exposes Hero's **infidelity** and rejects her as his bride. Don Pedro denounces her also and he and Claudio leave. Hero faints, Beatrice fears she is dead, and Leonato, devastated by this **shame** against his **family**, wishes she were dead. Hero swears her innocence and, believing her, the Friar devises a **deception** of his own to save her. They will pretend that Hero has died, hoping that such news will change Claudio's heart. Benedick counsels Leonato to accept the plan and Leonato swears **revenge** if Hero is innocent. Left alone, Benedick and Beatrice admit their love for each other, Benedick swearing that he will do whatever she requires for proof of his devotion. Resolute in her belief that Hero has been wronged, she asks him to kill Claudio. When he refuses, she wishes she were a man so that she herself could avenge Hero. Convinced by Beatrice's willfulness, Benedick resolves to challenge Claudio. Meanwhile, the Sexton hears the evidence against Borachio and Conrade and announces that Don John has fled.

Improvisation during Act 4 Reading

Beginning at a high pitch, Claudio accuses Hero of infidelity and brings intolerable public shame to Leonato's family. A variation of the mirror exercise makes it possible for students to assume the emotions of this tense situation and recognize the irony that adds to its gravity. For this purpose, it is most effective if students are in male-female partners who take on the roles of Claudio and Hero. Claudio stands before Hero, the mirror, who reflects back the image he wants in a wife. Before students enact this, involve them in a discussion of Claudio's image of Hero. What are the words that describe the woman Hero has appeared to be? The words are embedded in his accusation of her in Scene 1: gracious, fair, pure, beautiful, pious. Students can add their own words to this list. Further, what are the meanings that the name Hero implies? You might share its meaning from the Greek legend in which Hero was the true love of Leander for whom she drowned herself. This legend implies the meaning of Hero's name in Elizabethan times—fidelity in love. Against this background, ask those taking on the role of Hero to become mirrors, frozen without expression or gesture until the person in the role of Claudio steps in front of the mirror; at that point, coach them to very slowly transform themselves into the image that Claudio wants Hero to be and, once they have embodied that image, to freeze it. Then, direct those in the role of Claudio to perform the facial expressions and body gestures which communicate his disgust at her infidelity as you read lines and phrases from his accusation (e.g., "fare thee well, most foul," "thou pure impiety," "I'll lock up all the gates of love"). Those in the role of mirror in turn embody the shame and hurt that his words impose. Against the backdrop of students' earlier discussion of insults and put-downs, this experience can lead them to consider not only the power of words to transform one's sense of self but also the kinds of situations that might create in them a similar sense of shame and humiliation.

In this context, students can also expand their consideration of male-female relationships. How do men and women typically relate to each other in this play? Who has more power? How representative is Claudio and Hero's relationship? Is Claudio's fidelity ever at issue? Why is Hero so readily doubted and condemned? If Claudio does not recant, what will happen? How is the relationship between Benedick and Beatrice different, if at all? How might Beatrice respond in Hero's situation, and what prevents Hero from acting this way? Then, turning toward students' experience, how are male-female relationships different today? How much do males influence the images females have of themselves? To what extent have the females experienced the "mirror effect" in their own relationships where, like Hero, they have been defined by others' perceptions or expectations, and in what contexts? (Mary Pipher's *Reviving Ophelia* [1996] offers significant background information for such discussion.)

By the end of Act 4, the many deceptions on which the plot depends have nearly peaked and the line separating appearance and reality is sufficiently blurred. To construct a sculpture that reflects how the various deceptions have affected the different characters' relationships, ask students to first reconstruct the Act 3 sculpture in which they predicted these relationships. Next, ask them to revise the sculpture according to actual events and to evaluate their predictions. What happened that they had not anticipated? What outcome do they anticipate in the final act? What motive will ultimately win, revenge or repentance? With these speculations made, students are ready for the fifth and final act.

Act 5: The **comic** and **tragic** intermingle and **truth** and **illusion** vie for the final outcome. Leonato is inconsolable; Don Pedro and Claudio remain unmoved by his **grief**-fueled rage. Benedick challenges Claudio, resigns from Don Pedro's service, and accuses the two of having caused Hero's death. Borachio and Conrade are brought in and Borachio confesses. A remorseful Claudio begs to make amends; Leonato orders him to mourn at Hero's tomb that night and then marry his niece in Hero's place the following day. Meanwhile, anticipating a meeting with Beatrice, Benedick attempts a love **sonnet**. When Beatrice arrives, he hastily pockets his poor rhyme and, as the two survey the beginnings of their **love**, Ursula rushes in with the news that Don John's plot has been uncovered. In **repentance**, Claudio mourns all night and returns at dawn for the **marriage** ceremony. Leonato sends the women to **mask** themselves for the ceremony and Benedick asks him for Beatrice's hand. Claudio accepts the veiled figure as his wife and then discovers she is really Hero. Beatrice and Benedick discover the **trick** played on them as well; their love for each other is further exposed by the **revelation** of the love sonnets each has penned for the other. With Don John captured, the web of **deceit** is entirely unraveled and Shakespeare leaves nothing more to note. Claudio and Benedick, now reconciled, invite others into the dance that begins the celebration of their marriages.

Improvisation to Preface Act 5 Reading

Students may be immediately ready to read and improvise Act 5 and, if so, a warm-up exercise may interrupt their momentum. However, if you judge otherwise of your students, you might have them experiment with a sculpture that in some way portrays the war being waged in this final act between truth and illusion. That could involve students discussing situations in their own lives that have in some way involved the struggle between those two forces, which they can then translate into one or more physical images. One of the most effective of such sculptures I have seen was one depicting a tug of war, with the forces of truth on one side and, on the other, the forces of illusion. You could, of course, set up an actual tug of war including sound and movement. Whichever side wins, students can then speculate if the same forces will triumph in the final act.

Improvisation during Act 5 Reading

Shakespeare employs the motif of masks to end his play and, assuming students have made character masks, this is an effective place to use them. At the point in Scene 1 when Benedick has challenged Claudio and the sentiments of all of the characters are most polarized, ask students to identify the word, phrase, or sentence that most strongly expresses the point of view of the character for whom they have created their mask. Once students have selected their expression, engage them in creating a point-of-view sculpture for which they don their masks; once assembled, each person voices his/her character's point of view from behind the mask. A variation: After each character has voiced her/his point of view from behind the mask, the students remove the masks and each expresses something he/she believes the character is thinking but has, as yet, left unspoken. Another variation: Instead of doing a large-group sculpture, students create two-person sculptures. The exercise would proceed in the same way except, at the point where they remove the mask, they reveal a thought or feeling about the other character in their two-person sculpture that has not been expressed until that moment. This variation plays very close to the moment in Scene 4 when Beatrice and Benedick are required to publicly acknowledge their love for one another and, in doing so, remove the psychological masks which have previously protected them from each other's barbs. It further echoes the moment when Hero lifts her veil, revealing to Claudio yet another deception played on him.

Beatrice and Benedick's halting attempts at writing love sonnets for each other suggest the culminating activity and simultaneously set the stage for exploring a selection of Shakespearean love sonnets. The first step in this final activity is to expose students to sonnet form and content. A very accessible source for this is the *Handbook of Poetic Forms* (Padgett 1987) whose succinct description of the sonnet can be easily adapted to serve this purpose. Once students have an initial grasp of the sonnet form, which can be elaborated by showing them several modern-day sonnets, ask students to take on the role of either Benedick or Beatrice and write a sonnet for each other. Next, invite sharing of their sonnets in small groups (four to six students). Having heard each other's poems, ask them to select the one which appears to offer the most interesting dramatic possibilities. Each group is then given the task of dramatizing the selected sonnet, this time with the challenge of using *all three* basic improvisational techniques in their dramatization. Students' performance of their sonnets for each other becomes the finale of their study of *Much Ado About Nothing*.

Conclusion

There exist, of course, many more applications of the three basic improvisation exercises than I have been able to illustrate here. I would add that the effectiveness of such improvisations will be greatly enhanced by opportunities for focused preliminary discussion in which students have the opportunity to connect their own personal experiences with the various dramatic situations they will encounter in the text. Ultimately, you are limited only by your own and your students' imaginations. If you are willing to give both free reign, you will discover many more improvisational exercises of your own design and each teaching of this or any other Shakespearean play will result in a novel experience. As Bateson reminds us, "the excitement of improvisation lies not only in the risk involved but in the new ideas, as heady as the adrenaline of performance, that seem to come from nowhere" (9).

The essential point, however, is neither Shakespeare nor the improvisation exercises. Those are the vehicles through which students learn several crucial skills: the ability to more carefully observe what is happening, the capacity for more concentrated attention, and the willingness to open up to what is unfamiliar or unexpected—that state of expansion that will make it possible for them to create more viable futures for themselves and continue learning without us.

References

Alexander, R. 1969. Unpublished notes from an NCTE workshop in improvisational theater for the classroom. Washington, D.C.: The Living Stage Theatre Company.

Bateson, M. C. 1994. *Peripheral Visions*. New York: Harper Collins.

Padgett, R. 1987. *Handbook of Poetic Forms*. New York: Teachers and Writers Collaborative.

Pipher, M. 1994. *Reviving Ophelia*. New York: Ballantine Books.

Spolin, V. 1963. *Improvisation for the Theater*. Evanston, Ill.: Northwestern University Press.

Spolin, V. 1986. *Theatre Games for the Classroom*. Evanston, Ill.: Northwestern University Press.

III

Approaches In and Out of Literary Theory

CHAPTER 10

Transhistoricizing
Much Ado About Nothing

Finding a Place for Shakespeare's Work in the Postmodern World

PAUL SKREBELS

University of South Australia
Magill, South Australia

This section presents several different approaches to Shakespeare that reflect some of the most current trends in literary theory. Concerned about the distance between our students and the Shakespeare text and about the increasingly "optional" status of Shakespeare in the school curriculum, Skrebels identifies one challenge as that of "finding a place for his work in the postmodern world" and selecting an appropriate pedagogical approach. What he calls "transhistoricization" (which he demonstrates through his commentary on Much Ado About Nothing *and the foibles of certain members of today's British Royal Family) is his offering—a "use of the chronicles of our time to bridge the critical gap between 'universal human themes' and the specific historical and cultural circumstances of a text's production and reception."*

Teachers and students studying Shakespeare's plays in the classroom (and teaching is surely another form of study) face a crisis, but the crisis is not a new phenomenon. It has existed at least since the early years of the twentieth century, when bodies charged with implementing educational policies in English-speaking societies—the Newbolt Committee in Britain after the First World War is often cited, but each nation has its own equivalents—saw fit to reaffirm the place of "Shakespeare" in the school curriculum as a cornerstone of literacy and a mark of the educated citizen. The resulting establishment-sponsored educational programs, supported by the New Critical agenda of academics on both sides of the Atlantic, took root very quickly, so that the heads of English Literature departments in schools and colleges who declare Shakespeare study optional sooner or later find themselves called to account by concerned civic groups, often via the press.

The attitude of Professor Michael Wood, in a keynote address to British English teachers, that "Shakespeare can look after himself, he is not an endangered species, and doesn't need our protection" (Wood 1994, 19), may be refreshing to some and profoundly threatening to others. But without the daily classroom efforts of teachers, the species' gene pool surely would have diminished to the point where the creature would now be confined to a highly specialized

[handwritten margin note: a-politicizes the decision]

habitat and only occasionally observed at night. Our concern that this may already be the case is not eased by Wood's adding teasingly that if Shakespeare "couldn't look after himself, it would not . . . be at all a bad idea for someone else to have a spell as national poet. Marlowe, for instance, or Webster, or Aphra Behn" (19). Fine, but those of us in the rest of the English-speaking world committed to and charged with passing on Shakespeare to the next generation might be left crying, like Caliban, "The red plague rid you / For learning me your language!" (*Temp* 1.2.366–67), as we scratch around desperately looking for a replacement. Our "national poets" occupy a different cultural space from that allotted to Shakespeare, whose work, historically placed at the very brink of the English colonial project, is one of the few common links we have between "English" cultures that need not involve the names of fast-food chains or multinational media empires. And emerging anglophone societies (including economically advanced ones like Australia, struggling to define itself through concepts such as multiculturalism) seem constantly to find in Shakespeare a perfect forum for questioning and experimenting with the culture which, willy-nilly, is theirs as well.

Given the prominence of Shakespeare in our heritage and his place in our educational systems, what then is the "crisis"? It is simply when students find themselves unable to engage with a text—typically an early modern one—either at the formal linguistic level, or at the broader narrative or structural level, the elements of which are usually taught under the labels of plot, character, and theme. This in turn gives rise to a condition of aporia that causes many students to dismiss the text as boring, old-fashioned, and irrelevant.[1] They have a point. Recent critical discussion has reaffirmed the place of the reader/auditor/viewer in the process of making meaning, particularly in the interdisciplinary activity of sign system analysis called Cultural Studies. Antony Easthope, a proponent of the Cultural Studies line, explains the old "modernist" literary studies method as one which treats the text as "a self-defining object . . . sufficient to itself," and then brings the reader to the text to appreciate its inherent and unified meaning. This process Easthope diagrams as

Reader → Text (=Author)

because it also involves a wish "to disclose the personality within the poem, the author within the text" (Easthope 1991, 12).

The emphasis now is on the inherent pluralities of texts, which do not exist independently of readers. It is the reader who imposes unity on a text, and readers can interpret texts in many different ways according to the circumstances of their reading. The process is one "in which text and reader interact dialectically" (20–21), thus:

Reader ↔ Text

The equal place afforded to readership in this paradigm raises the issue of the place a text can have in the lives of those who either cannot read it or cannot identify with it. For while it may be argued that even a papyrus scroll to someone unversed in hieroglyphics may convey an aura of "Ancient Egyptianness," its inaccessibility as literary text must limit its role in the life of the observer. In our society, too, "Shakespeare" and "Shakespearean" can connote many things—usually associated with a hierarchy of cultural values—even for those who have never read a playtext or watched a performance. But what service are we doing students if our teaching of Shakespeare only reinforces such vague and possibly damaging associations, and fails to achieve at least a few points of reconciliation between them and the text?

Henry Giroux, in a recent article about the pedagogical value of cultural studies to modern youth, expresses urgency in his appeal for teaching practice to address students' changing needs:

> This is a world in which old certainties are ruptured and meaning becomes more contingent, less indebted to the dictates of reverence and established truth. While the circumstances of youth vary across and within terrains marked by racial and class differences, the modernist world of certainty that has traditionally policed, contained and insulated such difference has given way to a shared postmodern culture in which representational borders collapse into new hybridized forms of cultural performance, identity, and political agency. (287–88)

In a culture where "identities merge and shift rather than become uniform and static" (288), it is not—and probably never was—enough to "do Shakespeare" and trust that exposure to the great man's work will cast its civilizing spell. Objects preserved in glass cases, as beautiful and valuable as they may be, are still only the detritus of the past. In preserving them we render them fixed and lifeless, and leave to chance the possible impact they may have on people's lives. But to insist that a cultural product be maintained within the curriculum is to state *ipso facto* that it is of vital importance in the lives of our students. More than ever, students need strategies for understanding—or at least coming to terms with—the world in which they must operate. Writing about the place of historical novels in children's literature but expressing similar concerns, John Stephens says that ours is a "highly technological and extremely acquisitive society, with great personal mobility and information resources," but whose "systems and structures . . . tend to value doing and getting more than being" (203–4). A consequence of this has been "a loss of curiosity about and devaluing of interest in the historical past in late twentieth-century Western society caused by pressures to exist in the present and consider only the immediate future." His conclusion should be regarded as foundational for the present discussion: "For teachers, the question becomes a matter of how readings of the past can be offered as a corrective to living in a fragmented, reified world" (203–4).

The methodological basis for teaching Shakespeare has to be derived from finding a place for his work in the postmodern world, and I believe that this concern already drives, at least implicitly, most pedagogical approaches. Teachers and educational resource groups strive constantly to make literary texts "relevant." In the case of Shakespeare this involves strategies such as cartoon *Macbeth*s and rock-opera *Tempest*s, which under the formalist banner of New Criticism (the critical school which informed the learning of most teachers of English Literature) are scorned as paraphrase. Teachers may feel guilty that their classes are not really studying "literature"—perhaps they are not, and that may be a good thing. But while it is not the purpose of this paper to deal with the linguistic difficulties students may have in making meaning from Shakespeare, I hope to assuage some of the guilt by suggesting a way (or lending support for existing ways) of reading his plays within the specifics of the culture in which teachers and students coexist.

There is a certain irony underpinning this conciliatory process. Although students tend to feel more keenly any gaps between the teaching of literature and their perceived needs in the "real world," the theoretical positions of teachers and students often reflect the opposite. Michael Wood sums up this "most common clash between student and teacher in our discipline today" thus: "The teacher's a historicist and the student isn't. The student believes in universals and the teacher doesn't" (18). The point is well made, for even without the support of theory the teacher is more likely to promote a contextual approach simply through a wider knowledge of the circumstances of a text's production, setting, characters and so forth. This difference also, I suspect, has something to do firstly with the way people, particularly the young, are positioned by the media as "global villagers" and consumers of information, entertainment, and products promoted and distributed on a worldwide basis. Education and social status tend to make teachers more resistant to (but by no means immune from) this positioning, as does time of life, which is the second factor. Young adults are facing up to the "big questions" of existence for the first time, so that attention is directed to universal emotions at the expense of immediate cultural and historical circumstances. Nevertheless, as Wood points out, "The students are not wrong, of course; or rather the teachers are not simply right." Whatever our "different critical heritages, . . . we need a dialogue here, not a simple conversion experience" (18).

That students are better at dealing with universals than with contingent aspects of Shakespeare's plays is likely to become more pronounced when the play under study is not obviously historiographical. The romantic comedies of the 1590s are particularly difficult to historicize: they seem to be "about" universal binaries such as love/hate, loyalty/deceit, and trust/jealousy, with little concern for the precise time and location of the action and fairly tenuous links to the political and social issues of the era of their production. It is no wonder that so often they are produced with eclectic, ahistorical, or anachronistic costumes and settings ("When in doubt, choose the Edwardian era," I once heard a theater practitioner say), Kenneth Branagh's film version of *Much Ado About Nothing* being an obvious example. During my one opportunity so far to teach *Much Ado*, my efforts to deal with the play along broadly historicist lines proved rather limited. Students were able to describe the possible literary sources of the play, and to note that these in turn were indebted to classical sources.[2] Acknowledgment of the influence of Castiglione's *The Courtier* on the exchanges between Beatrice and Benedick elicited discussions about relations between the sexes among the aristocracy, and spilled over into considerations of Elizabethan notions of courtliness. But for the most part, there was the ever-present danger that students would regard the play rather as Ben Jonson damned the efforts of Shakespeare and other rivals as "a mouldy tale, / Like Pericles, and stale / As the shrieve's crust" (Jonson 1975, 283). This seemed particularly so when dealing with the linchpin of the plot, Don John's slander against Hero's virginity and Claudio's subsequent denunciation of her. While some students saw this as an inroad

[handwritten margin note: globalisation and how the young make meaning]

for considering Elizabethan sexual politics, their overriding reaction was that the incident no longer carried the same weight as it once may have. The significance of the episode was, for the students, grounded firmly in the past, and served to reinforce their sense of alienation from the text. Thus I ended the semester with a strong sense of missed opportunity, and a desire to historicize the play, and probably Shakespeare generally, from a different angle.

The poststructuralist critical project called New Historicism[3] in the American academy and usually equated with Cultural Materialism in the British calls for texts to be read not as simple reflections of larger historical movements or of unified world pictures, but as constituents of the thing itself we call "history." This thing in turn "is always 'narrated'," so that the past itself can only be "represented" as a text, and the concept of "history" as a single entity becomes instead a collection of "discontinuous and contradictory 'histories'" (Selden 1989, 95). A literary text should be seen "as largely replicating in its own dynamics and structure those of the culture at large . . . a molecular representation of the entire cultural organism, as it were" (Buchbinder 1991, 114-15). In other words, the tensions, contradictions, and struggles in the society in which the text was produced may be read in the text, as well as/instead of society's dominant and apparently unifying ideologies and philosophies.

There is another side to the new historicist agenda, however, which is of great value to the teacher of literature but which tends to get lost in the rush to revise our concepts of Elizabethan England or Romantic Europe. For if history is always a process of mediating the past, then

> We can never transcend our own historical situation. The past is not something which confronts us as if it were a historical object, but is something we construct from already written texts of all kinds which we construe in line with our particular historical concerns. (Selden 95)

Thus the new historicisms would seem to have more to offer the teacher of literature if the shift in emphasis moves away from analyzing past cultures through plays, popular songs, legal documents, iconography, travelers' tales, and so on, to examining aspects of our own culture and the way its texts are constantly shaped out of a reading of the past. Howard Felperin states the case well, in an essay which admits an important place in modern criticism for the often discredited romanticist notions of an idealized Shakespeare:

> At a certain level, the historical text must always offer itself, and be received, as timeless and universal textuality even as it remains at another level remote and specific historicity—*if it is to [be] interpreted at all*. Otherwise the historical text would remain mute and impenetrable to any but its own culture and movement. (14; original emphasis)

We are at last well on the way to reconciling the predisposition our students have for the universal qualities in texts with our own niggling concerns that somehow we must contextualize works within the specific cultures of their production. By allowing, as Felperin claims Coleridge and Hazlitt did, "for the possibility of analogy and communality between past and present based on linguistic and cultural continuity, . . . for a certain transhistoricity (as distinct from ahistoricity or transcendence)," we can be released from "the historical mean-ing of the text" (15), so that the culture we may concentrate on in our classes is our own.

Given this approach as a basis for classroom practice in the teaching of Shakespeare, the first step is to choose material from our own culture for reading (or viewing or hearing) in parallel with the play. The Cultural Studies agenda is concerned with "outlining ways high and popular culture can be studied alongside each other as forms of signifying practice" (Easthope 103), one of its premises being that "the split between high and popular culture—and the hegemonic effect likely from the superiority of high over popular culture—is vanishing in postmodern culture" (102). It might be added that this split was partly a product of time: what was "popular" once (commercial theater in Elizabethan times, for example) became "high" later; and partly of ideology: certain texts are privileged over others within a culture because they are seen to define a particular view of its "essence" ("conservative" Shakespeare is a compulsory part of the British school curriculum; "radical" Milton is not). The principle of a canon of literature works on what Easthope calls "the usual binary structure which includes one by excluding the other" (103), but in our eclectic world of information overload, can we justifiably study one text and not another on canonical grounds if "both . . . develop equally on the common ground of textuality" (103)?

I do not wish to promote, or be accused of, the idea that Cultural Studies and the new historicisms are merely different labels for the same set of practices. Nor do I have any illusions as to what we get up to as teachers of English Literature. As long as the discipline survives—and Easthope and others maintain that it has not much life left—English Litera-ture will be about privileging certain texts in a manner with which exponents of Cultural Studies need not (and certainly would not) concern themselves. This discussion, after all, is about maintaining such a position for Shakespeare. But in the postmodern eclectic spirit we can borrow from the shared aims and methodologies of the new historicisms and Cultural Studies to break down some of the elitism associated with "Eng. Lit." Both schools of crit-icism "defy traditional distinctions between high and popular culture by breaching disci-plinary boundaries" (Easthope 120) in their willingness to read non-canonical texts in conjunction with accepted literary ones. And the image of the "cultural materialist believ[ing] that his or her head is already under the water" rather than "standing safely on shore and gazing at the sea of history" (Hawthorn 1994, 134) is a valuable one for teachers adopting a historicist approach to literature. It

> requires that the investigator take full account of his or her historical location and of the historical life of literary works *(including their life in the present time of the investi-gator)*, not just the historical situation of the work's creation and composition. (134; my emphasis)

The approach outlined below does not dwell much on the theory that says that all text-making is ideological; nor does it prescribe necessarily "correct" readings based on class, gender, race and so on. Nevertheless, it is hoped that what follows upholds what Mellor and Patterson call "the right of English to claim for itself a specific type of pedagogy: one that focuses on developing in students the ability to interpret texts through the technique of

[margin handwritten note: the diff betw. eng lit & CS to the former requires a canon]

'problematisation'" which in turn gives rise to the "production of particular readings" (49). And for those who think this is ideologically too thin, remember that teaching practice *is* ideological: by bringing cultural studies/new historicist methods to bear in literary study, we are adopting a specific ideological stance in relation to traditional hegemonic views about "literature." This in itself should serve as a caveat to the unwary teacher who, casting about widely for texts from high and popular sources, may be called to account for those choices by students, parents, school heads, and the media.

The slur on Hero's chastity and her rejection by Claudio at the wedding is the aspect of *Much Ado About Nothing* which to modern readers might justify the play's title. This incident and the two characters involved are strongly tied to the generic formula of comic (but typically bordering on tragic) love complications and their eventual resolution. The whole originates from the older stories that make up the play's sources (reappearing in various forms in *Othello, The Winter's Tale* and *Cymbeline* [Cook 1980, 31]), and is an obvious target for the "mouldy tale" accusation. As such, it tends not to attract the same sort of interest as those things we like to think of as uniquely "Shakespearean," epitomized in *Much Ado* in the characters of Beatrice and Benedick and their verbal battles. It is, after all, the "gloriously witty couple" (Branagh 1993, vii) that many famous acting duos choose to play. The challenge, then, is to transhistoricize the characters of Hero—described by one actress as "A dull and boring girl" and "a terrible part which it is almost impossible to make interesting" (quoted in Cook 49)—and Claudio—"an impossibly *unromantic* figure" (Mulryne 1965, 35; original emphasis)—and their predicament such that postmodern readers can accommodate them within their own culture.

One solution lies in teaching *Much Ado* in concert with the vast amount of material about the Charles and Diana scandals in the British royal family. Leonato's household is for all intents and purposes a court in miniature, and the manners and attitudes of its members and guests represent the traditions and customs common to contemporary European nobility. These traditions, customs, and attitudes still exist in the form of the various royal families of Europe, and nowhere more so than in the British monarchy, its very large extended family, and the aristocratic system actively promulgated in British society. Attitudes that the members of this system no longer have any influence must be qualified not only by the fact of their still considerable wealth, but by the amount of media space they continue to occupy and the debates in which they feature, for instance in Australia, where the pros and cons of republicanism flare up with every royal indiscretion revealed. The place of gossip, slander, and scandal in any construction of fame or celebrity is an important aspect of research into the lives of "the rich and famous," and provides a convenient and, in terms of the popular culture in which our students are steeped, relevant point of entry for comparing the contexts and concerns of Shakespeare's era with our own.

Leonato may use the image of his daughter "fall'n / Into a pit of ink" (4.1.139-40) to describe the blackening of her honor, but the British royals would regard this as a very apt description of the gallons of printer's ink expended in exposing every aspect of their lives and reputations in recent years. The anecdotes, observations, surmise, gossip, and media "beat-ups" published in unchartable numbers are the modern equivalent of the old chronicles in which "most chroniclers tended to take their information as they found it, and made little attempt to separate fact from legend" (Abrams 1988, 26).[4] The brief analysis that follows draws on a number of the more "respectable" of these latter-day chronicles: mainly works that have appeared in book form—although a number have been serialized in newspapers, particularly the Murdoch press—some shorter news items, and a television documentary. The Branagh film merits attention not only because for many students it is likely to be the first, if not the only, means of dealing with the play as a performance text, but for its part in the current celebrity/royal-watching process. Less squeamish researchers will find the pit of ink getting deeper (and murkier) as they delve into the seemingly endless mass of related material appearing in the tabloid press, gossip magazines, current affairs television, and even the odd mini-series. Nevertheless, the value of such an undertaking in terms of the space that it creates for Shakespeare study in the postmodern world, and for the light it sheds on our own culture, cannot be overestimated, and should by no means be regarded as trivial or undignified.

The question of Hero's virginity is not simply one of whether or not she is a virgin. Don John's scheme involves Claudio's witnessing Hero supposedly playing the "contaminated stale" (2.2.25) the very night before her wedding, so the focus is not so much on virginity for its own sake as on "Hero's disloyalty" (2.2.48) and subsequent rejection in the interests of what "would better fit [Claudio's] honour" (3.2.104–5). Claudio's denunciation of her at the wedding is nevertheless couched in analogies of chastity and its opposite.

> You seem to me as Dian in her orb,
> As chaste as is the bud ere it be blown;
> But you are more intemperate in your blood
> Than Venus . . . .
>
> (4.1.57–60)

His classical reference begs for comparison with the Dian[a] of our own era, the Princess of Wales, who, despite attacks from her in-laws, the publication of a taped phone conversation with an alleged lover, and photographs of her bathing in the Caribbean or working out in a gym, manages still to maintain—as Hero does to Claudio, indicated in his use of "seem" and not "seemed"—an aura of the wronged heroine and the victim of the machinations of palace and media.

Diana's rise from "stunning mediocrity" (Dempster and Evans 1993, 58) to "Pop Princess" (Burchill 1992, 237) was a direct result of her suitability as a virgin bride for the Prince of Wales:

> Unlike some of the prince's previous girlfriends, she had no "past," no lovers to "kiss and tell". Nor had she been in love before; the prince could expect that, as her first love, he would also be her last. She was young enough to be moulded to the role of wife and mother according to the needs of the monarchy. (Dimbleby, 16 Oct. 1994: 2.1)

Innocence makes Diana malleable—grist to the monarchy's mill, to be refashioned into a future queen—and "in love." Yet, just as Benedick ironically calls the newly smitten Claudio

"Monsieur Love" (2.3.35–36) because one who "was wont to speak plain and to the purpose, like an honest man and a soldier" (18–19) has now become "the argument of his own scorn by falling in love" (11–12), so Charles, brought up in a family notorious for its lack of emotional display, was out of his depth in playing the Inamorato. Thus "the Prince's attitude towards women was hardly admirable," and according to "one of his polo friends," in a tone that might well be Benedick's, Charles "is shy, he is sensitive, he is sometimes devastatingly lonely, but he is also a shit" (Dempster and Evans 105). But what is not mentioned in the many unfavorable reminders of Charles's response "Whatever 'in love' means" in the television interview given after the announcement of their engagement, is that Diana choruses "Yes" (*The Windsors* part 4). The dynastic imperative forces love out into the margins of marriage—an optional, if desirable, extra; hence the importance of loyalty as the standard for judging the behavior of both Hero and Diana.

Claudio's efforts to assess Hero's suitability also seem quite loveless. He bothers Benedick with "Is she not a modest young lady?" (1.1.153) and "I pray thee tell me truly how thou lik'st her" (165–66), and to Don Pedro's recommendation that "the lady is very well worthy" he asks brazenly, "Hath Leonato any son, my lord?"—to be reassured that "she's his only heir" (274–75). In a similar mix of uncertainty and brashness, Charles formed one attachment after another, and had no qualms when "the faces [of his girlfriends] . . . were paraded—like bartered brides-to-be—before the populace for its delectation" (Dimbleby, 23 Oct. 1994: 2.2) by a story-hungry press.[5] Meanwhile, "The difficulties of finding a suitable bride were becoming larger every day, given the age factor—the older Charles got, the more difficult it was going to be to find a convincing and tasteful virgin—and given the press attention that by now was building up around the issue" (Dempster and Evans 106). Wilson obviously has missed the point in wondering "how or where this obsession with virginity developed" (Wilson 1994, 48), but he notes that "by the time Prince Charles was thirty years old, the mood had reached fever pitch" (48).

Charles at last made his choice in Lady Diana Spencer, and the fever pitch was such that their wedding on 29 July 1981 became "the greatest ceremonial event ever mounted in the history of the British monarchy" (Dempster and Evans 126). It was "the subject of the stupendous, unimaginably intense observation: 600 million people watched it on television" (Wilson 175), with the Archbishop of Canterbury—crosier in hand like Prospero's staff—declaring it "the stuff of which fairy tales are made" (Dempster and Evans 126). But if the romance comedy tradition as employed by Shakespeare in the 1590s demonstrates anything, it is that the story often does not end with the wedding:

> either a wedding is legalized or about to be celebrated, or a union is consummated, early or in the middle of the play, but then the completion of the marriage is abruptly interrupted, and the heroine or her allies must perform a difficult task or resolve a quandary connected with the law before there can be a celebration on the stage. (Salingar 1974, 302)

In *Much Ado*, Hero is denounced in the "overtly 'theatrical setting'" of the church wedding itself (Mulryne 35), and must "die" in order to be "reborn" as the chaste and fitting bride for a suitably chastened Claudio. Diana, "a real-life Cinderella—a bride who had so recently been the unhappy child of a broken marriage, miraculously reborn as an instant princess" (Dempster and Evans 126), soon found herself and her marital problems exposed to "all eyes, tongues, minds, and injuries" (4.1.243) on the stage of the world media.

In hindsight, there were signs threatening the fairy-tale image of the Wales' marriage from the outset. Charles, ever vacillating, and now lacking the guidance of his uncle the Earl Mountbatten, his Benedick and Don Pedro rolled into one but killed by an IRA bomb in 1979, came close to calling off the engagement, especially when Diana asked, "Would you marry me if I were not a virgin?" (Dempster and Evans 118). On a broader social scale, at the actual time of the wedding there were riots, looting, and burning in various parts of England, most notably at Toxteth, carried out by a "deprived, unhappy, disadvantaged population" (*The Windsors* part 4). The very minor position occupied by ordinary people in any construction of romance is made very clear in representations such as Branagh's film, where they are servants, revelers (only a step or two away from becoming rioters), and the crowd at the wedding, but voiceless and powerless otherwise. Their only champions in the play, Dogberry and Verges, are portrayed at the very least as ridiculous and in the Branagh film as "mad" (Branagh 58 and 75), and the household breathes a sigh of relief as they exit.

Phyllis Rackin notes that "In a chronicle, the story of England is the story of its kings" (24), and Salingar points out that during the 1590s, "Shakespeare was writing comedies in alternation with the national history plays . . . And his comedies are related in form to his chronicles of the national monarchy" (254). Both form a part of the publicity that the Tudor monarchs actively sought "to authenticate their questionable claim to the throne" (Rackin 1990, 4), and Steven Mullaney's observation about how this was achieved makes clear how the process of textualizing authority positions us—the "common people"—as outside looking in:

> In forums ranging from wonder cabinets to court masques and popular romances, from royal entries and travellers' narratives to the popular playhouses of Elizabethan London, the pleasures of the strange are invoked to solicit our attention as spectators, auditors, or readers. (Quoted in Rackin 15)

Here we are, too, peering through chinks in the palace walls by means of television (the "wonder cabinet"), newspapers, and fifth columnist royal observers. The Windsors have been branded "the greatest performing monarchy in history" (Dempster and Evans 126) in their own efforts to court popularity and publicity, but as the current chronicles tell, they have paid a heavy price. Instead of being satisfied with covering royal turns at special occasions and then going away, like the helpful but aggravating Dogberry, the media intensified its royal watching to the point where they have been accused of anything from causing the breakdown of the three Windsor children's marriages to actively plotting the overthrow of the monarchy itself in the interests of republicanism.[6] Shakespeare's plays, too, position audiences as royal watchers: his "stage world gravitates towards the great house or the court. He depicts the gentry from the outside, but they stand at the centre" (Salingar 255). But while "the Privy Council and the Court nourished the professional drama . . . because it served their own interests" (Montrose 58), the drama in turn could not always accommodate the wish-fulfillment of its patrons. The requirements of the genre, rather than "doctrinal ends" (66), determine the world-picture. Call the tale a romantic comedy and the protagonists are set "on the threshold of marriage and parenthood" but not yet at the stage of "the consummation and procreation which guarantee the continuity of the socio-economic order" (67). On the other hand, call it a chronicle and the dictates of time take over, and "Time reveals not the restorative action of romance but the destructive action of history" (Kastan 1982, 75).

In recording the action of time, the chronicles of Diana and Charles show how the marriage soon made Diana feel the opposite of the fairy-tale princess. In *Much Ado,* Hero's continued attraction for the menfolk despite (and maybe even because of) her supposed guilt is revealed in the curiously paradoxical terms of her denunciation at the wedding, where she is called "pretty lady" (4.1.98), yet "most foul, most fair" (103) and "pure impiety and impious purity" (104). Diana, rapidly acquiring star quality "of truly international magnitude" (Dempster and Evans 138) the more she was courted by the media and the public, and for whom "the world was now literally a stage" (Burchill 238), nevertheless felt herself "the biggest prostitute in the world" in having "to live someone else's idea of who and what [she] should be" (Morton 1994, 2:1). Although the target of Don John's calumny, Hero is more the victim of the credulousness of Don Pedro and Claudio and their puffed-up sense of honor, not to mention her own father's willingness to join in the denunciation. Similarly, whatever stories might be circulated in the media, Diana's feelings of guilt and inadequacy arise from the attitude of the royal household itself, exemplified by the "four stinging letters from the Duke of Edinburgh" which "argued that Diana was far from innocent in the breakdown of her marriage and that it was difficult to blame Charles for seeking comfort with [Camilla] Parker Bowles" (Morton 1994, 2:2). By contrast, the Duke wrote Charles "a long and sympathetic letter . . . praising what he saw as his son's saint-like fortitude" (Dimbleby, 23 Oct. 1994: 2.3). Small wonder that Diana "began to suspect plots against her" (Morton 1994, 2:2), or that the rest of the chronicles to date tend to deal with Diana's exacting retribution from the Windsors in ways that cast her as Hero, Claudio, and even Don John. The necessarily brief summary that follows is nevertheless sufficiently revealing.

As Claudio she becomes jealous and uncertain herself, suspicious "that her husband was persistently unfaithful" despite Charles's Hero-esque "declarations of loyalty and fidelity" (Dimbleby, 16 Oct. 1994: 2.2). As Hero she feels martyred to the cause of the monarchy: "Docile Diana" (Dempster and Evans 141) through whom "the royal family would be renewed, protected and loved for generations to come" (133). Yet just as Hero is reborn "Another Hero" while reasserting herself "a maid" (5.4.62 and 65), so Diana has re-emerged as "the Princess as Pop Star" and "an icon of sexy saintliness" (Burchill 240 and 243)—no longer a maid, to be sure, but one who attracts a loyalty that operates "beyond divorce and dishonour" (244). Part of this process of self-fashioning (to use a term of New Historicist guru, Stephen Greenblatt) involved Diana's almost certain active collusion in the production of that landmark chronicle of the Windsors, Andrew Morton's *Diana: Her True Story,* which painted the Wales' marriage as fraught with problems between an insensitive husband and a long-suffering wife (Wilson 1994, 54 and 143). Charles in turn authorized Dimbleby's biography, initiating "an extraordinary war . . . in print between the Prince and his wife . . . to bring [each] other into ridicule and contempt" (144). Like Don John, both parties cry out, "How canst thou cross this marriage?" (2.2.8).

It is as a potentially destructive influence on the Windsors that Diana plays Don John. In a secretly taped telephone conversation to a supposed lover in December 1989 published in the press as the so-called "Squidgygate" transcript in 1992, Diana bemoans the emptiness she feels "after all I've done for this fucking family" (Dempster and Evans 240), and makes other disparaging remarks about the Windsors.[7] New historicist criticism often focuses on the way rulers legitimize their authority by making use of "already constructed dichotomies which establish the deviance of certain classes and groups" in order to "cast out specific others" (Selden 97). One of these forms of deviance is perceived as "sexual liberty" (97); but if the "demonisation of sexual deviance" is a means of reasserting "the relations of power" (97), then the assertion of sexual liberty can be regarded as a means of establishing a form of autonomy from the main power structure. Diana's apparent adultery (in word if not deed) is an assertion of this autonomy, and reinforces the chastity/loyalty association that prizes the virgin with no other loyalties, past or present. The extent to which she has become powerful enough in her own right to resist being cast out by the palace (and of the latter's growing impotence in her case) may be gauged in comparison to the fate of her sister-in-law, Sarah, Duchess of York.

Sarah tried to follow Diana's example by getting the press onside in her own marriage breakdown with Prince Andrew. But with the publication of the notorious "toe-sucking" photographs, the demonization of Sarah was complete: "Her position was irrecoverable . . . and her sordid life . . . contributed to the general cheapening of the Royal House in the eyes of the Press" (Wilson 1994, 153).[8] Curiously, the Branagh film chose for its Margaret character a red-haired and freckled actress very reminiscent of Sarah. Yet in the film's depiction of the indiscretion which Borachio sets up to discredit Hero (which is only reported in playtext), there is no real possibility of an audience mistaking the Margaret-actress for the petite brunette cast as Hero.[9] The film (made in 1992, The Windsors' *annus horribilis*) seems to highlight the moralistic/voyeuristic dichotomy intrinsic to our constructions of celebrity: "Everyone agreed that it was morally insupportable that such photographs [of Sarah's St. Tropez holiday] should be in circulation, and everyone bought the *Daily Mirror* on the morning that they were published" (Wilson 152). Helped by the conventions of romantic comedy, Margaret finds forgiveness in Leonato's household; lacking the support of media, public, and palace, Sarah is banished from the royal circle "under a cloud" (Campbell 1993, 207).

The transhistoricization of *Much Ado* opens up many other possibilities for analysis. One is the use of trickery and deception as romantic comedy trope and for gathering news. In the Branagh film point-of-view camera angles, eavesdropping, masquerade, and decoying are all used to excellent effect, suggesting paparazzi with telephoto lenses, bugged telephones, leaked stories to the press, and other devices that have eked out the Diana and Charles chronicles. Another issue is the nature of status, privilege, and celebrity, which not only depend upon publicity yet are so easily its victim, but also seek legitimation through mutual association. Thus members of the royal family try to broaden their popularity base by sharing the spotlight with film and media stars, from the Mountbattens visiting Chaplin in the thirties to the Windsors taking part in a celebrity TV game show in the eighties. Again, the Branagh film is a useful springboard in its transatlantic mingling of old- and new-world dynasties of stars celebrating a common Shakespeare heritage.

This discussion has attempted to support and develop the ways in which classroom teachers keep open a dynamic space for Shakespeare in the postmodern world, which is much more than just helping him to maintain a precarious foothold associated with half-forgotten rituals in rarefied environments. As Hamlet urges Polonius to see the members of the acting troupe "well-bestowed" and "well used," because they ("and presumably their product" [Patterson 1988, 100]) "are the abstract and brief chronicles of the time,"[10] so should we teachers of Shakespeare—frequently in danger of becoming Polonius-like in our opinions of our own learning—not scorn the use of the chronicles of our time to bridge the critical gap between "universal human themes" and the specific historical and cultural circumstances of a text's production and reception.

Notes

1. See Hawthorn 6–7 for an explanation of aporia. My use here is in the generalized sense of "irresolvable doubts and hesitations thrown up by the reading of the text" (Hawthorn 7). While Hawthorn points out that the term is "not normally used . . . in a pejorative sense" by critics (7), I believe that my use of the term is apt. Getting students to the stage of using this condition as a "site" where they discover "the freedom to play with the text" (7) is of course the rationale of this paper.

2. See Humphreys 5–23 for a detailed discussion of the play's sources.

3. Throughout this paper, New Historicism/Historicist denotes the specific (mainly American) school of criticism; new historicism/historicist is used for the general poststructuralist movement regardless of national/cultural adherence.

4. Wilson also employs the term "chronicles" to describe these texts (for example, page 46).

5. Some idea of these "faces" may be gained from the photographs in Dempster and Evans and in Campbell. The photographs in Morton, *Diana: Her True Story,* not only parade the stages of Diana's life before the reader, but do so in an intimate and perhaps even questionable manner, in effect positioning the reader as "catalogue browser" and Diana as potential "mail-order bride."

6. See, for example, *The Windsors* part 4 for opinions about the role of Rupert Murdoch, whose News Corporation papers have regularly printed controversial material about the Windsors. Murdoch's status as Australian-turned-American citizen with huge interests and influence in Britain carries many resonances for an "empire writes back" perspective and critique. His father, Keith, a news correspondent in World War I, set a family precedent for attacks on the British establishment by daring to lay the blame for the military disaster at Gallipoli in 1915 on the ineptitude of British generalship; see C. E. W. Bean, *Anzac to Amiens* (Canberra: Australian War Memorial, 1946), 170.

7. Charles, of course was guilty of his own indiscretions in the "Camillagate" tape made at almost exactly the same time as Diana's conversation, and published in January 1993. While there was obviously a great deal of the double standard operating in relation to the two incidents in official circles, Charles seems to have lost much popular support as a result of the revelation, and

"A sense of shame tormented him for months" (Dempster and Evans 220). Transcripts of both tapes appear in Dempster and Evans 231–64. See also Campbell 157–58 for some startling claims about parts of "Squidgygate" not released for publication.

8. The details of the incident are described in Dempster and Evans 205–8, who claim that the revelation of "Squidgygate" four days later actually saved Sarah from further ordeal by the media (208). It should be bourne in mind that Sarah was already separated from Andrew at the time; Diana and Charles were not yet separated when the "Squidgygate" and "Camillagate" tapes were made.

9. "One seriously cool gal" claims the caption to an off-camera shot of her with sunglasses and cleavage (Branagh 126), as if desperately trying to offset the "boring girl" image of Hero and substitute instead a version of "pop princess."

10. I owe the use of this quotation from *Hamlet* 2.2 to Patterson's very fine New Historicist "recovery" of the circumstances surrounding Shakespeare's theater.

References

Abrams, M. H. 1988. *A Glossary of Literary Terms.* 5th ed. New York: Holt, Rinehart and Winston.

Branagh, Kenneth. 1993. Screenplay, Introduction, and Notes on the Making of the Film. *Much Ado About Nothing.* By William Shakespeare. London: Chatto and Windus.

Buchbinder, David. 1991. *Contemporary Literary Theory and the Reading of Poetry.* South Melbourne: Macmillan.

Burchill, Julie. 1992. "Di Hard: The Pop Princess." In *Sex and Sensibility,* 233–44. London: Grafton.

Campbell, Lady Colin. 1993. *The Royal Marriages: Private Lives of the Queen and Her Children.* London: Smith Gryphon.

Cook, Judith. 1980. *Women in Shakespeare.* London: Harrap.

Dempser, Nigel and Peter Evans. 1993. *Behind Palace Doors.* London: Orion.

Dimbleby, Jonathon. 1994. *The Prince of Wales: A Biography.* Serialized in *The Sunday Times* [London] *News Review,* 16 Oct., 2.1–2.3; 23 Oct., 2.1–2.3.

Easthope, Antony. 1991. *Literary into Cultural Studies.* London and New York: Routledge.

Felperin, Howard. 1990. *The Uses of the Canon: Elizabethan Literature and Contemporary Theory.* Oxford: Clarendon.

Giroux, Henry. 1994. "Doing Cultural Studies: Youth and the Challenge of Pedagogy." *Harvard Educational Review* 64.3:278–308.

Hawthorn, Jeremy. 1994. *A Concise Glossary of Contemporary Literary Theory.* 2d ed. London: Arnold.

Humphreys, A. R. 1981. Introduction. *Much Ado About Nothing,* 1–84. By William Shakespeare. The Arden Shakespeare. London and New York: Routledge.

Jonson, Ben. 1975. *The Complete Poems.* Ed. George Parfitt. Harmondsworth: Penguin.

Kastan, David Scott. 1982. *Shakespeare and the Shapes of Time.* Hanover, N.H.: University Press of New England.

Mellor, Bronwyn and Annette Patterson. 1994. "Producing Readings: Freedom versus Normativity?" *English in Australia* 109:42–56.

Montrose, Louis. 1980. "The Purpose of Playing: Reflections on a Shakespearean Anthropology." *Helios* 7:51–74.

Morton, Andrew. 1992. *Diana: Her True Story.* London: Michael O'Mara.

————. 1994. "Angry and Alone." *The Sunday Times* [London] *News Review*, 6 Nov., 2.1–2.4.

Much Ado About Nothing. Directed by Kenneth Branagh. Renaissance Films 1993.

Mulryne, J. R. 1965. *Shakespeare: Much Ado About Nothing*. London: Arnold.

Patterson, Annabel. 1988. "'The Very Age and Body of the Time His Form and Pressure'": Rehistoricizing Shakespeare's Theater." *New Literary History* 20.1:83–104.

Rackin, Phyllis. 1990. *Stages of History: Shakespeare's English Chronicles*. Ithaca, N.Y.: Cornell University Press.

Salingar, Leo. 1974. *Shakespeare and the Traditions of Comedy*. Cambridge: Cambridge University Press.

Selden, Raman. 1989. *Practising Theory and Reading Literature: An Introduction*. Hemel Hempstead: Harvester Wheatsheaf.

Shakespeare, William. 1964. *The Tempest*. The Arden Shakespeare. London: Methuen.

————. 1988. *Much Ado About Nothing*. The Arden Shakespeare, 1981. London and New York: Routledge.

Stephens, John. 1992. *Language and Ideology in Children's Fiction*. London and New York: Longman.

Wilson, A. N. 1994. *The Rise and Fall of the House of Windsor*. London: Mandarin.

The Windsors. 1994. Four-part television documentary. Thames Television.

Wood, Michael. 1994. "English for the 21st Century." *National Association for the Teaching of English News* (Autumn): 17–19.

CHAPTER 11

Making Sense of Shakespeare

A Reader-Based Response

CHARLES H. FREY
University of Washington
Seattle, Washington

Frey maintains that a type of reader-response approach to Shakespeare, one based on specific exercises he describes, can encourage students toward a close and caring engagement with Shakespeare's text. His exercises, for example, foster a heightened awareness of how metrical emphasis supports emotional emphasis and how many passages are "alive with much sense experience beyond or below the visual." As with so many of the chapters in this book, the illustrations are limited to one or two plays, but they could just as easily be adapted to almost any of the others.

To Engage Students as Readers of the Text

Suppose you have assigned the first scene of *A Midsummer Night's Dream* to your class to read tomorrow. You may, of course, provide background, watch a film, go over the plot, get the characters and their relations straight, talk about comedy then and now, and so on. Or you may choose to plunge in directly. Whatever your method, I suggest you consider employing one or more of the following exercises.

First, ask your students to notice what seems to them the most emotional part of the scene. This is a somewhat sneaky question! It silently *assumes* that Shakespeare contains emotion, of all things, as well as "Old English" and "a lot of boring speeches." Your students may, to be sure, come in the next day and proclaim they couldn't find any emotion whatsoever. Perhaps then you'd have to find some for them, but you could still proceed. Let's assume you ask Jimmy Jones to point to a line or two he thinks could be spoken with some emotion. He chooses Lysander's smart-alec remark to Demetrius (1.1.93–94):

> You have her father's love, Demetrius;
> Let me have Hermia's: do you marry him.

You ask Jimmy what emotion Lysander is expressing, and Jimmy says: "It's a put-down." Now, depending upon a thousand factors including your assessments of Jimmy's ways of relating, his relations to you and the class, your relation to him and the class, the age and maturity of the class, and the like, you can proceed in various ways. If Jimmy is with the program, you might ask him to read the two lines aloud with the emotion emphasized. See if he emphasizes "father's," "Hermia's," and "him," and then work with varying ways of saying the lines. If Jimmy is more defensive, you might try reading the lines aloud somewhat inappropriately, say, in a slight monotone or with a whine, instead of "scornfully" (note Demetrius' reply immediately below: "Scornful Lysander!"). Ask Jimmy if you've got it right. Tease him, politely, into correcting you, preferably by having him demonstrate better readings. However he may respond, it is likely that, by this time, more extroverted class members will be dying to "help" Jimmy, or offer "better" passages. Now, Jimmy may feel he has something to gain by keeping the floor. Or he may be all too willing to give it up. Or he may be wavering in between. That is to say, good teaching is always psychology, footwork, respect for persons, alertness, love of youth, looking for openings, the shaping of discourse, as well as knowledge of the subject. You're a teacher because you can do these things. So I hope you stick with Jimmy all the way to noting that "father's" and "Hermia's" occupy the same position in their respective lines.

If your students work well with such an exercise, you can use it easily to help them distinguish ways of verbally expressing emotion through increased loudness/softness or high pitch/low pitch or fast pace/slow pace or care in pronunciation or alliterative emphasis or changed timbre or use of pauses or adopting an "accent" or mimicry of a preceding speaker or using interjected sounds and so forth. By asking various students, for example, to express the scorn of "Do you marry him" through only one (at a time) of the above-mentioned traits of speech, you can teach them a great deal about the actual means of articulate emotional expression in our language (a topic arguably as relevant to the teaching of Shakespearean drama as is any other topic, including gender relations in the plays, connections of the plays to state authority, the use of boy actors, or the history of comic forms). You might move, moreover, from such an exercise into helping students note how significantly metrical emphasis supports emotional emphasis, and this could lead in turn to a better understanding of Shakespeare's rhythms in verse and prose and the importance of rhythm to creation of emotion and meaning (see the third group of methods, below).

Second, it helps to engage students with Shakespeare's texts and to liven up the class if the teacher devises means to have students read aloud substantial portions of text during the class meeting. Suppose that you as the teacher of *Romeo and Juliet* 4.3, the scene in which Juliet drinks the sleeping potion, ask your students ahead of time to practice reading the scene aloud. Depending upon contexts, they might practice at home or in the classroom. If you can bring all the students to read aloud together, perhaps after you have worked through the scene in front of them, they will discover that they stay together in the reading by sticking to a quite regular beat (the same isochronous reading style that church congregations and other groups employ to speak aloud in unison). That experience helps them hear and remember the living beat of Shakespeare's metrical art. You could begin the scene with the whole class reading the lines. Then you could divide the class in half and have one half read a line, the other half read the next line. Or you could assign groups of four or five students to read aloud together the parts assigned to Juliet and Lady Capulet. The idea here would be slowly to narrow responsibility for speaking Shakespeare aloud to smaller and smaller groups and finally to individual speakers.

You could shift from one group of student speakers to another at the point in a passage where self-debate takes place, as when Juliet wonders (4.3.25-30):

> What if it be a poison which the Friar
> Subtly hath ministered to have me dead,
> Lest in this marriage he should be dishonored
> Because he married me before to Romeo?
> I fear it is. And yet methinks it should not,
> For he hath still been tried a holy man.

At "And yet," the introduction of a new set of student speakers would emphasize the shifting stance or view in Juliet's thought. Such concretizing makes literal sense of Shakespeare.

You could also ask students to stand to read aloud, for standing often strangely increases perception and expression of emotion, intensifies energy, and heightens alertness. If an excuse be needed, choose passages wherein the speakers are obviously standing, as when Lady Capulet enters to Juliet (4.3.6). Or challenge the class to represent an aroused mob, as when the Citizens of Verona, perhaps milling about and obviously enraged that the Montagues and Capulets are fighting once again, shout (1.1.74-75):

> Clubs, bills, and partisans! Strike! Beat them down!
> Down with the Capulets! Down with the Montagues!

Differing sub-groups in your class could "memorize" one of the sentences in the two lines, and all the sentences could be spoken together. Or, taking a different example, to get at part of the physical dynamic of the balcony scene (and also to engender a good deal of physical excitement and high spirits in the classroom), you could have all the women in the class be Juliets who stand in a line to speak in unison (2.2.50-52):

> Romeo, doff thy name,
> And, for thy name, which is no part of thee,
> Take all myself.

The student Romeos, kneeling in a line before the standing Juliets, reply (2.2.52):

> I take thee at thy word.

Then, in a reminder of the gender-changed casting in Shakespeare's day, the former Romeos could stand upon chairs to be Juliets in the balcony, and the former Juliets could stand before them, each group to speak the lines again. And, again, you as the teacher might use smaller and smaller groups for a succession of such exercises, working toward individual speakers and wearing away the layers of inhibition and resistance.

Another approach to encouraging individual students to speak Shakespeare aloud in class is to begin by narrowing down the scope of "responsibility" to such an easy, and democratic, level that reasons for reluctance to speak are all but eliminated. Suppose you want your class to read aloud the first scene of *Hamlet*. You could arrange the chairs in a circle and ask one student to read aloud the first word of the play ("Who's"). The next student in line reads aloud the second word ("there"); the third, "Nay"; the fourth, "answer"; and the fifth (amusingly), "me." And so on. After the students laugh their way through the first few words, they will begin to speed up and smooth out the word sequence as it moves around and around the circle. After enough of that, shift to a two-word or three-word responsibility, or ask students to read from punctuation point to punctuation point, or read successive sentences, or two-sentence units, and so on up to responsibility for the successive speeches of characters. Such an exercise not only accustoms students to hearing themselves read Shakespeare successfully, with confidence, aloud, but it also teaches a great deal about the variety of sentence lengths and structures and the patterns of repetition to be found in Shakespeare's dialogue.

I find that I can further engage my students in reading Shakespeare's text by taking a part myself and inviting one or more students to read the part or parts in dialogue with mine. As they hear and feel the varieties of animation I introduce into my part, they often slowly abandon their tendency to read aloud in inhibited or monotonic ways. I may even pause and ask explicitly for a bit more emphasis or a description of tone or mood or sometimes even a substitution of pure feeling-sound for the words themselves. (How many ways, for example, might a student enact Hamlet's "windy suspiration of forced breath" with a sigh?) Or we may shift for a moment into silent miming of a gesture or movement appropriate to a bit of dialogue. Any movement is almost bound to enhance engagement, for motion yields emotion.

Such exercises make Shakespeare much more palpable and real for students who otherwise may tend to read too quickly or too abstractly for outlines of plot or vague theme or without any useful focus whatever. Nor are such exercises merely naive or touchy-feely attempts to create inauthentic enthusiasm. When Horatio sees the Ghost for the second time (1.1.131), we read:

I'll cross it though it blast me. *(It spreads his arms.)*

Ask two students to enact that line, complete with stage direction, and you may find the Horatio crossing the fingers of two hands instead of crossing the Ghost's path, and you may find either Horatio or the Ghost or both spreading arms. Such physical enactment is an ideal vehicle for raising questions about meanings of the line and stage direction, about nuances of "cross" and "blast," about sources and varieties of stage directions in Quarto or Folio or edited edition, and so on.

A third set of methods to help students achieve a close and caring engagement with Shakespeare's text invokes student memory and creativity. During a unit on Shakespeare (a unit that could vary from a few days to a whole semester or year-long course), you can ask students to memorize for each class period one sentence written by the Bard in the scene(s) to be discussed the next day. A sentence may of course consist of a single word such as "No!"

or it may be very long indeed. So the burdens on memory need not be challenging but may be so for any student whose readiness is all. If you ask further that each student bring to class the sentence written from memory, together with a paragraph explaining why this sentence was chosen and what emotion and manner of expression seem appropriate for it, then you are facing at the opening of class a little laboratory of subjects all presumably prepared to tell you and each other some very interesting things, from memory, about Shakespeare's text. You can easily imagine the kinds of conversations and exfoliations that may ensue.

You may also create a daily assignment that can prove enormously rewarding for the small amount of student time it consumes if you will ask your students to write and bring to class each day at least one line of iambic pentameter in imitation of Shakespeare's style and content in the scenes to be discussed. Listening to individual contributions read aloud and working with examples on the board allows everyone to perceive in the most graphic and memorable terms how it is that meter matters, how it functions, what Shakespeare could and could not do with his lines, how what seems to be formal constraints turn out to be opportunities for emphasis and music, how Shakespeare's verse connects to or disassociates from other verse and musical forms. Using analogies to music, rap, the regular rhythms of many rituals, and dance can help students see that the meter and prose rhythms are a large part of the message and that Shakespeare has little content separable from the living forms and the here/now experience of his text.

A final element in this third set of methods for student engagement invokes a distinction between visual and non-visual imaging. Here, you as teacher would challenge your students to hear, taste, smell, and touch while they read Shakespeare. A student considering the following passage might, if reading habitually, "see" in her mind's eye the character, Lady Macbeth, speaking on stage or standing in a castle. And the student might "understand" from reading the passage that Lady Macbeth is psyching herself up for the murder of King Duncan:

> The raven himself is hoarse
> That croaks the fatal entrance of Duncan
> Under my battlements. Come, you spirits
> That tend on mortal thoughts, unsex me here
> And fill me from the crown to the toe top-full
> Of direst cruelty! Make thick my blood;
> Stop up th'access and passage to remorse
> That no compunctious visiting of nature
> Shake my fell purpose, nor keep peace between
> Th' effect and it! Come to my woman's breasts
> And take my milk for gall, you murdering ministers,
> Wherever in your sightless substances
> You wait on nature's mischief! Come, thick night,
> And pall thee in the dunnest smoke of hell,
> That my keen knife see not the wound it makes,
> Nor heaven peep through the blanket of the dark,
> To cry "Hold, hold!"

As part of your challenge, you would ask students to circle all terms and phrases that seem to ask for an activity of perception other than seeing. Thus "hoarse," "croaks," and "cry" refer to hearing, not seeing. Similarly, "fill me," "make thick my blood," "stop up," "shake," and so on invoke sensations of inner feeling much more than sight. And "take my milk for gall" invokes taste, as "smoke" invokes smell and perhaps remembered sensations of irritated eye, nose, and throat membranes (as well as sight). Even the images of the "keen knife" and the "wound" are more tactile and feelingful than visual, especially, when the half-personified knife seems to perceive the wound explicitly through an agency other than sight. All in all, the passage is alive with much sense experience beyond or below the visual. Yet we are all trained, not only as readers but as citizens in our society, to let sight over-dominate all other sense experience.

Shakespeare often works below sight, internalizing imagery into somagery, requiring us to feel from the inside rather than to see from without. Macbeth, to take another example from this oft-taught play, says:

> withered Murder,
> Alarumed by his sentinel, the wolf,
> Whose howl's his watch, thus with his stealthy pace,
> With Tarquin's ravishing strides, towards his design
> Moves like a ghost.

Students need to perceive that the passage devotes its energy not only to the alarm of the howling wolf, which must be imagined in the mind's ear to have effect, but also to "stealthy" pace and "ravishing" strides, which can much better be felt, kinesthetically, than seen, visually. What makes a stride "ravishing" is the intent, the inner feeling of the strider; the sentence calls for kinesthetic and proprioceptive response within the reader, just as the creeping and walking and strutting in Macbeth's famous "tomorrow" speech call for a similar, muscular response.

Studies have shown that readers who are trained not just to see images and narrative action through detached, distancing sight but rather to focus upon a full range of sensuous, inner, feelingful responses actually produce measurably greater changes in breath rate, heart rate, muscle tension, skin conductance, and other indices of emotional arousal than the changes in readers who envisage the action and images as seen at a distance. If we teach uses of imagination partly to help students achieve understanding and sympathy for the experience of others, what could be more important than providing access to the key, perceptual bases of empathy? Macbeth speaks in pain and horror, but what do such terms mean physically and emotionally?

> For Banquo's issue have I filed my mind;
> For them the gracious Duncan have I murdered,
> Put rancors in the vessel of my peace . . .
>   (*Mac.* 3.1.66–68)

The typical gloss will give "enemies" or "enmities" or invite the image of poison, but "rancors" goes back to the Latin (which Shakespeare surely knew) for stench, stink, rancid and disgusting smell. Macbeth has defiled his mind. His wife will die tormented by "the smell of the blood still" (5.1.49). Unless your student readers sense the physicality of the Macbeths' torment, they will more than likely categorize (and toss off) their experience as one more example of abstract moral guilt, and thus they will make insufficient sense of Shakespeare.

To Make Sense of Shakespeare through Student Performance

Because Shakespeare was written to be performed, you as teacher of Shakespeare have every right to encourage performance by your students. And performance can easily make the best sense of Shakespeare, in all senses of the term "sense." After about twenty-five years of teaching Shakespeare intensively, I see no better way than to create student Performance Groups who will edit a scene or act, divide and double parts, assign roles, memorize lines, work out the stage movements, and perform for the rest of the class. I will describe what I take to be one good method and you may decide that your own method works as well or better, or you may find parts of this method adaptable to your own classroom contexts.

Divide the classroom into five Performance Groups, preferably having six to ten students in each group. Provide in-class time for group work. Assign one act of a given play to each group: group 1 does the first act; group 2 does the second, and so on. Have each group discuss independently various performance "concepts," that is, what time period, social situation, economic class, geographical location, and so on, they wish to portray. Have them choose a concept, edit the text down to about 200 lines (or a little more or a little less, depending upon student capabilities and available time), divide up the parts (with roughly equal numbers of lines and time on stage for each student) but keep most of the stage action (even if only mimed), memorize their lines (you can show them how), and take plenty of time to work out the blocking or precise and recorded movements on stage. Each group must make a Performance Program showing the assignments of parts and a Performance Notebook containing the edited text with annotations for stage movements and any technical effects (use of boom boxes for music, use of lights, etc.), a statement of the concept, a history of the meetings and progress at each, an analysis of each character played (by the respective actor), and an individual progress report and evaluation from each group member.

If your students are not mature enough to do all that, you can easily adapt the method to something much simpler but still containing the basic elements of group work, memory, and performance. You may wish to work up to the memorization demands by in-class memory work, brief out-of-class memory assignments, and a good deal of instruction as to how to memorize so that performance or unexpected happenings don't interfere with perfect recall. (For example, students can number each line in a part and learn to say each line independently of the others, learn to say the lines backward, have specific mnemonic images or sound associations for each last word of a line or sentence and first word of next line or sentence, memorize all cue lines and the line following the close of each speech, and so on.) You may also wish to attend various rehearsals of each group (if private or at least separated rehearsal spaces can be used without chaos, so much the better) to check up on progress and particularly to help with sight lines, appropriate stage business, and the like.

The main point is that students who successfully work in a group to put on a performance feel and exhibit an incredible exhilaration, almost without exception. They have made sense of Shakespeare in the most responsible and palpable way; they see at least part of what is involved in transferring Shakespeare from page to stage; they have moved inside the lines and spoken them with understanding and appropriate emotion; they achieve a better understanding of the writer's, director's and actor's arts (relevant to their thousands of hours of past and future TV and film watching); they have truly appropriated and made their own a heretofore alien bit of adult culture; they are rendered far less passive in the reception and evaluation of not only Shakespeare but other art; and their basic confidence in self, others, and cultural tradition becomes enhanced. That sounds like a lot to claim for such an exercise, but, if you try it or already do it, you will know that what I claim is true.

As you probably would imagine, I believe that these simple precepts for making sense of Shakespeare can apply across the board to the teaching of all poems, plays, and stories. Shakespeare makes an ideal place to start, however, precisely because Shakespeare is both suspect and pervasive, mistrusted but familiar, looked at askance by students yet still an object of curiosity, seemingly alien but actually accessible, emotional, dramatic, and meaningful. Shakespeare also employs, perhaps more than any other writer, a materializing, sensuous imagination that continually attaches abstract ideas to concrete realities and feelings. He speaks such sense that our sense breeds with it (cf. *Measure for Measure* 2.2.147–48). Of course Shakespeare raises a host of moral, political, social, and religious questions for all students, but Shakespeare also embeds those questions in aesthetic, entertaining, artful forms that deserve to be noted for what they contribute to the overall effects.

In this little essay, I have worked, as one teacher of Shakespeare, to address you directly, as another teacher of Shakespeare, and I want to close by conveying, as if in letter form, my hopes that at least some small portion of the methods recommended here prove useful to you. If you wish to gain more detailed information or discuss how these methods may be adapted to your particular situation, I will be glad to correspond with you by letter or through cyberspace. May your reading of this book and your experimentation with its suggestions help you and your students to make better, and more literal, sense of Shakespeare and, one may hope, of much other drama and literature.

CHAPTER 12

Textual Studies and Teaching Shakespeare

C. W. Griffin
Virginia Commonwealth University
Richmond, Virginia

Griffin begins by identifying some of the ways that modern, "sanitized" texts are made more "readable" (modernized spelling, stage directions, explanations of unfamiliar words and allusions). He then questions if such efforts are successful or if they create instead the opposite effect. He encourages teachers to spend extra time exposing their students "to some of the ways in which such texts were first produced, marketed, and received." Throughout his series of suggestions, he designates points where he uses transparencies to reinforce and illustrate his ideas; and he always offers sufficiently interested readers enough reference material to make their own if they so desire.

When our students study plays by Shakespeare or other Renaissance dramatists, they are typically exposed to them in texts rendered more "readable" than their originals by editors and publishers who have printed them in clean and attractive type faces, modernized their spelling, delineated acts and scenes, indicated stage directions, and offered definitions of unfamiliar words and phrases as well as explanations (often, in actuality, interpretations) of obscure allusions.

These sanitized texts, whose goal is to remove as many barriers as possible to careful reading, interpretation, and enjoyment of the plays, may actually be inducing just the opposite kinds of practices in our students: Encouraged to think of the task of decoding and interpreting such texts as an unnatural and artificial activity, they may be moving through their assignments at such a clip and in so perfunctory a manner that they are comprehending little and appreciating hardly at all.

One way to encourage students to engage more seriously and more intently in the study of the texts of Renaissance plays is to draw on work in current textual studies in order to expose them to some of the ways in which such texts were first produced, marketed, and received. Seeing, for instance, the ways in which the author of a particular text revised, or understanding how that text's first readers responded, might help to demystify it and to better situate it within the context of our students' own processes of reading and writing. Let me illustrate:

Purchasing a Play:

To give our students some sense of what it would have been like to purchase a Renaissance play-book, we might suggest that they do the following:

Imagine for a moment that it is late in the year of 1597 and that you are a visitor to London from the country or from abroad, someone who has recently seen a play by that popular new playwright William Shakespeare; you were so taken by the play's sharp characterizations and apt figures that you'd like now to reflect on the printed text at your leisure. In order to obtain a copy, you'd have to find your way to the bookstalls located in the heart of the city, near St. Paul's Cathedral **(Transparency of St. Paul's)**.[1]

What with the crowd (Thomas Dekker identifies for us "the knight, the gull, the gallant, the upstart, the gentleman, the clown, the captain, the apple-squire, the lawyer, the usurer, the citizen, the bankrout, the scholar, the beggar, the doctor, the idiot, the ruffian, the cheater, the puritan, the cut-throat, the high-man, the low-man, the true-man, and the thief. . . .") and the confusion (Dekker exclaims: "What swearing is there, yea, what swaggering, what facing and outfacing! What shuffling, what shouldering, what justling, what jeering, what biting of thumbs to beget quarrels, what holding up of fingers to remember drunken meetings, what braving with feathers, what bearding with mustachoes, what casting open of cloaks to publish new clothes . . . ," from Dekker's *The Dead Tearme* quoted in Evans 1990, 222–23), you'd have quite a time pushing your way up to the bookstalls that lined Paternoster Row, which ran along the north side of the cathedral **(Transparency of Paternoster Row)**.

If you could finally get to the stalls, though, your eye might be caught by the 1597 title page (posted on the bookstall post) of *Richard III,* which promised the story of Richard's treacherous Plots against his brother Clarence: the pittieful murther of his innocent nephews, his tyrannicall usurpation: with the whole course of his detested life, and most deserved **(Transparency)**.

Drawn by such a juicy description, but with no help from the lazy bookseller (whom Thomas Nashe pictures in his *Pierce Penilesse,* quoted in Wilson 1911, 153, standing with his "thumb under girdle," never stirring or even looking at the customer, but gesturing to his boy with his little finger), you might purchase that play-book for the price of sixpence. Such an amount is about what one would pay for the Arden edition of the same play (paper, of course) today, though the slim Elizabethan quarto edition, consisting of twelve sheets of cheap paper poorly stitched together, and indifferently printed (by two shops, one whose type fount was quite clean but "spectacularly short of certain letters," while the other's type fount was "by contrast, old and rather battered, but well stocked," Hammond 1985, 23), would seem a poor thing compared to its elegant modern counterpart. In content, the two editions would differ just as radically. In contrast to the Arden, with its introduction of over one hundred pages (containing a particularly detailed discussion of the textual dilemmas created by the existence of the very quarto that you are buying), its carefully edited and annotated version of the play, and its copious appendices, the Elizabethan edition consisted of a title page and forty-seven pages (some heavily blotted) of text **(Transparency of a quarto page)**.

The Popularity of Plays

Of course, if one weren't drawn particularly to *Richard III,* one could have chosen from a wide selection of other plays. Louis Marder tells us that in the years 1593-1616, more than sixty editions of Shakespeare's plays and poems were published (87). Professor Evelyn Albright (1927) estimates that "during the period 1580-1640 about 355 plays are known to have been printed for the first time" (286). Since many of the plays were published in multiple editions or impressions, we can be certain that literally hundreds of thousands of plays by Elizabethan and Jacobean dramatists must have been printed and sold during the approximately one hundred years from 1557 until 1660. Plays were so popular, in fact, that during the early seventeenth century, it became acceptable for the first time to publish collected editions, Ben Jonson's in 1616, Shakespeare's in 1623, John Lyly's in 1632, John Marston's in the next year, and Beaumont and Fletcher's a little later in 1640.

The Equivocal Reputation of Plays

Although plays were popular throughout the late sixteenth and early seventeenth centuries, demand for them never matched that of some other kinds of materials, particularly those that were religious or utilitarian in nature. In fact, at the hands of the kinds of people who valued these kinds of materials, the reputation of printed plays suffered considerably. Our students might be titillated, for instance, to discover that plays were considered to be immoral reading, with the most serious complaints against them lodged, as one might expect, by Puritans. The Puritan writer William Prynne complained, for example, about the "above forty thousand Play-books printed within these two yeares"; in the same pamphlet Prynne goes on to grieve that the plays are "now newprinted in farre better paper than most octovo or Quarto *Bibles,* which hardly finde such vent as they" (quoted in Albright 286).

Besides being immoral, published plays were considered of little interest or utility by some discriminating readers. One of the best-known contemporary judgments on plays was Sir Thomas Bodley's placement of them among the "idle books, and riff-raffs of his library," though he did concede to the keeper of his library that "haply some plays may be worth the keeping: but hardly one in forty" (Bentley 1984, 52). In his *Satyres: And Satyricall Epigrams* (1617), Henry Fitzgeffrey grouped plays along with popular journalistic literature such as ballads, cony-catching pamphlets, jestbooks, wonder books, and almanacs (Wright 1958, 97). Even playwrights admitted that their plays were to be read after "your serious affairs and studies" as Richard Jones, the printer of the 1590 edition of Marlowe's *Tamburlaine, Parts I and II,* put it (66). Echoing this sentiment much later, Richard Brome dedicates his *The Antipodes* (1636) to William, Earl of Hertford, for "your recreation at your retirement from your weighty employments . . ." (3).

Production of Plays

The authors of English Renaissance plays were among the first professional writers in English letters. Writing individually and in collaboration, and receiving, on average, about six pounds (equivalent to a little over one-third of the salary of Shakespeare's schoolmaster at Stratford), they produced approximately nine hundred plays during the period 1590–1642 (Bentley 25–26). One playwright alone, Thomas Heywood, claimed to have "either an entire hand or at least a main finger" in 220 plays (quoted in Albright 203).

As they study the plays, it would be helpful, I think, for our students to know how they were composed. Typically, Renaissance dramatists began with a "plot" of their play, a preliminary outline of the sequence of scenes. From that, they progressed to a rough draft, called "foul papers," of the whole play. We have, for example, the manuscript of the play called *The Book of Sir Thomas More,* including the pages believed to be in Shakespeare's hand. Students might be interested in the number of deletions and corrections made by the playwright **(Transparency of a page)**.

The next version of the play, the promptbook, used to prompt actors who had forgotten their lines, was sometimes produced from the manuscript itself and sometimes from a scribe's clean copy. In addition to the author's stage directions, promptors added their own directions to the prompt copy. Frequently these directions were anticipatory in nature, i.e., instructions to have an actor enter sometime before he speaks his first lines or to have certain props set out just before they would be needed. A page from the promptbook of Phillip Massinger's *Believe As You List* **(Transparency of pages 22–23)** reveals such directions as "Table ready; & .6. chaires to sett out" and "Mr Hobs: calld up." It was the prompt book that the official censor actually approved; the last page **(Transparency)** of the same play, for example, contains the signature of Sir Henry Herbert, the Master of Revels, who licensed plays for performance. Students will also be interested in another set of documents used by the company in their rehearsals; called "cues," these were individual actor's lines, preceded by the last word of the previous speech. Thus, actors never had the complete script, only their own lines with which to rehearse the play **(Transparency of some of Alleyn's lines in Orlando Furioso)**.

Revisions of Plays

In order to understand the most immediately useful aspect of textual materials, revisions that can actually affect the way a play might be interpreted, our students will also have to know that plays were published in two forms, quartos and folios. While showing transparencies of pages from quarto and folio facsimiles **(Transparencies of quarto and folio pages)**, a teacher might summarize the salient facts as follows:

> Because the smaller quarto edition was a good deal less expensive to produce than the larger folio, plays were usually first published in quarto form. Some quarto versions of the plays were actually stolen from the theatrical company that owned them, pirated, most scholars now think, by disaffected actors who had memorized the lines. Other quarto versions of the plays that we used to think were pirated, because of their differences from other, more authoritative versions, we now suspect were performance versions, some possibly used by the company when it was on the road. More expensive folio editions were most often used for collected editions of the plays. Many scholars

now agree that we have not one version of *King Lear,* but actually two, an earlier version published in quarto and a later, revised one in the folio; the later version lacks some 285 lines found in the quarto but contains another 115 not found there.

The fact that plays were often published first in quarto and only later in folio helps scholars identify playwright's revisions. Struggling, in the words of Stanley Wells, "to confer respectability upon the popular drama" (41–42), it was Ben Jonson, of all playwrights, who revised most carefully. The following passages from the quarto and folio editions of *Every Man out of His Humor* show how carefully Jonson revised the punctuation of a speech in order to direct and guide his readers' responses **(Transparency)**:

Quarto I	Folio I
Fast. Why do you see sir?	Fast. Why, doe you see, sir?
they say I am Phantastical:	they say I am phantasticall?
why true, I know it, & I	why, true, I know it, and I
pursue my Humor stil in con-	pursue my humour still, in con-
tempt of this *censorous* age:	tempt of this censorious age.

Speculations about Shakespeare's revisions are more conjectural, but certainly of interest. In his excellent "Shakespeare as a Reviser" (1985), Ernest A. J. Honigmann offers a series of speculations on Shakespeare's revisions, both his own and those of other scholars. Thus, he notes that Gary Taylor, in his comparison of the quarto and folio editions of *King Lear,* argues that Shakespeare "accelerates and intensifies" the movement toward war and also simplifies it, "deliberately excising an extraneous political complication," the French forces (4–5). Honigmann also summarizes the observations of another scholar, Neville Coghill, who argues that differences between the quarto and folio versions of *Othello* resulted from Shakespeare's attempt "to *endear*" Emilia to the audience, perhaps sensing that she would be blamed for giving Desdemona's handkerchief to her husband, Iago (5–6).

Two of Honigmann's most dramatic, and most detailed, examples of Shakespeare's possible revisions might be particularly useful to classroom teachers, since their texts could easily be put before the class on a transparency while the revisions were discussed. The first shows how Shakespeare may have added lines to one of Lear's speeches, lines which underscore the old king's criticism of hypocritical judges. Here, the bold-faced lines, from the folio version, fit perfectly into the earlier quarto version **(Transparency)**:

Through tatter'd clothes small vices do appear;
Robes and furr'd gowns hide all. **Plate sin with gold,**
And the strong lance of justice hurtless breaks;
Arm it in rags, a pigmy's straw does pierce it.
None does offend, none—I say none; I'll able em.
Take that of me, my friend, who have the power
To seal th'accuser's lips. Get thee glass eyes,

And, like a scurvy politician, seem
To see things thou doest not. Now, now, now, now!
    (4.6.162-170)

An even more famous example of textual revision Honigmann takes from the work of John Dover Wilson, who argues that Shakespeare revised Theseus's famous speech on the imagination in *A Midsummer Night's Dream,* adding the bold-faced lines that expand the speech to include the poet's imagination as well as that of lunatics and lovers (**Transparency**):

            I never may believe
These antique fables, nor these fairy toys.
Lovers and madmen have such seething brains,
Such shaping fantasies that apprehend
More than cool reason ever comprehends.
The lunatic, the lover and the poet
Are of imagination all compact:
One sees more devils than vast hell can hold,
That is, the madman: the lover, all as frantic,
Sees Helen's beauty in a brow of Egypt:
The poet's eye, in a fine frenzy rolling,
Doth glance from heaven to earth, from earth to heaven;
And as imagination bodies forth
The forms of things unknown, the poet's pen
Turns them to shapes and gives to airy nothing
A local habitation and a name.
Such tricks hath strong imagination,
That, if it would but apprehend some joy,
It comprehends some bringer of that joy;
Or in the night, imagining some fear,
How easy is a bush suppos'd a bear! (5.1.2-22)

The Reception of Plays

If one reads the prefatory material added by playwrights and publishers to the plays, one discerns their attempts to create a sympathetic readership for their plays. Although they frequently denigrated their *theater audiences,* calling them "the many-headed bench," "the vulgar," "those heavy-witted worldlings," or "the uncapable multitude," playwrights referred to their *readers* as "Gentlemen Readers," "My Equal Reader," "the honored few, lovers of drammatick poesie," and "the juditious." It was the garrulous Ben Jonson who labored most directly, in his preface to *Cataline,* to distinguish between his "ordinary" readers, whom he pictured insultingly, and his "extraordinary" readers, to whom "I submit my selfe, and worke" (5: 432). Jonson was wise enough to omit the distinction from the folio edition.

    It was truly an "extraordinary reader" for whom the playwrights and publishers of their plays yearned. It was perhaps the printer Richard Hawkins who expressed their ideal most accurately when, in his epistle to "the Understanding Gentry" who would read Beaumont and Fletcher's *Philaster,* he described his readers as a part of that group of "Seeing Auditors, or Hearing Spectators" who would possess the ability to understand and appreciate a play fully. The best of these poems, he continued, are like that "all-tempting Minerall newly digged up, the Actors being onely the labouring Miners, but you the skilful Triers and Refiners . . ." (1:372).

Students will be interested, I think, in the identities of some of the actual first readers of Renaissance plays. They included a king (King Charles while he awaited his execution), lascivious ladies (Louis B. Wright quotes an anonymous pamphlet that describes Mrs. Wanton's chamber as containing "'nothing but four or five naked Pictures, a Song book, A Play book, a Lute, a History, two or three great Looking-glasses,' and similar equipment" [151]), as well as noblemen, fellow playwrights and poets, tradesmen, even clergymen. Judging by their comments, a number of these readers became passionately involved in the plays they read. Thus, the Duchess of Newcastle says that Shakespeare

> presents passions so naturally, and misfortunes so probably, as he pierces the souls of his readers with such a true sense and feeling thereof, that it forces tears from their eyes, and almost persuades them, they are really actors, or at least present at those tragedies (Munro 1932, 2:132).

Other readers' responses to the plays suggest that they experienced the plays just as intensely in the theater of their minds. So moved by reading *Hamlet* or *Othello* that "my hair starts up, and my nerves shrink with dread," the poet Robert Gold describes how he sees Iago, hears the Moor, and scans "such-like scenes" (Salgado 1975, 57–58).

It would be an interesting study in reading tastes for students to contrast the way various readers responded to the plays. Students might contrast the passionate responses I quoted above, for example, with the less histrionic but still positive responses of the Anglican divine Abraham Wright (who liked particularly those plays that contained elegant lines, varied plots, and strong characterizations) and perhaps with the responses of such decidedly less sympathetic critics as John Dennis and Thomas Rymer. It was this last reader who has become so notorious for his responses to *Othello;* rather than edifying the audience as it should, claimed Rhymer, Shakespeare's poetry works "to delude our senses, disorder our thoughts, addle our brain, perfert our affections, hair our imaginations, corrupt our appetite, and fill our head with vanity, confusion . . . and Jingle-jangle" (Spingarn 1957, 2:254–55).

Through some of the experiences I have just described, our students might come to realize that in studying the plays of Shakespeare and other English Renaissance dramatists, they are, in actuality, witnessing a unique phenomenon in the history of literary studies—the emergence of the genre of the printed play in the late sixteenth and early seventeenth centuries. Through their exposure to a variety of primary materials, they could come to see how this new genre evolved amidst literary, moral, and social criticism; was shaped by the additions and revisions of playwrights; was given respectability by their prefaces, commendatory poems, and dedications; and was read by a variety of people in a variety of different ways.

Notes

1. Throughout this essay, I shall designate the points at which I use a transparency to illustrate something. Using my references, readers should be able to make their own transparencies if they wish.

References

Albright, Evelyn May. 1927. *Dramatic Publication in England, 1580–1640: A Study of Conditions Affecting Content and Form of Drama.* New York: D. C. Heath; London: Oxford University Press.

Bentley, Gerald Eades. 1984. *The Profession of Dramatist in Shakespeare's Time, 1590–1642.* Princeton, N.J.: Princeton University Press.

Brome, Richard. 1966. *The Antipodes.* Ed. Ann Haaker. Lincoln: University of Nebraska Press.

Evans, G. Blakemore, ed. 1990. *Elizabethan-Jacobean Drama: The Theatre in Its Time.* New York: New Amsterdam Books.

Hammond, John, ed. 1985. *King Richard III.* The Arden Shakespeare. London and New York: Methuen.

Herford, C. H., and Percy Simpson. 1971. *Ben Jonson: The Man and His Work.* 10 vols. Oxford: Clarendon Press.

Honigmann, Ernest. 1985. "Shakespeare as a Reviser." In *Textual Criticism and Literary Interpretation,* ed. Jerome J. McGann. Chicago and London: University of Chicago Press.

Kirsch, Arthur C. 1969. "A Caroline Commentary on the Drama." *Modern Philology* 66:256–61.

Marder, Louis. *His Exits and His Entrances: The Story of Shakespeare's Reputation.* Philadelphia and New York: J. B. Lippincott.

Munro, John. 1932. *The Shakespeare Allusion Book: A Collection of Allusions to Shakespeare from 1591 to 1700.* 2 vols. London: Oxford University Press.

Salgado, Gamini. 1975. *Eyewitnesses of Shakespeare: First Hand Accounts of Performances 1590–1890.* London: Chatto and Windus.

Spingarn, J. E. 1957. *Critical Essays of the Seventeenth Century.* 3 vols. Bloomington, Ind.: Indiana University Press.

Tamburlaine the Great. 1956. Ed. U. M. Ellis-Fermor. New York: Gordian Press.

The Dramatic Works in the Beaumont and Fletcher Canon. 1966. Ed. Fredson Bowers. Cambridge: Cambridge University Press.

Wells, Stanley. 1973. *Literature and Drama, with Special Reference to Shakespeare and His Contemporaries.* London: Routledge and Kegan Paul.

Wilson, John Dover, ed. 1911. *Life in Shakespeare's England: A Book of Elizabethan Prose.* New York: Barnes & Noble.

Wright, Louis B. 1958. *Middle Class Culture in Elizabethan England.* Ithaca, N.Y.: Cornell University Press.

———. 1931. "The Reading of Renaissance English Women." *Studies in Philology* 28:139.

CHAPTER 13

Team-Teaching Shakespeare in an Interdisciplinary Context

KATHY M. HOWLETT
Northeastern University
Boston, Massachusetts

Howlett combines two elements that today's teachers hear a good deal about: team-teaching and interdisciplinary course offerings. She describes a course — Exploring Humanities through Film — that draws together the disciplines of history, theater, philosophy, literature, and art. Four or five faculty team-teach the course; and Howlett, the representative English faculty member, is responsible for the two-to-three-week unit on Shakespeare. The goal of her section of the course is to "investigate the relationships between the written word, its theatrical incarnation, and the medium of film in interpreting Shakespeare." And in fascinating detail she describes the efforts of a literature professor and a theater professor as they work together to teach Henry V.

*I*n recent years the academic community has been extolling the virtues of interdisciplinary teaching, but I find that few English faculty actually team-teach interdisciplinary courses. Whether English professors are reluctant to engage with the faculty from other disciplines in their classrooms or merely lack the opportunity for such an experience, I cannot tell. But what I can offer in this essay is testimony to the excitement and challenge of team-teaching Shakespeare's works in an interdisciplinary context. For those lucky enough to be able to engage their colleagues in discussions in a classroom of eager and curious students, the results can be rewarding for the faculty who participate in the course as well as for the students who experience the play through a kaleidoscope of interpretations and perspectives.

The English professor who normally considers Shakespeare's plays under a conventional course rubric, such as "Renaissance Drama" or "Introduction to Shakespeare," will discover that the experience of interdisciplinary team-teaching can free him or her from the narrowness of vision that those categories may represent. Interdisciplinary teaching can liberate the teacher of the Shakespearean text from what Stanley Fish has described as "the confining perspectives of the ideologically frozen divisions of intellectual labor," into the open range of intellectual inquiry and exploration (Fish 1989, 16). Critics of interdisciplinary teaching, however, fear that its effects are ultimately destabilizing; they argue that interdisciplinary teaching assaults the boundaries of academic fields of study and succeeds only in the "blurring of genres." Yet my experience in *sharing* a course with several faculty from different disciplines contravenes those dangers described by its critics. On the contrary, the overall effect of examining Shakespeare's drama in the context of an interdisciplinary course setting is to stimulate and reaffirm the varied critiques of the teacher-participants within their individual disciplines. The aim of interdisciplinary team-teaching is an assessment of Shakespeare's drama in relation to alternative understandings of culture and art, without necessarily rupturing the traditional boundaries of established disciplines. Yet, at the same time, the varied approaches highlight the Shakespeare text itself as the site of conflicting ideologies and approaches.

The Course: "Exploring Humanities through Film"

As the syllabus of "Exploring Humanities through Film" states, the purpose of this interdisciplinary course is to "investigate the ways in which the methods of the humanities can expand one's awareness of the sources, statements, and meanings of popular films." An assumption basic to this course is that literary, historical, sociological, philosophical, and artistic perspectives are a natural part of film's methodologies. Students see a series of films under the direction of faculty members from the humanities, and analyze and evaluate the films according to the various approaches presented by the instructors. Each unit of the course, which can focus on films as varied as *The Tin Drum, Henry V, To Kill a Mockingbird, Khartoum,* or *Golddiggers of 1933,* covers the ways in which a specific humanities discipline can illuminate the forms and messages conveyed through the medium of film.

The disciplines represented in "Exploring Humanities through Film" are history, theater, philosophy, literature, and art, but the particular units can vary. The four or five faculty who team-teach the course select works that not only highlight the interpretative differences between our disciplines but also demonstrate a connection to the final unit on the film *Cabaret,* which is taught by all of the faculty involved. In designating the centrality of a given text at the end of the course (in this case, *Cabaret*), we draw together conventionally separate fields of inquiry—history, philosophy, literary studies, theater, and art history—into interactive and interdisciplinary forms of knowledge. The student's final essay on *Cabaret* should demonstrate the student's ability to synthesize the approaches from the various humanities disciplines. Students soon recognize that the relationships between the visual, performing, and literary arts are as rich and varied as the methodologies of the faculty who oversee the individual film units.

As the representative English faculty member in "Exploring Humanities through Film," I teach a two-to-three week unit on one of Shakespeare's plays and on two film versions of that same play. For my section of the class designated as the unit "Shakespeare on Film," I have taught *Henry V* for several years now, although occasionally I have experimented with teaching different Shakespeare plays and films within the context of this course. Typically, I will show the class Laurence Olivier's 1944 version of *Henry V* and Kenneth Branagh's 1989 production of *Henry V,* although I have used Orson Welles's film *Chimes at Midnight* (1965) when Branagh's *Henry V* was as yet unavailable for class use. However, the visual and audio quality of copies currently available of Welles's film is poor. Also, when the class has compared Olivier's film with Welles's film, discussions invariably center upon Henry's rejection of Falstaff and the contrast between the battle sequences, rich elements in themselves but perhaps too complex for most of the students to comprehend in the short time allotted for the study of Shakespeare on film in this particular course.

I have discovered that *Henry V* works best in connection with the final film of this course, Bob Fossi's film *Cabaret*. Both films are concerned with the theatrical aspects of political power, both employ a "Chorus" whose commentary subverts or is subverted by the accompanying scenes, and both examine the issue of leadership through the voices and perspectives of characters outside the political mainstream. Students who have closely attended to the Shakespeare lectures are alert to *Cabaret*'s more contemporary representations of the problems of history, power, charismatic leadership, and moral responsibility. If our discussions of *Henry V* have been successful, the evidence is clearly demonstrated by the quality of the final essays that I receive on *Cabaret*.

Team-Teaching Shakespeare's Drama in an Interdisciplinary Context

The goal of the section of the course focusing on "Shakespeare on Film," as stated in the syllabus for the course, is for students to "investigate the relationships between the written word, its theatrical incarnation, and the medium of film in interpreting Shakespeare." In order to accomplish this goal, I share the Shakespeare lectures with a professor from the Theatre Department, who, I must confess, has a significantly different approach when she teaches the same play and films to the class. Whereas I emphasize interpretations of the written text as the site of "meaning," the theater professor teaches the play from the perspective of the actor and the dramaturg, who find the "meaning" of the play in performance. Whereas I draw the students' attention to the details of the text and the subtleties of interpretation, the theater practitioner, as my colleague reminds the class, must ignore the array of possible readings to reach for the "pith" of the character. The often stark differences between the goals of the theater practitioner and the goals of the English professor may confuse a few of the students, particularly those who wish to be "told the answer" and are consequently resistant to a multiplicity of perspectives or approaches, but for the majority of the students the exploration of the text in this manner can be illuminating.

As the literature professor in the course, I emphasize the need for students to be aware of the textual language as the concrete embodiment of the play's experimental meaning. My lectures and discussions on *Henry V* encourage the reading of the play as an active process of constructing meaning. Although the students must be guided through the play's more difficult and ironic passages on Salic Law or shown a genealogical table in order to grasp the problems in the line of succession that haunt this play, the class discussions work to discourage the notion that there are any encoded textual truths to be derived from this play. By emphasizing the possibilities and richness of the textual language, I seek to demonstrate that "meanings" of dramatic texts are never stable, and consequently open the way for various cinematic interpretations of the same Shakespeare play.

Recent criticism on *Henry V* supports this perspective; I will sometimes assign those secondary readings to the interested and ambitious students in the class. Norman Rabkin's essay on *Henry V* in *Shakespeare and the Problem of Meaning* (1981) provides the best starting point for students grappling with the ambiguities of the text. I realize that once students view Kenneth Branagh's *Henry V* they are resistant to less celebratory interpretations of the king, often refusing to see the darker aspects of Henry's character even in Branagh's representation. Therefore, my initial lectures on the play underscore the discontinuous and self-contradictory impulses in a play that purports to idealize and legitimate state power. I detail the inherent problems for Henry as son of a usurper, the spectre of Mortimer as contender for the crown, and ways in which the play continually gestures towards Henry's possession of power as the inversion of legitimate authority. Close readings that include a studied awareness of historical or topical reference (such as the Chorus's reference to Essex's Irish campaign in Act 4) prepare the students for Olivier's and Branagh's interpretations of *Henry V*. Recent articles on Branagh's and Olivier's *Henry V* that I sometimes suggest as further reading, such as Sara Munson Deat's essay "Rabbits and Ducks: Olivier, Branagh and *Henry V*" (1992) and William Shaw's "Textual Ambiguities and Cinematic Certainties in *Henry V*" (1994), provide the students with useful examples that confirm the interpretative aspects of film as working within the frame of current literary critiques of the play.

I have found that I need to discuss the play in some detail before the students actually view Olivier's and Branagh's films, if I want them to demonstrate some autonomy in their critical appraisal of the plays and films. I emphasize four to five key elements that will surface in those cinematic productions. First, I begin with the function of the Chorus in this play. Students scrutinize the words of the Chorus in relation to the text, assessing the "truth" of the Chorus's relation of the events that the audience views in the subsequent scenes. I ask the students to consider the relevance of the Chorus's request for imaginative participation when the play moves from the limits of theatrical representation to the possibilities of the cinematic screen. Second, the students discuss the representations of Henry created by the cacophony of voices of the minor characters in the play. I point out specific examples, such as the subversive implications of Fluellen's comparison between Henry and "Alexander the Pig." At this point I might direct some students to Stephen Greenblatt's essay on the Henriad in *Shakespearean Negotiations,* since it provides many useful ways in which to discuss the function of the minor characters. Third, I discuss the role women have in *Henry V* in "framing" the discussion of territorial "right," in the discussion of Salic Law in Act 1 and in the "wooing" of Katherine in Act 5. And, fourth, we examine the scenes of war, which include the battle of Harfleur as well as the scenes in preparation for the battle of Harfleur. Embedded within these discussions are critiques of what I call the "sexualized language of invasion" in the scene before Harfleur and in Katherine's English lesson. Inevitably, these "sections" overlap in our discussions, but they prepare us for the ways in which Olivier and Branagh, the two directors whose films we view in class, will manipulate, suppress, or exaggerate these images and issues.

On the basis of these discussions and lectures, students begin to consider the elements within the play that might work to subvert Henry's glorification. Students are particularly interested in the relationship between the ending of the play, which resembles those of

Shakespeare's romantic comedies, and the political relations in the play. Students perceive Princess Katherine of France as playing a pivotal role as they assess Henry's rhetorical strategies in producing political order out of sexual and political relations. A few students have written interesting and insightful papers on "Katherine's Role as Critic" in the play and its cinematic incarnations. In writing their essays, students may be directed to recent essays by Karen Newman, Phyllis Rackin, Peter Donaldson, Katherine Eggert, and even Peter Stallybrass's influential essay "Patriarchal Territories," which does not specifically address *Henry V* but is clearly useful in developing student discussions regarding the "colonized" female body.

If my aim is to demonstrate that the language of drama is verbal, my colleague in the Theatre Department works to demonstrate that the language of drama is an expressive art that encompasses a wide range of practices. She may discuss the relevance of music to *Henry V,* for example, and suggest how a director like Branagh may manipulate our emotional involvement in the battle through Henry's specific directions for two psalms to be sung, "Non nobis" and "Te Deum" (4.8.125). As a theater practitioner, she is committed to performance as the only true medium by which dramatic literature can be understood or experienced. She demonstrates for students the process by which an actor prepares for a dramatic role, insisting upon the self-exploration that is part of the performing artist's engagement with the text. Ultimately, she argues, engagement with Shakespeare's play will yield the experiential "truths" of the play that the actor seeks.

As a self-described "dramaturg," the theater professor discusses the characters in the play and their motives with the students as if she were advising actors on how to prepare for their roles. Her emphasis upon character analysis demands that the student deal with issues of motivation (always problematic in discussing Henry V), but within a belief-system that would be acceptable for the actor as "Henry" to internalize. Too many contradictory interpretations—that bugbear ambivalence—would prevent a coherent performance of the character for the audience. The student assignments that spring from these lectures and discussions emphasize the actor's reading of a character and its translation on the stage or screen. A typical assignment for students entails consideration of the ways in which Branagh's performance concretizes the actor's understanding of the qualities of a great leader: "As he was preparing for the title role in *Henry V* for the 1984 Royal Shakespeare Company production, Kenneth Branagh remarked that he wanted to explore the 'highly complicated and ambiguous . . . nature of leadership.' After viewing the subsequent film *Henry V* (1989), do you believe Branagh was successful in exploring the rich psychological nature of Henry?"

The interdisciplinary approach to Shakespeare's text prepares the students for the array of interpretative possibilities in the cinematic representations of Shakespeare's plays, but it also drives home the point that performance *is* interpretation. From the very first class we want the students to have a sense of the enormous possibilities contained within the lines of the play. To emphasize this point we sometimes invite a professional actor into the classroom to demonstrate the way an actor prepares for the Chorus's Prologue in *Henry V.* These lines are usually the first stumbling block for students who have difficulty with the

Shakespeare text and with the conception of the function of a "Chorus." The immediate and tangible experience of a live "Chorus" in the classroom is crucial in overcoming the students' resistance to the text. Faces light up with recognition and interest, as if the students are hearing the words for the first time. This classroom "Chorus" strides through the aisles of the classroom as he explores the various possibilities in the language, altering tone and emphasis with the expressive gestures of his body. In order to force the students to feel and understand the immediacy of the words, this actor crawls on his hands and knees on the floor as he huffs the word "fire, fire, fire," permitting his body to feel the image itself. Each time he refines his performance of the lines he draws the students' attention to the particular words that inspire his interpretation. I was struck to find that the words or lines I would emphasize in my lectures (for example, the Chorus's charge to the audience "to *judge* our play") were not considered imagistically or emotionally significant (and therefore went unemphasized) in the actor's interpretation of the lines of the Chorus.

At any point during the lectures and discussions on *Henry V* the other faculty in the course are free to make their contributions to understanding the Shakespearean text and the films. For example, when we have shown Laurence Olivier's 1944 film *Henry V,* the theater practitioner illuminates some of the more confusing issues of staging in Olivier's recreation of the Shakespeare's Globe Theatre, or comments upon the differences in acting styles evident in our two cinematic versions of *Henry V*. The history professor who attends the class draws our attention to the elements of war-time propaganda evident in the opening scene of the film, in which a playbill flutters from the sky into the Globe Theatre in a parody of Hitler's descent in an airplane in the German propaganda film *Triumph of the Will*. The historian may also alert the students to the political and historical dynamic that shaped Olivier's and Branagh's interpretations, from the crisis of World War II to the Falkland Conflict, or raise the psychological and political implications of growing up in war-torn Ulster for a young man who would later direct a film about the English colonization of foreign lands.

The contributions of my colleagues have forced the discussions into directions I could never have anticipated and deepened my own understanding of the material. When I have taught *King Lear* as the Shakespeare component in "Exploring Humanities through Film," for example, the philosophy professor in the class has explored some of the more subtle concepts of human relations in this play. Students are prone to assess the emotions that torment Lear and Gloucester as "guilt," but my colleague guides the class to understand that these characters do not behave in a way that we may associate with that particular emotion. As the philosopher examines the shading of human response, the students find that the overwhelming emotion that Lear and Gloucester experience is that of "shame," a more social response than guilt. As we discuss the possible manifestations of shame in human behavior, I am able to point back to the Shakespeare play and the ways in which Shakespeare exposes "shame" as the emotion that drives these two fathers.

The two films that I have shown when teaching *King Lear* in "Exploring Humanities through Film" are Akira Kurosawa's *Ran* (1985) and Grigori Kozintsev's *Karol Lear* (1970), films that illustrate cross-cultural adaptations of the Shakespearean text. As Kozinstev re-marked after meeting Kurosawa and studying his films, "Influence in art is not only the result of one artist learning from another, it is the threads of the twisting spiral of history, the continuit of life where old contradictions develop new forms and new generations ask once again the age-old and very simple question: 'What does man live for?'" (1977, 14). The cultural experience of historical dislocations and human misery that these two directors discover in the national expression of Japanese and Russian art and literature is also a central tenant of Shakespeare's *King Lear,* and explains why both directors were attracted to this particular play.

I anticipated some difficulty in conveying the richness of Japanese culture—particularly the nature and form of Noh drama—to my class. For elements of Japanese Noh drama that appear in both films, I turned to my colleague in the Theatre Department, who had spent a year of her graduate training studying Noh drama. She brought several Noh masks to class and explained their representative characters in the Noh narratives. She discussed the nature of theatrical training under the Noh master, a disciplined and difficult course of study that unites the mind and body behind the Noh mask in a concentrated intensity.

However, my experiment with *King Lear* in "Exploring Humanities through Film" only stood one trial. The material was too dense and difficult for students in the short amount of time that the class allowed. Students had difficulty understanding the more philosophical questions posed in the play, and they disliked the "multicultural" component imposed upon them. In their view, Shakespeare was enough of a "foreign" language. To compound their difficulties in understanding Shakespeare's play with subtitled films and a range of cultural symbols and artistic representations to which they had little previous exposure made their experience confusing and unpleasant. I have consequently reserved such in-depth explorations of interdisciplinary materials in cinematic versions of *King Lear* for my graduate students. My experimentation with teaching various Shakespeare plays in the interdisciplinary classroom has forced me to acknowledge the limits of my own expertise as well as the limits of the students' ability to absorb the richness of the materials explored within the context. Shakespeare's drama in the interdisciplinary classroom is never fully appreciated without an awareness of its variables in performance, experienced in conjunction with the written text and the students in the course.

For the faculty who stand before a classroom and "represent" a chosen discipline, the experience of team-teaching serves to remind them that Shakespeare's drama is primarily experiential and fluid. As others who have team-taught drama have discovered, "a work of theater—no less than an essay in a composition class—should be regarded not only as a product but also as a complex, vital, living process" (Davis and Hutchings 1984, 569). The information the English teacher's lectures impart to the students, culled from historical sources and literary theory, is only one element in their overall experience of Shakespeare's drama, only one contribution in a classroom tableau represented by subtle shadings and striking contrasts. The exchange of critical perspectives within the classroom reaches to the heart of what "Exploring the Humanities through Film" hopes to teach: the richness of the humanities and the centrality of Shakespeare's plays within any curriculum.

References

Davis, Ken and William Hutchings. 1984. "Playing a New Role: The English Professor as Dramaturg. *College English* 46.6:560–69.

Deats, Sara Munson. 1992. "Rabbits and Ducks: Olivier, Branagh and *Henry V.*" *Literature/Film Quarterly* 20.4:284–93.

Donaldson, Peter S. 1991. "Taking on Shakespeare: Kenneth Branagh's *Henry V.*" *Shakespeare Quarterly* 42.1:60–70.

Eggert, Katherine. 1994. "Nostalgia and the Not Yet Late Queen: Refusing Female Rule in *Henry V.*" *ELH* 61.3:523–50.

Fish, Stanley. 1989. "Being Interdisciplinary Is So Very Hard to Do." *Profession 89*, 15–22.

Kozinstev, Grigori. 1977. *King Lear: The Space of Tragedy.* Trans. Mary Mackintosh. Berkeley and Los Angeles: University of California Press.

Newman, Karen. 1991. *Fashioning Femininity and English Renaissance Drama.* Chicago: The University of Chicago Press.

Rabkin, Norman. 1981. *Shakespeare and the Problem of Meaning.* Chicago: University of Chicago Press.

Rackin, Phyllis. 1990. *Stages of History: Shakespeare's English Chronicles.* Ithaca: Cornell University Press.

Shaw, William. 1994. "Textual Ambiguities and Cinematic Certainties in *Henry V.*" *Literature/Film Quarterly* 22.2:117–28.

Stallybrass, Peter. 1986. "Patriarchal Territories: The Body Enclosed." In *Rewriting the Renaissance: The Discourses of Sexual Difference in Early Modern Europe,* ed. Margaret W. Ferguson, Maureen Quilligan, and Nancy Vickers, 123–42. Chicago: University of Chicago Press.

CHAPTER 14

An Inquiry-Based Approach

MARIE A. PLASSE
Merrimack College
North Andover, Massachusetts

Plasse describes her frustrations with her students' level of interest and responses in her undergraduate Shakespeare classes and her work to improve the situation. In Plasse's words, "My efforts to make the students' interaction with Shakespearean texts the backbone of the course and the basis of our daily class work have yielded the inquiry-based course structure I now use." Her new approach "focuses on teaching students how to develop their own inquiries into the plays and locates these at the center of the course rather than at the margins of a course built mainly around the instructor's agenda."

*A*fter several years of conducting my undergraduate Shakespeare course as a traditional Socratic lecture/discussion requiring midterm and final exams and two four- to six-page papers, I became frustrated with what I perceived as my students' low level of responsive engagement with Shakespeare. Most of them did their work, appeared to be learning, and claimed in their course evaluations to have been satisfied with the class. But there was always something slightly oppressive about the experience for them and for me, and something vaguely contrived about the classes and the work that students produced for them.

Many students, English majors included, seemed to approach the course with trepidation about the difficulty of Shakespearean texts, and with negative experiences of Shakespeare fresh in their minds from past classroom encounters. As a result, they were often simply too intimidated or put off by Shakespeare to respond at all in class. Others seemed to enter the course with such reverence for Shakespeare as a "great author" that they, too, were reluctant to respond actively to his works, preferring that the instructor fill them with wisdom about the master. I prepared exhaustively for class meetings in which students seemed dutifully attentive, but not genuinely involved. There was little class discussion, students would almost never have genuine questions or concerns of their own to pursue (aside from the usual queries about plot), and I ended up having to answer my own questions all too often.

After discussing these frustrations with colleagues who were experiencing similar problems in their own classes, I began to see that the Socratic method I had been using was at least partly responsible for the students' hesitancy to strike out on their own paths of inquiry. As many teachers do, I usually brought a set agenda to every class, and while I welcomed questions and other deviations from that agenda, my approach to the plays and my sense of which topics and questions were important completely governed what we did in class, what options for paper topics the students received, and what was on the final exam. Although I believed then (and continue to believe) that there is nothing wrong with the professor's exercising this degree of control over the course, I have learned that my students tend to engage more fully with Shakespeare when I step back from my customary position of control and call off the Socratic hunt for my own fully formed interpretations and insights. My efforts to make the students' interaction with Shakespearean texts the backbone of the course and the basis of our daily class work have yielded the inquiry-based course structure I now use.

This new structure focuses on teaching students how to develop their own inquiries into the plays and locates these at the center of the course rather than at the margins of a course built mainly around the instructor's agenda. I am not suggesting that we give students total responsibility for "teaching themselves" Shakespeare, nor do I mean to imply that my own contributions to the discussions, assignments, and overall structure of the course are minimal. Rather, I want to show how a shift from the pursuit of my interests and insights to the identification and development of students' observations, questions, and interpretations has significantly improved my students' and my own experience of teaching and learning Shakespeare.

In order to bring about the changes in emphasis I have been describing, I radically altered the kinds of writing assignments I use in the course. Like many teachers of traditionally structured undergraduate Shakespeare courses, I had been asking students to complete writing assignments which required them to have mastered, without much prior training, not only difficult Shakespearean texts, but also the complex process of composing a cogent piece of literary analysis. Such assignments, typically in the form of short papers or essay exams that asked students to respond to a topic I had already formulated (e.g., analyze Mercutio's role in *Romeo and Juliet;* trace Hamlet's development through several soliloquies), were often little more than one-shot endeavors, completed and forgotten, in which the student either hit or missed the mark. My comments on the graded papers offered the writer some sense of the strengths and weaknesses of the piece, but formal opportunities for students to sharpen and develop their ideas during the semester were rare in these courses in which each writing assignment operated as a relatively isolated performance.

I abandoned these traditional assignments in order to build into the course a series of writing tasks that would engage students in learning how to interrogate Shakespearean texts before requiring them to create a fully polished product of such work. To replace the old assignments, I designed a sequence of writing tasks inspired by the process- and revision-oriented pedagogy I use as a matter of course in my composition classes, but which had always seemed difficult to adapt to my much larger literature courses. Instead of assigning two short essays of four to six pages (one at midterm and one at the end of the term), plus midterm and final exams, I instituted a three-part sequence of what I call, for lack of a more elegant term, inquiry-based writing assignments. I now use the first part of this sequence as the basis for nearly 50 percent of the work we do in class. This three-part sequence consists of:

1) short pieces of writing (1–2 pages), which I call "seed papers," in which students pose a productive question about the text and then attempt to answer it.

2) longer, more formal essays (4–6 pages) developed directly from seed papers, in which students expand and refine a seed paper idea.

3) a final exam essay (4–6 pages, take-home) in which students analyze a selected group of seed paper questions posed during the semester, explaining which questions were most productive and why.

A more detailed explanation of each phase of this sequence follows.

1. Seed Papers

I designed these short writing assignments with two principal goals in mind. First, since I had learned through experience that my students would rarely come to class prepared to answer my questions on the spot, nor would they respond well to study questions I distributed prior to class discussion, I instituted seed papers as a mechanism that would compel them to come to class with something substantial to say about the play at hand. Second, I wanted students to engage regularly in the processes of observation, inquiry, discovery, and collaboration that form the basis of any productive literary study. These short papers, which asked students to pose and then answer a question growing out of their reading, were intended to catalyze such processes. The papers did not have to be formally polished essays, nor did they necessarily have to reach solid conclusions. They just had to offer, with detailed reference to the text, the student's initial exploration of an idea that would be worthwhile for the class to discuss.

Typically, each student does two seed papers over the course of the term. I schedule two or three members of the class for seed paper assignments per day and plan the course so that approximately half of the class sessions on any one play are devoted to seed paper assignments (e.g., three out of six classes on *Richard III*, four out of six classes on *Othello*). I reserve the remaining days to present historical and theatrical contexts, to introduce important ideas not raised in seed paper discussions, and to synthesize and review. On the day their seed paper assignments are due, students come to class with their questions and answers typed up, ready to hand in to me. During class, I ask them to: 1) pose their questions to the group; 2) allow us time to think through the question and to go back through relevant passages in the text; 3) listen to the ensuing class discussion; and 4) contribute the work of their seed papers to the discussion at an appropriate moment. (A circular seating arrangement, incidentally, is crucial to this classroom procedure, as is the understanding that individual seed ideas will receive varying allotments of class time depending on the progress of discussion.)

I prepare the class for seed paper work during the first two weeks of the semester by explaining the goals of the assignment and evaluating some sample seed questions I ask them to bring to class after they read *A Midsummer Night's Dream*, the first play on the syllabus. We discuss the difference between limited or "dead end" questions that will elicit only descriptions, reiterations of "given" features of characters and events, or plot summary (e.g., "What happens to the lovers in the woods?") and more productive questions that will generate interesting and useful inquiries into the significance of various features of the play (e.g., "Why do all the characters eventually end up in the woods and what do the woods represent in the play?"). Our criteria for evaluating questions grows out of the course goals stated on the syllabus, namely to develop students' understanding of Shakespeare's theme, dramatic techniques, and their Renaissance contexts, with emphasis on both the literary and theatrical dimensions of Shakespeare's art. These criteria form the basis for a predominantly formalist inquiry into the plays, a skill I want to build before introducing any other critical approaches in the course.

Students receive written responses to their seed papers from me in the form of marginal and end comments, along with a numerical grade from zero to four, roughly equivalent to the grades in the traditional A through F system. I use these numbers, and distribute prose explanations of what each numerical grade signifies, in the hope of discouraging students from focusing exclusively on a letter grade after I return their papers to them. More significantly, however, before they receive a grade and formal response from me, students receive informal feedback on their seed papers from their peers during the course of class discussions in which they present their questions and responses. Writers of seed papers often report, as they hand in their papers after class, that having heard the class discuss their questions, they now have much more material they wish they had included in their papers. One of the advantages to using the short seed papers as part of a sequence that also includes longer essay assignments is that I am able to remind these students that the upcoming longer essay assignment will be a good opportunity for them to revise and expand their seed papers according to what they have learned from class discussion.

Classes built around this process of asking and answering seed questions are lively, not focused on the teacher, and prompt more dialogue among students than the traditional Socratic discussions I have led in the past. For example, early in the current term, a seed question that pondered the significance of Puck in *A Midsummer Night's Dream* led one class to consider Puck's role as a catalyst for the plot, a link between the lovers', mechanicals', and fairies' stories, and a personification of love, as well as his connection to the play's vast network of sight imagery and the significance of his two names (Puck and Hobgoblin). Later in the semester, a question about how female characters in *Othello* are treated by male characters opened up a discussion in which students made connections between the play and their reading of secondary sources on women's roles in Elizabethan culture. These connections led them to widen their conception of the play's theme, moving from a narrowly conceived focus on Othello's gullibility and Iago's villainy to a broader view that included the play's dramatization of gender stereotypes.

In each of these discussions and many others, the class raised many issues that I would have introduced myself in a more traditional lecture/discussion format. These sessions sparked investigation of structures, themes, dramatic techniques, and cultural contexts that I consider essential to any study of the plays. The important difference between the discussions I have just described and the more traditional classroom formats I have used is that in seed paper sessions, genuine inquiry transpires during class time, with the entire group (including me) working together on the spot to develop responses to the question posed. Class meetings are animated by dialogue in which students listen to, develop, refute, and refine one another's ideas rather than dominated by lectures or leading questions from me. Students learn not only about Shakespeare's plays but also about the processes through which useful discussion of the plays can be generated.

As a way of suggesting just how substantial a change in classroom procedure this seed paper assignment has created for me, let me summarize how this approach has altered my routine as the teacher. My role in class sessions, in addition to articulating my own answer to the questions posed without suggesting that my response is the best one, is to refine questions that could be better formulated, suggesting and explaining more productive word-ing or focus; to push students to clarify and develop their responses as much as possible; to make connections among questions posed earlier in the course, and to look ahead toward issues pertinent to upcoming plays. Instead of coming to class, as I usually did, with a well-planned set of questions and notes whose content and goals I had carefully devised, I now go to "seed paper" classes not knowing exactly what the focus of each day's discussion will be. (I do not ask students to inform me in advance of the questions they are planning to ask.) I bring to class pages of material in "modular" form—groups of notes on major characters, central issues, and key dramatic techniques in the play at hand, which summarize my own perspectives on these topics and note textual references that will support explora-tion of them. After a student poses a question and the class sets to work for five to ten minutes singly or in small groups to develop responses, I sift through these notes to prepare a contribution to the ensuing discussion and make further notes and reminders inspired on the spot. Once we finish discussing a given play, I provide students with a list of all the seed questions that have been submitted on that play, along with the names of the authors of those questions. (Students use these lists later as part of their longer essay assignments and they need them to complete the final exam for the course.)

Although this inquiry-based class procedure was nerve-wracking at first, especially for a compulsive class-preparer like me, I soon began to enjoy the excitement and the virtue of these looser class sessions that placed the students, their questions, and the group's responses center stage. The anxiety and tension of having to respond on the spot keeps most of us engaged and interested, and helps me produce fresh thoughts rather than the canned riffs that so many of us come to rely on in our teaching. Moreover, the process of working through questions alongside students makes me feel much more like a true participant in my classes than ever before; it removes some of the loneliness of "being a teacher." These sessions also help me see what my students find puzzling, interesting, strange, and compelling about Shakespeare, things that I had begun to lose touch with after years of teaching my own agenda so assiduously. Perhaps most importantly, this process allows the class to be more precisely geared to the students' needs and interests as we work our way through a play. (The earliest seed question days, for example, tend to feature basic questions, while later days focus on more complex and sophisticated issues.)

2. Short Essays Built on Seed Papers

For the two longer, more formal writing assignments in the course, I ask students to develop four- to six-page essays built on one of their own previously completed seed papers or on a seed question posed by another member of the class. (I advise them to take careful notes on our discussions so that they will be able to use one another's work for this essay assignment if they choose.) My goal in connecting the longer paper to the seed papers is to encourage students to develop their initial inquiries into analyses that are more clearly conceived and fully supported than those produced in the shorter, more exploratory seed papers. In doing this, I hope that they will come to understand something of the process by which genuine scholarly inquiry into literature proceeds: that is, by means of observations and questions pursued over a sustained period of time, refined by discussions with others, and fed by repeated readings of the text. I also want to avoid giving out "paper topics" that ask students to write in response to paths of inquiry I have already formulated for them. I want them to see that a full-fledged essay can be built on the basis of a question or observation that they have generated themselves.

Some students choose to develop their own seed papers into fuller, more carefully argued essays, adapting material originally conceived for their seed papers and incorporating new ideas generated during class discussion. One student, for example, recently wrote a short seed paper on *Romeo and Juliet* in which she offered the following observation and question: "While reading *Romeo and Juliet,* I came across an interesting paradox. While night symbolizes death and sadness, it also provides the cover for all of the love in the play. What is the significance of this love in the darkness?" The paper went on to identify several different references to darkness, love, and night in the play, ranging from examples in which darkness connotes sadness (Romeo's "artificial night" of daytime pining for Rosaline in 1.1.143), dream and fantasy (Mercutio's Queen Mab speech), and a safe cover for Romeo and Juliet's love (2.2; 3.5). For the longer paper assignment, she developed her seed paper into an essay that analyzed the role of darkness in *Romeo and Juliet,* expanding and revising her original observation/question about love in darkness. She began the longer essay with this more comprehensive and carefully structured conceptualization of the topic: "Dark imagery plays a very important role in *Romeo and Juliet.* Essentially, darkness is used in four ways: as an opposition to light, as a cover for love (and a time for dreams), as a metaphor for death, and a foreshadowing of tragedy." This student and others who choose to rework their seed papers for the longer essay are engaging in processes of revision and development of ideas for which traditional "one-shot" writing assignments in literature courses do not allow, but which have become standard procedures in beginning and advanced composition courses. This sequenced use of seed papers and longer essays is the most feasible method I have found to import a useful strategy from composition pedagogy into the heavily enrolled Shakespeare courses I teach without creating an impossible paper-reading burden for myself.

Other students prefer to fulfill the longer essay assignment by pursuing lines of inquiry their classmates have opened up in their seed papers. I ask students who take this approach to acknowledge the work of their peers in their papers, explaining that such acknowledgments are routine in scholarly writing. I also ask them to be sure to distinguish their own ideas carefully from those of their classmates. Many students seem to take great satisfaction in citing classmates' work in their own papers, especially when they follow such acknowledgments with emphatic declarations of how their own approach to a given question differs from their classmate's.

3. Final Exam Question

The third phase of this assignment is a take-home final exam question which asks students to choose three plays from among those that we have studied during the term and, for each of these plays, to select three seed questions from among those posed during the semester that they believe are especially useful for helping them enjoy and understand that play. The exam then requires them to explain why these seed questions are productive and to provide detailed references to the important issues and insights the question has led them to. If students have trouble finding three especially productive questions from among those that were asked during the term, they are free to include and analyze new questions of their own. My aim in assigning this exam question is to follow up on the work that we do all semester on formulating an interesting and productive line of inquiry into a play. In order to answer the question well, students must revisit the plays and the discussions we have had about them, be able to distinguish clearly among weaker and stronger questions, and discuss some of the key issues and features of the plays. Students who write strong answers to the exam question demonstrate that they have not only learned something about the subjects, characters, themes, and dramatic techniques of three plays, but also that they have grasped the principles of conducting a fruitful interrogation of any Shakespearean dramatic text.

Teaching an undergraduate Shakespeare course structured by the inquiry-based assignments I have described often means having to give up a number of things that perhaps have become familiar and comforting features of a course more fully driven by the instructor's agenda. Among these things are: "comprehensive" coverage of individual plays; ordered, predictable class sessions; extended class time available for showing substantial portions of video or film versions of the plays. Placing students' observations and questions at the center of the course means that sometimes it will take a long time for the class to arrive at an understanding of an idea the instructor could quickly explain in a lecture. It means that when a student asks a weakly conceived seed paper question, the class must struggle together to find and pursue a stronger line of inquiry based on that question. It also means that sometimes a full class period will be spent discussing something that the instructor finds uninteresting or only marginally relevant to what she wishes students to understand about a given play.

However, in the process of giving up some familiar things and occasionally enduring an unfocused or uninspiring discussion, teaching an inquiry-based Shakespeare course opens up the possibility of inspiring greater engagement among students with the processes of reading, discussing, and writing about the plays; exposes them to a wide variety of their peers' perspectives and encourages them to rely on one another as sources of knowledge; and builds their ability to respond critically to all the literature they will read and study, including Shakespeare. For me, at least so far, the trade-off has been worthwhile.

CHAPTER 15

A Whole-Language Approach to *A Midsummer Night's Dream*

JOHN WILSON SWOPE

University of Northern Iowa
Cedar Falls, Iowa

Swope claims that Shakespearean tragedy dominates traditional high school English offerings and argues for a greater consideration of the comedies. He then notes that A Midsummer Night's Dream *presents secondary school students with issues they can relate to just as well as those of* Romeo and Juliet *or* Macbeth. *Finally, because traditional approaches often presume that students are fluent readers, he recommends that teachers try a whole-language approach; and he provides a detailed discussion of* A Midsummer Night's Dream *and of the theories and activities that are part of such an approach.*

*A*ny of us who have either been through or taught in traditional high school English programs know that Shakespearean tragedy dominates the curriculum. Too often, we may not have considered either what we teach or how we teach it. Applebee's study (1989) of the book-length works taught in high school confirms our recollections that *Romeo and Juliet, Julius Caesar, Macbeth,* and *Hamlet* are the plays that students are most likely to study. It may be simply the intellectual snobbery that tragedies are a higher art form than comedies or histories; however, there are other choices: thirty-two other plays, fourteen of them comedies.

The arguments for teaching *Romeo and Juliet* or *Macbeth,* the most commonly taught works in Applebee's study, apply equally as well to teaching *A Midsummer Night's Dream.* In selecting *Romeo and Juliet* we point to ways that our students, most often ninth graders, can relate to the play. We point out that the pursuit of true love forces Romeo and Juliet to meet in secret, just as Hermia and Lysander do. Or that Romeo originally pines for the unrequited love of Rosaline, just as Helena does for Demetrius. Our students understand Juliet opposing the marriage Lord Capulet arranged for her, just as Hermia opposes Egeus's desire that she marry Demetrius.

In presenting our case for teaching *Macbeth,* we're likely to mention that adolescents are attracted to the magic of the witches: the same sort of device that enables Oberon and Puck to cast the spell upon the unsuspecting lovers and Titania. Similarly, adolescents understand the rivalry, jealousy, and seeking of retribution: precisely what motivates Oberon to squeeze the flower's juice upon the eyelids of his queen and have her fall madly in love with a transformed Nick Bottom.

In addition, students love to laugh. *A Midsummer Night's Dream* provides ample opportunities. Under the magical spell of the flower, the lovers fall for the wrong match and Titania falls for the bewitched Bottom. The droll humor of the mechanicals in their performance of "Pyramus and Thisbe" is equal to any routine of either the Three Stooges or Jim Carey.

More important than which plays we select is how we teach them. Traditional approaches presume that all students are fluent readers, and the teaching begins after the students read all or some portion of a text. Teachers often become frustrated when they can't discuss the play because they're too busy explaining the plot. Instead, we need to recognize and to address the problems our students are likely to have in reading *A Midsummer Night's Dream,* and we need to better prepare them to participate in discussion of the text and other activities that follow.

However, effective reading involves a great deal more than recognizing individual words. And reading Shakespeare involves more than looking at the lines of verse and consulting the footnotes. When we assign our students portions of Shakespeare to read we are also assigning them an array of problems to solve as readers. Shakespeare's characters, settings, and plots draw upon and reflect a world view that few students embrace today. In *A Midsummer Night's Dream,* Egeus appeals to Theseus, an enlightened but nonetheless absolute monarch, to force his daughter Hermia to marry Demetrius although she's in love with Lysander. Egeus is willing to impose the ancient Athenian penalty: obey or die. Theseus offers a slightly different set of choices: obey, die, or enter a convent. Although contemporary teens are likely to understand the source of this conflict, they are unlikely to submit completely or automatically to the wishes of any outside authority.

Additional reading problems students must overcome include foreign vocabulary, place, and character names; contextual shifts in the use of what appear to be familiar words; multiple, interrelated plots, often interrupted with long digressions; and blank verse that uses inverted syntax, literary allusions, figurative language.

One means to address these problems is for the teacher to intervene actively in the students' reading processes. This intervention also needs to provide opportunities for students to employ all their skills in using language. Whether we call this approach *whole language, integrated language instruction,* or *balanced instruction,* these terms describe a student-centered philosophy about language instruction rather than a discrete set of instructional strategies. Within a secondary English classroom, *A Midsummer Night's Dream,* like any of Shakespeare's plays, provides opportunities for students to develop their language skills by integrating reading, writing, speaking, listening, critical thinking, and viewing within meaningful contexts. For example, students develop their comprehension of what they've read and critically evaluate it by completing reading- and writing-to-learn activities, talking about it (speaking and listening), and processing audiovisual media.

Integrating reading among the other language arts promotes a broader, psycholinguistic view of reading that Weaver (1994, 15) defines as "learning to bring meaning to a text in order to get meaning from, or understand a text." Promoting students' understanding of *A Midsummer Night's Dream,* like any other difficult literary text, involves deliberate teacher intervention into the active process of reading before, during and after students read assignments. Although exploring any literary text with students focuses first upon reading, the exploration also provides opportunities to develop and reinforce other language skills.

Reading Process Instruction

Over the past quarter century, we have come to recognize both reading and writing as recursive, complementary processes. In writing instruction, *prewriting, writing,* and *rewriting* are common terms. In reading process activities have corresponding counterparts: *prereading, during reading,* and *postreading.* **Prereading activities** serve two goals: to organize the reader's prior knowledge related to the selection that will be read and to provide a genuine purpose for reading. **During reading activities** help students make better sense of what they've just read. At this stage, reading, writing, speaking, listening, viewing, and critical thinking activities allow students to transact with the written word within the social context of the classroom. **Postreading activities** allow students to make sense of their earlier explorations and to place them within the context of reading the rest of the play, connecting it to other works of literature previously studied, and to their lives. **Extending activities**, like any other summative project, allow students to demonstrate and apply what they've learned to new situations or contexts.

Prereading Activities

The prior knowledge that students bring to *A Midsummer Night's Dream* obviously varies. Some students may have studied a Shakespearean play already. These students are familiar with more than just plot. Ideally, they will have had positive experiences processing the Elizabethan verse. Others may have seen a production of the play. Still others will have no experience with the play, its language, or plot. However, all students do possess, as part of their own life experience, knowledge of characters and situations that relate directly to the characters, situations, and themes of the play.

In Act 2, scene 1, Puck delivers the exposition for the feud between Oberon and Titania, king and queen of the fairies. Puck warns a fellow fairy to keep Titania out of this part of the forest because Oberon is jealous that Titania will not give him the changeling boy she's stolen. Although we, as teachers, may be familiar with the Celtic mythology that allows Puck (a.k.a. Robin Goodfellow) in particular or the fairies in general to steal children from unguarded cradles, our American students probably won't be. However, students do understand jealousy and covetousness. Therefore, encouraging students to recall a situation in which they were either jealous or covetous provides a basis for comparing Oberon's emotions and desire for revenge.

To vary the student-centered instruction, *improvisations, speculation journals,* and *small-group discussion questions* help students tap into their own experiences prior to reading a scene. Consider the following examples, all of which help set up the conflict between Oberon and Titania in 2.1. Because they all address the same instructional goal, students need to complete only one prereading activity. Once students complete the activity, direct them to consider how the characters in the play act in a similar situation. This direction helps students establish a purpose for reading: to learn whether the action of the play confirms or contradicts their experience.

Improvisation. Students may work on improvisations in pairs or small groups. Give the students a prompt and let them discuss it briefly before performing. More willing students will volunteer to act in front of the class. Less willing students may find working from their desks less intimidating.

> **Scene:** The local park, vacant lot, or backyard where children gather after school to play football, baseball, softball, or soccer.
> **Characters:** Pat and Kim, best friends, age ten, and avid ball players. Tony or (Toni) the child who owns the ball.
> **Action:** A group of ten children gather each afternoon to play ball. This afternoon Tony (Toni), the one who owns the ball, got angry because s/he wasn't chosen first and took the ball and left. Decide how you will get even with Tony (Toni) for ruining your game.

Speculation Journal. As a writing-to-learn activity, encourage students to accumulate their work in a journal, so they can review it once they've read a section. This type of journal allows students to work individually or in pairs or small groups. Working from a written prompt on the chalkboard, overhead, or handout, allow the students to write for a few minutes and then encourage them to share before moving on to read the play. The following prompt also sets up Act 2, scene 1.

> Recall a time when either you or someone you knew was envious or jealous of someone else's talents or possessions. Briefly describe why you felt as you did and what you wanted to do to "get even" with the other person.

Small-Group Discussion. To generate a brief small-group discussion, I could present the following prompt:

> What would someone else have to do to make you really jealous or envious of either their talents or possessions? What might you do to "get even" with them?

As students become more familiar with the play, its characters, and their actions, similar activities allow students to apply what they've learned about the play and to speculate about other reading assignments. These speculations continue to guide the students' purposes for reading. The goal is not to guess the plot events correctly; instead, it is to provide an assertion that textual evidence affirms or contradicts.

For example, once students have seen Titania refuse to give up the changeling boy to Oberon (2.1), they can speculate how the nectar of the flower might make her behave when she falls in love with the next person or animal she sees upon awakening. To set up Act 3, scene 1, here are prompts for *improvisations, speculation journal,* and *small-group discussion.*

Improvisation.
Scene: Titania's bower, early morning.
Characters: Titania and some animal in the forest.
Situation: Oberon has squeezed the magic juice of a flower into the eyes of Titania while she slept. When she awakes, she will fall madly in love and dote on whatever animal or person she first sees. Decide what animal she falls in love with and how she might make a complete fool of herself in doing so.

Speculation Journal.
   Oberon has squeezed the juice of the magic flower into Titania's eyes while she slept. Under its power, she will fall immediately and completely in love with whatever animal or person she first sees. Describe how she makes a fool of herself when she awakes.

Small-Group Discussion.
   Once Oberon squeezes the juice of the magic flower into the eyes of Titania, she will awake and fall madly in love with the first animal or person she sees. How will she have to act for Oberon to have his "best" revenge? How would she have to act for it to be his "worst" revenge?

Students' familiarity with the language they read is another important type of prior knowledge that enhances students' comprehension. Margaret Early and Diane J. Sawyer (1984) point out that a "large part of the prior knowledge that a student brings to reading a specific selection is familiarity with language structures and codes" (62). Clearly then, another challenge for the teacher of Shakespeare's plays is to have the students examine the language—its syntax, its imagery, its encoding of human emotions, motivations and experiences.

   Because so much of Shakespeare is a foreign language to students, showing scenes on video or film prior to reading or distributing prose summaries employs familiar avenues to establish a preliminary understanding of the play.

   Videotape. Three versions are available on videotape: a live BBC (1960) broadcast with Benny Hill as Bottom, the Joseph Papp Public Theater (1982) version and PBS/BBC production from the Shakespeare Plays. Productions done specifically for television possess two advantages over film adaptations. First, the productions present the entire play, rather than eliminating or transposing scenes to make a better film. Second, these productions were designed and produced for television, so the visual details originally intended for the big screen of the theatre aren't lost to students in the back row when the film is reformatted for television.

   Showing scenes on video may be done as either a prereading or postreading activity. As a prereading activity, it may take little or no setting up, for the goal is to have the students develop an overall sense of how the scene progresses. Therefore, once the students look at the scene, simply asking "what seems to be going on here?" becomes a means to begin to assess their visual comprehension.

   Because the students have difficulty with Shakespeare's language, giving the students a prose summary of a scene before they read it imparts an overall framework that assists them in their reading and processing of the text. Again, the logic is the same for giving students a prose summary before reading a scene: it is an accessible reference that uses familiar language as a bridge to Shakespeare's.

Plot summary, Act 1, scene 1:

Theseus, Duke of Athens, enters with Hippolyta, Queen of the Amazons. He announces that he will marry her with great pomp and ceremony in four days with the coming of the new moon. Egeus interrupts and tells the Duke that he wishes his daughter, Hermia, to marry Demetrius. Hermia, however, is in love with Lysander and refuses. Egeus asks Theseus to impose the ancient penalty for disobedience upon Hermia: obey or die. Theseus instructs Hermia that she has four days to agree to marry Demetrius, die, or enter a convent and become a nun. Theseus leaves with Egeus and Demetrius.

Once alone with Hermia, Lysander reveals that he has a wealthy aunt who lives in another city and regards him as her heir. They plan to meet in the forest outside Athens the next night and flee to the aunt and be married. Just as they are ready to part, Helena enters. She tells them that she is hopelessly in love with Demetrius. To comfort her, they tell her of their plans to escape. Knowing the plans, she then plots to tell Demetrius of the meeting in the woods, hoping that he will be grateful to her for the information, and perhaps look more favorably on her.

During Reading Activities

While prereading activities help set up the reading for the students, during reading activities allow the students to test the predictions, speculations, and assumptions they've made while they read. These activities engage students in comprehending and exploring the play.

Organizing Class Reading Sessions. Reading any play aloud is common classroom practice. The typical pattern is for the teacher to assign one role to a student and have the whole class read it together. This certainly gets the eight or so students who are in any given scene involved; however, the remainder of the class is at best engaged in primarily passive activities: reading along silently and/or listening to other students read aloud.

Instead, have students work in groups of eight, and have three groups reading aloud simultaneously. For example, divide up the speaking parts for Act 3, scenes 1 and 2 among eight students in three groups:

Roles	Group 1	Group 2	Group 3
Titania	Lizzie	Carmen	Kim
Snug, Cobweb, Lysander	Jesus	Tim	Orlando
Bottom, Moth	Sanjay	Steve	Dwayne
Flute, Mustardseed, Hermia	Tanya	Alicia	Lynnette
Snout, Oberon	Richard	Jaime	James C.
Starveling, Demetrius	Hector	Alan	Marquis
Puck	Angelina	Stephanie	John

Having students discuss their reading, whether in small or large groups, is common practice in most literature classes. These discussions are more valuable when students prepare for them by reading actively and keeping some sort of reading journal. When students read portions of the play silently, they tend to regard the reading as a passive activity: pass their eyes over the text, turn pages, and then close the book when done. Using journals provides a means for students to read and contemplate the text as they read. Further, the journal provides a means for students to record their immediate reactions and concerns about the reading to review later. Provide students who are unaccustomed to keeping reading journals with specific prompts, like the following one for 3.1.

> Look back at the prereading activity that you completed before reading Act 3. In what ways did the plot confirm your view of Oberon's revenge upon Titania? How did the plot contradict your view? What other influences that you may not have foreseen, affected the characters?

Another way to structure a reading journal is to have students complete a character diary. In this type of journal, the students keep a journal from the perspective of one of the characters throughout the play. In keeping the diary, two things need to happen: the student accurately summarizes the action of the play and provides a means or explanation for learning of the action. For example, Puck's diary for 1.1 might look like this one.

> Something's afoot in the city. Peaseblossom, who accompanied her majesty, Titania, on a recent journey to the city, said that there's a wedding coming soon between Theseus and Hippolyta. They also overheard an old man demand that his daughter marry one man even though she was in love with another. The young lovers plan to escape to the woods tomorrow night. I just love it when I can play pranks upon mortals, especially the ones who don't believe we fairies exist.

Journals also provide a way to hold students accountable for reading assignments without resorting to reading quizzes. Collect journals and quickly review them, commenting briefly in the margins, making an effort to comment at least once in each student's journal. As with any writing-to-learn activity, don't evaluate these journals on grammar, usage, or mechanics. Emphasizing errors diverts the students from exploring ideas about the reading and taking risks related to interpretation.

The reading journal prepares students to discuss what they've read. Good discussion does more than simply review the action of the play; it provides opportunities for students to process what they've read and make fuller sense of it. Students need opportunities to hear divergent views about literature. Discussion also allows students to "talk out" interpretations that may have been only tentative in their reading journals. Encourage students to have their journals with them when they discuss their reading. Also encourage students to record their own questions in their journals and ask them as a part of the discussion or in an individual conference.

Postreading Activities

Once students have read and made sense of what they've read, they can then return to explore specific elements of the literature, momentarily isolating them before relating these elements to the play as a whole. Two areas worth examining after students have processed the action of the play include **character development** and the **use of figurative language**. Both activities require students to review sections they have read and draw conclusions that they can relate to the play as a whole.

Character Development. Within *A Midsummer Night's Dream,* students can examine how both major and minor characters are developed and/or revealed. Logical candidates include Hermia, Helena, Demetrius, Lysander, Oberon, Titania, Puck, Egeus, Theseus, and Bottom. Because not all characters appear in each act, encourage students, working in pairs or small groups, to examine several different characters. The sample below examines several of Oberon's actions during Act 2, scenes 1 and 2:

Scene	What Oberon says, does, or what others say about him	What this reveals about Oberon's character
Act 1, scene 1	Oberon sends Puck to get the flower; when its nectar is squeezed into anyone's eyes it makes the receiver fall madly in love with the next creature the victim see.	Oberon is spiteful, plotting revenge upon Titania, wanting to watch her make a fool of herself.
Act 2, scene 2	Oberon tells Puck to squeeze the flower's nectar into the eyes of Demetrius	Oberon wants to rectify an injustice: Demetrius to return Helena's love.

Use of Figurative Language. Teaching students about figurative language such as similes, metaphors and the like helps them become better readers. During the first reading, students are concerned with understanding the overall action of the play; therefore, return to study Shakespeare's language after students have a general understanding of the play. So this study doesn't become tedious, select only a few literary devices that you wish to review with the students. Within *A Midsummer Night's Dream,* students can apply their understanding of similes, metaphors, and personification, for example, developing their abilities to decode figurative language as an advanced reading skill.

Begin these activities by selecting specific passages and then assigning one or two to each group who work to solve two broad problems:

1. Isolate the figurative language and determine its structure. For example, in the following passage, Helena compares herself directly to a spaniel, using a metaphor.
2. Determine how the figurative language functions. How does the students' understanding of the metaphor affect their interpretation of the passage, scene, and play: What does this conceit reveal about Helena's character at this point in the play?

To illustrate this type of activity, consider how the metaphoric conceit in the following passage reveals Helena's character and her love for Demetrius.

> I am your spaniel; and Demetrius,
> The more you beat me, I will fawn on you.
> Use me but as your spaniel; spurn me, strike me,
> Neglect me, lose me; only give me leave,
> Unworthy as I am, to follow you.
> What worse place can I beg in your love—
> And yet a place of high respect with me—
> Than to be used as you use your dog?
>
> (2.1)

Extending Activities

Reading process activities help students understand the play as a whole. Once they've completed the play, they're ready to do something with what they've learned through **extending activities**. Whether we call these activities projects or extending activities, they serve a definite purpose: they allow students to apply what they've learned during the study of *A Midsummer Night's Dream* to new and additional situations.

Students complete these activities individually or in groups. These activities should be fun for the students. Extending activities also provide the teacher with an alternative to a unit test as a means to assess students' learning. The range of possible activities also provides opportunities for students to perform in accordance with their individual strengths. For example, some students may wish to write an interpretive essay, others may want to produce a newspaper featuring stories related to the action of the play: "Local Weaver's Story: 'I Was Kidnapped by Fairies.'" Some students may wish to act out specific scenes for the class; others may be more comfortable presenting ideas in the text through improvisations, reader's theater, or using simple puppets or masks.

Improvisation. In addition to being a productive prereading strategy, improvisations or skits based on unseen situations also provide means for students to demonstrate their understanding of characters and situations related to the play. Here is a sample situation that students might try.

> How might Bottom explain his being out all night to his wife once he returns from his experiences in the forest?

Puppets and Masks. Although students enjoy acting out scenes on their own, some often feel that they need to have costumes and props. While this is possible when the teacher has her own classroom, it is not for those teachers who move from room to room. Puppets and masks often are more comfortable for students to use in classroom performances because the student actor literally has something to hide behind and use to become someone else.

Students can make simple puppets from paper bags. Any size brown paper bag that has a flat bottom can serve. Using any type of stiff drawing paper, draw and cut out the head and upper face of the puppet and mount on the flat bottom of the bag. The mouth and lower part of the face, as well as the body of the puppet, are mounted on the side of the bag with the crease where the bottom folds. Insert a hand into the bag, keeping the bag partially folded, and move the upper part of the hand to make the puppet talk. Turning a table on its side makes an adequate stage for the puppets. Placing the table in front of a bulletin board or blank wall makes an ideal place to hang a mural, if the students feel the need for a backdrop.

Students can also make simple masks from large white paper plates. They can cut two eyeholes and draw on the plates with markers or crayons and decorate them with yarn or paper hair. The students may wish to attach strings to tie on the masks or mount them on dowels and hold them in front of them while performing. Even the most reluctant students get involved when they can use puppets or masks.

A Midsummer Night's Dream is a valuable addition to the current canon. As with the study of any of Shakespeare's plays, overcoming the language is a major hurdle. By placing students actively at the center of this study and helping them through a structured approach that includes prereading, during reading, and postreading activities in addition to postreading discussion, they come to see themselves as readers and interpreters of Shakespeare's language and humor, making them more receptive to the next play they study, whether it's *Hamlet* or *The Taming of the Shrew.*

References

Applebee, Arthur N. 1989. *A Study of Book-length Works Taught in High School English Courses.* Report Series 1.2. Albany: Center for the Learning and Teaching of Literature.

Early, Margaret and Diane J. Sawyer. 1984. *Reading to Learn in Grades 5 to 12.* San Diego: Harcourt Brace Jovanovich.

Shakespeare, William. 1953. *A Midsummer Night's Dream.* In *William Shakespeare: The Complete Works,* ed. Charles Jasper Sisson, 208–30. New York: Harper & Row.

Weaver, Constance. 1994. *Reading Process and Practice: From Socio-Psycholinguistics to Whole Language.* 2d ed. Portsmouth: Heineman.

IV

Beyond Traditional Settings and Approaches

CHAPTER 16

"So Quick Bright Things Come to Confusion"

Shakespeare in the Heterogeneous Classroom

Michael W. Shurgot

South Puget Sound Community College
Olympia, Washington

> *To a great extent, making the teaching of Shakespeare a success is making him interesting to our students. In this section, we offer suggestions from several teachers who have felt it necessary to go beyond traditional approaches to Shakespeare or who have had to teach his work in nontraditional settings. Shurgot examines the challenge of "the growing heterogeneity" of the classes he encounters in community college courses. He urges teachers to encourage the "multiple possibilities" of interpretation that the Shakespearean text supports, and he offers a number of comments on* A Midsummer Night's Dream *and* Othello *to illustrate his observations.*

My title is the final line from Lysander's speech in *A Midsummer Night's Dream* (1.1.141–49; *Riverside*) about the fragility and vulnerability of youthful love, that wonderfully idealistic and fleeting emotion we all recall from our teen years. Anyone who has been in a literature classroom lately knows that the "text" that, like youthful love, we used to idealize, has become just as fragile and vulnerable as any youthful passion we can recall. More's the pity, perhaps. However, the explosion of "isms" in literary criticism has tremendously expanded our consciousness and hence our teaching of literature and drama, including Shakespeare, just as our classrooms have themselves expanded to become far more heterogeneous than they were just a few decades ago. The growing heterogeneity of America's classrooms is especially evident at community colleges, such as my own, where for the past decade I have taught extremely diverse groups of students. In the hope that some of my work will prove useful to my colleagues, I herewith describe recent classroom experiences with *A Midsummer Night's Dream* and *Othello*.

In his superb essay "Teaching Shakespeare in America," Charles Frey writes:

> At the present moment [1984], teachers of Shakespeare might do well to consider critically the concept of "the text itself" and the many lingering appeals for "close" reading of it. I believe that the search for and the appeals to Shakespeare's "text" are too often based upon desires for authority and ownership, or "possession," desires inappropriate to student-centered teaching. (553)

Consider now Lysander's line. First, what parts of speech are "quick" and "bright"? "Bright" seems safely adjectival, but what form of "quick"? If an adjective, then with "bright" it modifies "things." So then quick, bright things (such as "lightning in the collied night" [1.145]) and love come to confusion quickly. What if "quick" is simultaneously adjective and adverb? Then, like lightning, love is quick and bright, yet its very quickness and brightness emphasize its nearly simultaneous extinction.

Further, this line images both the play itself, a quick, bright thing that succumbs to confusion in the Athenian woods, and its audience of teachers/students/viewers. Shakespeare's play has the structure of a dream: vivid, confusing, frightening, desirable, and nearly intractable. When I ask students how the middle acts of the play resemble a dream, they inevitably recount their confusions while reading it initially, especially trying to keep straight who loves whom, who is supposed to be with whom, and why, and trying to decipher Puck's and Oberon's intentions throughout Acts 3 and 4. For students in their initial course, Shakespeare—the course, the playwright, the script of this play—may seem, if not quick and bright, then hopelessly confusing. Nothing is but what is not.

Whatever Lysander's line is, it is certainly not stable. Yet in its very instability is its value—poetically, dramatically, symbolically. Lysander's line resists what Professor Frey calls "desires for authority and ownership, or 'possession,'" and thus images the heterogeneous script we teach in our classroom. If I insist that "quick" is an adjective, modifying "things," I rob Shakespeare's line of its marvelous poetic complexity, and simultaneously deny my students the opportunity to deduce their own meanings from it. If, on the other hand, I teach all Shakespearean dramatic poetry by saying that since all interpretation is personal anyway then "anything goes," I take two huge risks: first, encouraging the heresy of mere paraphrase of characters' lines; and secondly, denying students the intellectual rigor necessary to understand the richness and complexity of poetic drama. Shakespeare's lines and play do bear meaning and do have value, and we must insist that any "interpretations" be grounded in the scripts students read, however indefinite, complex, and shifting those scripts may be, and regardless of what critical fashion prevails during the hour we are in class.

Let me return to *A Midsummer Night's Dream*. In his essay "Teaching Differences" (1990), Edward Pechter contrasts three radically different critical responses to the play: C. L. Barber's, Terry Eagleton's, and James Kavanagh's. Summarizing their different interpretations of Bottom & Company's artistic endeavors, and the play's critique of the instability of human identity, Pechter writes:

> The polarities in Barber [serve] to create a protected space, "master[ing] passionate experience" by excluding it. In Eagleton and Kavanagh, however, passionate experience won't respect such boundaries, and the space of the play is overwhelmed by a threatening reality that cannot be kept at bay. (163–64)

While these critical polarities can be frustrating enough in the classroom, consider an even more difficult (and therefore more pedagogically fascinating) problem, one far more "student-centered." During spring term, 1991, I taught *Dream*, and in one class I asked my students, who ranged in age from early twenties to mid fifties, these questions: 1)Why don't Hermia and Helena speak during the "play-within-the-play" in Act 5? 2)What do you make of this fact, and how would you communicate your answer to a theater audience? Most of the younger women in the class insisted that these two marriages—Lysander/Hermia and Demetrius/Helena—are in some trouble by play's end, and that Shakespeare signals this fact in several ways. First, Demetrius, the "spotted and inconstant man" of Act 1, has not changed much in the play; his threatened violence during the dream sequence is consistent with his harsh criticism in Act 5 of those he considers socially inferior, mere "entertainers." His comments about the playlet are nastier than Lysander's, and he seems overall an unpleasant man whom Helena should have dumped long ago. Secondly, the two women see their lovers chastising the poor, bumbling actors who are, after all, only trying their best; Bottom et al. never before labored in their minds, insists Filostrate, and, as Theseus (of all people!) reminds us, the worst in this kind are but shadows if imagination mend them. Lysander and Demetrius seem incapable of mending, of imaginative sympathy, and are likely to be harsh critics of their wives' human imperfections. At this point in our discussion, I mention John Russell Brown's observation in *Shakespeare and His Comedies* (1957) that in both *Dream* and *Love's Labour's Lost*, Shakespeare tests the imagination of his onstage audiences by their reaction to impromptu stage plays, thereby indicating something of their ability to respond imaginatively to the passions and demands of love. My younger female students' reactions support Brown's point about how Shakespeare seems to be using playlets in these two comedies. The female students offered several possible methods of communicating these emotions, but most agreed that Helena and Hermia could be scowling, perhaps overtly distressed, holding their heads in disbelief or chagrin, perhaps resembling Hippolyta in 1.1 as she becomes increasingly angry at Theseus's treatment of Hermia in her conflict with Egeus.

The majority of the men, however, and several older women (forty-five to fifty-five years old), resisted this interpretation, wanting to believe that these two marriages would be successful. Asked for evidence, the older women pointed to Demetrius's and Lysander's awed reactions to their awakening; their emphasis on strange, unfathomable changes; the sensitivity of Demetrius's images of the metamorphosis of mountains into clouds, suggesting belief in profound changes and ethereal existences; and above all the suggestion of a religious sanction for their marriages: they are to meet Theseus in the "temple." The older women in the class claimed that Lysander and Demetrius had learned too much in their nightmarish trek through the Athenian woods to abandon their lovers now, or to risk such frightening journeys again should they be unfaithful or inattentive. Should Lysander again abandon his sleeping Hermia, she certainly would not trust him a second time, perhaps not even let him explain himself.

The men in the class, most of them young (twenty to thirty years old), adamantly defended Demetrius and Lysander. They insisted that the young men's actions during the playlet should be viewed as an attempt to demonstrate their wit to their wives; as rather typical, if snobbish, male bravado; and perhaps as the men's attempts to relax momentarily their sexual anticipation, as they endure the evening's tedious entertainment before retiring to bed.

Which "view" does one teach here? Or, indeed, does one "teach" one over the other? Is not the silence of the two young women here, in Philip McGuire's term, "open" like that of Hippolyta's in 1.1 ("Hippolyta's Silence," 1985)? If one approaches the last act visually, as I did spring term, one can devise a lively debate. Encouraged by Edward Rocklin's superb discussion of students' different ways of staging Hippolyta's stage presence in 1.1, I asked students to prepare a similar exercise: to block Act 5 for a Friday class, using a diagram approximating the shape of the Globe's three-sided, thrust stage. I then asked for volunteers to draw their designs on the board. If one supposed a happy ending to these marriages, one could then have the men and women sitting closely together, and the women simply enjoying the men's criticism, laughing along with the fun. However, if one thought the marriages might not be genuinely happy, or that, at the very least, Act 5 signals some romantic distance for these couples still to travel, one could place the men and women separately on stage, perhaps, as several women suggested, grouping Helene and Hermia with Hippolyta, thus suggesting, as I mentioned above, that these three have much to share regarding the insensitivity and occasional tyranny of their lovers.

This exercise gave my students the opportunity to "complete" Shakespeare's "script," to fill in what he left "unwritten" and thus open to interpretation. Such "openings" allow students to participate actively in creating the "meaning" of a Shakespearean play; as Philip C. McGuire explains, "Hippolyta's silence [in Act 1] . . . helps to endow *A Midsummer Night's Dream* with the capacity to change significantly while retaining identity and coherence—to remain itself yet be 'translated' not just from performance to performance and production to production but even from era to era across the centuries" (18). *Dream* is thus a "quick bright thing" whose apparent "confusion" in Act 5 may indeed be essential to its meaning, and our task as teachers is to open up Shakespeare's plays to these multiple possibilities. As Norman Rabkin (1972) insists:

> We need to embark on a large-scale reconsideration of the phenomena that our technology has enabled us to explore, to consider the play as a dynamic interaction between artist and audience, to learn to talk about the process of our involvement rather than our considered view after the aesthetic event. (102)

A second example of how my students and I pursued "multiple possibilities" in a Shakespeare play sharply illustrates Rabkin's point about a "dynamic interaction" between artist and audience, or rather audiences. In a recent class I had the most heterogeneous group of students I have ever taught. The majority of the thirty-nine students were female, and two of them were (I think) in their late sixties or early seventies. These two women were quite intelligent and articulate, and, I was to learn, ardently feminist; further, I gathered from their conversations that each had been married and divorced at least once. Of the remaining thirty-seven students, 65 percent were female, the majority of them in their late twenties or early thirties, with one or two probably fifty years old. From conversations during and out of class I learned that several of the women in their thirties were in second marriages. The men, however, were much younger, most in their early twenties and, I gathered, single or recently married. Here then was a group of people in varying age groups and with vastly different personal experiences, some much more sexually "experienced" than others: some, perhaps, rather bitter; others resembling the young lovers of *A Midsummer Night's Dream*. Our discussion of *Othello* in this class remains the most exciting and stimulating Shakespeare teaching experience I have ever known.

During many discussions with these students about Othello and Desdemona, and the role of Othello's jealousy in this relationship, I generated diverse and often heated discussion about the degree of Othello's sexual possessiveness. (For a much fuller discussion of my remarks here, see my "Othello's Jealousy and the 'Gate of Hell,'" *The Upstart Crow* 12 [1992]: 96–104). The most frank comments occurred when I suggested that Othello's remarks at 3.3.270 ff. and 4.2.57 ff. portray Desdemona as a sexual object, and that some of the images are specifically genital. At 3.3.270–73, Othello says: "I had rather be a toad / And live upon the vapor of a dungeon / Than keep a corner in the thing I love / for others' uses." At 4.2.57–62, in the "brothel scene," he cries: "But there, where I have garner'd up my heart, / Where either I must live or bear no life; / The fountain from the which my current runs / Or else dries up; to be discarded thence! / Or keep it as a cestern for foul toads / To knot and gender in!" One cannot be certain that the adverb "there" in the second excerpt is a genital reference, although the context, and Othello's earlier remark about keeping a "corner" in the "thing" he says he loves, strongly supports this suggestion. I want to focus now on my students' responses to these lines.

These responses were quite varied. Many female students, especially the two oldest women and several younger women in second marriages, argued stridently that Othello's references here are definitely genital, and furthermore that Shakespeare had captured in Othello's language a pervasive, if unspoken, element in men's sexual attitudes towards their wives: i.e., that despite their claims to the contrary, and their insistence on the multidimensional nature of married love, men still view their wives at some subliminal level as sexual possessions, and that this possessiveness is implicitly genital. The males objected equally stridently. Indeed, many of the male students protested too much, suggesting, perhaps, an unwillingness to admit what they suspect may be true. What was most fascinating about these discussions was not just the division of opinions by gender, but by age and extent of personal/sexual experiences. The two oldest women vilified Othello; the younger women in second marriages were convinced that Othello's love was "too sexual"; and the men, regardless of age or married status, thought this criticism of Othello unfair and my (and the women's) readings of these lines too slanted. One younger man said I was finding sexual meaning in the text just to spice the class discussion.

I found myself quite stimulated by these discussions, and introduced into class some Medieval/Renaissance and contemporary views of jealousy. Andreas Capellanus says "He who is not jealous cannot love," and adds that jealousy is "the very substance of love, without which true love cannot exist" (17). Thus, for Capellanus, romantic love should not be the basis for marriage, because it leads to jealousy. Several contemporary psychologists agree. Nena and George O'Neill (1972) characterize jealousy as a "destructive cancer" which is "never . . . a function of love but of our insecurities and dependencies. It is the fear of a loss of love and it destroys that very love" (237). Abraham Maslow (1968) identifies jealousy as inherently destructive; he places it within what he calls "D-Love," which is "dependency love, deficiency love," and which is opposed to "B-Love," or "Being Love" which seeks the good of the partner and is devoid of jealousy (42 ff).

Other researchers characterize specific male and female differences in jealous behavior. Gordon Clanton and Lynn Smith (1977) argue that men are more apt to express jealous feelings, and to "focus on the outside sexual activity of the partner, and they often demand a recital of the intimate details" (Introduction; 11). Gregory White (1981) finds that "vaguely formed suspicions or expectations about the likelihood of partner involvement with another reflect an underlying fear of sexual inadequacy" (29). I should add that none of the researchers I read mentioned racial or age differences in their analyses of the causes of jealousy, while all found men much more prone than women to destructive behavior caused by jealousy.

If we examine Othello's actions and words in light of these observations, what do we find? And how might these views of jealousy reflect on my students' own heterogeneous reactions to Othello's jealousy?

Most readers of *Othello* would agree that his jealousy implies insecurity and dependence; he is a stranger to Venetian society, and is thus vulnerable to Iago's innuendoes. Othello also fears, at least temporarily, his sexual inadequacy; he is prone to anger and violence once convinced that Desdemona has betrayed him; and he asks Iago for "intimate details," which Iago luridly provides in his "dream."

Consider again 3.3.270 ff. "I had rather be a toad / And live upon the vapor of a dungeon / Than keep a corner in the thing I love / For others' uses." Othello says he loves a "thing," often in Shakespeare a genital reference, as Partridge explains, and then subdivides this "thing" into "corners," one of which he now seems to imagine himself sharing for others' "uses." (Note that this is a *plural* possessive, suggesting the "general camp"?) This last word is most striking, horrifying, and perhaps, revealing. Desdemona in this sentence is a "thing" to be, not loved, but "used." Does Othello in this crisis forged by Iago reveal how he actually "loves" Desdemona? Is this the kind of truth about his marriage that this crisis reveals? Does he love Desdemona *only* sexually, and can one locate in his sudden rage of Acts 3 and 4 a passionate anger at being rejected sexually from that "thing" which he sees as existing for only his "use"?

Consider again 4.2.57–62: "But there, where I have garner'd up my heart, / Where either I must live or bear no life; / The fountain from the which my current runs / Or else dries up: to be discarded thence! / Or keep it as a cestern for foul toads / To knot and gender in!" Othello's fury propels him into three consecutive "either . . . or" assertions which exemplify—at least here—the brutal simplicity of his mind, suggest why he resolves to murder Desdemona, and herald his frightening dichotomy as he stands over Desdemona in 5.2: "Be thus when thou art dead, and I will kill thee / And love thee after" (18–19). I suggested above that the "there" of 1.57 is genital; if I am right, then Othello has "garner'd up" his heart, not in Desdemona the person, but specifically in her vagina. The following lines, especially the image of the fountain, suggest, with the admitted difficulty of the preposition "from," Othello's seminal fluid, which will be forever "dried up" if Desdemona is a whore. The *Riverside* gloss of "fountain" as "source, spring," i.e., source or spring of his semen, further supports this reading, as does the circular shape of "cestern," where Othello grotesquely imagines foul toads knotting, a brutal, animalistic reduction of Desdemona's sexuality to a thing which he imagines himself "keeping" for "others' use" and from which he has been discarded.

I conclude with two other examples. At 4.1.41 ff., near the end of his nearly incoherent ravings and just before his trance and fall, Othello utters: "It is not words that shakes / me thus. Pish! Noses, ears, and lips. Is't possible?" Noses, ears, and lips are orifices, and may be seen here as vaginal displacements, especially "lips." In his ravings, Othello's conscious mind imperfectly masks his unconscious genital fixation. Finally, at 4.2.90-92, just 33 lines after the first of Othello's "there" in his assault upon Desdemona's chastity, he turns to Emilia: "You, mistress / That have the office opposite to Saint Peter, / And keep the gate of hell." "Gate of hell" is, in context, an obvious genital reference which echoes the verbal puns in "cunning whore" and "office" and hideously reduces Desdemona to a satanic, sexual object, her vagina an entrance into hell which will surely corrupt other men. Thus she must die.

My own readings of these lines, the research I introduced into class, and the sometimes fierce reactions to Othello's images prompted an intense, animated examination of *Othello*. I often found myself aligned with the women who severely castigated Othello for his sexual attitudes. But at other times I had to admit, with the men, that the extraordinary oxymoronic tenderness of Othello as he stands over the sleeping Desdemona in Act 5 ("Be thus when thou art dead, and I will kill thee / And love thee after"), and his remarks in 1.3.261-62 ("I therefore beg it not / to please the palate of my appetite"), mitigate the argument that his love is only a sexual brutishness and argue rather that it is, like all human love, frighteningly complex. Yet, that Othello can say these words in Acts 1 and 5, and apparently mean them, accentuates the sheer horror of his reducing his wife to a "thing," in a corner of which toads "knot and gender."

The obvious question here is: what difference did gender, age, and sexual/marital experience make in our interpretations of Othello? The obvious answer is *every* difference. And who am I to minimize the importance of these factors in evaluating criticism of Othello and *Othello*? If, as Sharon Beehler (1990) urges, we "de-authorize the teacher" (195), and realize that we all—teachers and students—read from a "personal and linguistic context" (198), our aim in the Shakespeare classroom should be to guide our heterogeneous students to weigh for themselves the critical soundness of the scripts that their cultural contexts evoke and thus to create their own Shakespearean art as complex, perhaps, as their own lives, yet constant in its ability to create quick, bright images that continually fascinate and beckon.

References

Beehler, Sharon. 1990. "'That's a Certain Text': Problematizing Shakespeare Instruction in American Schools and Colleges." *Shakespeare Quarterly* 41:195-205.

Brown, John Russell. 1957. *Shakespeare and His Comedies*. London: Methuen.

Capellanus, Andreas. 1957. *The Art of Courtly Love*. Trans. John Jay Parry. Ed. Frederick W. Locke. New York: Frederick Ungar.

Clanton, Gordon, and Lynn G. Smith, eds. 1977. *Jealousy*. Englewood Cliffs: Prentice-Hall.

Frey, Charles. 1984. "Teaching Shakespeare in America." *Shakespeare Quarterly* 35.5:541-59.

Maslow, Abraham. 1968. *Toward a Psychology of Being*. New York: Van Nostrand.

McGuire, Phillip C. 1985. *Speechless Dialect*. Berkeley: University of California Press.

O'Neill, Nena and George. 1972. *Open Marriage*. New York: M. Evans.

Pechter, Edward. 1990. "Teaching Differences." *Shakespeare Quarterly* 41:160–73.

Rabkin, Norman. 1972. "Meaning and Shakespeare." In *Shakespeare: 1971,* ed. Clifford Leech and J. M. R. Margeson. Toronto: University of Toronto Press.

Rocklin, Edward. 1990. "'An Incarnational Art': Teaching Shakespeare." *Shakespeare Quarterly* 41:147–59.

White, Gregory L. 1981. "Jealousy and the Partner's Perceived Motives for Attraction to a Rival." *Social Psychology Quarterly* 44:24–30.

CHAPTER 17

Building Shakespearean Worlds in the Everyday Classroom

CHRISTINE D. WARNER

The Ohio State University
Columbus, Ohio

Warner identifies the role of the middle and high school teacher of Shakespeare not as translator but as pathfinder, someone to facilitate students' "attempts to make connections between themselves and a Shakespearean play, between his play and the ideas it embodies, and between the world of the play and the students' world." To that end, she recommends group improvisational strategies called process drama, activities "whose outcome is not any kind of presentation, but the exploration of an improvised dramatic world for the opportunities, insights, and learning it offers." She argues that this teaching technique can often produce very positive results in the classroom.

> English is about working on the knowledge we have acquired from
> the unsystematic processes of living, about giving expression to it
> and making it into a firmer and more conscious kind of living.
> (Peter Medway 1980, 8)

Several years ago when I was teaching a senior literature class in an inner-city high school in Washington, D.C., I came to the decision that my class was ready to explore and experience a Shakespearean play. One morning I wrote in big letters on the backboard: "William Shakespeare: *As You Like It*." As I was turning around to greet my students, a desk from the back of the classroom came flying up and hit what I had just printed on the board. I was quick to assess that the student *did not like it!* I could not put much blame on the student's conduct because I will wager that more than half of my class wanted to do the same thing.

When it comes to the teaching and learning of Shakespeare, many people on both sides of the desk are nervous, bored, overwhelmed—or all of the above. Often the teacher's job ends up being that of a translator for Shakespeare's plays. As middle and high school teachers of Shakespeare our job should not have to be to act as translators of Shakespeare for our students, but as pathfinders. As pathfinders, we need to enable our students to make connections between themselves and a Shakespeare play, between his play and the ideas it embodies, and between the world of the play and the student's world.

Some of the best techniques for teaching Shakespeare in English classrooms derive directly from the world of theater. Perhaps this is because actors are continually forced by their profession to realize, in a way most literature students do not, that plays are intended to be dramatized before and with groups of living people. By using dramatic activities in the classroom, students can encounter Shakespeare on his own ground, which is inside the play. All kinds of students do best when they are able to make their own seminal connection with Shakespeare—that is to say, with his words in their mouths.

This chapter is not about acting, it is about doing. The form of drama that I will discuss in this chapter is called *process drama* (O'Neill 1993, 1); it is a group improvisational process whose outcome is not any kind of presentation, but the exploration of an improvised dramatic world for the opportunities, insights, and learning it offers. This chapter has two basic parts. In the first part I will offer a clear theoretical base from which a teacher can develop his/her work and include brief examples. Secondly, I will demonstrate dramatic possibilities and illustrations of actual student responses from *The Tempest, Macbeth,* and *Hamlet* in order to demonstrate the exciting potential of using process drama with Shakespeare in the English classroom.

A Theoretical Base for Using Process Drama

Patrice Pavis (1982) has usefully defined a dramatic text as one which lends itself to a fiction and is capable of being translated into a possible or "as if" world. When Shakespeare's plays are encountered through process drama, the result is a complex interpenetration of at least three alternate worlds. First, the Shakespearean play that students encounter in the classroom is a fiction and is capable of evoking possible worlds. While using process drama students are asked to create an "as if" world in response to the world that Shakespeare presents in the play. This possible or parallel world operates as a "pre-text," whose existence is the reason for the action in Shakespeare's play (O'Neill 1991). Shakespeare often used pre-texts as a basis for his plays, pre-texts that often came from myths, legends, and history. In the classroom, Shakespeare's play becomes the pre-text that will define the nature and limits of the world that arises from it and will help frame the participants in appropriate roles in relation to the action (O'Neill and Rogers 1993).

The second world is the parallel drama world created in response to the play. This parallel world will share some significant features with the world in the play Shakespeare presents, but may not appear in the original text. This parallel world provides the means for students to personalize a dramatic situation by converting the Shakespearean world from an obscure time and place to a parallel setting in the comfort and security of the present. The final world that is created in the classroom is the result of using drama. It is the personal world of the students, which emerges in the encounter of the literary and dramatic worlds. While working with process drama, students' response can be seen in terms of their exploration of three distinct but interpenetrating worlds: the world of the original text; the dramatic world that developed parallel to that text; and their own personal worlds, which remained a touchstone for the truth of their experience in the imagined worlds of Shakespeare's play.

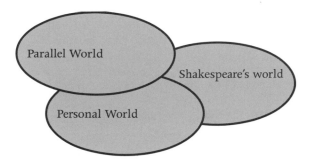

Figure 1. Interpenetrating Worlds

When these three worlds are integrated, students are able to render the elements of a particular scene intelligible with its contemporary context, and then they are guided back to the language and action of Shakespeare's original verse, always keeping in mind the emotional rhythm of the scene.

Several basic strategies can be readily employed in the classroom to make the students producers of the drama and then can be transferred to the different Shakespearean plays. These strategies are all intended to provide opportunities to explore the play through the retelling, extension, elaboration, or enactment of events in the original play, as well as the exploration of individual characters' motives and behaviors.

The first strategy, teacher-in-role. The teacher-in-role involves the teacher participating in the drama activity in role as someone else while the students are also in role. In this way the teacher will engage in the progress of the drama alongside his/her pupils and can thereby more effectively support their contributions, challenge the students' thinking, and move the drama on. The teacher-in-role strategy does not require acting skill, since what it implies is not so much the creation of fully rounded characters as the adoption of a set of attitudes and taking of a stance (O'Neill et al. 1987). A teacher selects a dramatic situation for the class to engage in and conveys information through his/her role.

For example, a teacher could role-play an editor of a local newspaper. The editor assigns his/her students, who are role-playing reporters, to investigate how the servants in Macbeth's castle react to the news of Duncan's murder.

The second strategy, interviewing. Interviewing can be carried out with students working in pairs or small groups; it requires commitment and interaction, but no presentational skills. This strategy promotes question-making on the part of the student, rather than solely from the teacher (Morgan and Saxton 1987).

For example, all students are separated into pairs; one student would role-play a servant in Macbeth's household and the other student would be the reporter who is writing a story. A possible dramatic situation incorporating the interviewing technique would be the following: reporters looking for information on how the servants in Macbeth's household feel about how Macbeth's elevation to the throne will affect them. Later, the reporters would come back to the editor (the teacher-in-role) and report either orally or in written form the information they learned from the servants.

A third strategy, tableaux. A still image, or tableau is created by the students, working in small groups. In devising these images students use their own bodies to create a significant moment in the story, an abstract idea, or a mental state. This strategy requires the students to become involved physically, but does not demand any great theater skills. In composing these images, students are using their knowledge and understanding of the text to engage in a highly selective, economical, and controlled form of expression that must be read and interpreted by the rest of the class (O'Neill and Rogers 1993). Tableaux can be used to discover and display what the students already know about a topic or theme.

For example, students would be asked to divide into groups of four or five each. A possible dramatic situation using the strategy of tableaux might be to have students create Macbeth's personal photo album. What kinds of pictures would Macbeth find meaningful? From his pictures, can one detect when the seeds of his evil ambition were first planted— when he was a child, when he was a young man, when he got married to Lady Macbeth, or all of the above? As each group shared its tableau, the class would read and interpret the still images.

A fourth strategy, inquiry. A particularly useful and essentially dramatic strategy is to set up an inquiry about the events in the play. The question that can be asked about many of Shakespeare's tragedies is, "Who is to blame?" In order to answer this question it may be necessary to put a character or a community on trial, to establish a tribunal or a people's court, or, where any misdeeds have remained secret, to bring a character before the court of conscience.

For example, in the case of *Macbeth,* at the climax of the play, Macbeth discovers that he has been the victim of the "equivocation of the fiend / That lies like truth" (5.5.43-44). Is there anyone else who might be partially responsible for Macbeth's rejection of morality? Parents of Macbeth? Past teachers or clergy members? His advisors and/or role models? An examination of other characters who could have contributed to Macbeth's character, whether they actually were characters in the play or extensions from those characters, enables students to examine and reconsider the play in more depth.

In the next section, the activities and student responses demonstrate that by using process drama to uncover meaning, a typical group of ninth-grade students were able to understand what is happening in a scene from the *inside* out.

Dramatic Possibilities and Student Responses

It may be possible to bring these strategies together by adopting a media frame as a context for the dramatic activities. As an illustration: in one of my ninth-grade English classes we examined Ferdinand and Miranda's second meeting in *The Tempest* (3.3), where the young man has been enjoined by Prospero to carry heavy logs as a test of his virtue and sincerity. Instead of beginning the discussion on meter, verse form, or imagery, it was helpful to approach the scene by asking the questions which actors and actresses would ask themselves: "Who are these people?" "What are they doing and why?" "What do they want, and how will they acquire it?" Students were then asked to split into groups of four or five each; their task was to come up with television news reports of the action that had taken place. As teacher-in-role, I played a producer who was only interested in the network ratings and Nielsen surveys. The reporters' jobs were on the line if they failed to report action that would entice viewers. These news reports fashioned themselves after *Current Affairs* and *Entertainment Tonight* and were often accompanied with personal interviews conducted with magical animals who lived with and knew Miranda and Ferdinand. When the context of the literature is put into a drama, the focus of attention suddenly moves from a rather distant, academic dissection of the text to a more immediate concern with its characters as ordinary people.

Building upon the previous drama experience, the students were ready to examine closely the importance of Ferdinand and Miranda's meeting; a further inspection of the scene was necessary. The class and I role-played archaeologists who had just found an abandoned island; on this island were mysterious statues. During one particular class session, a student suggested that these tableaux or statues were humans who were now turned to stone and were the only things left on Prospero's island. Because the statues were stone, they could not speak, so we as archaeologists had to investigate closely what these pieces of stone might have meant. Several statues depicted two people in close proximity, facing each other and holding something between them. From the look of their posture, the item they were pantomiming as being in between themselves seemed very heavy. Behind this statue was another statue; it appeared as if someone was hiding and listening. "Someone wanted to be private," one role-playing student volunteered. "Looks like they want to talk to each other. But why?" "They're really trying to find out all they can about each other," stated another observant, role-playing archaeologist. And that, of course, is the scene's main action: Ferdinand has been enslaved by Prospero and has had his social standing downgraded from prince to servant. Miranda is lovely, naive, and demonstrably shy. In this brief scene, they "discover" each other's beauty, and they pledge their love.

How do students perceive this, and are they able to transfer this theatrically? Shakespeare's principal device is the pile of logs Ferdinand carries. Students are quick to perceive that these logs function as props which allow the two young lovers to be physically close during the scene. During the students' process of shaping themselves into statues to communicate their understanding ("discover"), these logs grant physical proximity in which students can experience and see with their own eyes that Ferdinand and Miranda do indeed discover each other.

In order to provide the opportunity for students to examine Shakespeare's written word, I often begin a drama by having students look at a particular scene. Students are to read the scene and determine in small groups what the action in the scene is. Students are then responsible for finding one verb that describes the action in the scene. Instead of communicating orally what this verb was, each group of students is instructed to construct a tableau depicting the verb, all within the context of the scene. During one exploration of *Hamlet*, several groups of middle school students were outraged that Hamlet lacked ambition to seek revenge for his father. The crucial scene in which Hamlet accidentally comes across Claudius while he is praying (3.3), proved to be an emotional and thought-provoking experience for some of the students. Students were split into four groups of four to five students each and each group was assigned the task of finding a verb that motivates the action in Hamlet's monologue in this scene. The students were then involved in the task of using this verb to create a silent tableau; the questions and comments that were generated by the students were as follows: "He is very angry and tormented." "He wants revenge!" "No, he doesn't." "He hates Claudius." "He just doesn't want to do anything that will make the situation worse!" "He is watching!" "He wants to take control."

"He wants to take control." That is exactly one of the scene's main functions. C. S. Lewis has described Hamlet as a man given a task by a ghost. The ghost of Hamlet's father requests that Hamlet seek blood revenge, have Gertrude repent, and restore order to the state of Denmark. Students are quick to perceive that Hamlet's tragedy does not lie in the fact that he is capable or incapable of carrying out any of these tasks. Rather, the tragedy lies in the fact that what he is told to do and what he is inwardly impelled to do are decidedly two different things. Though talking is not encouraged by the participants in the tableaux, one student, just before the group posed, announced that their tableaux was of a statue that is placed in Hamlet's music box that he keeps in his room. This particular tableau was made up of four students. Two participants were posed as Hamlet raising his sword over the praying Claudius; the other two students were posed, back to back, as Hamlet in defeat carrying his heavy sword like a cross across his shoulders. The student who was role-playing Claudius was smirking while praying. The students in the tableau turned round and round like a turntable in a music box to depict Hamlet's frame of mind. Several observing students pointed out that Hamlet was split in two and that is what has caused his torment, his anguish and his heavy burden. Not only is Act 3, scene 3 the turning point in the play, it is exactly what the play is about.

Conclusion

By incorporating drama into the English classroom, new worlds are created in the classroom that intersect to foster new knowledge and new understandings of Shakespeare's plays. This teaching technique of using process drama to uncover meaning can often produce stunning results in the classroom. The moments of quiet intensity can speak volumes about a scene's potential for meaning within its proper dramatic context. The process of students generating their own questions and ideas, and posing answers, puts students on the same level as scholars, actors, and directors. As teachers we learn that our students are really up to it. We also learn that we are up to it too. On several occasions colleagues have told me that certain Shakespearean plays may be too difficult for middle or high school students. However, because of the experiences I have had with students, I unequivocally assert that Shakespeare is for all students, of all ability levels, all reading levels, and of every ethnic origin in every kind of school. In 1623, John Heminge and Henry Condell, two members of Shakespeare's acting company, compiled thirty-six plays and had them published in the "First Folio." Their introduction to this book (reprinted in the Yale *Shakespeare*) is entitled, "The great Variety of Readers"; it begins, "From the most able, to him that can but spell . . ." They knew what they were talking about in 1623.

Additional Recommended Readings for Using Process Drama in the Classroom

Byron, Ken. 1986. *Drama in the English Classroom*. London: Methuen & Co., Ltd.

Lambert, A., and C. O'Neill. 1982. *Drama Structures: A Practical Handbook for Teachers*. London: Hutchinson Education Ltd.

Morgan, N., and J. Saxton. 1987. *Teaching Drama: "A Mind of Many Wonders . . ."* Portsmouth, N.H.: Heinemann Educational Books.

Excerpt from "Experiencing Shakespeare with Middle Schoolers" by Christine Warner reprinted with permission from *Ohio Journal of the English Language Arts* 35.2 (Autumn 1994).

References

Byron, K. 1986. *Drama in the English Classroom*. New York: Methuen.

Heathcote, D., and P. Herbert. 1985. "A Drama of Learning: Mantle of the Expert." *Theory into Practice* 24.3:173–80.

Lewis, C. S. 1942. *Hamlet: The Prince or the Poem*. Production of the British Academy.

Medway, P. 1980. *Finding a Language*. London: Writers and Readers Publishing Co-operative.

O'Neill, C. 1994. "Process Drama." In *Reflections* booklet. Columbus, Ohio: The Ohio Drama Education Exchange.

O'Neill, C., A. Lambert, R. Linnel, and J. Warr-Wood. 1976. *Drama Guidelines*. London: Heinemann Educational Books.

O'Neill, C., and F. Rogers. 1993. "Creating Multiple Worlds." In *Exploring Texts: The Role of Discussing and Writing in the Teaching and Learning of Literature,* ed. G. Newell & R. Durst, 69–89. Norwood, Mass.: Christopher Gordon Publishers, Inc.

Pavis, P. 1982. *Languages of the Stage: Essays in the Semiology of the Theater*. New York: Performing Arts Journal Publications.

Shakespeare, William. 1917. *The Complete Works of William Shakespeare*. New Haven: Yale University Press.

Smith, D., R. Corbin, and J. Ebbs. 1967. *Greek Myths and Legends*. (Literary Heritage Series.) The Macmillan Company.

CHAPTER 18

Enhancing Response to
Romeo and Juliet

LARRY R. JOHANNESSEN
Benedictine University
Lisle, Illinois

Along with several other authors in this section, Johannessen begins by questioning the effectiveness of standard approaches to Shakespeare outlined in many secondary literature textbook anthologies. He has found that, following such textbook approaches, secondary students often "have learned only two things: they do not understand the play and they hate Shakespeare." And he offers a detailed description of the instructional activities he uses in place of the typical textbook approach in his teaching of Romeo and Juliet. *Finally, he offers suggestions for building writing instruction into this series of activities.*

*M*any secondary literature textbook anthologies advise teachers that the best way to prepare students for reading a play such as *Romeo and Juliet* is to lecture to them about the author, about historical and/or philosophical background, and/or about the work itself before they begin reading. If the teacher feels inadequate to this task, then she might simply have students read the appropriate sections out of the text. The Teacher's Guides for these anthologies indicate that this introductory material will help students with reading problems and motivate them to read.

According to most of these textbooks, the focus of instruction ought to be on having students learn "the elements of literature," which seems to mean memorizing terms such as "aside," "pun," "meter," "iambic pentameter," "allusion," "irony," and "tragedy." The implication seems to be that students need to know these terms in order to understand and appreciate the play. To help students learn the terms, there are handy definitions provided in the "Handbook of Literary Terms" in the backs of these textbooks, plenty of study guide questions and quizzes, and, of course, an objective test at the end to ensure students have memorized the definitions. Presumably, at the end of this sequence of instruction, students will have mastered the play.

After looking at what many of the anthologies have to say about how to teach Shakespeare's *Romeo and Juliet*, it is not difficult to understand why, after struggling through the play, many students have learned only two things: they do not understand the play and they hate Shakespeare.

But what is wrong with this standard approach? As Louise Rosenblatt (1968) argues, this approach often puts the students' focus on a great deal that is "irrelevant and distracting."

In fact, in a recent analysis of this approach as used in most secondary literature anthologies, Michael Smith (1991) describes it as "very reductive" and argues that it does little to prepare students to cope with the complexities involved in understanding literary texts.

In contrast to this approach, Rosenblatt talks about the need to foster what she calls "fruitful . . . transactions between individual readers and individual literary works" (1968, 26–27). The question is, how do we accomplish this? One way to help students have "fruitful" involvements with *Romeo and Juliet* is to focus instruction on a theme or concept that will be of interest to them and is critical to comprehension of the play. This means, of course, eliminating most or all of the traditional "irrelevant and distracting" background lectures and/or readings that normally precede the reading of the play and dispensing with the traditional focus on memorization of literary terms and superficial application of the terms to the text. According to Smagorinsky (1989 and 1993) and Smagorinsky, McCann, and Kern (1987), ensuring that students have "fruitful" experiences with literature involves creating instructional activities that tap into their prior experiences and engage them in interpretative problems related to the concept or theme that is the focus of instruction.

I have been able to break with the traditional textbook approach and achieve Rosenblatt's goal for student involvement with literature. What follows is a description of the instructional activities I have used, how they tap into students' prior experiences, and how they involve students in solving interpretive problems key to comprehension of the play. In addition, I describe how I have been able to help secondary students link their study of the play to modern poetry, which helps them to see how Shakespeare's characters and themes are relevant to them and modern literature.

What Is Loyalty?

Smagorinsky (1989 and 1993) argues that students should explore a theme or concept from upcoming literature prior to reading. He states that this provides a framework or cognitive map for understanding that is critical to comprehension. I decided to focus my instruction on the theme of love. I decided on this focus for two primary reasons: First, for many young people no topic fascinates them quite as much as the relationships between the sexes—not sports or automobiles or rock groups. Yet their knowledge of pop stars, athletes, and cars far exceeds their understanding of love. I knew, therefore, that teenagers would be drawn to this play that explores the concept of young love. In addition, if students are going to comprehend the play, then they will need to be able to interpret what Shakespeare wants readers to understand about the theme of love.

I knew from past experience that many students find the protagonists' ostracism from their families hard to understand, and perhaps because of this, many students fail to appreciate key elements of Romeo and Juliet's love relationship. Therefore, I decided to begin my instruction with an introductory activity that would help students gain an understanding of the conflict between the Montagues and the Capulets and the protagonists' conflict between their love for one another and their duty to their parents. Elizabeth Kahn of James B. Conant High School, in Hoffman Estates, Illinois, and I designed a set of six scenarios all concerned with loyalty. The scenarios are designed to parallel the situation Romeo and Juliet face in the play (see Figure 1).

To begin the activity, I have students individually answer the questions posed after each of the scenarios in the "Loyalty: What Is It?" activity sheet (Figure 1). After they have completed their answers, I divide them into small groups of three to five students. I ask them to discuss each scenario in their groups and try to reach a consensus on their answers. This is not easy since there is no one obviously best answer to any of the questions. As students try to convince other group members that they are "right," they must elaborate the reasons for their answers. In deciding why, for instance, Bruce in scenario 6 should flee to Canada to avoid having to fight in a war that he thinks is wrong, students discover characteristics they think are essential for an action to be loyal or disloyal and the criteria that can be used to judge whether an action is loyal or disloyal.

After the small groups complete their discussions, I lead a class discussion of their answers. At this point the debate begins again as groups defend their answers. As the debate continues, I lead students to a discussion of the qualities or criteria for deciding if an action is loyal. As students generate ideas, I list these on the board and have students copy them for future reference. As students read the play, I or other students often refer back to the criteria the class has generated and to the loyalty scenarios. They serve as an anchor to help students make sense of the play.

This activity provides a context for understanding the turmoil between the families of Romeo and Juliet, the protagonists' conflict between their love for one another and their duty to their parents, and the motives behind the characters' actions. As students read the play, they usually have a good understanding of the feud, and they have been able to understand how the actions of the protagonists are influenced by the feud and by the conflict between their duty to their parents and their love for one another. In addition, they have been able to understand why the young lovers were ostracized by their families, and why their love was forbidden and had to remain hidden. They also have been able to understand the Friar's motivation for marrying the young couple secretly and his hopes of reconciling the two families. In fact, in subsequent discussions of the play, students often refer back to particular scenarios from the activity in trying to explain their interpretations. In other words, once students understand the Montague-Capulet feud and the protagonists' conflict between their love for one another and their duty to their parents, they have a context or framework to begin examining the theme of love in the play. In brief, having students do this activity prior to reading the play results in more purposeful reading when students begin the play. They have something to look for—the attitudes, behavior, motivation, and actions of characters presented in the play.

How Students View Love

After students had read and discussed the first four scenes of Act 1 (the events leading up to Romeo's first encounter with Juliet at the Capulet party), I wanted to prepare them for how Shakespeare handles the theme of young love. To accomplish this, I utilized an opinionnaire activity. I use an opinionnaire activity that I adapted from Johannessen (1984,

15–16) and Kahn, Walter, and Johannessen (1984, 35–38). Originally designed to be used as an introduction for a unit on love poetry and fiction, I modified the opinionnaire to introduce the theme of love in the play and to achieve some other instructional goals.

The idea behind the opinionnaire is simple. Students have ideas and opinions about the subject of love, and the activity attempts to use their ideas and opinions to create interest in the characters, themes, and issues in the play. It also attempts to link student attitudes and opinions about love to how Shakespeare deals with this theme in the play. The "True Love Opinionnaire" contains eleven generalizations about love, everything from "Love is blind" to "Teenagers cannot experience 'true' love" (see Figure 2).

I have students complete the "you/before" column of the opinionnaire by indicating their agreement or disagreement with each statement. Then I compile the results on the board and lead a class discussion of their opinions, focusing on the statements for which there is the most disagreement. The discussion is lively and generates considerable debate among students. I encourage students to express their opinions and to challenge opinions expressed by others. Even normally timid students actively participate. For example, in one class, I called on usually quiet Mary, who sat in the back of the room, and asked her to explain why she disagreed with the statement about young people obeying their parents. She readily responded by saying, "Teenagers should obey their parents because parents sacrifice so much for their children." Her statement triggered considerable debate among her classmates. Because the statements require students to take a stand and because there are no right or wrong answers, this activity ensures a lively discussion. Students become actively involved in thinking and discussing. Furthermore, the opinionnaire activity unlocks the door for finding meaning in Shakespeare.

Many of the statements are designed to apply directly to *Romeo and Juliet*. For instance, the statement "Love at first sight is possible" is an obvious example, and it raises many issues among students. In one class a student raised her hand and said with great conviction, "I believe in love at first sight because that's how I fell in love!" Another student added, "My mom and dad fell in love at first sight at a dance." A skeptical listener replied, "How can you fall in love at first sight? You don't even know the person." Another student agreed by saying, "You just fall in love with a person's looks if you fall in love at first sight. You don't even know the real person." In discussing the idea of love at first sight prior to reading how Shakespeare handles this idea in the play, students are thinking through how they feel about this issue and closing the gap between their experiences and their experience of the play.

The teacher's role in this kind of pre-reading discussion activity is not to tell students how to think about these issues, but rather it is to encourage them to explain and defend their viewpoints, ensure that a variety of viewpoints are expressed and discussed, and, of course, provide synthesis when necessary and appropriate.

Once students have discussed most or all of the statements on the opinionnaire, I point out that the statements deal with problems and issues that the characters face in the play, and that they should keep them in mind as they read. Then, I have them read the last scene in Act I when Romeo and Juliet meet at the Capulet party. When I lead a class discussion of the scene, students are quick to note the drastic change in Romeo from a lovesick youth who pouts over his unrequited love for Rosaline to a swooning teenager infatuated with his new love Juliet. Perhaps as a result of the opinionnaire activity, students seem to enjoy reading this scene. Also, the satisfaction students gain from understanding Act 1 has a positive influence on their interest in the play and their self-confidence. In fact, many students even begin to enjoy and appreciate the play.

How the Characters and Shakespeare View Love

As students read the rest of the play, I have them return to the opinionnaire for a series of activities designed to help them understand how various characters view love, and how a character's viewpoint is similar to and different from other characters' views. I also designed these activities so that students would to be able to compare their own views to those of various characters in the play, and, ultimately, to enable them to interpret what Shakespeare wants readers to understand about love. At different points during their reading, I ask students, in small groups, and then individually, to complete the opinionnaire as they think a particular character would respond: Romeo, Juliet, Capulet, Lady Capulet, Friar Laurence, and the Nurse. After they have completed the opinionnaire for a character, I lead a class discussion of their responses. However, now I also ask them to cite evidence from the play to support their viewpoints.

Small-group and whole class discussions of how these characters would respond to the statements on the opinionnaire are nearly as lively as those that deal with how students themselves respond to the statements. One reason for this may be that students have thought about these issues prior to reading and have already gained confidence in discussing them in class. In addition, the statements on the opinionnaire provide students with specific and concrete ways to talk about the actions and motives of characters.

These discussions are often at a high level, which leads me to conclude that the opinionnaire activities help students gain a more sophisticated understanding of the characters, their actions and motives. For example, there is usually considerable debate over how Juliet would respond to the statement, "Children have a duty to love and obey their parents." Some students argue that Juliet would agree with this statement. They point to Juliet's response to her father's request that she consider Paris for marriage. Students point to the line in which Juliet dutifully tells Capulet, "I'll look to like if looking liking move." Other students argue that while Juliet would have gone along with her father's wishes early in the play, she changes and becomes more independent as the play develops. They point to the balcony scene, when Juliet says that if Romeo would refuse his name, she "would no longer be a Capulet." Other students offer differing viewpoints and evidence to support their interpretations, often refuting previous interpretations. In other words, the series of opinionnaire activities helps students to construct a framework for understanding the characters. More important, perhaps, these activities help to bring the characters alive for students.

One of the pleasant aspects of doing the series of opinionnaire discussion activities comes when students discuss the characters of the Friar, the Nurse, and Capulet. Many students cite similarities between the opinions of their parents and those of these three characters. Without prompting, many students go beyond the text. They apply what they learn in class to their own lives. In addition, these discussions help students see the range of viewpoints Shakespeare includes in the play.

Once students have finished reading the play, I ask them to fill out the opinionnaire again. This time, however, I ask them to complete it as they think Shakespeare would respond to the statements. In discussing their responses, students begin to formulate important conclusions about Shakespeare's message regarding love. As we discuss various statements from the opinionnaire in light of the play, most students recognize that the suicide was an immature and impulsive act, and many feel that the real tragedy involves the destruction of love in a world filled with hate. As one of my students concluded one year, "Shakespeare wants us to see that you shouldn't hate because hate can destroy love." The "True Love Opinionnaire" activities and the "Loyalty: What Is It?" scenarios activity helped this student establish a framework for understanding that enabled her to come to this conclusion. Once again, the teacher's role in these discussions is not to tell students what various characters think or what Shakespeare wants students to think about these issues; rather, it is to facilitate the discussion, help them inquire, think about, and solve the problem, and synthesize ideas brought up in the discussion.

As a final step, I ask students to complete the opinionnaire one last time for themselves, and I have them compare their responses to how they responded before they read the play. Most often, their opinions have changed. In looking back at how they marked the eighteen statements on the opinionnaire prior to reading the play, most students usually change their opinion on at least one statement as a result of their study. I lead a class discussion asking them to explain how and why their opinions have changed. This discussion is important because it helps students see the impact that the play has had on them.

The positive results I have had with these activities stand in striking contrast to my previous efforts following the approach suggested in widely used textbook anthologies. These past efforts, which have included weeks of lectures and readings, including various audio-visual aids, on the historical and philosophical background, Shakespeare and his theater, and the themes and elements of literature in the play, had not done much to help students even begin to understand, appreciate, or enjoy the play.

Writing about/in Response to the Play

Writing is an important part of the instruction I designed to help students understand and enjoy the play. In fact, because my past experiences with the typical writing assignments in widely used textbook anthologies have been largely negative, and because I know how difficult it can be for students to translate their interpretations of literature, particularly Shakespeare, into effective compositions (Kahn, Walter, and Johannessen 1984; Johannessen 1993), I have attempted to build writing instruction into my series of activities. Consider for a moment what students do in the activities I have described that prepares them for analytic writing: In the scenarios activity, students argue their viewpoints to an audience of peers (small-group and whole class discussions) regarding the actions of characters in the scenarios, present evidence and reasoning to support their views, and refute opposing viewpoints with evidence and reasoning. In a similar manner, in the initial opinionnaire activity, students argue their viewpoints to an audience of peers (whole class) regarding the statements on the opinionnaire, present evidence and reasoning to support their views, and refute opposing viewpoints with evidence and reasoning. In addition, in the opinionnaire activities dealing with the characters in the play and Shakespeare, students argue their interpretations of how each character and the bard would respond to the statements to an audience of peers (again, in small-group and whole class discussions), present evidence from the text to support their interpretations, provide reasoning to link their evidence to their interpretations, and refute opposing interpretations with evidence and reasoning. In other words, in these activities students orally practice the skills necessary to turn their personal viewpoints and interpretations into effective literary analysis compositions.

What I try to do is to get students to use what they have learned through these activities. One effective assignment I have used is to have them compare and contrast their own views on love (two of the statements from the opinionnaire) to the views of either Romeo or Juliet, and to provide reasoning for their own views and reasoning and evidence from the text to support their interpretations of the views of the character they are writing about.

I usually spend a little bit of time helping students understand how they might organize their comparison and contrast composition. Other than this bit of preparatory work, I have been pleased to find that students are interested in the assignment and anxious to get going. One reason for this may be that students see the assignment as an extension of what they have been doing in class. In other words, students see the assignment as a continuation of the classroom dialogue of their own viewpoints on love and their interpretations of the characters' and Shakespeare's views.

I have always been very pleased with the results. Not only have all the compositions been different, but nearly every one has been interesting and thoughtful. Instead of writing about the play as if it were something completely unrelated to and separate from them, which is what they do when they are given typical textbook assignments, students personalize the assignment and critically examine the messages in *Romeo and Juliet*. The success of the assignment is certainly related to the fact that students have practiced the skills they need for the assignment. As a result, they have not been afraid to take risks in their writing. When I have students share their writing with other students, I have been pleased to note that most of them are eager to read their compositions and to hear their classmates' papers.

Another possible writing assignment is to have students write a composition in which they explain how their own opinions have changed, and why, regarding one or two of the statements from the opinionnaire after reading the play. I ask them to explain what their opinion was before reading the play and why, what their opinion is now after reading it, and what specific evidence from the play accounts for how and why their opinions have changed. This assignment involves both personal response and some literary analysis. Students have success with it because they have thought about and discussed their opinions before and after reading the play, and they are able to explain how their opinions have changed as a result of their study. Without the opinionnaire activities, which require them to articulate and defend their opinions and interpretations, their written responses to this assignment would not be very effective.

In addition to these assignments students might also examine the issue of loyalty. I ask students to explain what they learned from the play about both the positive and negative aspects of loyalty, using specific evidence from the play to support their ideas. Students have success with these analytical assignments because they have critically examined conflicts of loyalties and the positive and negative aspects of loyalty prior to reading the play through the scenarios activity and again when they encountered these issues as they read the play.

Students experience success with the writing tasks I have described because they are not simply assignments for the sake of assignments, which is often the case with many textbook writing assignments; rather, they follow naturally from the activities students have been doing all along. Students use and practice the skills and strategies they have been learning in the activities.

From Shakespeare to Poetry to Self

After students study the play, I have them read and analyze a series of modern love poems. These poems include Dorothy Parker's "The Choice," Amy Lowell's "Carrefour," Robert Graves's "Symptoms of Love," Edna St. Vincent Millay's "Love Is Not All," and Mikhail Kvlividze's "In the Metro." (These poems are collected in and available for classroom use in Kahn, Walter, and Johannessen 1984.) Once again, I use the "True Love Opinionnaire." In small-group and whole class discussion activities, I ask students to determine how each of the poets would respond to the statements. The moans and groans that usually occur in the classroom whenever the word "poetry" is mentioned are noticeably absent. The self-confidence students gain from their previous work enables them to tackle these new problems with enthusiasm and an intellectual vitality that is very gratifying. As a result of their previous work, students are able to arrive at some fairly sophisticated interpretations of the poets' views of love, and often they relate their interpretations of the poems to characters in the play or what they thought Shakespeare might say.

What about the students themselves? Does their study of the play and poetry have an impact on them? At the conclusion of this unit, I again ask students if they have changed their views about love as a result of studying Shakespeare and the poems. In looking back at how they have marked the eleven statements on the opinionnaire prior to the unit, most students say they have changed their opinion on at least one statement as a result of their study. As students discuss how and why their views have changed, it becomes clear that the play and poems have affected them; that they have matured and grown. As one student put it: "I always thought that when two people fell in love nothing bad could happen. It was like love could conquer anything. But now I think it is a lot more complicated than that."

I also have students complete anonymous evaluations of the unit. Most students express a good deal of satisfaction and enjoyment. One student wrote, "You made learning fun and easy to understand. I especially enjoyed *Romeo and Juliet,* the poems and of course the questionnaires." Another student particularly liked the way I "related school to personal things in life." Again and again students made comments such as the following: "From what my sister told me, I thought I wouldn't like Shakespeare, but I loved *Romeo and Juliet,*" and "I actually looked forward to English class."

These responses are interesting for a number of reasons: first, they illustrate that as a result of this approach these students do not hate Shakespeare; and further, that they have learned some important lessons about love; it also suggests that they understand and enjoy the play and poetry; in addition, it shows that they grew as readers and writers; but it also shows that what these students learn is as much, or perhaps more, a powerful affective response as it is intellectual. If one of our goals in teaching classic literature like *Romeo and Juliet* is that it will have a profound impact on students, that it will move them, that it will be more than a rote exercise in memorizing literary terms, then these student responses stand as a testament to the fact that the problem isn't with what we teach, but rather with how we teach it, particularly when we rely on textbooks to tell us how to teach literature. The approach I have described here is one way to break away from the textbook approach and to foster fruitful involvements between students and literary works.

Figure 1. Loyalty: What Is It? Scenarios

Loyalty: What Is It?

Directions: Read the following scenarios and answer each of the questions that follow them. Be prepared to explain your answers to the class.

1. Tiffany has a friend who has recently been severely depressed. One day her friend confides that she has a bottle of tranquilizers from her mother's medicine cabinet in her purse. She makes Tiffany swear not to tell anyone, and Tiffany agrees. Later, however, she worries that her friend might try to kill herself so she tells her school guidance counselor. Her friend confronts her the next day in a rage. She says that Tiffany has betrayed her trust and that she wasn't going to kill herself, she was just joking around. She says that if Tiffany were a true friend she would never have broken her word to her. She tells Tiffany never to speak to her again. Do you agree with Tiffany's decision to tell the counselor? Why or why not? Was Tiffany disloyal to her friend when she reported her? Why or why not? Do you agree with her friend's definition of loyalty? Why or why not?

2. Sharon's grandparents are having a big party to celebrate their fiftieth wedding anniversary. Unfortunately, the big bash is scheduled for the same night as her senior prom. Her parents tell her that her grandparents will be very hurt if she goes to the prom instead of their anniversary party but that they will not force her to go. They say it will be a meaningless gesture if she only attends because they make her go. Sharon decides that she will have more fun at the prom, and that there will be people she doesn't even know at her grandparents' party. Her decision is to attend the prom and miss her grandparents' party. Do you agree with Sharon's decision? Why or why not? Is she being disloyal to her family by choosing to attend the prom? Why or why not?

3. McAuley was a cadet at the United States Military Academy in Fort Frontier, Arkansas. Cadets at the academy are studying to become officers in the U.S. military. They all swear to live up to this code: *We will not lie, steal, or cheat, or tolerate among us those who do.* Violation of any aspect of the code means dismissal from the academy. McAuley and two of her friends found out that another student had cheated on a final exam. McAuley told her friends that they were bound by the code to report the

cheating. But her friends refused. They said it was wrong to "snitch" on others. They said McAuley should be loyal to her fellow cadets, especially after all they had been through together. After much agonizing, McAuley decided she had to uphold the code she had sworn to honor. She reported the cheaters as well as her friends who knew about the cheating and broke the code by not reporting it. As a result the cheaters and McAuley's two friends were expelled from the academy. Do you agree with McAuley's decision? Why or why not? To whom does she owe more loyalty: the code, her two friends, her fellow cadets? Why?

4. Shaw is an army officer fighting a guerrilla war overseas. As a soldier he was taught that he must obey all orders of his superior officers. To disobey is a crime. While his unit is searching a village, three of their men are blown up by a booby trap. An investigation uncovers evidence that the village is inhabited by only women and children and also points to a woman and her eleven-year-old child as the possible culprits. Shaw's superior officer orders him to shoot the woman and her son to make an example of them. Shaw is appalled at the idea of killing women and children, especially when there is a chance they might be innocent. He voices his opinion, but his superior officer says that as a good soldier he must follow orders. He tells Shaw that he owes more loyalty to his fellow soldiers than to a bunch of murdering enemy villagers. Shaw decides to carry out the orders. Does Shaw make the right decision? Why or why not? Do you agree with what the superior officer tells Shaw? Why or why not?

5. Samira's family sacrificed everything to bring their children to the United States from their country. When they arrived, most of Samira's friends were not American but others who had also immigrated from her homeland. Her parents worked long hours each day to make a good life for their family. Over the years, Samira learned English, excelled in school, and made many new friends from many different backgrounds. Her parents encouraged her friendships but told her that she had to marry someone of her own ethnic and religious background. They explained that they had much knowledge and experience in the ways of the world and that they knew it was the only way her marriage would be truly happy and lasting. This expectation never really bothered Samira until college when she fell in love with Chacote, a boy from another culture—a group that is an ancient enemy of those from her homeland. She and Chacote want to marry, but her parents forbid her to marry him. When she refuses to obey their wishes, they say she is being disloyal to her country and family who have sacrificed so much for her. Samira cannot deny her love for Chacote and decides she will marry him against her parents' wishes even if they refuse to speak to her ever again. Do you agree with Samira's decision? Why or why not? To whom does Samira owe more loyalty, her parents or Chacote? Why? Is she being disloyal to her family if she marries Chacote? Why or why not?

6. Bruce was drafted into the United States Army at the age of eighteen. He knew that he would probably be sent into combat overseas. Bruce believed that the war his country was involved in was wrong. He decided to flee to Canada to avoid the draft. Do you agree with Bruce's decision? Why or why not? Were Bruce's actions disloyal to his country? Why or why not?

Figure 2. True Love Opinionnaire

True Love Opinionnaire

Directions: Read each of the following statements. Then Write A in the column under "you" if you agree with the statement or D if you disagree with it.

	You Before	Characters from the play C#1 C#2 C#3 C#4 C#5 C#6	The Bard	You After
1. People who are in love often do foolish things.				
2. Physical attraction must precede true love.				
3. People who love each other are best friends.				
4. Children have a duty to love and obey their parents.				
5. Teenagers cannot experience "true" love.				
6. You should do anything to make the person you love happy.				
7. All's fair in love and war.				
8. If you truly love someone, you will not be attracted to anyone else.				
9. Love at first sight is possible.				
10. Love is blind.				
11. Love never changes.				

References

Johannessen, Larry R. 1993. "Digging into *Julius Caesar* through Character Analysis." In *Teaching Shakespeare Today: Practical Approaches and Productive Strategies,* ed. James E. Davis and Ronald E. Salomone, 207–17. Urbana, Ill.: NCTE.

———. 1984. "The Nature of Love: Two Short Stories." *NOTES Plus* 2.1:14–15. Rpt. in Ruth Cline, ed., *The Best of NOTES Plus* (Urbana, Ill.: NCTE, 1989), 40–43.

Kahn, Elizabeth A., Carolyn Calhoun Walter, and Larry R. Johannessen. 1984. *Writing about Literature.* Urbana, Ill.: ERIC/RCS and NCTE.

Rosenblatt, Louise. 1968. *Literature as Exploration.* New York: Noble and Noble.

Smagorinsky, Peter. 1993. "Preparing Students for Enriched Reading: Creating a Scaffold for Literary Understanding." In *Exploring Texts: The Role of Discussion and Writing in the Teaching and Learning of Literature,* ed. George E. Newell and Russel K. Durst, 153–74. Norwood, Mass.: Christopher-Gordon Publishers, Inc.

———. 1989. "Small Groups: A New Dimension in Learning." *English Journal* 78.2:67–70.

Smagorinsky, Peter, Tom McCann, and Stephen Kern. 1987. *Explorations: Introductory Activities for Literature and Composition, 7–12*. Urbana, Ill.: ERIC/RCS and NCTE.

Smith, Michael W. 1991. *Understanding Unreliable Narrators: Reading between the Lines in the Literature Classroom*. Urbana, Ill.: NCTE.

CHAPTER 19

Teaching *King Lear*

Michael J. Collins
Georgetown University
Washington, D.C.

Collins admits that King Lear *is a long, complex, and difficult play, one that poses special challenges for both students and teachers. One problem is that students wish for a presentation of the single timeless meaning of the play, yet teachers can choose from among a number of plausible readings and find ample critical commentary to support many interpretations. But, as Collins also illustrates, some of these views are contradictory. He urges teachers to "resist the desire for certainty," and to help students recognize that* King Lear *does not have one "right reading" to the exclusion of all others.*

*A*s I always tell my students, each time I begin teaching the play, with *King Lear* literary critics and English teachers get found out. *King Lear* is a long, complex, and difficult play, particularly for those who have neither read it nor seen it performed before. After years of sitting in classrooms, however, students have faith: they expect their teachers (older, wiser, more experienced with the play) and the critics (if the students read the criticism or even the introductions to some of the standard texts) to explain the play, to make sense of it, to offer an interpretation of it, and so to put their difficulties to rest.

But if reading the critics, who among them offer remarkably different and often contradictory interpretations of *King Lear,* will only compound their difficulties, students will not do much better in the classroom, for the best their teacher can do (if he or she hopes to fulfill the ordinary expectations of students) is to offer a plausible (but never compelling) reading of the play, a reading against which students, if they are at all interested in doing so, can offer equally plausible (but never compelling) readings of their own. *King Lear* puts a teacher, to a greater degree than usual, in the awkward and sometimes uncomfortable position of having to admit that his or her reading is at best a plausible reading and that other equally plausible readings are always possible.

Some years ago, a *Peanuts* cartoon showed Peppermint Patty, the perennial D– student, giving an oral report to her class. "This is my report on *The Brothers Karamazov,*" she begins, "of which there were three. It reminded me of a similar story, *The Three Little Kittens,* because there were three of them also." The teacher, whose words we do not hear, interrupts the report, and Peppermint Patty, in the last frame, responds, "I'm surprised the similarity never occurred to you." Although she will probably get another D– for her report, Peppermint Patty, I propose, has the makings of an English teacher or even a literary critic, not simply because she has a sophisticated sense of the negotiations among texts, a new historical sense of intertextuality, but because she has done what critics and teachers always do—noticed similarities, parallels, echoes, analogies, image patterns within and between texts. (Indeed, the successful literary critics, for better or worse, are those who notice things that no one, often for good textual or theatrical reasons, has ever noticed before.)

Luckily for Peppermint Patty, however, she is stopped from taking the next step, the step that critics and teachers inevitably take: she never gets to tell what the similarities mean (and thus, by implicitly challenging the teacher's reading, risk another D-). And that is one way teachers of *King Lear* get found out: while we are adept at noticing all sorts of similarities in the play—parallels, echoes, analogies of language, image, character, and plot—we do not have the good sense to stop there, for our attempts to find meaning in those similarities (which may work simply to bring coherence and the feel of significance to the play) leave us, once again, with readings that are at best plausible, at worst ingenious, but never compelling.

In the fourteenth chapter of his Gospel, as Jesus, taken prisoner in the garden where he has been praying with his disciples, is about to be led away to the high priest, Mark momentarily interrupts his story to describe another event: "And a young man followed him, with nothing but a linen cloth about his body; and they seized him, but he left the linen cloth and ran away naked" *(The New Oxford Annotated Bible,* Revised Standard Version, 51–52). The boy in the linen cloth, who comes from nowhere in the story and never appears again, momentarily running naked across salvation history, cries out to the literary critic, to the teacher, as the psychiatrist puts it in *Equus,* "Account for me. Account for me." In what is for many a sacred book, a book that has meaning, that proposes to reveal to its readers the truth about their lives, such an odd detail seems inevitably to be telling us something, to be meaningful, to have some significance.

Biblical critics propose several plausible (but never compelling) readings. The event is Mark's reticent signature, like Alfred Hitchcock's momentary appearances in his films. It is a detail to confirm the truth of the story: no writer of fiction would break the continuity of his narrative at so climactic a moment if the boy did not actually happen by. It is an allusion to Amos 2:16: "'and he who is stout of heart among the mighty/shall flee away naked in that day,'/says the Lord". And finally, most telling of all (telling because it seeks, by giving it a name, to make orderly and reasonable something that is clearly disorderly and unreasonable), it is an enigma. And that is a second way teachers of *King Lear* get found out: we propose answers to questions the play itself never answers, we find certain meanings in things the play seems to leave open, ambiguous, even unmeaningful, instead of saying simply and more honestly, "We just don't know."

From another point of view, however, if we are satisfied with plausible readings, *King Lear* is a satisfying play to teach because by simply reading the play in the way we ordinarily read plays in the classroom, making the interpretive moves we as teachers and critics ordinarily make on plays, we not only can have the *King Lear* (and, for that matter, the world) we want, but we also can find some of the best critics of Shakespeare to agree with us. Here, for example, are two well-known, frequently cited, and, I believe, representative articulations of what the critics say *King Lear* tells us about itself and about the world in which we live. The first is G. Wilson Knight in "*King Lear* and the Comedy of the Grotesque":

Sometimes we know that all human pain holds beauty, that no tear falls but it dews some flower we cannot see. Perhaps humour, too, is inwoven in the universal pain, and the enigmatic silence holds not only an unutterable sympathy, but also the ripples of an impossible laughter whose flight is not for the wing of human understanding.[1]

The second is J. Stampfer in "The Catharsis of *King Lear*":

And with Lear's death, each audience . . . shares and releases the most private and constricting fear to which mankind is subject, the fear that penance is impossible . . . , because its partner has no charity, resilience, or harmony—the fear, in other words, that we inhabit an imbecile universe. It is by this vision of reality that Lear lays down his life for his folly.[2]

Although they offer entirely different understandings of the play, both articulations, growing out of readings that are intelligent, sensitive, and alert to the complexities of the text, are entirely plausible. With *King Lear*, we can, if we wish, choose the reading we want to teach and the world we want to live in.

Let me offer some examples of the difficulties we encounter in reading *King Lear*. First, as Peppermint Patty would surely recognize, the play clearly parallels (in an inverted way) the family of Lear and the family of Gloucester. (An old man has three daughters, the two older turn against him, the youngest one tries to save him. An old man has two sons, the older one tries to save him, the younger one turns against him). But once we have recognized the parallel, we are on our own, for the play never intimates what meaning we are to take from it, what it tells us about the world of *King Lear* and, by extension, our own. Any good teacher, any good literary critic can propose a plausible meaning or, for that matter, a variety of meanings that will, in turn, lead to a larger reading (or readings) of the play. But then another teacher, another literary critic, another student can propose another plausible meaning or, for that matter, a variety of plausible meanings that will, in turn, lead to a different reading (or readings) of the play.

Then the Fool, like the boy in the linen cloth, puzzling, enigmatic, textually and theatrically insistent, cries out in at least two ways to the teacher, "Account for me. Account for me." First, although his words at times seem apt and meaningful, at others they seem either nonsense or related to their dramatic context in ways we cannot fathom. If, as Alec McCowen, who played the Fool in Peter Brook's production, has suggested (in a talk at Georgetown University), it is impossible to know at every moment what the Fool's words mean, it seems more honest and more true to the play not to propose complex and (sometimes ingenious) meanings for them, but to say simply we cannot know what they mean, nor how (or even whether) they might relate to or comment on the people and events of the play.

The Fool also cries out to be accounted for in another way, for the play never tells us what becomes of him after he speaks his last words, "And I'll go to bed at noon" (3.5.84).[3] On the stage, he (or sometimes she) is to some degree accounted for: found dead when Kent says "Come help to bear thy master / Thou must not stay behind" (3.5.98-99); left (in Nicholas Hytner's production for the Royal Shakespeare Company in 1990) folded in a chair on a revolving stage, her arms waving spastically; exiting for the last time with Lear, Kent, and Gloucester; hanging himself on the stage (in Jude Kelly's production in London in 1995); or turning sharply around and walking deliberately off the stage after his last words (in David Hare's production for the Royal National Theatre in 1986). But the script leaves the Fool's fate a mystery that grows still more mysterious through the opening words of Lear's final speech, "And my poor fool is hanged" (5.3.307), and through the possibility that on Shakespeare's stage the actor who played Cordelia doubled as the Fool.

Finally, the blinding of Gloucester, in a play whose characters make repeated and contradictory references to the role of the gods in human affairs, raises a larger question about the play, one to which the words of G. Wilson Knight and J. Stampfer point: Is the story of *King Lear* (and by extension our own stories) played out in a sane or a lunatic universe; can we draw any light from the darkness of Gloucester's cruel and violent blinding? Edgar's conclusion,

> The gods are just, and of our pleasant vices
> Make instruments to plague us:
> The dark and vicious place where thee he got
> Cost him his eyes,
>
> (5.3.172-75)

which proposes an austere justice, a ruthless sanity for the world, seems no more plausible than the conclusion that the gods are unjust: Gloucester's heroic charity in helping Lear cost him his eyes. The play gives no answer to such questions; rather, it holds out sanity and lunacy, light and dark as equal possibilities. If we choose an answer, if we propose an answer, a reading, an interpretation to our students (as did the director who chose to have Gloucester blinded upright, with his arms tied out in cruciform), then we ought at least to admit to them that the answer is not the one the play gives, but one we believe or desire or hope to be true. The death of Cordelia raises the same question and leaves us with the same uncertainty, for while we might plausibly—through her lines in 4.4.24-25 that allude to Luke's Gospel, 2:49 ("O dear father, / It is thy business that I go about") and the reversed Pietà of the final scene—associate her with Christ, we can never know with certainty how we are to understand that association, what meaning it might have, whether we are to take it literally or ironically.

If we resist then both the absolutism of teaching one plausible reading and the relativism of endorsing any plausible reading, where do we end up in the classroom? We end up finally at the end of the play, with Lear kneeling over the body of Cordelia, speaking his final lines, raising the play's final interpretive question:

> Do you see this? Look on her. Look, her lips,
> Look there, look there."
>
> (310-11)

What does Lear see, what does he ask us to look at, in the last moments of his life? What is the tone of his words here? For some readers, Lear's words suggest that he sees some transcendent vision, as Robert Stephens, playing Lear in Adrian Noble's production for the Royal Shakespeare Company in 1993, implied when he crawled upright toward the apron of the stage, pulling Cordelia behind him, looking diagonally up and out over the audience, pointing to something unseen in the far corner of the theater. For other readers, they suggest that Lear sees only the absurd insult of Cordelia's body lying dead before him. And while both readings seem plausible, the play compels neither.

In discussing *Waiting for Godot,* a play with certain affinities to *King Lear,* Samuel Beckett said, "There is a wonderful sentence in Augustine. . . . 'Do not despair: one of the thieves was saved. Do not presume: one of the thieves was damned.'" *King Lear* leaves us poised between the fundamental possibilities of the human condition, between sanity and lunacy, between light and dark, telling us at once: Do not despair: Lear may see Cordelia living. Do not presume: Lear may see Cordelia dead. And here, in its refusal to answer the fundamental question it has raised through the story it has told, lies a reason to value *King Lear* and a reason to teach it as well.

As we struggle in the classroom to read the meaning of the play, we replicate our struggle to read the world outside it, and, in the end, we are left in the same uncertainty, facing the question whose answer, in the play and in the world, we most need and desire to know—whether we live finally in a sane or a lunatic universe. Like audiences at the end of *King Lear,* we live inevitably in uncertainty, in the classroom as we struggle to teach the play, in the world as we struggle to live wisely and justly, and we can do no more than read both the play and the world with care and make what seem the right choices along the way. While our students inevitably look to us for certain answers about the play and sometimes about the world as well, we ought to have the courage to say that we do not have them, that we, like all who live, live in uncertainty and what answers we have—to illuminate the play, to guide us through our lives—are at best guarded, tentative, subject always to revision, our best guesses in the face of an ultimately impenetrable mystery. Do not despair, we have answers to our questions. Do not presume, our answers remain always uncertain.

If we resist the desire for certainty, in our classrooms and in the world, if we can bring students to recognize that *King Lear* leaves us precisely where our own lives inevitably leave us—poised, as the critic Barbara Everett, quoting Pascal, puts it, "between everything and nothing"[5]—then we might help them not only to read more wisely, but perhaps to live more wisely as well. As we resist the desire for certainty, then, we might thus dissuade our students, in the classroom, from either presuming that one reading is the right reading or despairing that any reading is as good as any other. At the same time, we might also dissuade them from holding as certain, outside the classroom, what no one can ever know to be certain and thus falling victim to one of the pseudocertainties that threaten the world today—absolutism and relativism, presumption and despair. If the readings which we offer them, both of the play and the human condition, seem, as a result, finally less comforting than we or they would wish, we shall have at least helped our students to read more honestly and perhaps also to recognize that the questions we ask (about a play or about the world) tell us more than any answers we might give to them.

Notes

1. *The Wheel of Fire* (London: Methuen, 1949); rpt. in Laurence Lerner, ed., *Shakespeare's Tragedies: An Anthology of Modern Criticism* (Harmondsworth: Penguin Books, 1968), p.146.

2. "The Catharsis of *King Lear*," *Shakespeare Survey* 13 (1960); rpt. in *Shakespeare's Tragedies: An Anthology of Modern Criticism,* p. 160.

3. Citations of *King Lear* are from *The Tragedy of King Lear,* ed. Russell Fraser, Signet Classic Shakespeare (New York: New American Library, 1963).

4. Quoted in Martin Esslin, *The Theatre of the Absurd,* 3d ed. (Harmondsworth: Penguin Books, 1980), p. 53.

5. "The New *King Lear*," *Critical Quarterly* 2 (Winter 1960); rpt. in Frank Kermode, ed., *"King Lear": A Collection of Critical Essays* (London: Macmillan, 1969), p. 200.

CHAPTER 20

Images of *Hamlet* in the Undergraduate Classroom

LOREEN L. GIESE

Ohio University
Athens, Ohio

Giese recognizes both the exceptional popularity of teaching Shakespeare through performance and the increasing prevalence of feminist interpretations. In her teaching of Hamlet, *she suggests that "feminist approaches combined with performance approaches can be extremely effective in making this play more accessible to undergraduates." The classroom project she describes includes, among other things, the discussion of gender roles in the play, the viewing of different video versions of a specific scene, and small group classroom performances that she videotapes.*

*I*n the last decade, teaching Shakespeare through feminist and performance approaches has become much more widespread. Essays on teaching Shakespeare through performance, for instance, dominated a special issue of *Shakespeare Quarterly* edited by John F. Andrews that was published in 1984 (issue 5). Andrews noted that "A decade ago 'performance-oriented' pedagogy was relatively unfamiliar among Shakespeareans and was anything but universally accepted as the wave of the future. Now it is difficult to find a dissenting voice: virtually everybody acknowledges the need to approach Shakespeare's plays as dramatic rather than literary works" (515). In the preface to the next issue of *Shakespeare Quarterly* that was devoted to teaching Shakespeare, published in 1990 (issue 2), guest editor Ralph Alan Cohen comments that he surprisingly received few papers devoted to performance pedagogy, concluding that "Performance pedagogy seems to have attained the status of a given" (iii).[1] Several of the essays in the 1990 issue also attest to the increase in feminist approaches in teaching Shakespeare.[2] Feminist approaches can be combined effectively with performance approaches in making *Hamlet* more accessible to undergraduates.

In this essay, I shall explain a classroom project involving both feminist and performance approaches that I use when teaching *Hamlet* in an upper-level, undergraduate Shakespeare survey. The course averages about thirty-five students with a wide variety of majors and meets twice a week for two hours a session, so that I devote two and a half weeks or five meetings to this play. With both approaches, the students gain a much deeper understanding of *Hamlet* and of the genre of drama itself, particularly how the practical, materialist conditions of theater—costuming, the stage, lighting, and the like—produce meaning.

Moreover, this project helps them to formulate critical responses to the play, to overcome language barriers, to apply theory, and to experience collaborative learning.

In the first part of the assignment, we devote three two-hour classes to closely reading the text itself. I am particularly concerned that students understand the text as a cultural product, not as an ahistorical text. Such an understanding of *Hamlet* is often more difficult for students, because they usually consider it as a sanctified, aesthetic masterpiece with an objective, fixed, and timeless meaning. Before they read the play, I have the students write one paragraph on why they think we are reading *Hamlet* and another on what they think the play means. I then ask for a few volunteers to read their paragraphs, which usually include answers pointing to the universality of human nature and of Shakespearean drama. During these three sessions of lecture and discussions, examination of the play through feminist approaches not only helps students understand the gender roles in the play, but also serves as a useful approach to make the play more accessible: Leah Marcus, for example, maintains that

> The value of interrogating Shakespearean drama in terms of its portrayal of women can scarcely be overestimated in the classroom. It provides an almost instant recipe for successful discussion because it opens up the plays to ideological investigation of a kind that is immediately accessible to our students. . . . The multiplicity of recent feminist approaches to Shakespeare provides students with a rich interpretative matrix from which they can come to their own conclusions about the patterning of gender roles both within the plays and outside them. (110)

In classroom practice, I also try to contextualize the play and introduce the issue of the transmission and instability of the text itself. The latter topic is particularly appropriate to this drama, since the text is one of the many uncertainties of *Hamlet*. One way to introduce such instability is to have the students read the 1603 version of the "To be or not to be" soliloquy alongside the one in their editions. The students do not become overwhelmed when they analyze a piece rather than an entire variant version. The analysis of two differing texts also opens up discussion to the shift from manuscript to print culture and the status of drama in the sixteenth and early seventeenth centuries. In order to highlight the social and political contexts of the play, we consider issues such as Hamlet's position to take revenge and the status of women in early modern England in light of contemporary tracts; for example, before studying Act 1, in relation to Hamlet's situation, the students read two excerpts from contemporary political tracts—Jean Bodin's *The Six Bookes of a Commonweale* (1576) and Philippe Duplessis-Mornay's *Vindiciae Contra Tyrannos* (1579)—that take different positions on the right of the subject to overthrow a monarch. A few selections from William Gouge's *Of Domesticall Duties* (1622) will certainly ignite discussion regarding the roles of and gender definitions for men and women.

As we finish Act 5, the students again write paragraphs on why we should read *Hamlet* and what the play means to them. I again ask for a few volunteers to read their paragraphs. After we briefly discuss these readings, I introduce them to other critical perspectives such as Marxist and psychoanalytic readings of the play. The different theoretical perspectives allow students to understand better the range of opinions on the play and encourage debate in our class discussion. I then have the students write for five minutes on how their arguments relate to the three critical perspectives—feminist, Marxist, and psychoanalytic—and the implications of these relationships in terms of the significance of their arguments, namely: How do their findings relate to that of the other perspectives? What similarities and differences are there? What is the significance of these similarities and differences? We then discuss what they have just written. Through this comparison, they realize that they too are critics of the play who produce meaning.

While we study the play, they are to work on their first essay, which focuses on the nunnery scene. The nunnery scene works well as a focus for their assignments for several reasons: it is open to diverse interpretations, thus inviting critical and creative thinking; it is manageable in length; it is accessible in terms of subject matter; and it makes the students deal directly with one of the uncertainties in the text that continues to provoke intense debate—the relationship between Ophelia and Hamlet. J. Dover Wilson's observation—"The attitude of Hamlet towards Ophelia is without doubt the greatest of all the puzzles in the play" (1935, 101)—continues to be made by readers of the play today. The students write a four-page essay on the nunnery scene based on the evidence in their texts and the contemporary tract we examined. This essay requires the students to examine: What is the exact relationship between Hamlet and Ophelia as demonstrated in this scene? And how is their relationship relevant to the play itself? How do the gender roles defined in the play relate to Hamlet and Ophelia? What is the significance of the pattern they see?

The next two parts of the assignment involve different productions of the scene they have just analyzed. After the students turn in their essays at the beginning of the next class session, we discuss the differences of reading, staging, and filming a drama. This discussion includes alerting the students to compare the camera work, decor, landscapes, setting, lighting, blocking, music, body language, tone, pace, costumes, and textual additions and deletions in the different productions. We then watch three different interpretations of the nunnery scene: the Laurence Olivier (1948), the BBC (1979), and Franco Zeffirelli (1990) productions. By studying more than one performance, students can see a range of possibilities in interpretation that enables them to understand better how the director's choices impact their reading of the scene and the gender definitions and roles within the play, an understanding that helps prepare them for their performances. Ophelia, for instance, in each of these productions represents a different view of women's roles. These versions also promote debate about the differences between film and television as media. We then discuss the different versions as I reintroduce the questions on which they have just written: What is the exact relationship between Hamlet and Ophelia as interpreted in each version? In what gender roles are they portrayed? How does the director achieve this meaning?

After these discussions, the students break up into groups of three or four for the third part of this unit: their own performances that I videotape. They have the remaining hour of class to work on their performances, although most students continue their rehearsals outside the classroom. Since my class averages about thirty-five students, I end up with eight or nine groups. To involve all the students in some manner is important. J. L. Styan identifies one of the benefits of using performance as an increase in the intellectual commitment of the students: "when [students] see their peers at work, they will be pleasantly alert and critical because they will be involved in the same effort with the same material" (1993, 62). Usually most students are eager to participate; however, those who are reluctant can play Polonius (who has few lines in the scene) or take turns operating the video camera. The students are their own directors and can cut whatever lines they choose and use whatever costumes and props they deem appropriate. This scene is particularly provocative for student performance since it encourages them to make some difficult critical judgments; for example: What exactly is Hamlet's attitude towards Ophelia? Does Hamlet know they are being watched? When does he discover this? Does Ophelia give him a clue? If so, when and how? What is his demeanor? How does he know that she is at her "orisons"? What is her demeanor? Is his treatment of her in this scene all part of his act? Or does he show some real concern for her by changing the tone of his lines? What exactly are the "remembrances" that Ophelia "longed long to redeliver"? In the past, I have not graded the performances, since I was worried that the students' concern about grades could stifle their creativity. If I do decide to grade them in future, I would tell them before they start working on their performances that the group will receive one grade based on how well they present a coherent, well-thought-out reading of the scene that is consistent in its execution.

During the next class, the students perform. With eight or nine groups performing, we usually comment generally on each production for a few minutes before going on to the next, focusing our comments on the production's interpretation of the relationship between Hamlet and Ophelia and how the physical considerations of theater influenced the meaning of the scene. Students are often struck by the extent to which the use of space and props can influence meaning. In terms of the "remembrances," for instance, some students will have Ophelia return a letter, basing their choice on Act 2, scenes 1 and 2, while others are more inventive: in one group Ophelia returned sexual aids and condoms, while in another she returned very expensive jewelry, including an engagement ring. The students in each performance are asked to explain how the text supports the props they chose for the scene. After all of the performances, we then discuss how these productions influenced their own understanding of the scene itself and their interpretations of the play.

In the final part of this project, the students rewrite their earlier papers on the nunnery scene. In a ten-page essay, they reexamine the questions from their earlier essay, now drawing their evidence from three different texts: their editions, one of the television or film productions, and one of their stage productions. I leave the videotapes on reserve for students to watch, a viewing which also encourages them to realize how the camera produced meaning in their performances—by focusing on specific characters, zooming in on certain facial expressions, and the like. To witness several versions of the same scene underscores how meaning is negotiated, not fixed, an understanding that will inform and enrich their subsequent readings.

When teaching *Hamlet* to undergraduates, I have found that this project helps students to understand better both *Hamlet* and the fluidity of meaning in Shakespearean drama both on the page and on the stage, so that in order for us to "teach [students] to drink deep ere [they] depart," "Playing is the thing!"

Notes

1. In addition to these two issues of *Shakespeare Quarterly,* see Jay L. Halio (1977), Charles H. Frey (1993), and J. L. Styan (1993) for further discussions of performance pedagogy.

2. See, for example, essays by James Hirsh (1990) and Ann Thompson (1990).

References

Andrews, John F. 1984. "From the Editor." *Shakespeare Quarterly* 35:515-16.

Bodin, Jean. 1989. *"The Six Bookes of a Commonweale."* In *Shakespeare's World: Background Readings in the English Renaissance,* ed. Gerald M. Pinciss and Roger Lockyer, 119-31. New York: Continuum.

Cohen, Ralph Alan. 1990. "From the Editor." *Shakespeare Quarterly* 41:iii-v.

Duplessis-Mornay, Philippe. 1989. *"Vindiciae Contra Tyrannos."* In *Shakespeare's World: Background Readings in the English Renaissance,* ed. Gerald M. Pinciss and Roger Lockyer, 108-18. New York: Continuum.

Frey, Charles H. 1993. "Goals and Limits in Student Performance of Shakespeare." In *Teaching Shakespeare Today: Practical Approaches and Productive Strategies,* ed. James E. Davis and Ronald E. Salomone, 72-78. Urbana, Ill.: NCTE.

Gouge, William. 1622. *Of Domesticall Duties.* London: Bladen.

Halio, Jay L. "'This Wide and Universal Stage': Shakespeare's Plays as Plays." In *Teaching Shakespeare,* ed. Walter Edens et al., 273-89. Princeton: Princeton University Press.

Hirsh, James. 1990. "Teaching Paradoxes: Shakespeare and the Enhancement of Audience Skills." *Shakespeare Quarterly* 41:222-29.

Marcus, Leah. 1994. "Disestablishing Shakespeare." In *Teaching with Shakespeare: Critics in the Classroom,* ed. Bruce McIver and Ruth Stevenson, 98-114. Newark: University of Delaware Press.

Styan, J. L. 1993. "Shakespeare off the Page." In *Teaching Shakespeare Today: Practical Approaches and Productive Strategies,* ed. James E. Davis and Ronald E. Salomone, 61-71. Urbana, Ill.: NCTE.

Thompson, Ann. 1990. *"King Lear* and the Politics of Teaching Shakespeare." *Shakespeare Quarterly* 41:139-46.

Wilson, J. Dover. 1935. *What Happens in Hamlet.* New York: Macmillan.

CHAPTER 21

What Happens in the Mousetrap

Versions of Hamlet

Robert Carl Johnson

Miami University
Oxford, Ohio

As in the previous chapter, Johnson also discusses Hamlet *and suggests an approach to the play that focuses on a single scene. He recommends the mousetrap scene and shows his students four productions of the play that "offer us completely different versions" of it. In this way he emphasizes how "readings of the mousetrap scene (and perhaps all of Shakespeare) are open to individual interpretation," and he highlights "the difficulty of interpreting and performing Shakespeare's text."*

For many students *Hamlet* is an overwhelming play, difficult to understand and too complex to comment upon intelligently. The mousetrap scene, coming so closely upon the berating of Ophelia in the nunnery scene, is especially difficult for many students. Hamlet has supposedly told us what he hopes to accomplish with the play the roving players will perform. In soliloquy he promises the audience that through the play he will catch the conscience of the king. And he has also written a short speech that the main actor has agreed to insert at the appropriate point in the play. And further demonstrating his concern for the success of the performance by the troupe, he spends considerable time with the actors, explaining the way he would want his speech conveyed to the audience:

> Speak the speech, I pray you, as I pronounc'd it to you, trippingly on the tongue, but if you mouth it, as many of our players do, I had as lief the town-crier spoke my lines. (3.2.1–4)

Immediately before Claudius, Gertrude, and the court enter, Hamlet carefully instructs Horatio what he expects from Horatio during this special court performance. He expects Horatio to observe carefully the king, as he witnesses the part of the scene that "comes near the circumstance / Which I have told thee of my father's death" (3.2.81–82). So the audience has been carefully prepared for what Hamlet has planned and what he expects to accomplish. If all works well, then, at the end of the sequence Hamlet can boast with complete confidence that he will "take the ghost's word for a thousand pound" (3.2.297–98).

But between Hamlet's instructions to Horatio and his confident boast, a scene unfolds that is much more complex and controversial than this framing of the events by Hamlet suggests. For students reading the play there is no way to appreciate the tension inherent in the situation, nor to understand fully Hamlet's three-fold concerns during the scene: Ophelia, Gertrude, as well as Claudius. At certain moments even the reader has to wonder if either Hamlet's relationship with Ophelia or with Gertrude is not more important than his attempt to trap Claudius. All students recognize that simply reading the text cannot do justice to the scene, so in class I have my students attempt to act out the scene with special attention to what the stage audience is observing and where members of the theater audience are directing their attention. The reactions are interesting. "I was curious how to interpret Rosencrantz and Guildenstern's reactions," one student comments. Another student wonders what the rest of the court is doing during Hamlet's exchanges with Ophelia. The result of our exercise is that we agree that Hamlet's plans have not been fully completed, and we question the degree of his success in carrying out his plan. And, of course, the students who are Horatio or Polonius have different concerns as court observers, since Horatio has specific instructions and Polonius is still concerned about the possibility of a relationship between his daughter and Hamlet. My imaginary theater audience is not sure whom to watch as we struggle through all the lines of the traveling troupe. A student inevitably asks how the scene has been performed by professional companies, since at the undergraduate level there is often the desire for a definitive answer. I respond that I have seen no performance which attempts to use the entire scene in the order of the text that we are reading, and we then explore how we could change our understanding of the scene by changing or eliminating parts of the scene.

Fortunately, there are four readily available versions of the play that offer us completely different versions of the scene and thus challenge our interpretations. The starting point of any comparison is the Laurence Olivier version. Olivier's abbreviated version of the play uses the bad quarto ordering of the soliloquies and places the "to be or not to be" soliloquy before "the play's the thing" soliloquy. This change has the immediate effect of forcefully changing the impression we have of Hamlet. The bad quarto ordering suggests a person who moves from contemplation to a specific plan of action, whereas the normal order suggests the hesitation and vacillation we traditionally associate with Hamlet. More important, Olivier has eliminated the text of the one soliloquy, and in a dramatic and compelling moment, Olivier dominates the screen with but one line from the soliloquy: "The play's the thing / Wherein I'll catch the conscience of the king" (2.2.584–85).

Olivier's version of the mousetrap scene offers an excellent starting point for the comparison of the versions and our attempts to understand this scene, since he obviously simplifies the problem. When the members of the court enter, Hamlet leads Gertrude to the throne, and the scene starts with Claudius's question, "How fares our cousin Hamlet?" Olivier combines the exchanges between Hamlet and Ophelia, using before the dumb show the exchange about the brevity of woman's love (3.2.160–63) with a much later exchange:

O: You are keen, my lord, you are keen.
H: It would cost you a groaning to take off my edge. (3.2.259–60)

After that combined exchange the players enter to perform the dumb show we read in the text. There is no dialogue and we witness the anguished reaction, the obvious guilt of Claudius and also watch the observing court, especially the concern of Polonius. Olivier dispenses with all of the dialogue from the players or from Hamlet; he depends entirely upon the dumb show and the anguished reaction of Claudius. There is no problem with Hamlet's relationship with Ophelia or with his mother; the question of Claudius's guilt is clear: he has reacted to the play and has left the scene in fear and in complete confirmation of his guilt. In this version it is clear that Hamlet has succeeded in his plan to catch the conscience of the king.

In direct contrast to Olivier's shortened and, I would argue, simplistic rendering of the scene, Derek Jacobi's interpretation of the mousetrap is strikingly different. The scene in this Time-Life BBC version is much longer, using significantly more of the text. Jacobi makes no changes in the order of the text, although much of the players' text is necessarily omitted. However, the emphasis on the player queen's unfaithfulness is germane, and Hamlet interrupts his concentration on the guilt of Claudius to question the reaction of his mother to the play.

When Claudius asks whether or not there is any offense in the play, Hamlet engages the debate. When he starts to tell Claudius that Lucianus, nephew to the king, is about to enter, the tension is keen, and that intensity cannot be interrupted by the exchange between Hamlet and Ophelia (255–62). Jacobi recognizes, as the other three versions of the scene also concede, that the sexual relationship between Ophelia and Hamlet cannot interrupt the confrontation between Hamlet and Ophelia. The exchange itself is important, but when I discuss with my students how it would work in the entire scene they (and I) are confused. Our feeble attempts to act out this part of the play in class had resulted in confusion for all. We agree that it is more appropriate in Jacobi's version for Hamlet to move from "This is one Lucianus, nephew to the king" to his anguished cry, "Begin, murderer." Why at this point, at the climactic point of his attempt to catch Claudius, is he concerned about his sexual relationship with Ophelia:

> O: You are as good as a chorus my lord.
> H: I could intepret between you and your love, if I could see the puppets dallying.
> O: You are keen, my lord, you are keen.
> H: It would cost you a groaning to take off my edge.
> O: Still better, and worse.
> H: So you must take your husbands. (3.2.255–62)

My students and I agree as we watch Jacobi's version that it is impossible to interrupt Hamlet's obvious concentration on the players' performance and his confrontation with Claudius with what we now see as an extraneous concern with Ophelia.

Jacobi at this point is obviously concerned that his plot to catch the conscience of the king is in danger of failing. Claudius (superbly played by Patrick Stewart) has not displayed any undue reaction to the dumb show and has not been affected by the ensuing dialogue.

When Hamlet calls on Lucianus to begin, the audience feels that this is Hamlet's last chance to complete his initial plan to confirm Claudius' guilt.

But Jacobi's version of the mousetrap directly contradicts the Olivier version. Patrick Stewart's Claudius does not react to the players' version of the death of a player king. When Claudius rises, he does not do so in panic. He has asked for light as he rises, but instead of fleeing, he approaches Hamlet in a completely calm manner, stares directly into his eyes, shakes his head, and then says, "away." The effect of the scene is obvious on the theater audience, completely ambiguous for the court audience. Hamlet has failed to catch the conscience of the king; the court audience is bewildered. And Hamlet's boast at the end of the scene that he will trust the ghost is empty bravado.

If these two versions represent the extremes of interpretation of the mousetrap (complete success and abject failure in confronting Claudius), the performances of Nicol Williamson (1969) and Mel Gibson (1990) offer interesting intermediate interpretations and also help students understand not only the complexities of the scene, but also the variety of options.

Williamson's version also recognizes that it is difficult to include the exchange between Ophelia and Hamlet before the entrance of Lucianus, so he takes those lines and uses them in a variation of the first exchange between Hamlet and Ophelia:

> H: Shall I lie in your lap? (105)
> O: No, my lord. (106)
> H: That's a fair thought to lie between maid's legs. (111)
> O: You are keen, my lord, you are keen. (259)
> H: It would cost you a groaning to take off my edge. (260)

As I and my students attempt to recreate our struggle to include all of the lines of Shakespeare's play, many of us conclude that this combination is appealing and striking in the presentation.

Williamson's version does suggest the guilt of Claudius, but Claudius also approaches Hamlet in a calm manner, before Hamlet delivers the line, "What frighted with false fire!" Establishment of Claudius's guilt is obviously somewhere between the certainty of Olivier and the absolute failure of Jacobi.

At this point students realize that readings of the mousetrap scene (and perhaps all of Shakespeare) are open to individual interpretation. We then turn to Franco Zeffirelli's 1990 version of *Hamlet* with Mel Gibson as Hamlet and Glenn Close as Gertrude. Gibson's version of Hamlet is the one that students may have seen since Gibson himself is a screen attraction for today's youth. And this version depends in part on the audience's lack of familiarity with the sequence of this scene. The players enter to juggle, tumble, and entertain; Hamlet turns to Ophelia and instructs her "to get thee to a nunnery." The purists among my students are appalled, but on reflection the lines, recalling the earlier nunnery scene, seem in some way absolutely appropriate. Can Shakespeare be changed, improved, challenged?

This version further challenges our understanding of the scene when Hamlet responds to the prologue's introductory comments, "Is this a prologue, or the posy of a ring?" We are stunned when Gertrude, not Ophelia responds, "'tis brief, my son." The substitution of son for Ophelia's lord is appropriate, but how do we react to the idea that it is Hamlet's mother who has responded? One student commented that he preferred that reaction since it emphasized the concern of Hamlet for his mother's sexuality.

Gibson's version also emphasizes the idea that Hamlet has trapped Claudius. Again dropping the exchange between Hamlet and Ophelia before the final confrontation between Hamlet and Claudius, the Gibson version has Hamlet lean close to Claudius and confide: "This is one Lucianus, nephew to the king." But it is Claudius who takes Ophelia's line and replies, "You are as good as a chorus, my cousin" (for Lord). In the performance at that moment on the screen, if we willingly ignore our knowledge of the text, I and my students conclude that it works, for it emphasizes what is most crucial at that moment, the confrontation between Hamlet and Claudius.

Is it worth it to spend so much time on this one scene for an undergraduate course? Each student or teacher will have to answer for himself or herself. And, of course, there are other scenes from many other plays that could be used, but what is clear is that students do come away from the exercise with a sense both of the difficulty of interpreting and performing Shakespeare's text and of the many possibilities of creative and challenging rereadings of a particular scene. Is it wrong to conclude that Mel Gibson or Derek Jacobi has actually improved Shakespeare for our students?

References

The Riverside Shakespeare. 1974. Ed. G. Blakemore Evans. Boston: Houghton Mifflin Co.

Hamlet. 1948. Directed by Laurence Olivier. Hamlet played by Laurence Olivier. 155 minutes.

Hamlet. 1964. Directed by Tony Richardson. Hamlet played by Nicol Williamson. 114 minutes.

Hamlet. BBC Series. Directed by Rodney Bennett. Hamlet played by Derek Jacobi.

Hamlet. 1990. Directed by Franco Zeffirelli. Hamlet played by Mel Gibson. 135 minutes.

CHAPTER 22

Problems with *Othello* in the High School Classroom

Leila Christenbury
Virginia Commonwealth University
Richmond, Virginia

Christenbury explores matters of race in the teaching of Othello *at the secondary level. It is her belief that "the specter of race" is central to the play and that this "uncomfortable fact is . . . one of the major reasons that Shakespeare's great and grave play is not taught more frequently in high school English classes." She argues for honesty and completeness in classroom presentations and urges teachers not to "sidestep the issue of race." She provides a useful series of questions that will help teachers introduce the issue and help students begin to recognize connections between their own experiences and those dramatized in the play.*

> The black man insists, by whatever means he finds at his disposal,
> that the white man cease to regard him as an exotic rarity and
> recognize him as a human being.
>
> *James Baldwin, "Stranger in the Village" (1993, 72)*

*V*ersion the First: The title character of this play is a mature general, veteran of many battles. The main female character is a sheltered young woman who is impressed by the warrior's tales of war and danger. Against all probability, they fall in love. Shortly after, in an audacious act, they defy her father and marry. Yet love does not conquer all: in a series of tragic misunderstandings, largely due to the general's inherent character flaws and the wife's unshakable naiveté, the marriage disintegrates. Mars and Venus are incompatible. In despair, the general kills his wife and then, when he realizes his misunderstanding and her complete innocence, kills himself. The marriage is thus dissolved, and the society mourns the tragedy and the loss to humanity.

Version the Second: The title character of this play is a black man. The main female character is white. Against all probability, they fall in love. Shortly after, in an audacious act, they defy the surrounding white society and marry. Yet love does not conquer all: in a series of tragic misunderstandings deliberately engineered by the black man's secretly racist white "friend," the husband comes to distrust the wife. Black and white are incompatible. Egged on by his friend, and scorned and isolated by white society, the black man kills the white woman and then, when be realizes he has been duped and betrayed, kills himself. The marriage is thus dissolved, and the white society quietly returns to the status quo.

To What Degree Does Race Matter in *Othello*?

While there are a number of versions and explanations of *Othello, Moor of Venice*, if we were to circumscribe the interpretive world to the above two, which would be the more accurate? Does *Othello* largely turn on the issue of race? Does it, on the other hand, deal only with the subject of the difficulty of love and trust and with the arenas of war and society and their incompatibility? Is Othello's race central to the play? Is it peripheral? Borrowing from the inventive title of Cornel West's influential 1993 book, to what extent does *Othello* address race matters and, further, to what extent does race really matter in this play?

It is my belief that race does indeed matter in *Othello*. And that intransigent, uncomfortable fact is, I think, one of the major reasons that Shakespeare's great and grave play is not taught more frequently in high school English classes. *Othello* raises the specter of race and that fact, for many teachers, overshadows its literary merit, its relative difficulty, or even its relevance to secondary students. Like its sister *The Merchant of Venice*, which touches on the unpleasant subject of anti-Semitism, part and parcel of *Othello* is the topic of racism. While, as mentioned before, there are a number of important additional themes (appearance vs. reality, good and evil, innocence and knowledge, the consequences of a tragic flaw, the conflict between the military and domestic life, the limits of friendship between and within the two sexes), a central question of the play is the degree to which *Othello* is the story of a black man confronting a white world—and losing. As Cornel West tells us, race indeed does matter.

Race Matters, Teachers, and Students

I have no definitive answer to what degree race matters in *Othello*. This is, appropriately, the territory of a reader's interpretation and a reader's experience, and while I have reacted over the years in varying ways to *Othello*, my point here is that teachers need to be aware of race, the topic of racism, and must be prepared to let their students explore, argue, and debate not just the themes of the tragic flaw, of trust, innocence, friendship, and self-deception, but, inescapably, also the theme of race.

For teachers and students reading *Othello*, the question of race can be an uneasy one. Certainly, any reader's answer to that question greatly influences the interpretation of the play. Further, different students and different classes will—and can—come to markedly different interpretations of *Othello, The Moor of Venice*. Regardless of differing interpretation, however, it is simply not acceptable to read and discuss *Othello* and sidestep the issue of race. While not every line of the play hammers home the point that Othello is black—and every other character in the play is white—there is quite sufficient comment and remark within the dialogue as well as underlying the plot to make the race of the characters a significant, if not the most significant, factor in this tragedic masterpiece.

Background and Summary

Othello, known as the Moor of Venice (the subtitle of the play and a phrase which recurs repeatedly throughout the five acts), is a renowned general from foreign parts who is in service to the city of Venice. The war business is currently slow, however, and Othello has found himself in town with time on his hands. In the company of one of his lieutenants, the faithful and kind Michael Cassio, he has wooed—and won—the beautiful and shy Desdemona, daughter of Brabantio, one of the town luminaries. Desdemona and Othello, at the play's opening, have eloped in an interracial marriage, the fact—and scandal—of which is reported at night to Desdemona's unwitting father. Brabantio, awakened from sleep to hear that his only daughter has taken off with the "sooty" (1.2.70) Moor, is horrified.

The news of the couple's elopement comes from one of Desdemona's disappointed suitors, Roderigo, and, more importantly, from one of Othello's ostensibly faithful ensigns, Iago. The two meet in the street and, under Brabantio's bedroom window, shout the details— including bawdy speculations regarding the couple's nocturnal embraces. It is not a decorous scene, and Brabantio, shocked and alarmed, rushes to the Duke of Venice to force the eloped pair to return and to nullify their union.

Othello, greatly in love with Desdemona and confident that "my parts, my title, and my perfect soul / Shall manifest me rightly" (1.2.31–32) appears calmly before the Duke with his bride. Both detail their courtship, declare their love and harmony and, while Brabantio is bitterly disappointed in his daughter's choice of husband, the Duke allows the couple to continue their union in peace.

But peace is not to be had. Iago, Othello's ensign, is, for varying reasons (all of which he offers at differing times in the play and none of which is wholly convincing) determined to bring the great general down. Now that Othello is married to Desdemona, Iago sets cunning trap after trap and, expertly using Othello's own explosive nature, he makes the general believe that the young bride Desdemona is unfaithful and treacherous. Along the way, Iago schemes against the gullible Cassio, getting him drunk and causing Othello to suspect him. Further, Iago funds some of his plans using the money of the yearning suitor Roderigo, who pays Iago a small fortune in the vain hope that he will be able to bribe Desdemona's affections away from Othello. Iago also gets his unsuspecting wife, Emilia, Desdemona's maid, to cooperate in his plans. Finally, Desdemona, truly unschooled in the treachery of the world, walks blindly into compromising scene after compromising scene and, unwittingly, perfectly cooperates in the deceit and the resulting tragedy.

At the end, Cassio is wounded, Bianca is under suspicion for plotting murder, Roderigo and Emilia are dead, Othello has strangled Desdemona. Othello comes to recognize the web in which he has been trapped and then, in a horrific scene of comprehension and bottomless remorse, he commits suicide and falls upon the body of his dead bride. For his part, Iago is arrested and taken away for punishment but, in one of Shakespeare's great strokes of genius, he refuses to detail his true motivation for the carnage and treachery. Iago exits the stage in silence, forever leaving us to puzzle over the real source of his evil animus.

An Interpretation: Race Does Not Matter

We return to the question to what extent race matters in *Othello*. Certainly, a central issue in the play is the reason Iago would take it upon himself to plot so effectively against Othello, as well as why Iago would so completely desire not just Desdemona's disgrace but her death (he even urges Othello not to poison but to strangle her, 4.1.220-21). Also unanswered is why Othello would so quickly and thoroughly believe Desdemona could be immediately and repeatedly unfaithful to him ("a thousand times committed," 5.2.212) and the swiftness with which others, on the basis of a single incident, lose faith and trust in Othello and believe he has indeed run mad.

Iago, for his part, is clearly out for revenge: "I follow him to serve my turn upon him" (1.1.42). Iago tells Roderigo that he hates Othello because he has been passed up for promotion (1.1.8-11) and that he suspects Othello may have been intimate with his own wife, Emilia (1.3.392-93), a suspicion Emilia acknowledges but scorns. Possibly, however, it is Iago's feelings of hatred for the good which inspire him to plot against the great Othello. As he remarks of Cassio, "he hath a daily beauty in his life which makes me ugly" (5.1.19-20), a nasty little sentiment that certainly reveals Iago's patent dislike of the good and the innocent.

Iago's animus against Desdemona can be explained by his misogyny, his dislike of women and of wives. He taunts Emilia with her "changeable" nature and scorns Bianca repeatedly for being promiscuous. Yet he notes that he knows Desdemona is pure and that, in a way, he loves her (2.2.300).

Why Othello could believe Desdemona's unfaithfulness can be seen as part and parcel of his character. Like the Duke, who makes his unchangeable will explicit (1.3.65-70), Othello is a man who makes up his mind and then sticks to his decision. While some could see this as an admirable trait, it can surely backfire if the facts upon which such inflexible decisions are based are incorrect. Othello, once convinced, believes surely and completely. Why Othello needs to kill Desdemona—not just disgrace her—may be part of his warlike character.

The distrust of others can be explained by their unfamiliarity with Othello in domestic matters: they know the general on the battlefield, not in the drawing room. Perhaps seeing him in a less warlike scene, they judge him quickly and harshly.

An Interpretation: Race Does Matter

The explanations for the above could also be attributed to racism: as a black man Othello is not playing on a level field. Beyond the usual envy of those less successful for those who are brilliant and achieving, Othello attracts a high degree of animosity. Certainly it is plausible that others hate and despise him in particular because of his color. This hatred, it can be argued, is intensified when the black Othello moves from being a brilliant hired gun for Venice to presume social parity (through marriage to Desdemona) within its society. By attracting, winning, and marrying a well-born, desirable white daughter of Venice, Othello has crossed a barrier. He has violated, in essence, a code, and others are only too willing to believe the worst of him in questionable circumstances.

Aware that he indeed may not be treated as others are, Othello is only too vulnerable to the possibility that his beautiful, white wife might be unfaithful. Certainly he has watched others turn on him once he "overstepped" his bounds and married Desdemona: Brabantio and others turn away in disgust. It is only, actually, Cassio, Desdemona, and the Duke who continue steadfast in their high opinion of Othello. But, thanks to Iago, Cassio and

Desdemona are vanquished and, in Shakespeare's play, the Duke ceases to be a force after the first act.

Othello the Man

Within the context of the play, Othello the black man does not verbally confront his white world. He does not, as Shylock does, call upon the characters—and the audience—to witness to his universal humanity and treat him as they would treat others. Othello does not trumpet his race nor highlight it nor rail against what might have been previous inequities and difficulties. At the opening of the play, we see him at his height: he has been successful in the service of Venice and, clearly, enjoys the great respect of the Duke. While he has endured much as a military man, including slavery, if anything, his comments about himself reveal self-deprecation and a wistful understanding of the limitations his race places upon his success. He notes, regarding Desdemona, "For she had eyes, and chose me" (3.3.189), apparently marveling at the miracle that such a beauty could choose such as he. In another observation, he remarks that "Haply, for I am black" and thus does not understand the subtleties of the court (3.3.263–67).

The white world, however, is not so reticent to discuss the race of the general. In the first act and first scene Othello is derided as "thick-lips" (66), an "old black ram" (87), the "devil" (90), and a "Barbary horse" (112) who has literally stolen Desdemona (79–81). Iago speculates that Othello has married Desdemona to advance himself (1.2.50–51) and calls the bridegroom a "barbarian" (1.3.362). So repulsive and ugly is Othello, Desdemona's father asserts, he must have used magic to entrance his bride who, unthinkably, has fled to the "sooty bosom / Of such a thing as thou" (1.2.70). Even when defending the marriage and allowing the couple to remain husband and wife, the otherwise supportive Duke remarks to Brabantio, in a backhanded compliment of sorts, "If virtue no delighted beauty lack / Your son-in-law is far more fair than black" (1.3.290–91).

One of the most consistent and telling pieces of evidence that race is not benign in *Othello* is the fact that the great general is most often identified not by his name nor by his military rank—which has won him fame and renown—but by the fact that he is black, that he is a Moor. Early in the play, in the very first scene when Iago is complaining that Othello did not promote him, the general is scornfully termed "his Moorship" (1.1.33), and the title "Moor" recurs repeatedly (1.1.39, 57, 127, 148, 164, 178). At the end of the play, when all is in disarray, Othello ceases to be a person or even a military man: he is, in multiple separate references in Act 5, scene 2, the "dull Moor" (225), the "cruel Moor" (249), and the "Moor" (167, 240, 249, 366). The use of this term by itself signals a clear reliance upon identification of the man, to quote Martin Luther King, Jr., with the color of his skin, not the content of his character.

Othello's personality is one that makes him fairly rigid. Susceptible to suspicion, once he makes up his mind, he cannot modify or change. As he describes himself to Iago, he is like a tide that cannot turn back (3.3.453–62). Othello is also vulnerable to self-hatred. If Desdemona is unfaithful, her visage is not only dark like Othello's, it is dirty, as we assume he sees his own face: Desdemona is "begrim'd and black / As mine own face" (3.3.387–88). Certainly at the end of the play, when Desdemona is dead and Othello realizes he has been cruelly, completely deceived, he attacks his own self-image. As Peter Erickson argues:

Othello's military vocation keeps him at the margins of the society. He serves Venice at the borderline between "civilization" and "barbarism." Himself an outsider on the inside, he protects Venice from outsiders. The difficulty in maintaining this identity shows in Othello's consternation at the disruption on Cyprus. . . . At the end of the play, Othello crosses back over the line and imagines part of himself as "a malignant and a turban'd Turk" (5.2.353) in order to kill himself. His self-image is destroyed when he himself is pulled into the category of a non-Christian alien against whom he had been commissioned to defend Venice. And this tragic culmination originates in the initial paradox that although Venice needs Othello to defend its purity from foreign barbarism, he is also a source of impurity as defined by Brabantio's unabashed exhibition of racial prejudice. (1985, 86)

Betrayals in a White Society

And, as a black man, Othello is uniquely vulnerable to betrayals in a white society. While we know that Othello was invited frequently to Brabantio's house to eat and share discussions of his notable exploits, that Brabantio "lov'd" (1.3.128) him, once Othello has assumed equal status to his white host (i.e., by marrying his host's daughter), he is despicable, "such a thing as thou." Certainly Brabantio knew that his daughter, in the company of Cassio, listened frequently and avidly to Othello's tales, yet he never assumed that such contact could lead to affection and then love.

Additionally, Emilia, who, we can assume, must have had some kind of cordial relationship with Othello, her mistress's husband, turns bitterly on him at the end and calls Desdemona's marriage to the now-hated Moor a "filthy bargain" (5.2.157) and Othello an even "blacker devil" (5.2.131) than before.

And, when emissaries from Venice, headed by Desdemona's cousin Lodovico, observe Othello both upbraid and strike Desdemona, they are appalled and alarmed. With Iago's help and interpretation, the single incident causes Lodovico to remark, "I am sorry that I am deceiv'd in him" (4.1.293) and to question, "Is this the noble Moor whom our full Senate / Call all in all sufficient?" (4.1.275). One could wonder if a white general, who acted similarly, would lose others' confidence so quickly. As it is, Othello is returning to Venice not in triumph but under a cloud of suspicion and a question, "Are his wits safe?" (4.1.280).

For her part, Desdemona is also irrevocably compromised by marrying out of her race. Because she has chosen Othello, she is akin to the heroine in the original *Hecatommithi* (Giraldi Cinthio's mid-sixteenth-century tale upon which *Othello* is based), who cautions others against following her example and by marriage separating oneself from the group, the tribe. Desdemona, by marrying Othello, has wholly isolated herself. As others remark, Desdemona has sacrificed herself and has "forsook so many noble matches, / Her father and her country and her friends" (4.2.125–26).

Further, it is plausible to at least some of Iago's hearers that Desdemona, who appears shy and reticent and upright ("A maiden never bold; / Of spirit so still and quiet that her motion / Blush'd at herself," 1.3.94–96), is actually a sex-craved woman who has married the Moor out of lust, not love or respect. She has embraced the horrible and the forbidden, doing the impossible and falling "in love with what she fear'd to look on" (1.3.98). Sex, it is assumed, must be the culprit, and even Emilia, who loves Desdemona, wonders about her mistress's choices. Desdemona's own father, too, is puzzled that his chaste daughter could apparently, willingly, choose the black general. While enchantment is mentioned as a possible source of attraction, sex, it is assumed, is the only credible reason that Desdemona could love Othello, the Moor of Venice.

Iago repeatedly sounds this theme although, in private, he gives it little credence. The wedding nuptials, as envisioned by Iago, are crudely termed "making the beast with two backs" (1.1.117–18), and Iago extensively speculates on Desdemona's lust and lechery (2.1.223–65). It is thus easy for Iago to make others believe Desdemona is lascivious and promiscuous. Using, appropriately enough, racial imagery, Iago's hope is that through sexual innuendo he can "turn her [Desdemona's] virtue into pitch," (2.3.366) and thus destroy Othello.

Teaching *Othello*

It is hoped that the above outlines the degree to which the issue of race can be addressed in the teaching of *Othello*. Certainly senior high school students are ready to tackle this important and often difficult subject. Shakespeare does not make Othello's race incidental or unimportant; thus, when we teach the play we must teach it fully and, essentially, honestly.

James Baldwin's words, cited at the opening of this piece, are pertinent. Othello is, most importantly, a human being and not an exotic rarity. He is also, however, a black human being, and that inescapable fact shapes him, shapes the play, and must shape our reading and reaction to *Othello, Moor of Venice*.

Some questions which students might want to consider before and during reading *Othello* follow. While final answers are more than likely unattainable, considering the issue of to what degree race matters in *Othello, Moor of Venice* will more authentically serve a reading of this great play.

Discussion Questions for Students

Race as a Concept.

We often refer to a person's "race." What is "race" and how is it defined in the dictionary? By you and your peers? How descriptive is *race* in today's society? Does it mean the same in your school as in, for example, a school in Miami or New York City or San Francisco or Seattle? What does *race* mean in *Othello*? In any of these settings, how does *race* function: what are its limits? advantages? disadvantages?

The Limits of Race.

Thinking of what you know and have experienced of *race*, how do you think it specifically influences a person and his or her attitudes? values? perceptions? Turning to *Othello*, in your opinion to what degree can we separate what is Othello's "core" character or personality and what is Othello's experience as a black man? Can you speculate how differently Othello might have reacted to certain events if he were *not* black?

Interracial Relationships.

In Cornel West's *Race Matters,* the writer has a chapter entitled "Black Sexuality" in which he observes that "White fear of black sexuality is a basic ingredient of white racism. . . . Social scientists have long acknowledged that interracial sex and marriage is the most *perceived* source of white fear of black people" (1993, 86). To what extent do you agree with West's assessment? What in your opinion are the limitations (if any) on interracial friendships? Interracial romantic relationships? Interracial marriage? Integrated workplaces? Integrated churches? Integrated schools? How willing do you judge your school community to be to tolerate interracial institutions and couples?

Changing Race Roles.

Imagine Othello is white and the locale is no longer white Venice but black Dakar. To what extent would Othello's professional standing be altered? His relationship with his men? His marriage to Desdemona? His feelings?

"Race" in Other Literature: Three Examples

1. James Baldwin's "Stranger in the Village" is an essay about the black American writer living in the Caucasian Swiss Alps and a meditation on black and white relations in the United States. Read "Stranger" and consider this passage:

> The cathedral at Chartres . . . says something to the people of this village which it cannot say to me; but it is important to understand that this cathedral says something to me which it cannot say to them. Perhaps they are struck by the power of the spires, the glory of the windows; but they have known God, after all, longer than I have known him, and in a different way, and I am terrified by the slippery bottomless well to be found in the crypt, down which heretics were hurled to death, and by the obscene, inescapable gargoyles jutting out of the stone and seeming to say that God and the devil can never be divorced. I doubt that the villagers think of the devil when they face a cathedral because they have never been identified with the devil. But I must accept the status which myth, if nothing else, gives me in the West before I can hope to change the myth. (76)

What is Baldwin's point about cultural differences? About the myth of black people being identified with the devil? How might his point relate to today? To the issues and perceptions of those issues raised in *Othello*?

2. During Dr. Martin Luther King, Jr.'s "I Have a Dream" speech made during the March on Washington in 1963, King spoke for many African Americans when he said that he hoped his four children would one day "live in a nation where they will not be judged by the color of their skin, but the content of their character." What did he mean? How might this relate to *Othello*?

3. Young adult writer Julius Lester's *Othello: A Novel* has turned Shakespeare's play into fiction, placing it in sixteenth-century England. In his interpretation (which Lester calls a

"reconceptualization"), he adds two characters, the King and Desdemona's mother, makes Iago and Emilia Africans, and more clearly highlights the issue of race and racism. Read Julius Lester's *Othello: A Novel* and consider how it is different from Shakespeare's play. To what extent do you agree with Lester's reconceptualization? Does it deepen your understanding of the original work? Does it change it? If you were William Shakespeare, would you approve of what Lester has done? Would you object to it? Why or why not?

References

Baldwin, James. 1993. "Stranger in the Village." In *In Depth: Essayists for Our Time,* 2d ed. Edited by Carl Klaus, Chris Anderson, and Rebecca Faery. New York: Harcourt Brace.

Erickson, Peter. 1985. *Patriarchal Structures in Shakespeare's Drama.* Berkeley: University of California Press.

King, Martin Luther, Jr. 1992. *I Have a Dream: Writings and Speeches that Changed the World.* Ed. James Melvin Washington. San Francisco: HarperSanFrancisco.

Lester, Julius. 1995. *Othello: A Novel.* New York: Scholastic.

Shakespeare, William. 1942. *Othello.* In *The Complete Plays and Poems of William Shakespeare,* ed. William Allan Neilson and Charles Jarvis Hill. New York: Houghton Mifflin.

West, Cornel. 1993. *Race Matters.* Boston: Beacon Press.

V

Beyond the Text

CHAPTER 23

Uses of Media in Teaching Shakespeare

H. R. COURSEN
University of Maine
Augusta, Maine

This section focuses on a variety of extra-textual possibilities: stage, film, television, animation, and festivals. Coursen describes some of the advantages of comparative productions; when students contrast elements of different productions, he claims, "their writing takes a leap towards maturity." He also recommends a further use of television in the teaching of Shakespeare: "the trial format for dealing with the issues of a given play." In this approach, an issue is identified (for example, Othello's killing of Desdemona), the class is formed into the components of a trial (judge, jury, witnesses, etc.), and the exercise can be videotaped for further discussion and analysis. Coursen concludes that "the media, even if anti-creative in themselves, can be part of the process of education."

Where two or more productions of the same script are available, the contrast between productions can suggest invaluably to students of Shakespeare that no "right" version of a scene or a speech exists, indeed that manifold options are available to actors. Those options are themselves conditioned by the medium—stage, film, television, or some combination—of the production.

We teach what we enjoy, what we feel comfortable doing—the trick is to empower ourselves. This power then can become available to our students. One option is to have students pick an element as it occurs in different productions. As they do so, students notice differences and begin to describe them. Their writing takes a leap towards maturity, an inevitable consequence of their suddenly enhanced powers of observation. If they present their contrasting versions on cassette to the class—a good approach in a small seminar—the class itself contributes to the process of perception, so that a "corporate mind" is energized, as opposed to the single student struggling at the eleventh hour with a paper he or she is not interested in based on a topic only dimly defined, at best, or selected from a list of the instructor's devising.

However, "researchers have concluded that watching any TV show is a meaninglessly passive activity" (Tashman 1994, 21). Indeed, Paul Robinson argues that, rather than promote the illusion that television can educate—"it can't," he says—"Complete ignorance really would be preferable, because ignorance at least preserves a mental space that might someday be filled with real knowledge, or some approximation of it" (1978, 14). TV can be an element in the educational process, however. "On a recent Sunday, Joanna Cleveland made sure she had a supply of chips and soda at home because her daughter, Meghan, was expecting friends. The teenagers, sophomores at South Portland High, spent the afternoon talking, joking and having a marvelous time—all over a video of '*Julius Caesar*'" (Lau 1994, 1A).

Many teachers in the late 1970s and early 1980s plopped their students down to stare at some very bad BBC-TV productions. The students were bored and the teachers were put in the false position of trying to defend, say, that terrible *Romeo and Juliet* or that cramped *Julius Caesar*. But the quality of the productions was not the only issue. TV as static medium induces passivity; like any machine it has to have a purpose and—in most cases—the content of the machine does not provide purpose, even on a cathode tube. The radar sweep showing the weather, for example, does not recommend response. Response is a function of interpretation.

Here is a simple project that a student might select: contrast two versions of the "Yorick" sequence, as rendered by Olivier in his film and McKellen in the 1971 television version.

Olivier the performer never lets us forget that he is an actor playing a role, greatly playing a role, of course, chuckling ever so slightly as some dirt falls from Yorick's skull. The dirt reminds us of the sand falling in an hour glass and is a metonymy for the lawyer's fine pate full of fine dirt, a line cut in the film. Olivier does not make the mistake of the amateur actor of knowing what comes next, but he is always in control, and, at the end, sits in the throne in a production without Fortinbras. McKellen permits his character to go out of control, totally fascinated by the skull with a finger, sniffing that finger, then thrusting the grisly object at a Horatio who is clearly not enjoying this pause and whose own gorge may be rising? We get two very different acting styles—each right for the actor and his conception of the role and for the moment in which the play is being sent outward into its *zeitgeist*—the late forties in one instance and the early seventies in the other.

The Yorick sequence permits other questions to be raised. The design of the scene brings Hamlet from disquisitions about death to increasingly specific confrontations with it—to Yorick, whom he knew and loved, to Ophelia, whom he knew and loved—and into contact with the men who will kill him and whom he will kill—Claudius and Laertes. The sequence permits the historian of ideas to talk about "Yorick" as the culmination of the *memento mori* tradition, made remarkably available here by dint of its being rendered in a theater by a character the audience would, in all probability, have identified with. Why is Ophelia buried in Yorick's grave? She has been a jester, of course—a speaker of truth in song and rhyme—and may represent "the feminine," as it has been argued Yorick did to the very young Hamlet.

Some students really are knowledgeable about the media that dominate our culture. Excerpts from *different* media—film, which emerges from the silent screen, where images alternated with the print of title cards; television, which stems from radio and absorbs more of the spoken word than does film; and stage, with its recent movement out from under the proscenium arch—can engage students in the important questions attendant on the conceptual spaces in which the plays are produced. Space defines what can occur within it. In the Yorick contrast, some students will notice that Olivier's deep-field, black and white photography allows for considerable depth of field, while the McKellen color version for television is much more a close-up version of the play. It should be obvious that teaching with taped performance materials complements the approach wherein students deploy themselves in available spaces to make the moves that the scenes seem to dictate. The two approaches inform each other. It is a good idea, it seems to me, to have students look at a professional production on tape after they themselves have mastered a scene in their own way. They will probably prefer their own way and be able to defend it cogently.

If we contrast two versions of a line by Fortinbras, one in which Robert Coleby (in the 1970 Hallmark production) says "Take up the bodies," and another in which Don Reilly (in the 1990 Kline production for PBS) says "Take up the body," we can make some points about texts and the options they present.

One is clearing an open stage of bodies, even on television. The other is, perhaps, using a single body that would have proved "most royal had *he* been put on" the throne as part of a combination funeral/coronation, similar to the one that Claudius, obviously, conducted much earlier. Fortinbras, knowing that he has the "voice" (or vote) of the men, who was briefly King Hamlet the Second, will use that fragment of body politic to consolidate his own "rights of memory in this kingdom." The choice between Q2's "bodies" and F's "body" is not a quibble. The decision as to singular or plural tells us whether, in choosing the singular—meaning Hamlet's body—Fortinbras is thinking of his own plurality as king. The moment in contrasting performances permits us to talk about textual variations, to introduce the concept of the king's two bodies, and to ask students to defend their own choices on this and other notorious textual alternatives, like the "Judean/Indian" crux in *Othello*.

One goal in having students look at Shakespeare in different media is to get them to examine the nature of the media themselves. As one who remembers World War II vividly, I am haunted by the possibility that the German people might have understood how they were being manipulated—by Leni Reifenstahl's *Triumph of the Will,* for example—if they had had a grasp of how the media work. This is probably an ongoing fear, and a growing one, since we seem to be educating the manipulators, the people with a stake in the system of indoctrination, as Noam Chomsky would say, and making sure that the proliferating underclass lacks any vestiges of formal education. When students recognize that television is an outgrowth of radio, they can begin to understand some of the assumptions and limitations of TV. If students know that films come from the *silent* screen they can answer other questions. Special effects, so important to recent films, from *Raiders of the Lost Ark* to *Frankenstein,* are a product of the silent screen, though techniques have become more sophisticated since 1925. But elaborate special effects, so powerful in the darkened auditorium that faces a huge screen, are diminished on television, where the depth of field is shallow. Television has a "normalizing" tendency, so that the supernatural tends to become, on television, the product of a single disturbed psyche, as opposed to an aberration in the cosmos. Television should be a good medium for Shakespeare because, coming from radio as it does and having a small screen, it can and must contain more words than film. Television, however, unlike film, cannot contain the larger scenes of a Shakespearean script or suggest the supernatural, as film, obviously, can. The shots in television are simpler and tend, with the development of standard techniques, to incorporate a close-up, a reaction shot, and a two-shot in their three-camera format. Films *made* for television tend towards televisual values—their camera techniques, "naturalism," and shallow field. All of these considerations, of course, impinge on the question of Shakespeare on film or on television and on the complicated issue of televised live performance of a Shakespeare play, of which many examples are available. Does the fact of an audience help recreate a sense of live performance? Does stage performance, with its tendency towards exaggeration and projection, translate to a medium where "micro-acting" tends to be the rule? Can the three-camera format work with a stage production? Suffice it that we cannot begin to evaluate the production until we examine the medium into which the script is projected. These may seem like very sophisticated questions, but they can elicit enthusiasm and intelligent response from students. Film and TV are, after all, the media they claim for their own. We teachers can enlist that claim and energize it within agendas that help students deconstruct effectively as opposed to vegetating.

I stress the issue of media because a new and influential book on teaching Shakespeare, *Setting Shakespeare Free,* is dangerously ignorant on this point.

A further field that students enjoy exploring and writing about is Shakespeare in contemporary culture. In *Star Trek VI: The Undiscovered Country,* for example, Kirk and McCoy are sentenced to the lithium mines on the penal asteroid of Rura Penthe—"The Aliens' Graveyard." Martia, a fellow captive, offers to help them escape beyond the security shield so that they can be beamed up to their home ship. She is a Chameloid, or "Shapeshifter," who shifts from her green-eyed basis to alien male, to young girl to get rid of her leg irons. When she becomes Martia again, Kirk questions whether she really *is* as she seems. "I thought I would assume a pleasing shape," she says. The line is Hamlet's, of course: "The devil hath power to assume a pleasing shape," and represents an extension of Shakespeare's treatment of appearance versus reality into the 40th Century. When Kirk sees through her plot to betray him and McCoy, she becomes Kirk. "I can't believe I *kissed* you!" says Kirk. "It was probably your lifelong ambition," says his alter ego in a neat allusion to his narcissism. Fortunately for the real Kirk, the Rura Penthe constabulary vaporize his hapless imitator and Kirk and McCoy are beamed up in the nick of time.

Another possible use of television in the teaching of Shakespeare is the trial format for dealing with the issues of a given play (cf. Boynton and Carducci 1993). Here, an issue is defined. The class is formed into the components of a trial: judge, jury, defendants, witnesses, defense and prosecution teams. Topics are manifold, of course; a sampling of the possibilities includes Bolingbroke's defense of his premature return from banishment to England, Othello's defense of his killing of Desdemona, Caliban's suit against Prospero for damages and recovery of property, Angelo's culpability in *Measure for Measure,* etc. The trial, of course, with its intrinsic dramatic form, formatted setting, stereotypical characters, and opportunities for reaction shots, has long been a standard subject for film and television, from Fritz Lang's *Rage* to Perry Mason and *The Defenders.* The recent rise of *Court TV,* and its televising of the trials of Pamela Smart, William Smith, the Menendez brothers, et al., provides a possible format for a camcorder here, and the recent mock trial of Hamlet, held in an elegant room at the Supreme Court, could serve as a model.[1]

In the latter case, the tape itself will reward careful study and comment. Associate

Justice Anthony M. Kennedy, who presides, defines the case against Hamlet around a "narrow issue": Was Hamlet, at the time of his killing of Polonius, capable of understanding the criminality of his conduct or of conforming his conduct to the requirements of the law?

Hamlet has been allowed to survive Laertes' apparently fatal thrust, but "all questions of his accession to the throne of Denmark have been held in abeyance" until his criminal responsibility has been established. If he is found to be insane at the time of his killing of Polonius, he will be committed to a mental institution. If the jury finds him sane, he is criminally responsible and will be tried for anything from involuntary manslaughter to first degree murder. If the latter charge were to be brought, it would be based, one assumes, on Hamlet's soliloquy as he decides not to kill the apparently praying Claudius and on his belief that the person behind the arras *is* Claudius ("I took thee for thy better").

The jurors are the arbiters of fact, Kennedy suggests, the judge merely the interpreter of the law. The evidence is made up of the text of *Hamlet* (the conflated text, one assumes) and the testimony of expert witnesses. The facts in this instance are not contested. Hamlet did kill Polonius. The mental condition of the defendant at the time of the killing is the jury's only concern. In this case, the defense has the burden of proof to show that the preponderance of evidence demonstrates that Hamlet was not criminally responsible at the time he killed Polonius. That means "more probably than not," as opposed to "beyond a reasonable doubt."

The defense, represented by the expert testimony of Dr. Thomas Gutheil of Harvard Yard, is that Hamlet shows no emotion as he kills Polonius — "how now, a rat?" — nor remorse afterwards. Those who know Hamlet best all attest to his madness. He is "mad as the sea," his mother says. Furthermore, Hamlet hallucinates, as proved by his seeing the Ghost in Gertrude's closet, an apparition invisible and inaudible to her. Hamlet suffers from what was once called manic depression, now termed bi-polar illness in Hamlet's case, of the rapid cycling form. This is a disease of the mood in which the victim alternates between elation and depression. Its manic phase manifests itself in hyper-sexuality, babbling speech, episodes of inappropriate hostility, and a grandiose sense of mission. The depressive symptoms are suicidal tendencies, loss of pleasure, bad dreams, loss of contact with the environment, and loss of a sense of right and wrong. Results of this illness for Hamlet are his inability to understand that he has killed someone, meaning that he a) did not have the mental capacity to appreciate his criminality or b) did not have the ability to conform his conduct with the requirements of the law. If a policeman were standing next to him at the time he heard Polonius behind the arras, he would have behaved the same way. To *fake* mental illness, the defense argues, is for the mentally ill person to claim mastery over his illness. The secondary gain is that the faking achieves something for its practitioner. But Hamlet gains nothing from it, as proved by his inappropriate hostility to Ophelia. "To conclude that his conduct is sometimes inappropriate is like saying that his father died of an earache."

The prosecution argues that Hamlet's "antic disposition" is a defense against a King who has killed Hamlet's father, and against Polonius and Rosencrantz and Guildenstern and even Ophelia, who are spying on Hamlet. He is an intelligent man constantly aware of the precariousness of his situation. His feigning does not show diminution but enhanced capacity. It is essential to his survival. What triggers his melancholia are actual events, and, according to Dr. Alan Stone, also of Harvard Yard, if someone did not respond as Hamlet has done, "we would have a madman on our hands." Hamlet *is* spied upon and is therefore not delusional. He *is* a prince and does not then embrace a grandiose vision ("O cursed spite, that ever I was born to set [the time] right.") That's his mission. As a student of philosophy, Hamlet is profound, not merely suicidal. Camus's statement on suicide would be a modern example of Hamlet's exploration of the consequences of human action, including "self-slaughter." Hamlet does experience a grief reaction, complicated by his mother's behavior. Madness means that a person is trapped within himself—as *Ophelia* is—but Hamlet devises a "reality check," the play-within-a-play, and appoints an independent witness, in Horatio, who agrees with Hamlet's interpretation of Claudius's reaction to "The Murder of Gonzago." He shows a remarkable ability to *control* his impulses when he decides not to kill an apparently praying Claudius. As for those who claim that Hamlet is mad, Polonius is "mistaken and wrong-headed," says Stone. Although Ophelia goes mad after her father is slain by someone close to her who goes unpunished for the crime, Hamlet, a victim of similar circumstances, does not go mad. It is a matter of contrast, not a parallel case.

The prosecution argues that to hold Hamlet responsible is to offer him his only chance at vindication, presumably at a trial at which he could be acquitted. The defense counters that Hamlet "is a sick boy who needs help." It is enjoyable to see lawyers do with *Hamlet* what literary critics have done for years, that is, take the same evidence and draw from it diametrically different conclusions.

The verdict of the jury, which includes Associate Justice Ruth Bader Ginsburg, is that Hamlet is "criminally responsible" for killing Polonius. The jury recommends to the prosecution that it "investigate whether Hamlet should be held criminally responsible for the destruction of Ophelia."

The latter recommendation represents a knotty assignment, as does the question of Ophelia's suicide. *Is* it suicide?

The prosecution's case could be strengthened in several ways. That Dr. Stone believes in ghosts does not mean that Hamlet is not hallucinating the Ghost in Gertrude's closet. If the written text—as opposed to the performed script—is the evidence, however, one must argue that the Ghost's lines, which are there in the text, constitute a remarkable feat of ventriloquism on Hamlet's part. He projects a voice out that returns from his hallucination only to him. "It is not possible," says the defense's witness, Dr. Gutheil, "for a hallucination to tell you something that you don't know. It's your mind." While it can be argued that the Ghost represents Hamlet's repressed a) anxiety about delay and b) empathy with his mother, the Ghost's words on the parapets and later in Gertrude's closet do exist on the authority of the text, not just on the basis of Hamlet's belief that he hears them. In the John Barton production of 1980, Gertrude *did* see the Ghost, but kept that to herself. Suffice it that a key argument of the defense—that the hearing of voices is a classic symptom of manic depression—can be refuted on the basis of the evidence. Dr. Stone counters the defense's claim that Hamlet accosts Gertrude "on her bed," but could have been more assertive. The bed, after all, does not appear until Gielgud's famous production of the 1930s. In the illustration in Rowe's 1709 edition, based on a stage *Hamlet,* the Ghost enters what is obviously a sitting room. On that point, Michael Kahn, under whose auspices this trial was conducted, might have been helpful. Furthermore, the prosecution could have adduced some "precedents"—the protective "madness" of Junius Brutus, and of characters like Hieronimo and Malevole. Furthermore, Hamlet does say of Polonius, "For this same lord, I do repent me," and it could be argued that Claudius knows Hamlet's behavior is "not like madness," but that the useful official view must be that "Madness in great ones must not unwatch'd go." It may be, as Dover Wilson argues and as the Olivier film shows, that Hamlet knows that Claudius and Polonius are eavesdropping on his meeting with Ophelia and that that knowledge motivates his otherwise inappropriate hostility. Furthermore, if others at the play scene can hear his remarks to Ophelia, his "hyper-sexuality" can also be explained as part of his antic disposition, and not a symptom of mental incapacity.

In the hubbub after Justice Kennedy gavels the trial to a close, the actor playing Hamlet can be heard telling Kennedy, "I had a great time." We notice, however, that he is not called to testify in his own defense.

Since this trial is very much an anachronism, applying recent psychiatric theory to an early-seventeenth-century killing, it would have been helpful for someone to "historicize" the moment, giving us a sense of how the law, as Justice Kennedy says, "was beginning to change when Shakespeare wrote." Early modern England was, in this instance as in so many others, a testing ground for the new or evolving concepts that so deeply inform these plays. It would have been helpful as well for someone to provide an outline of the "insanity defense," beginning with Henry de Bracton in the 1400s on the legal consequences of mental disorder, moving on to Lord Hale's "child of 14 test," and Justice Tracy's "wild beast test," which stems from Bracton. Perhaps the first real insanity defense was in the Hadfield Case (1800), where Thomas Erskine put forward the concept of "delusion" as the "true character of insanity," and convinced the court. The McNaughton Rules, formulated in 1843, became the basis of subsequent jurisprudence. They say that "the party accused . . . was laboring under such a defect of reason, from disease of mind, as not to know the nature and quality of the act he was doing; or if he did know it, that he did not know he was doing what was wrong." The issue, of course, is the condition of the defendant at the time of the crime, and the debate has diverged—in the U.S. "morality" has tended to be the definition of "wrong," while in Great Britain it has been "contrary to the law." Critics point out that the problem with the McNaughton Rules is that they stress the element of "rationality," and present an old-fashioned model of how mind and psyche function. One of the first "modern" insanity defenses was that of Clarence Darrow in 1925. In defending Leopold and Loeb, Darrow argued they murdered Bobby Franks: "They killed him as they might kill a spider or a fly," Darrow said. In the U.S. the "irresistible impulse test" has emerged out of dissatisfaction with the McNaughton Rules. "Partial insanity" or "diminished responsibility" can affect the element of premeditation, a factor of great importance in capital cases. And so on—the topic is a good one for research for future law students or defendants in murder cases.

The media dominate our lives and those of our students. We can deplore that fact or we can do our best to befriend it. The media, even if anti-creative in themselves, can be part of the process of education.

Notes

1. For information on obtaining the tape: C-Span Viewer Services, 400 North Capital Street, Suite 650, Washington, D.C. 20001, (202) 737-3220.

References

Boynton, Vicki, and Jane Carducci. 1993. "Angelo and the Mock Trial Experience in the College Classroom." *Shakespeare and the Classroom* 1.2:13.

Lau, Eddie. 1994. "Parents Part of Teaching Team." *Portland Press Herald,* 4 October, 1A.

O'Brien, Peggy, ed. 1993–94. *Setting Shakespeare Free,* vols. 1 and 2. New York: Washington Square Press.

Robinson, Paul. 1978. "TV Can't Educate." *New Republic,* 5 and 12 August, 13–15.

Tashman, Billie. 1994. "Sorry Ernie—TV Isn't Teaching." *New York Times,* 12 November, 21.

CHAPTER 24

Teaching Shakespeare through Film

LINDA KISSLER

Westmoreland County Community College
Youngwood, Pennsylvania

Kissler encourages the teaching of Henry V, *a play that is not anthologized often and one frequently disparaged or ignored by critics. She claims that, with some of her suggestions for the use of videotapes, it can be "an amazingly simple one to teach at almost any level." Class session by class session, she details her approach, the specific videocassette clips she shows, the homework assignments, student mock interviews of characters, and other useful activities.*

"Once more unto the breach, dear friends, once more, / Or close the wall up with our English dead!" With these dynamic words Shakespeare's King Henry V of England urges his half-starved, dysentery-ridden soldiers to continue storming the French town of Harfleur. Rousing as these words may seem to someone well-versed in Shakespearean rhetoric, to the average student—alone with a text—they sometimes fall alarmingly flat. How to make Henry's bombastic patriotism—and the overwhelming heroics of the play itself—come alive for today's students? Ah, there's the rub . . .

Henry V is not a play that is anthologized often. It has been ignored by scores of critics, disparaged or misunderstood by countless others. It has presented challenges for both actors and directors. Yet, it is quite simply a good play—and an amazingly simple one to teach at almost any level. It also offers teachers a unique opportunity to utilize videotapes in the classroom setting, often with very positive results. By adapting even a few of the ideas we're about to offer—the most important one being the use of two videocassette versions of the play—you can share a unique learning experience with your students. You will find yourself teaching much more than Shakespeare's play; *Henry V* offers a marvelous opportunity to share geography, history, politics, and a host of other disciplines in addition to the added bonus (especially with a video-oriented audience of today's students) of discussing film-making techniques and directoral intent.

If you are not accustomed to teaching Shakespeare via videotape, one of the first—and most important—rules to follow is never to introduce the film before your students are comfortable with the text. In the not-too-distant past, many educators, excited by the prospect of presenting Shakespeare on film, usually fell prey to one of two pitfalls: (1) they read the play with the class, then turned on the 16mm projector and sat back while most of the class went not to Agincourt—or to Elsinore—but to sleep; or (2) they ignored the text altogether and hoped that somehow (through a kind of literary osmosis?) their students would understand the play by watching it for two hours without interruption. Hopefully, these outdated techniques have been retired with the old 16mm and 8mm films. Today, with the variety of easily accessible videocassettes of Shakespeare's plays, the teacher is able to reach out to students in a multitude of ways. The basic rule is simple: NEVER view any film in its entirety, unless you do so at the end of a unit as a special event. Begin with the text, read aloud. Shakespeare was meant to be heard—and performed—and the worst case scenario is that solitary student who is faced with reading an entire act of a play, silently . . . and alone.

When introducing *Henry V*, do not begin with Act 1, scene 1. Do not assign the play as homework (at least not initially), but rather, begin in class on Day #1 by introducing them to 3.1: Henry's battle cry at Harfleur. Read through the first eight lines, with either a very good student reader or the teacher doing the reading. The first obvious question—"What's a breach?"—should be brought up immediately. Explain that while Henry may be king of England, he also feels it is his right to be king of France. Harfleur is a seaport town in France; it is a typical town of the Middle Ages, which is when this story takes place. At this point, slip a videocassette of Kenneth Branagh's 1989 film of *Henry V* into the VCR, set to begin with the Harfleur sequence. You may want to hit the Pause button rather quickly to create a freeze-frame effect of Henry with the breach behind him. Point out that the primary objective of the English is to blast through the stone walls surrounding the town. Considered the key to Normandy, Harfleur was extremely well fortified; it was surrounded by a wide, impassable moat. Peter Earle notes that "Efforts to climb the walls were met with showers of sulphur and lime poured into the faces of the grappling English" (128). You should be careful to remind your students that this battle actually happened historically. Henry's troops had landed at Harfleur on 13 August 1415; it was not until 22 September that the town finally surrendered. The English tried tunneling under the walls; ultimately they managed to blast holes through them: "Once more unto the breach . . ." Remind your students—via maps if necessary—that Henry brought a complete army, including horses, cannons, and all sorts of military equipment on ships across the choppy waters of the Channel. During the time you have been talking, the frozen picture of Henry's determined face urging his soldiers to the breach has been paused on the TV screen in front of your students. Push the play button and let them listen to Henry's whole speech (complete with dazzling pyrotechnics). Assign students to read the same passage, 3.1.1–34, for the next class session.

By using this method, we have accomplished several important objectives. First, and most important, you now have your students' interest. Because the clip we've selected is relatively short (under five minutes playing time), no one in your class is going to fall asleep. Secondly, they've got Shakespeare's words (thanks to Branagh's impeccable diction) ringing in their ears. Finally, they've seen what a breach is—and a good replica of a medieval French town—so they can visualize the action much more realistically.

For your next session, change the pace totally. This time we'll begin with Laurence Olivier's 1944 film of *Henry V*. Olivier, of course, had a different objective than did Branagh; his film was produced while Britain was deeply entrenched in World War II. You may want to point out to your students that Olivier wanted his wartime audience to "escape" into his film; his movie, unlike Branagh's more recent version, is not MEANT to look realistic. It looks like a fairy-tale world; in other words, expect comments from your students that Olivier's version looks "fake." To accomplish this effect, Olivier uses a technique of presenting us with the "play" within the "movie." As Olivier's film begins, we are treated to an aerial view of Elizabethan London, before focusing in on the Globe Theatre. You might want to begin today's lecture with some background information on Shakespeare as a playwright, the Globe Theatre, Elizabethan stagecraft, or a discussion of "groundlings."

With Olivier's film you want to make sure that you've fast-forwarded through the somewhat lengthy credits at the opening to the cut of a playbill floating down from the sky. As the camera moves in, point out the Globe Theatre and note the fact that a flag is flying—there will be a play performed today. Olivier offers us a marvelous panorama of English society in the 1600s; first, we see a shot of a typical gentleman, complete with lace and velvet doublet; next we are given a glimpse of his societal opposite—a common woman selling oranges to the playgoers. Point out the various kinds of seating; note in particular the groundlings lounging about the stage area. If you look quickly, you will see the prompter sitting off to the side of the stage; he looks surprisingly (and intentionally) like William Shakespeare, complete with feather pen.

As the play begins, you may want to discuss the use of a Chorus, perhaps interjecting some background on the Greek theater conventions. Shakespeare uses this technique rarely—in *Romeo and Juliet* and in *Henry V*. Play the Olivier video through until the Chorus urges us "Gently to hear, kindly to judge, our play!" Now your students are ready to begin studying *Henry V*. Assign Act 1 for homework.

Your next class session can go in a variety of directions. You may want to begin your discussion with a definition of the Salic Law. See if your students can name any females who hold positions of power in today's world. Most likely, many students will name Queen Elizabeth. Make sure you have done your homework and can also offer modern females who hold high office. Explain Henry's feeling of the subject: he claims the throne of France through his great-grandfather, Edward III; more importantly, the claim is through Edward's mother, Isabella—obviously, a woman. Depending on your class, you may want to open the discussion even further by debating women's rights. Shakespeare can take us in a multitude of directions.

One of the complaints issued most often about *Henry V* is that it generally does not make sense to students who have not previously read *1 Henry IV*. However, after pointing out some of the Archbishops' comments about Henry's somewhat miraculous conversion from playboy Prince to perfect King, you may want to treat your students to a view of Falstaff via Branagh's videotape. One of the most praiseworthy techniques incorporated by Branagh was his creative use of the flashback. Branagh obviously felt that audiences who had not read the earlier plays would be confused at the lines about Falstaff. By using his flashback technique, Branagh shows us the young Prince Hal; the lines concerning conversion in *Henry V* suddenly take on an added significance. Show your students the tavern scene from Branagh's *Henry V*. You will strengthen the concept of Henry's metamorphosis; you may also want to read them a few lines from Hal's initial soliloquy in *1 Henry IV*. He tells us that when the time is right, he will be a good king. Remind them of Henry's charge to the breach; has he not fulfilled his promise? Some students will inevitably feel sorry for Falstaff; you must remind them of Henry's position as monarch. Where could Falstaff possibly fit in? Talk about friendship. Was Hal ever really Falstaff's friend? Assure them that while it may be sad—especially in Branagh's film—Henry really cannot have his former cronies as friends once he becomes the king. Do you see Henry in a slightly different way now? What are the qualities that a king should have? Does Henry have these qualities?

You might open a discussion on the use of flashback in other films or television shows they might have seen. What purpose does it serve? Would the film work equally well without the Falstaff flashback? In answer, show them the cut from Olivier's film. It is much shorter, showing only Falstaff's death. Hal does not appear; we hear only a voice-over, cold and harsh: "I know you not, old man." If you are showing both Branagh's and Olivier's cuts on the same day, you might want to conclude by having your students write a compare-contrast essay on the two directors' interpretations.

Since the class has been assigned Act 1, you may also want to have them turn to the gift of the tennis balls from the French dauphin. Does this scene—and the gift—make more sense now that you know something of Prince Hal? Choose several students to alternate reading Henry's lines from 1.2.259-97. Concentrate on the sibilant sounds. Does this indicate anger? Notice how he seems to "hiss" in some lines. Remark on Henry's obvious control, and suggest that his anger, once released, might be a real factor with which to be reckoned. Talk about Henry's repetition of the word "mock" in this scene. What does "mock" mean? What part of speech is it? Why do you think Henry uses "mock" twice on the same sentence? Time permitting, rewind the Branagh tape to the sequence of the tennis balls. Listen to his precise diction. Point out and discuss how an actor can convince us of emotions that we may not derive from the text alone. By the time you're finished with today's class, you can almost rest assured that at least a portion of your students will have read other parts of the play, and/or rented either Olivier's or Branagh's film at their local video store. Homework: Read Act 2.

For today's class you will be concentrating on two scenes from Act 2, the traitor scene and the French court. Have the students identify the three traitors: Scroop, Cambridge, and Grey. Make sure they realize that Scroop has been especially close to Henry; he is called his "bedfellow." Why do they want to betray Henry? The obvious pun on guilt/gilt should be emphasized, but make sure to tell them that there were those in the kingdom who felt that Henry shouldn't be the king of England, much less the king of France. Without going into a treatise on English history, you can simply point out that Richard II was not a very good king; Henry's father, Henry Bolingbroke, decided to become the king instead, had Richard put in prison and usurped the crown. Some believed, therefore, that neither Henry Bolingbroke, nor his son, Henry V, had a right to the throne. Show them Branagh's cut from 2.2. Note especially his excellent use of the Chorus at the beginning of this scene, and how the camera pauses on each of the traitors as the Chorus names them.

Pause the video as King Henry physically attacks Lord Scroop and pushes him down on the table. Why is Henry so angry at him in particular? Have you ever had a friend betray you? Raise the question: Isn't this the same thing Henry did to Falstaff? You may want to have your students write a short essay on the theme of betrayal either from personal experience or about Henry/Scroop or Henry/Falstaff. After watching the rest of the scene, discuss Henry's punishment of the traitors. Students are sometimes appalled and/or fascinated by medieval executions, so use your own judgment about where the discussion will go from here. It might be noteworthy to mention at this point that the so-called "traitor scene" or Southampton plot of 2.2 has been omitted from Olivier's film version. Critics over the years have accused him of propaganda, of presenting an unrealistic, "too-perfect" king for his audiences. Yet we must bear in mind that England in 1944 was entrenched in a war of its own; any hint of traitors in a film about "this star of England" would never have been acceptable. Olivier felt that he had a duty to perform: "I knew what I wanted to do . . . my country was at war" (1986, 275). If your class has been interested in the differences in Branagh's versus Olivier's interpretations of the play, show them the way Olivier manages to eliminate the three conspirators. If they view both films, consider assigning a short essay defending the decision of one director or the other.

The second film clip you want to view deals with the French court. Make sure the students have read 2.4 thoroughly. You might begin by having them jot down on paper some of the characteristics Shakespeare assigns to the English. For example, the English are called "fatal and neglected" (13); Henry is described as "a vain, giddy, shallow, humorous youth" (28). On the other hand, the old French king remembers with horror the defeat of the French at the Battle of Crecy by "that black name, Edward, Black Prince of Wales" (56), and he describes Henry as "a stem of that victorious stock; and let us fear / The native mightiness and fate of him" (62–64). From this scene, do you think the French are really afraid of Henry? Do they take his threat seriously?

This is the ideal time to utilize Olivier's storybook scenes of the French court. His depiction of the French as weak and effeminate characters may cause some students to laugh, but remind them that Henry's army will soon be reduced to only a small band of men who will ultimately go up against more than ten thousand French knights and men-at-arms. Point out that the French king, Charles VI, suffered bouts of insanity and may have been very much like the weak, crouching imbecile Olivier depicts in his film. It is important to remember that each of the French dukes wanted to be the king. Therefore, they will fight against, rather than for, each other when the Battle of Agincourt takes place. Many historians agree that the division among the French dukes was one of the major causes of defeat at Agincourt.

You are now ready to assign Act 3 (where we actually began!) for homework. Students will be delighted to recognize these familiar lines and put them into context. They may ask to see Branagh's Harfleur speech again, but show them Olivier's instead. They will immediately note his theatricality, and most especially, the absence of mud or blood. Remind them of Olivier's purpose—his war was not to be viewed in realistic terms. Note that Olivier's scene differs from Branagh's in other ways as well; Olivier is removed from both the breach and his men. The camera intensifies this isolation, by backing away from him, rather than focusing in for close-up. The shot encompasses all the men—united behind their monarch in a spirit of true brotherhood. A very different approach—with a very different motive.

If you have included some of the minor characters in your class discussions, this might be an ideal time to talk about Fluellen, the Welsh commander. Have the students read through 3.2.53–139. What nationalities are represented here and why? A map of the British

Isles may prove helpful. Note also that Henry and Fluellen are "kinsmen" because Henry was born at Monmouth Castle, Wales. You may wish to show a clip from Olivier's film as it is particularly useful in identifying the four nations of England, Scotland, Ireland, and Wales. Have the students read Act 4 for the next session.

Act 4 is obviously where most of the war action takes place. This can be an ideal time to discuss medieval warfare, the concepts of which may seem strange to some students. Stress Henry's belief in his right to the throne of France. The deciding battle looms near, at Agincourt. Henry's men are exhausted, sick, and half-starved. It has been raining; it's nearing the end of October and it is also cold. Morale is at an all-time low. It is Henry's job to motivate his troops, just as he did at Harfleur. Is Henry afraid? Since Act 4 has been assigned as homework, you might want to have the students write an essay answering this very question. However, a more interesting approach is to have them act out the parts of the English camp and the French camp. Choose a student to portray Henry as he walks among his soldiers on the eve before battle. At this point, a little modernization can actually intensify the experience for your class. Choose an additional student or two and have them prepare interview questions for both the French and English soldiers, for the Dauphin (or the Constable or Mountjoy) and, of course, for Henry. It might go something like this:

Interviewer: Excuse me, sir, you are the Dauphin, is that right? I understand you and Henry are old enemies. Is it true you once sent him an insulting gift?

Or perhaps:

Interviewer: King Henry, I saw you praying over there a while ago. Can you share some of your thoughts with our viewers on this, the eve of the biggest battle of your life?

This can be done as a group project, and written ahead of time. Remind the students that while the modern television interviewer may speak 1990s English, the characters in the play should answer in Shakespearean language. This kind of assignment can be extremely effective in getting the students to use Shakespeare's words.

Obviously, the Battle of Agincourt will be the highlight of your study of the play, so you want to make sure you devote sufficient time to both videos. Of special importance is the initial sequence in both films in which you are treated to an impressive and frightening sight: the French army, thousands upon thousands of them bedecked in their shining armor, with colorful banners unfurled. Contrasted with this opulence is Henry's meager band: "We few, we happy few, we band of brothers" (4.3.60). You need not dwell on some of Branagh's more graphic battle scenes; to demonstrate the contrast with Olivier's sunny, picture-book Agincourt, about three minutes of each film should be sufficient. To reinforce the magnitude of the French losses, you may fast-forward to Branagh's or Olivier's reading of 4.8.

Act 5 will come as somewhat of a letdown. Yet your students must realize the importance of the final act. Director Joseph Papp maintains that in the final act Shakespeare must also show that Henry is "a tough negotiator, ruthless in the conditions he demands for France's surrender" (Bevington 1988, xv). The Princess Katherine is simply one of the conditions. The marriage of Henry and Katherine symbolizes the jointure of the kingdoms of England and France.

If you have been using the videos throughout the course of this study of *Henry V,* you must do one more compare and contrast with the Olivier and the Branagh adaptations. Students will be tempted to look for a storybook ending of "They lived happily ever after." If you view the Olivier film, the marriage of Henry and Katherine will quickly fade to a return to the Globe Theatre, a form of happy-ever-aftering. The Branagh film, on the other hand, includes the Chorus presenting the ominous Epilogue:

> Henry the Sixth, in infant bands crowned King
> Of France and England, did this king succeed;
> Whose state so many had the managing
> That they lost France and made his England bleed . . .

If you have done your job well, you have given your students a unique and memorable experience: you, with the help of Laurence Olivier and Kenneth Branagh, have made Shakespeare—and his Henry—come alive. And perhaps you have whetted their appetites not just for the study of Shakespeare's plays, but for history . . . geography . . . linguistics . . .acting . . . directing . . .

References

Allmand, Christopher. 1992. *Henry V.* Berkeley: University of California.
Bevington, David, ed. 1988. *Henry V.* By William Shakespeare. New York: Bantam.
Branagh, Kenneth. 1989. *Henry V: A Screen Adaptation.* London: Chatto and Windus.
Earle, Peter. 1972. *The Life and Times of Henry V.* London: Weidenfield and Nicolson.
Mast, Gerald. 1981. *A Short History of the Movies.* 3d ed. Indianapolis: Bobbs-Merrill.
Olivier, Laurence. 1986. *Laurence Olivier on Acting.* New York: Simon and Schuster.

Videotapes

Branagh, Kenneth, director. 1989. *Henry V.* Renaissance Films.
Olivier, Laurence, director. 1944. *Henry V.* United Artists, 1945.

CHAPTER 25

When Images Replace Words

Shakespeare, Russian Animation, and the Culture of Television

MARTHA TUCK ROZETT
University at Albany–SUNY
Albany, New York

Rozett describes a recent cross-cultural collaboration of Europeans, Americans,
Japanese, and Russians that produced a series of thirty-minute animated adaptations
of six Shakespeare plays. As Rozett explains, "for many young people, these films
will serve as a first . . . encounter with Shakespeare." She asserts that "because so
few of Shakespeare's words survive the paring-down process, images necessarily
become a medium for conveying the themes." She also claims that the patterns of
images have a unique capacity to communicate much about the plays.

Starting in 1990, an unusual cross-cultural collaboration involving an international community of European, American and Japanese financiers, a Welsh television production team, actors from the Royal Shakespeare Company and the National Theatre, the distinguished Shakespeare scholar Stanley Wells, the children's book author Leon Garfield, and Russian animators, artists, and musicians at Soyuzmultfilm and Mosfilm studios in Moscow produced a series of thirty-minute animated adaptations of six Shakespeare plays: *A Midsummer Night's Dream, Romeo and Juliet, Twelfth Night, Hamlet, Macbeth,* and *The Tempest.* The project survived the anti-Gorbachev coup in August 1991, although the rumble of tanks near the studio made the cameras shake, and the films, called "Animated Tales," were aired beginning in the fall of 1992. They have been shown on HBO and energetically marketed for educational use by Random House, along with print abridgments and a free study guide.

For many young people, these films will serve as a first, and perhaps most memorable, encounter with Shakespeare, much as comic-book adaptations of the "classics" did for an earlier generation. The international culture of television has acclimated even the youngest audiences to a set of cartoon conventions—conventions of character types, facial expressions, gestures, movement, scene shifts, and special animation effects—which the Russian animators were able to incorporate into their design concepts. But rather than resorting to a stylized, Disney-like homogeneity for the series, the designers and producers decided to create a different look for each film, by using six teams of artists, and a variety of animation techniques, camera movements, drawing styles, and color schemes. The result is a series of films that look and sound sufficiently different from popular commercial cartoons to make children take notice, yet with enough of the familiar cartoon conventions that they will pick up the visual and audio cues even when the language is over their heads.

Leon Garfield's abridgments reduce Shakespeare's text to a mix of paraphrased narration and excerpted lines or abbreviated speeches. As is typical in cartoons, non-verbal action accompanied by musical cues that signal conventional moods accounts for a substantial portion of each film. Often, these non-verbal sequences draw on cinematic techniques that are not unique to animation, particularly when the camera lingers on details of scenic location, for each play is set in a very distinctive and elegantly drawn group of interior and exterior scenes. Even in the short space of twenty-five minutes, the audience can become familiar with the Verona of *Romeo and Juliet,* inspired by the architecture and color schemes of Italian Renaissance paintings, or the tiny, rock-strewn, wave-swept island of *The Tempest,* or the shadowy recesses of the castle in *Hamlet. Hamlet* is the most visually interesting of the six films, due to its painting-on-glass technique, which causes the spectator to experience the illusion of entering into a book of drawings or engravings. Because so few of Shakespeare's words survive the paring-down process, images necessarily become a medium for conveying the themes that Garfield and his collaborators chose to emphasize. Thus while the extraordinary range and complexity of Shakespeare's imagery is sacrificed, the films do offer their viewers a manageable number of strong, recurrent, audio-visual effects and visual themes that interpret, transform, and indeed "teach" the playtexts. Here are some examples of how this happens.

"The Animated *Twelfth Night*" begins with a violent storm at sea. A high-masted wooden ship buffeted by the waves splits in half, and two identical little puppet figures fall into the ocean. Rather than offering a close-up of the puppets, the camera lingers for a significant moment on the carved figurehead attached to the ship's prow: a large, voluptuously rounded female torso. This image appears twice during the storm sequence, and so becomes fixed in the viewer's mind. The figurehead contrasts in very interesting ways with the animated puppets, most of which have stylized, angular, unisex bodies, with the exception of Maria, Sir Toby, and Malvolio, whose comic roles are signaled in the visual language of cartoon conventions by their fat round bodies or exaggerated protruding stomachs. The figurehead at the beginning is nicely complemented by the final image of the film (which remains on screen longer than any other since it serves as the backdrop for the credits). This is a stone Cupid with poised bow, placed on a pedestal in Olivia's beautifully detailed walled garden, where much of the action occurs. These two icons, each crafted from inanimate materials (like the puppets), invoke a complex of associations regarding the arbitrary, dangerous, and life-transforming power wielded by nature and the emotions, a power humans try to harness by representing it anthropomorphically. Neither image is mentioned in the text, yet for the viewer who first experiences *Twelfth Night* through this performance, both become memorable parts of the play.

The motif of artificial figures invested with meaning is sustained by another visual image, this one inspired by the language of the playtext; in Act 1, scene 4, when Orsino sends the now-disguised Viola/Cesario to woo Olivia on his behalf, the film shows him gazing upon a full-size portrait of her, framed by a red velvet curtain (cf. Olivia's line to Viola/Cesario in Act 1, scene 5: "You are now out of your text, but we will draw the curtain, and show you the picture. Look you, sir, such a one I was this present").[1] The portrait reappears in Act 2, scene 4, as the backdrop against which Orsino listens to Viola/Cesario speak of her father's daughter's unrequited love and comforts her with an embrace that anticipates the comic resolution. Taken together, the buxom figurehead, the formal portrait, and the androgynous Cupid signify a welter of ideas about sexual attraction, gender confusion, the authority invested in images, comic blindness, and the helplessness of lovers caught up in forces beyond their control. And unlike Shakespeare's language, such signs are accessible to viewers unfamiliar with the play, due in large measure to the ubiquitous culture of television.

These same viewers would also know how to interpret the expanded bird imagery of "The Animated *Hamlet,*" probably inspired by Hamlet's fifth-act speech "We defy augury. There's a providence in the fall of a sparrow . . . " The familiar cartoon cliché of a bat flapping noisily and ominously upward through a high, vaulted castle stairwell appears fairly early in the film, as the camera moves in a vertiginous, circling movement while Hamlet's voice delivers excerpts from the "O what a rogue and peasant slave" soliloquy. This circling camera movement, with its bird/flight associations, is a reiterated motif in the film, suggesting not only the flight of birds and bats but also the confused, disorienting atmosphere of the play.

A different sort of bird imagery occurs in the non-verbal scene that immediately precedes Gertrude's description of Ophelia's death. The camera follows Ophelia's white silhouette down a long, dark, cloistered corridor that is used several times in the film, then cuts to a marsh full of reeds into which the white figure disappears. Our attention is now focused on a long-legged white bird in the foreground. We hear a splash, and then the bird spreads its wings and takes flight along a shaft of light through the clouds. The camera pauses on this image, then takes us back to the castle and an abbreviated version of Gertrude's speech. What is interesting about this scene is that Shakespeare has provided a wealth of imagery the adapters could have used: the "pendant" boughs of willow on which Ophelia "clamber[s]" to hang her crown of flowers, her "mermaid-like" figure in the brook, with "clothes spread wide," "chaunt[ing] snatches of old lauds," and finally, her garments pulling her "To muddy death," the image of descent with which the speech ends. But the film makers opted for a more uplifting image, one that, in the international language of animal symbolism, offers the audience a reassuring vision of the soul's escape from bodily limitations and ascent to heaven.

The third occurrence of bird imagery begins in the graveyard scene: a cawing raven perched on a monument flies off as the camera pans toward Hamlet and the gravedigger. As the camera recedes upward, leaving the small crowd below gathered around the bier, the raven circles into the sky, its insistent cawing foreshadowing the tragic events to come. A few moments later, just as Hamlet says "There's a special providence in the fall of a sparrow," we see the bird for the last time, dipping down from the sky to touch a wave and swoop upward again. This, clearly, is a very different "fall" from the one implied by Hamlet's biblical allusion. What has occurred in the transformation from text to film is a substitution of conventional images of white and black birds as symbols, respectively, of transcendence and foreboding, for what was originally a considerably more complex and philosophical use of imagery. Hamlet defies augury—that is, he refuses to act upon the signs that predict events, even as he ascribes "a special providence" or meaning to such signs. Eventually, he takes a curious kind of comfort in knowing that each event, however inconsequential ("the fall of a sparrow") is part of a larger pattern of inevitable causality. Some of this feeling comes across in the film, but not because of Shakespeare's language; rather, a combination of visual and sound effects leaves the viewer with a sense of Hamlet's "readiness."

The bird imagery is not the only visual motif in "The Animated *Hamlet*." A heavy gold goblet appears frequently, always accompanying the sinister-looking Claudius, and suggesting a train of associations among excessive drinking, moral turpitude, sexual seduction (the camera lingers on Claudius and Gertrude toasting one another as the Ghost delivers the lines "won to his shameful lust the will of my most vicious queen"), out-of-place festivity ("the funeral meats did coldly furnish forth the marriage feast") and of course, poisoning. The film omits Hamlet's "dram of eale" speech, which explicitly refers to the King's drunken revelry, but the metonymic cluster of the goblet, drinking, and moral corruption is nevertheless visually reinforced so that by the last scene the goblet is an obvious vehicle for Claudius's final act of treachery.

Part of the reason for focusing so much on the goblet, I suspect, is that the animation techniques in all the films, but especially this one, don't lend themselves to very articulated facial movement. Hence the camera often lingers on objects or architectural details rather than faces while characters are speaking. Sometimes these directorial choices create entirely new, non-Shakespearean imagery, such as in the closet scene, when the camera cuts from the slain Polonius to a tapestry of hunting dogs swarming over a stag. The tapestry depicts a non-verbal cruelty comparable, perhaps, to the murder that has just occurred but also less harrowing than the verbal cruelty excised from the text in Garfield's adaptation. In place of the striking verbal images with which Hamlet berates Gertrude the film reduces the main point of the scene to the neat couplet we hear as we gaze upon the fallen stag: "I must be cruel only to be kind / Thus bad begins and worse remains behind" (3.4.56–178).

Other films contain patterns of imagery generated from hints in the text, although not always parts of the texts that survived Garfield's radical cutting. The drumbeat is a recurring audio-visual motif in "The Animated *Macbeth*" although the witches' wonderfully rhythmic line "A drum, a drum, Macbeth doth come!" is omitted. In scenes corresponding to Act 1, scenes 6 and 7 and at intervals thereafter the striking figure of a jester beating a drum and wreathed in flames flashes onto the screen; this motif, I later realized, is adapted from the 1948 Orson Welles film. The enigmatic jester/drum image contributes to a series of interlocking images in what is arguably the most graphically experimental and imaginative of the six adaptations. The film begins with a mask disintegrating into bold abstract patterns that metamorphose into clouds or rising smoke, as three disembodied mask faces appear, and, while speaking the play's opening lines, dissolve to a circle of arms, then spin off into space. When the witches reappear a scene later they take the shifting forms of skeletons and fragmented body parts that are constantly reassembling themselves into shapes and patterns as they address Macbeth and Banquo in high-pitched, cackling cartoon voices. One witch face is a white mask, removed by a bodiless hand to reveal another, darker, sinister-looking face beneath, reinforcing the theme of metamorphosis. This sequence is repeated a few moments later; just as Lady Macbeth gets to the line, "that shalt be king hereafter," the white mask appears on the letter. All of the faces in "The Animated *Macbeth*" look mask-like, for the team of artists employed a contour-drawing technique that relies upon bold, geometrical blocks of contrasting color rather than shading to denote the shadows and curves in bodies and faces. Macbeth's face is particularly striking, its tortured, angular lines and stark white eyes with tiny pinpoint irises setting him apart from the other characters and conveying an expression of horror and emptiness. Circle, mask, and flame images recur—in the cauldron scene, of course, but more interestingly, when Lady Macbeth says "Come to my woman's breasts, . . ." Her breasts, which the contour drawing represents as two perfect circles, become disks that explode toward the viewer and burst, flame-like, into a wolfish monster face just as she says "you murth'ring ministers." The harsh flames of torchlight throughout the film culminate in the flame which becomes a branch which becomes a naked crowned babe in the final witches' scene; then, the animated metamorphosis recurs, as the child repeats its prophecy about Macduff to the anguished Macbeth just before the battle begins. Instead of a moving forest, however, we see soldiers emerging from flames, and then the red and gold colors echoed seconds later by Macduff's red hair and beard. This is a curious departure from the Shakespeare text, particularly since the moving Birnam wood lends itself so obviously to animation effects. I suspect that American or British animators would have been less likely to take such liberties with so familiar and famous a scene than did the Russian artists, who seem to have let their design concept take precedence over Shakespeare's language.

Only occasionally do the animated Shakespeare films produce new characters and text, though nearly all of them alter the plays' endings. *Hamlet* ends with the line "The rest is silence," omitting all mention of Fortinbras (not unusual for abridged *Hamlet*s), just as it omits Rosencrantz and Guildenstern, Osric, and virtually all of Hamlet's antic behavior. *Twelfth Night* ends with a recognition scene that contains only the four lovers; Maria, Sir Toby, Sir Andrew, Feste, Malvolio, and Antonio are nowhere in evidence. And *Romeo and Juliet* ends with the lovers lying side by side on a bier, ascending upward into the sky as music swells. During the credits, the audience gazes upon a rosy glow of sunrise and the last twinkling star, a rather different image than the one Shakespeare gives us in the Prince's closing speech: "A glooming peace the morning with it brings / The sun for sorrow, will not show his head" (5.3.305-6). The ending of *Macbeth* is even more upbeat and reassuring, perhaps in an effort to offset the horrors and bloodshed of the preceding scenes. To the accompaniment of soothing flute music, an old, white-bearded man with a staff walks toward us across a bright and peaceful landscape, as the narrator says "At last the darkness was lifted from Scotland." The old man raises his arms in a gesture of benediction and says, "God's benison go with you and with those that would make good of bad and friend of foe." Like the images associated with Ophelia's and Romeo's and Juliet's deaths, this ending seems designed to smooth over the tragedy of violent death with reassuring audiovisual effects.

Some teachers may be reluctant to use the animated films because they simplify and exaggerate. Oddly enough, the study guide distributed by Random House assumes a greater range of interpretive possibilities than the films offer. Here, for instance, is an exercise focused on Malvolio:

Malvolio is not in himself a great man: he doesn't have a tragic ending. Yet actors have sometimes founded their reputations on playing him. He is a priceless mixture of dignity and pathos, and sometimes your feelings about the play when it's over depend on how deeply he is left in pain after Maria's trick. He seems to draw the pain, the love and the laughter of this story into himself, and in this way he stands for a little bit of almost everybody. Did you care for him?

In small groups, discuss which of these views of Malvolio is the one that the film makers chose to bring out:

* Is he a passionate man, full of dreams, misunderstood by everyone?
* Is he self-important, pompously judging everyone and ending up plain tiresome?
* Is he genuinely honest, efficient, and dignified, surrounded by fools?
* Is he hopelessly funny, a true comic part?[2]

No viewer of the film would recognize in the cartoon Malvolio a "priceless mixture of dignity and pathos" or "a passionate man full of dreams." Malvolio struts comically about with his large protruding stomach, a conventional cartoon figure accompanied by comic cartoon effects; for example, when he sets aside his walking stick after using it to pick up the planted letter, the stick stands up by itself. Later, he dances around the garden looking at himself in a hand mirror, just prior to his scene with Olivia. His exit from the play comes when Olivia summons Maria to have him "look'd to," at which point Maria pops up from behind a wall, and pulls a large, striped bag over his entire body. This conventional image of silencing and entrapment, derived from Saturday morning cartoon conventions in which the aggressor moves swiftly and wordlessly to obliterate or transform the victim, collapses a much longer and essentially verbal sequence into the film's single comical image of the capable Maria whisking Malvolio out of Olivia's presence and out of the play.

Children, of course, would enjoy this moment enormously, just as they would enjoy Viola's "Cinderella" twirl into her "woman's weeds," or the magic fairy dust Puck uses to transform Bottom to an ass, or the way Oberon slowly disappears into the vegetation as he becomes invisible, or other instances of cartoon magic, such as Romeo's mask at the Capulet's ball, which disappears the moment he begins talking to Juliet and then reappears just as she is called away, after their tender love sonnet. They would enjoy the comical Caliban, an impossible mix of different animal traits, with froggy limbs, crab-claw arms, feathery hair, an ape-like stance, and a croaky cartoon voice; and they would notice that when he begins his wonderful "Be not afeard, the isle is full of noises" speech, a large stone outcropping in the background with a recognizably human face opens it eyes and looks askance at him, as if to confirm his words. They might be surprised, though, by how "adult" the animated characters look in comparison with American cartoon figures, especially the lovers in *A Midsummer Night's Dream,* who are ugly and unromantic with angular features and visible body hair, for this film rather deliberately distances itself from the prettiness of so many stage and ballet renderings of the play by emphasizing the grotesqueness and disorientation implicit in it.[3]

Since their release in November 1992, the six "Animated Tales" have been sold to fifty-two countries, dubbed into ten languages, and have won several awards, including two prime-time Emmys and the New York Gold for Best Animation, according to the project director, Christopher Grace of S4C, Channel Four Wales. To date, forty thousand videos and sixty thousand books have been sold in the English language edition, and a large percentage of primary and secondary schools in the U.K. are using the films and special BBC Education editions of the books. A representative of the Writing Company's Shakespeare catalogue (an extensive collection of teaching materials testifying to the widespread inclusion of Shakespeare in American school curricula) told me that the films are selling well to elementary schools in the U.S. Six more films have been produced, and the first of these, *Richard III,* animated with the same painting-on-glass technique used for *Hamlet* and exhibiting some visual echoes of the Olivier film, was shown with much fanfare on BBC in early November 1994 with *As You Like It, Julius Caesar, Othello, The Winter's Tale,* and *The Taming of the Shrew* scheduled for release in 1995.[4]

It would not be an exaggeration to say that the teaching of Shakespeare has been and will continue to be changed by the existence of the "Animated Tales," just as it was undoubtedly changed by the full-length films produced by the BBC in the 1970s, and that the international distribution of the series has the potential to create a "global village" of students who will go on to read translations of Shakespeare with their preconceptions colored by those first encounters with the striking images I have been describing. There's a study here, for someone who wants to undertake it, of the way children from different cultures are responding to the "Animated Tales" — children who belong to the next generation of adapters, translators, directors, and actors around the world.

Notes

1. All quotations from Shakespeare's plays are taken from *The Riverside Shakespeare,* ed. G. B. Evans et al. (Boston: Houghton Mifflin, 1974).

2. "Shakespeare: The Animated Tales: Study Assignments for Students" (Random House Inc., n.d.)

3. This film was begun in Armenia, but had to be completed in a Moscow hotel room because of the civil war there. This may help explain the atmosphere of the film. Teresa L. Waite, "Tempest and Others the Size of a Teapot," *The New York Times,* November 9, 1992.

4. Private correspondence with Christopher Grace, February 8, 1995. Mr. Grace adds that Channel Four Wales has gone on to produce a six-part animated opera series and a Bible series, and is planning to animate such works as *Moby Dick, The Canterbury Tales,* and *Don Quixote.*

CHAPTER 26

Different Daggers
Versions of Macbeth

HARRY BRENT

Baruch College–CUNY
New York, New York

Brent has designed a writing assignment for college freshman based on a viewing of
two or more film versions of Macbeth, *selected from Verdi's opera* Macbeth *and*
three film versions of the play. He is interested in the range of student responses and
how these responses compare with traditional criticism. To elicit these responses, he
created short assignments that build incrementally toward a long, comprehensive
paper, and he includes excerpts from several student commentaries as illustrations of
the success of his approach.

I find myself hesitant to write on *Macbeth,* and for good reason. A number of years ago, a friend of mine who is a member of the company at the Royal National Theatre of Great Britain in London invited me backstage for a drink in the company's private pub. After a few pints, I casually mentioned that I had always wanted to perform at the National Theatre, at which point somebody said, "Well you shall sir, you shall." Thereupon I was ushered out of the pub and onto the stage of the Olivier Theatre, arguably the most prestigious set of boards in the world. I wanted to recite Hamlet's "To be, or not to be . . . " soliloquy but couldn't remember past ". . . who would fardels bear . . . ?" So instead I launched into "Is this a dagger that I see before me?" and did a pretty intense job of it in front of the empty seats. Then the trouble began. I innocently asked as I began walking off the stage, "Well, how did you like my Macbeth?" My frowning friends grabbed me by both arms and quickly ushered me backstage. You do not, I learned, utter the title of "the Scottish play" in a theater. To do so is bad luck. I tried to calm my friends with the Scholastic explanation that I had meant the name of the character, not the title of the play. Frowns eased a bit, but not entirely.

I have since learned that the curse that accompanies the mention of the real name of "the Scottish play" applies only if the title of the play is uttered *in* a theater. With that distinction in mind I decided to go ahead with the project upon which this article is based, a writing assignment which required my second-semester college freshmen to discuss *Macbeth* based on their reading of the text and their viewing of two or more of the following films based on the play: *Macbeth,* directed by Orson Welles; *Macbeth,* directed by Roman Polanski; *Throne of Blood,* directed by Akira Kurosawa; and finally, Verdi's opera, *Macbeth,* conducted by Riccardo Chailly and starring Leo Nucci and Shirley Verrett. I was interested to see how my students would react to four relatively contemporary, but markedly different, renderings of what is perhaps Shakespeare's most disturbing play. I was also interested to see how their responses would compare with the traditional criticism.

Macbeth continues to arouse critical debate. Phrases like "textual indeterminacy" and "interpretative will to power" which have marked the critical literature for well over a decade (Carr and Knapp 1981) might lead us to wonder whether the criticism of this play has outrun itself, and whether the extreme relativism of the contemporary critical climate legitimates *any* critical response whatsoever. One of my students noted the ambiguity of today's critical context when she wrote, "*Macbeth* is a story that sets questions to be asked and answers to be analyzed but leaves a certain liberty for the reader or interpreter of the play. We make the play become what it will become." The problem with this starting point in teaching Shakespeare is that it very quickly leads students off on tangents about personal experience. In planning my *Macbeth* project, I thought that I could keep students closer to the text (and thereby help them to learn to write analytically) by giving them a series of short assignments requiring close analysis of the four films mentioned above. I designed these short assignments to build incrementally toward a final long, comprehensive paper. By arranging things this way, I had hoped to let the students construct, as it were, a mosaic of interconnected ideas and arguments from which they could later draw for the final paper. I hoped that they, once having developed several independent kinds of analytical observation, would be less likely to go off on relativistic tangents.

I began the project by having the students read the text, watch the Welles film, and write a two-page paper on differences between the experience of reading the text and viewing the film. Next, I screened the Polanski film and invited a two-page paper comparing it with the Welles version. I assigned another two-pager after the screening of *Throne of Blood,* but this time I let the subject become less exact. Some students had already become enamored of a particular topic (differences among the various Lady Macbeths was a popular one). Others began to stall or to write disorganized essays that tried to do too much, or they continued to go off on tangents. But by the time I assigned the final two-page paper after screening the Verdi opera, the students had gained so much familiarity with the play that they ceased to stall or wander, and class discussion became very rich and highly analytical with respect to the text. The students had learned their way around with the play, so it was easy to point them toward closely reasoned arguments for the final assignment, a paper in which they had to follow a theme, image, character, or line of thought through the text and at least two of the filmed performances screened in class. What follows here is a sampling of some of the topics the students developed.

The earliest two-page assignments tended to be more general and vague than those that came later. Students were not yet very familiar with the play, and even those who kept to the text tended to write about amorphous subjects such as the "atmosphere" of the play. Vague as this topic is, I encouraged the students who chose it, suspecting that as they got to know the play better they would take the distillations of their early, overgeneralized writing and incorporate the finest bits and pieces into their final essays. Indeed the subject of the play's "atmosphere" could, in good critical hands, constitute a suitable topic itself. Contemporary critics have noted the psychological nature of dream-like contexts within the play (Stockholder 1987). With this in mind, I screened the Welles film first, as it readily allows for commentary on atmosphere and symbolism. Students found it easy to make connections between the physical climate of Welles's film and the actions of the characters. One of them wrote, "The sky is constantly gray and cloudy. The ground is muddy and there is not much vegetation. The trees are bare and there is hardly any grass or shrubs. There is a lot of rain, lightning, and thunder. All of this foreshadows events to come." Another student, recognizing, as has the criticism (Manville 1979), that Welles enhances the play's atmosphere by using various electronic techniques to magnify and distort the sound, wrote, "Orson Welles begins this version of *Macbeth* with rain, thunder and lightning. Even though he gave the movie a very gloomy start, viewers' attention is captured. Various 'Halloween' subjects help create the background. Loud and dark music complements the scene. This is all very stirring and captivating." Another student wrote, "The Welles film began grim and remained grim throughout. It feels right to assume that the evil was represented by the darkness. Also, the uncomfortable screams of the owl, the cries of the crickets, and the cries of the 'weird sisters' suggest an atmosphere of evil."

In the early papers, several students made comments that spoke in surprising ways to reader-response theory. Many of them wrote about the differences between reading the text and viewing its representation in film. One student, disturbed that his viewing of the film destroyed the characters he had created in his imagination, wrote, "When I started reading the first act of *Macbeth,* I created my own images of the characters. The book provides an easier way to picture and create faces for your characters. One could say that you are making your own film. It is stimulating to imagine how your characters act and how they look. You build your own landscape, you dress them in clothing that you have chosen and you are somewhat the master of the play. This is intellectually and mentally stimulating. The film, however, does not let you play with your fantasy. It tells you how the characters looked and the way they were. All the images I built up were more or less destroyed." Another student felt exactly the opposite and wrote, "The actual sound of the witches' voices in the Welles film creates that spine-tingling sensation that you don't get when reading the play. The mental image that I had of Macbeth while reading the play was that of a courageous man. Macbeth also had an aspect of evil to him that I didn't quite capture while reading the play. In Welles' film version you pre-sense his madness through the expressions on his face. In a way you can also feel it through the thunder and lightning. In the murder scene, or in the scene just before when Macbeth is contemplating the act, you again pre-sense his further direction in life from the worried expression on his face."

As the project moved on, students began to make direct comparisons between the Welles and Polanski versions. One of them, discussing symbolism, wrote, "In the Welles film when the thane of Cawdor is executed the scene starts off showing a drummer beating the drum. Then we see the Thane's head on a flat wooden surface and we know he is about to be beheaded. Instead of actually showing the Thane's head getting cut off, the camera once again returns to the drummer. When he hits the drum with a hard stroke, it is implied that the Thane is beheaded. When the Thane is executed in the Polanski film, however, it is not at all expressed through symbols. He realistically stands on a platform from which he jumps . . . and he is left hanging for all to see." Another student applied the same kind of thinking to the murder scene: "In the Polanski film, we see Macbeth stab Duncan to death very graphically. The fact that Welles does not show this scene is another example of his symbolic depiction of the play as opposed to Polanski's actual acting out of the scene."

Some students surprised me by their preference for the Polanski film, which I have always thought of as overdone and needlessly bloody in a Sam Peckinpah sort of way (though not as bloodily good as my favorite Peckinpah film, *The Wild Bunch*). One of my best students wrote, "Orson Welles' version of *Macbeth* in comparison to Roman Polanski's seemed sort of dead. I do not believe that making the play lively or even realistic was one of Welles' intentions. His characters don't eat, don't sleep, don't go to the bathroom. When they read monologues or dialogues from the original play, real emotions seem to be absent from their voices. Their lines are read in a clear diction and monotonous intonation. Even in the dinner scene you can't see food on the table. . . ." Another student developed this point when he wrote, "Those who criticize Polanski for reducing this pivotal scene [the murder of Duncan] to one of blood and gore miss Polanski's point, which is to emphasize Macbeth's hesitancy and fear, by taking the audience along with the murderer and watching, even feeling, his indecision. It is not until Duncan awakens that Macbeth finally decides to strike." Yet another student did some research on Polanski's life (cf. Synard 1986) and wrote, "Perhaps due to his own dark personal history, Polanski seems to stress more the carnage rather than the tragic nobility of the characters. The horrific scene where Lady Macduff and her small son are murdered was based, says Polanski, 'on a childhood experience. . . . I suddenly recalled how an SS officer had searched our room in the ghetto, swishing his riding crop to and fro, toying with my teddy bear, nonchalantly emptying out the hatbox full of forbidden bread. The behavior of Macbeth's henchmen was inspired by that recollection.'"

The fact that the Welles film is in black and white and the Polanski film in color provided ground for abundant commentary. One student wrote, "Every significant event in the Welles version takes place in dark, or not-so-sunny times. This strikes me as pointing ultimately to the darkness that awaits mankind in some future great calamity that Shakespeare must have been thinking about." Students who discussed color contrast often branched out to related technical points. One wrote, "Welles' use of black and white conveys the story with harsh and intimidating weight that works especially well against a backdrop that emphasizes height. Camera angles point upward toward the percussionist who pounds out the moments leading to Cawdor's decapitation. Camera angles point downward to the abyss into which Lady Macbeth throws herself. For Welles the action of the play is put in terms of either/or, black/white, high/low. The contrasts are as pointed as the spikes of the modernist crown placed by Welles on Macbeth's head." Yet, other students preferred Polanski's use of color. One wrote, "The sparkle of the knife, the redness of the blood and Duncan, the king of Scotland is murdered. It happens right in front of the viewers' eyes. It is so obvious, so real, you can almost feel it yourself."

As we moved on to the third and fourth short papers, students began to focus more on the play's characters, especially Lady Macbeth, a focus of attention one would expect given criticism of the play in recent times (Greene 1984). In contrast to some of that criticism, which tends to view Lady Macbeth as a "victim" who is refused participation in the world of male power and who thus is forced to turn to her inner devices (Asp 1981), none of my students had any sympathy at all for the woman. Nevertheless, they were keen to point out differences between the Lady Macbeths in the various versions and to discuss her character in terms of the theme of innocence and experience that continues to be a central critical consideration (Wintle and Weis 1991). Many students wrote their final papers by comparing all four incarnations of Lady Macbeth. The second paragraph of one such paper reads, "Shakespeare gives Lady Macbeth ambition and greed, courage and a little conscience. In the Kurosawa film she is a young girl dressed in a kimono and in a dreamy white gown. In the Welles version she sits in the world of darkness also in a flowing white gown, a presence that is evil, dominant and cold, always with a devilishly serious expression on her face. In the Polanski film she is nude, an indication of her innocence and weakness. She is not malevolent enough to keep dark secrets inside. Like her body, her mind is naked. In Verdi she is neither superior nor inferior to her husband, but his absolute equal."

If the students had to vote on their favorite Lady Macbeth, I'm sure the Polanski film would have won. One student wrote, "Francesca Annis, the 25-year-old actress is perfect for the role, with her petite frame, smooth ivory skin and long strawberry hair. She delivers Lady Macbeth's lines with a natural ease, as if they were her own. By using a young fragile actress, the director gives his audience a touch of promiscuity that Shakespeare left out. Polanski's Lady Macbeth has a sublime sexual presence about her. She gives an air of a woman who is aware of her sexuality and its effect on those around her; she is a sort of femme fatale."

Orson Welles's Lady Macbeth also proved a fascinating creature for some students. One wrote, "Lady Macbeth, played by Janet Nolan, is introduced lying in bed dressed in some dreamy white nightgown. The suggestion is not so much one of madness but of unreality. She does not seem a creature of this world, a state of being that is supported by her own words, '. . . come to my woman's breast and take my milk for gall. . . .' She transcends womanhood and humanity and is a creature of some other kind."

Other students concentrated on the Kurosawa Lady Macbeth, who is called Lady Asaji. One student wrote, "Kurosawa unmistakably suggests that Lady Asaji has a deviant mind, prompted by urgings that are in part sexual. Freud might say that her murderous impulses find their origin in sexual repression. Her stony facade lends truth to her demand to become 'unsexed,' a request not as convincing when it comes from her more sensuous counterpart in the Polanski film."

Another student wrote, "The Kurosawa Lady Macbeth differs radically from the Lady Macbeths of the other portrayals and from the text. Kurosawa, in presenting Asaji as a woman able to rule her husband, goes against the grain of Japanese cultural tradition. To make her believable he balances Asaji's un-Japanese needling and domination against body and head movements that suggest she maintains her humble wifely position. She sits in a respectful position relative to Washizu and almost never makes eye contact with him. This maintenance of the external forms of Japanese propriety lends all the more strength to her promptings."

Another student noted that Kurosawa is apparently able to maintain the contradiction noted above through borrowings from the traditions of Noh theater: "Although Noh has had little effect on Japanese film, Kurosawa has obviously been influenced by this ancient school of theater. Throughout his version of *Macbeth,* he uses a number of obvious Noh elements: Lady Asaji's white face resembles a Noh mask for a young woman."

I was somewhat hesitant to even attempt to use Verdi's opera. I thought the students might be bored since most of them had never seen an opera performance. But it turned out that the students, who by this time had become thoroughly familiar with *Macbeth,* liked Verdi. One of them wrote, "Music liberates feelings, in this play notably fear. The witches are like a chorus in the background. Filthy and foul, they resemble dirty animals and at a point become associated with rats. Perhaps the point being made here has to do with the animal nature of man." As was the case with the earlier screenings, many students directed their comments to the character of Lady Macbeth. One wrote "The Verdi Lady Macbeth is a powerful and strong character. Her regal bearing and her eyes tell it all. She is the personification of inwardly-directed, wondering emotion." Another wrote "The Verdi Lady Macbeth is in control of herself, someone who can handle any situation well. Yet, as strong as she is, she cannot be said to manipulate her husband who is more forceful from the beginning, more determined of what he wants. He does not need Lady Macbeth to convince or encourage him to murder. Yet she remains a strong external force to validate his actions."

My students wrote on other themes, but the limits of this paper do not allow me to explore those subjects at length. For example, much time during class sessions was given over to examining the language in some of the major soliloquies, a task that even recent criticism has not been able to successfully accomplish (Fawkner 1990). Because much of the current criticism has turned again to the character of Banquo (Blythe 1991), several students wrote about him. But by far the chief object of interest was Lady Macbeth.

In summary, the project worked out well, but I might cut its scope the next time, using perhaps only two of the films. Four films take up too much class time. But which two would be best? The Welles and Polanski versions provide an exceptionally good contrast with each other. Then again, either one of these used together with the Kurosawa film would make for a nice cross-cultural set of explorations. Either the Welles film or the Polanski film juxtaposed to the Verdi opera would provide a good contrast in media. I would not attempt to use the Kurosawa and Verdi versions together because the problems inherent in cultural displacement and in the appreciation of opera, coming together all at once, might make things too hard. Perhaps the best answer is to use three of the films, or to move on to the Shostakovich opera, *Lady Macbeth of Mtsensk*. Shakespeare is unending.

References

Asp, Carolyn. 1981. "'Be bloody, bold and resolute': Tragic Action and Sexual Stereotyping in *Macbeth*." *Studies in Philology* 78:153–69.

Blythe, David-Everett. 1991. "Banquo's Candles." *English Literary History* 58:773–78.

Carr, Stephen Leo, and Peggy A. Knapp. 1981. "Seeing through Macbeth." *PMLA* 96:837–47.

Fawkner, Harald William. 1990. *Deconstructing Macbeth: The Hyperontological View.* Rutherford, Madison, Teaneck: Fairleigh Dickinson University Press; London and Toronto: Associated University Presses.

Greene, James J. 1984. "*Macbeth*: Masculinity and Murder." *American Imago* 41:155–80.

Kurosawa, Akira, director. 1956. *Throne of Blood.* The Toho Company and Brandon Films.

Manvell, Roger. 1979. *Theatre and Film: A Comparative Study.* Rutherford, N.J.: Fairleigh Dickinson University Press.

Polanski, Roman, director. 1986. *Macbeth.* RCA/Columbia Pictures.

Shakespeare, William. 1974. *Macbeth.* In *The Riverside Shakespeare,* edited by G. Blakemore Evans. Boston: Houghton Mifflin.

Synard, Neil. 1986. *Filming Literature.* New York: St. Martin's Press.

Stockholder, Kay. 1987. "*Macbeth*: A Dream of Love." *American Imago* 44:85–106.

Verdi, Giuseppe. *Macbeth.* 1987. The Decca Record Company.

Welles, Orson, director. 1948. *Macbeth.* Republic Pictures Corporation.

Wintle, Sarah, and Rene Weis. 1991. "Macbeth and the Barren Sceptre." *Essays in Criticism* 41:128–46.

CHAPTER 27

"Our Lofty Scene"

Teaching Modern Film Versions
of Julius Caesar

SAMUEL CROWL
Ohio University
Athens, Ohio

Crowl recommends two film versions of Julius Caesar *as part of his approach to the play. The play itself has had a fascinating history in the classroom. In the late 1800s it was the most widely read play in American high schools: a century later it had fallen only to third place. At the same time, it has had "few successful realizations on stage." Crowl discusses the elements of the play that make it "so resistant to modern production"; he suggests two modern film versions for classroom use; he offers advice to teachers for arranging small-group response activities, specifically what he calls a "pairing approach" (that can also be used with other plays); and he provides useful commentary on each film's production.*

Julius Caesar is a curious play: widely read and studied in the schools, largely ignored by contemporary Shakespeare critics, and oddly resistant to successful realization on the modern stage. Even in an era when political ideology has become an official item on the agenda of Shakespeare studies, *Julius Caesar*'s obvious and direct engagement with political issues and themes has drawn scant attention.

The play does have a long history of speaking to contemporary issues. In America, Franklin, Jefferson, and Washington found parallels in *Julius Caesar* with their revolutionary experience, and John Wilkes Booth had the play feverishly stirring in his imagination as he jumped to the stage of Ford's Theatre after fatally wounding Abraham Lincoln. Gary Taylor reports that in 1886 *Caesar* was the most widely read Shakespeare play in American high schools; by 1988 it had only fallen to third place (behind *Romeo and Juliet* and *Macbeth*) and was still being read in 71 percent of the high schools across the country.[1] Shakespeare's play has served, from Jefferson and Washington to the present, as a key source for linking the American democracy with the Roman Republic in the popular imagination.

For a play that has such resonance with popular myths in both England and America it is surprising that *Julius Caesar* has received so few successful realizations on stage.[2] The most famous American version of this century remains Orson Welles's 1937 production for the Mercury Theatre, which galvanized both critics and audiences by its brash assimilation of the rise of fascism into its modern-dress production. In our own time, the Royal Shakespeare Company has found the play repeatedly intractable to successful realizations, and The Public Theater/New York Shakespeare Festival's production in 1988, with an all-star cast headed by Al Pacino and Martin Sheen, was an "embarrassing failure," according to *The New York Times*'s Frank Rich. Why does *Julius Caesar* appear so resistant to modern production? The Roman setting is certainly part of the problem as directors and designers seem either fixated on togas, columns, and alabaster statuary or incapable of successfully imagining the play against a less specific landscape. The play's focus on political oratory is difficult to capture in an anti-rhetorical age and is incompatible with a modern style of producing Shakespeare that emphasizes the conversational tone rather than the lyrical flourish. Interestingly, though film and television are even less receptive to public oratory than the contemporary stage, we have two modern film versions of the play, directed by Joseph Mankiewicz (1953) and by Stuart Burge (1970), which are available on video and offer an instructive visual contrast, from Joseph Mankiewicz's sleek formalism to Burge's view of the play through a postmodern lens.

In the past twenty years films of Shakespeare's plays have increasingly found their way into our classrooms not simply as a complement to teaching the text, but as production scripts deserving independent study and scrutiny. Many high school teachers have often used Shakespeare's *Julius Caesar* as a launching pad for class projects devoted less to the play itself than to recovering information about the Rome it appears to dramatize. Now Mankiewicz's and Burge's films of the play can be used to investigate how modern productions of Shakespeare inevitably reveal issues alive in the world at the moment of their creation.

Although only seventeen years passed between the making of the two films, each clearly represents the differing political and aesthetic assumptions of its cultural era. The films make a wonderful study in contrasts and can be creatively used to show how unstatic, how fluid and plastic, Shakespeare's text becomes when it is lifted off of the page and given life on stage or screen.

I suggest that teachers who might wish to use the films when teaching the play divide the class into three groups. The first group would be responsible for reporting and writing on the Mankiewicz film and locating its interpretive approach against the American political background of the 1950s. The second group would do the same for Burge's film, allowing the students to see its connections with the Vietnam War era; and the third group would he charged with defining and detailing the ways in which the two productions present quite different "readings" of the same textual material. A similar "pairing" approach can be followed with other film versions of some of Shakespeare's frequently taught plays: Laurence Olivier's 1944 *Henry V* with Kenneth Branagh's 1989 version; Tony Richardson's 1969 *Hamlet* with Franco Zeffirelli's more romantic 1990 film; and the Warner Brothers 1935 *A Midsummer Night's Dream*—its cast full of Hollywood stars—with Peter Hall's very different approach to the play in 1968 with actors from the Royal Shakespeare Company. What follows is my own detailed analysis of these *Julius Caesar* films, reading them against the background of the cultural and political issues prominent when they were made.

John Houseman originally came to Hollywood in 1939 as part of Orson Welles's Mercury Theatre team. He survived longer than Welles and had become, by 1952, a successful producer at Metro-Goldwyn-Mayer anxious to tackle a Shakespearean project. Houseman's earlier collaboration with Welles on the famous stage version of *Julius Caesar* made his choice of the play a natural one, like the choice of the erudite Mankiewicz as director. Houseman reports that he and Mankiewicz successfully battled MGM in their desire to shoot the film in black and white so as to better underline the play's parallels with recent history.

> In our eagerness to stress the historical parallel between the political intrigues of the last years of the Roman Republic and recent European events, we were drawn irresistibly to the use of black and white. Hitler, Mussolini and Gano at the Brenner Pass; Stalin and Ribbentrop signing the pact—we had seen these and other personal meetings that soon turned to violence and death in the press photos and newsreels of the past decade; they were hauntingly similar to the tense confrontations of Shakespeare's conspirators before and after the assassination. For the Forum scenes the parallel was even more obvious: inevitably these would evoke memories of the Fuhrer at Nuremberg and of Mussolini ranting from his high balcony overlooking the wildly cheering crowd that would presently spit on his dead body as it hung by its feet outside a gas station.[3]

Unfortunately, nothing in the film works to remind us specifically of these contemporary parallels and one might as easily suppose that the play was selected not for its parallels with pre-war Europe, but with post-war America. America was left, by war's end, as the inheritor of the power and the problems associated with Europe's various empires. By the early 1950s the country was being internally consumed by the communist witch-hunts sponsored by the House Un-American Activities Committee and Senator Joseph McCarthy. Hollywood was intimately involved in both the extension of America's international influence and the internal hysteria about supposed subversives. Mankiewicz explicitly refuses to give us the spectacle version of Rome we might expect from Hollywood; he concentrates instead on a tightly focused formalist approach eager to explore the play's irony and ambiguity.

Mankiewicz came to directing after a long career as screenwriter and producer and is known for having made literate films, ones which often deftly employed literary devices like the flashback and multiple points of view with rare film success. Interestingly, his great contribution to his version of *Julius Caesar* was to resist film's natural tendency to open such a work up to spectacle and epic grandeur. What captures Mankiewicz's imagination is not Rome, but the remarkable play of politics and personalities among the play's central characters: Caesar, Cassius, Brutus, and Antony. The film is at its best when it is in tight focus on the interplay within this quartet. Jack Jorgens accurately describes its subdued style:

> Mankiewicz's shots are often rigidly frontal and composed in geometric patterns— circles, triangles, and squares. In general, however, individual shots call little attention to themselves. In classical Hollywood style, the force and movement are linear as the action is propelled forward and emphasis placed on the actors and their lines.[4]

The way Mankiewicz's camera introduces us to the play's principals is instructive. After the opening scene the camera cranes up from the street to catch the procession to the Forum from above. Very briefly the screen is filled with the festive spectacle of packed streets with people leaning out of windows and hanging from the sides of buildings (the sets from *Quo Vadis* were in fact still standing on the MGM backlot and thus were given double service). But the camera quickly cranes back down to shoot Caesar (Louis Calhern) and Casca from the rear as they proceed toward the archway leading into the Forum. As Caesar spies Antony—our first view of Marlon Brando—standing with the other runners he stops and turns back toward the camera to summon Calpurnia. As he does, Casca circles behind him in the frame (one of the geometric patterns Jorgens points out), thus brilliantly anticipating the way Caesar will be encircled by the conspirators (and specifically Casca) at his assassination. As the camera finds Calpurnia and swings back with her to Caesar, Antony is called to join them. Calhern underlines the crassness of Caesar's public humiliation of his wife by delivering his remarks about her sterility in a haughty tone with his head tilted at an imperial angle. As Calpurnia moves out of the frame, we watch Brando's eyes lower and compassionately follow her in a silent acknowledgment of her embarrassment.

The parade resumes and the camera then catches the backs of Cassius and Brutus, who are immediately behind Caesar in the procession. When the voice of the soothsayer calls out from the crowd, Caesar again stops and turns back to the camera, following the same pattern we observed moments before. This time it is Cassius who circles behind Caesar and our first frontal shot of John Gielgud comes as he pivots to turn back to the camera and peers over Caesar's shoulder with a look of utter contempt.

As Caesar inquires "What man is that?" James Mason's Brutus slides into the frame from the left to repeat the soothsayer's prophecy about the Ides of March, and Caesar is now caught between Cassius and Brutus. The camera then moves into the crowd on "let me see his face" as Brutus leads the soothsayer out from the crowd into the street; the soothsayer's blindness is defined by a staff topped with a series of jangling bells. When Caesar dismisses him as a "dreamer" the procession continues into the Forum, parting to pass the soothsayer and Brutus stranded in the middle of the street. The camera then cuts to the two figures as the soothsayer takes Brutus's head in his hands and begins to touch his face for identification; his hands jump back as soon as they recognize who it is. The soothsayer moves off as Brutus stands puzzled at his reaction, and the camera finds Cassius leaning with his arms folded against the archway at the rear of the frame waiting to make his move. In this sequence it is Brutus who has been caught at the center of the frame and encircled by forces he does not yet comprehend.

In the midst of a scene which might easily have been swallowed up in epic spectacle, Mankiewicz and his camera have opted instead for what Lorne Buchman has termed film's special ability to create a "spectacle of multiplicity" by deftly presenting the play's four central characters and the spatial and physical relationships that will come to define their interaction.[5] Here, each character has existed within the same horizontal plane, their relationships suggested by their movement and positioning within the frame. As Mankiewicz moves to capture the next sequence in 1.2 he will employ film's ability to work vertically as well as horizontally. Shakespeare brilliantly uses an inner-outer contrast both spatially and psychologically at this moment. Caesar has entered the Forum to receive the adulation of the festive crowd gathered for the race. Cassius and Brutus remain outside to begin to explore their mutual dissatisfaction with Caesar—the man and his politics.

As Brutus moves away from Cassius he takes a book out from the folds of his toga and begins to ascend a set of the Forum's exterior stairs. The book neatly anticipates 4.3 while at the same time distancing the contemplative Brutus from the gamesome Antony. It also underlines Caesar's soon-to-be-expressed fears of men who read too much. The camera shoots from above as Cassius pulls even with Brutus on the steps on "I have not from your eyes that gentleness," and then moves up ahead of him on "You bear too stubborn and too strange a hand / Over your friend that loves you." Brutus joins Cassius on "Be not deceived" and the two men continue to climb together as Brutus apologizes for and tries to explain his recent distant behavior. This provides Cassius with the opening, and the momentum, he was seeking as he stops and asks "Tell me, good Brutus, can you see your face?" We get our first cut since they began to ascend as the camera now shoots up from Cassius's perspective capturing Brutus as he stops and turns back to Cassius's question and the camera. Cassius then comes up behind Brutus and the camera comes around to catch them both in medium close-up as Cassius purrs in Brutus's left ear about mirrors and hidden worthiness. The subtle shifts in control between the two men during these exchanges are perfectly mirrored in their movement up the steps, which constitutes as well an imaginative anticipation of the image of "ambition's ladder" evoked by Brutus in 2.1. The Forum crowd roars for the first time as Brutus and Cassius reach the last level before the final ascent into the Forum itself. Here Brutus sits on a bench and Cassius leans over him as he begins his treatise on Caesar's failings. When he reaches the Tiber story he moves away and stands before a huge statue of Caesar and nods at it derisively on "Caesar cried 'Help me, Cassius, or I sink'"; then in a stunning reversal of angle, Mankiewicz has the camera shoot down over the statue's shoulder as Cassius spits out:

> And this man
> Is now become a god, and Cassius is
> A wretched creature, and must bend his body
> If Caesar carelessly but nod on him.
>   (1.2.115–18)

Cassius, who has carefully controlled the scene to this moment, in his gradual physical and psychological dominance of Brutus, is now reduced by the camera to one of those petty men who walk under Caesar's huge legs and peep about to find dishonorable graves. The film here graphically captures Caesar's powerful, looming presence, which dominates the play both in this early pivotal sequence as well as in its mirror scene in 4.3 long after his assassination. In this moment, Mankiewicz captures Caesar's centrality to the play and to the lives of the very conspirators who seek to topple him. Cassius's and Brutus's inability, in dealing with Caesar, to separate the divine from the human leads them, in C. L. Barber and Richard Wheeler's astute formulation, to create "a hideous parody of blood sacrifice, from which the Ghost of Caesar emerges as a demonic power."[6] The death of Caesar destabilizes not only the state but also the psychological identities of his principal opponents, so that when "rivalry erupts between Brutus and Cassius [it can] be reconciled only in their common recognition that they are both bereft, lost inwardly without the center Caesar gave their lives."[7]

This extended analysis has meant to reveal how fluidly and effectively Mankiewicz's polished film style has worked to capture the dynamics at work in his Shakespearean material. Mankiewicz's treatment is augmented by the way he skillfully blends the contrasting acting styles of Calhern, Brando, Gielgud, and Mason. Ironically, though Gielgud was the greatest Shakespearean actor in the quartet, he had the least film experience and, in fact, only became a great film actor during the latter years of his long and rich career. His performance is finely chiseled, well spoken, and broken only by a few moments—especially in the quarrel scene—when his acting becomes too stagy. Gielgud's Cassius has a touch of vanity about him, which may be why he is so easily provoked by Caesar's. Gielgud and Mankiewicz create a fine moment at the end of 1.2 when Gielgud quietly delivers his brief soliloquy with his body leaning back against the very archway where we first glimpsed Mark Antony, and then moves forward on "I will this night" as the camera tracks back and up through the now empty street as the wind begins to rise and the flower petals earlier showered upon Caesar are picked up and blown about the moving figure as the prelude to the coming storm he has done much to initiate.

Not surprisingly for its historical moment, the film presents James Mason's brooding, soft-spoken Brutus as the classic conscientious liberal trapped between his pure ideals and dirty politics. Mankiewicz visually complicates several moments in Brutus's famous "It must be by his death" soliloquy by shooting him first through the limbs of a bare tree and later with the shadows cast by a grape arbor falling across his face, each image suggesting the tangled nature of Brutus's tortured reasoning. Calhern's Caesar certainly bears little relationship to the tyrants who provoked World War II. He seems much more the familiar garrulous legislator who enjoys the rewards of attention and influence his position provides and the ability to dispatch favors and advice to his sycophants rather than a brutal figure who relishes the wielding of power. Calhern repeatedly emphasizes that mortality which so provokes Cassius. He twice draws attention to his bad ear, leans on Antony for support as he exits the Forum, and is wonderfully eager for the morning cup of wine once the messy business of attending the day's Senate meeting has been resolved.

A production that seeks to emphasize the play's irony and ambiguity will inevitably come to center on the play's most ironic and ambiguous figure: Mark Antony. Marlon Brando's performance is a stunning example of cunning and calculation and is film acting at its best. His youthful handsomeness, his passion and intelligence, his ability to absorb the dynamics of a moment and turn it to advantage all help make his performance the driving energy of the film for my students.

As Steve Vineberg has observed, Brando "is a sleek, ultramasculine, soldierly Marc Antony, as well as intelligent and watchful; he stalks the streets and the Senate slowly, in a way that implies strength in repose."[8] "Watchful" is the key word in Vineberg's assessment, as Brando's eyes carry the essence of his performance. I have already indicated how those slightly lowered eyes follow Calpurnia and in so doing provide a judgment on Caesar's boorishness. When Brando enters the Senate after the assassination, Mankiewicz shoots him in a long shot down a narrow corridor seen from the perspective of the conspirators huddled around Caesar's body. As Brando begins slowly to move toward them he passes through light and shadow—a powerful mystery figure come to disrupt the conspirator's lofty scene. Brutus rises and moves around the group to greet Antony, but Antony's gaze is fixed on Caesar's body, and he glides by Brutus as though he were not there. The conspirators are frozen by his presence and do not stir until he slowly raises his eyes from the body and fixes them in his stare on "I know not, gentleman, what you intend." The camera then shoots from behind each conspirator as Antony constructs his own ironic counter-ritual by shaking each of their hands and calling out their names, thus completing the parallel trio of greetings earlier performed by Brutus (2.1) and Caesar (2.2) When he has finished he quickly looks down at his right hand and, after registering its bloody reality, slowly closes it into a fist.

Brando's treatment of the conspirators is at one with his later manipulation of the crowd. Both are distinguished by a controlled irony in which he manages to transform his personal anger into public revenge. The power of Brando's anger leaps out on "pardon me, Caius Cassius," after Cassius has interrupted his lament, but is quickly brought under control on "cold modesty." Brando effectively employs this pattern of releasing and then subduing his anger not only here with the conspirators to keep them off guard, but later with the mob when he wants to elevate their passions from anger to fury. The scene with the conspirators concludes in a fine reverse angle shot in which we first see the conspirators exit in a long shot over Antony's shoulder, which then cuts to Brutus's perspective as he looks back on Antony and Caesar while shutting the central doors to the Senate. Now, as Brando turns back to Caesar, he gives us a ferocious reprise of the bloody open hand being closed into a tight fist as he raises fist, arm, eyes, and voice for a powerful release of "A curse shall light upon the limbs of men." The camera then cranes back and up to allow him full voice on "Cry 'Havoc,' and let slip the dogs of war" but then quickly moves back down to a close-up to relish Brando's final disdain: "That this foul deed shall smell above the earth / With carrion men, groaning for burial."

Maynard Mack has written that in a school for demagogues Antony's funeral oration "would be the whole curriculum." Mankiewicz turns the crowd into a wonderful choric character with several proletarian faces—male and female—selected to give it voice. Brando plays upon it magnificently as his intelligence discovers that irony is the perfect mode to whip the crowd into a vengeful mob. His eyes flash fire on "Ambition should be made of sterner stuff," and he provides a daring stutter on "p . . . p . . . pause" in "My heart is in the coffin there with Caesar, / And I must pause till it comes back to me." Here he turns his back on the crowd, and the camera catches his cunning expression as he listens intently for their response to his theatrics. Brando provides a similar ironic moment when his voice and posture mock the crowd on "O, now you weep . . . ," which also gets the intended reaction. By the time Antony is approaching the climax of his oration, words like "wise," "honorable," and "reasons" are dripping with irony. He repeats, now publicly, the posture and gesture that crowned his private vow to Caesar as he raises the will in his right hand and cries out in full voice: "Here was a Caesar! When comes such a-a-n-n-n-o-other?" As the mob swirls into destructive action, Antony quietly climbs back up the steps of the Senate and the camera catches on his face a chilling half smile which, as Jack Jorgens reports, allowed Mankiewicz to let the smile speak for itself and to leave Shakespeare's "Now let it work" on the cutting room floor.[10]

Jack Jorgens and Steve Vineberg are both correct in calling attention to one final detail in Brando's performance. Act 4, scene 1 is set in Caesar's house, on the balcony overlooking the city. Perched on the center of the balcony's railing is a bust of Caesar facing into the house. After Octavius exits, Brando moves out onto the balcony and stretches out his arms as he takes in the commanding view. Spying Caesar's bust, he reaches out and moves it a quarter turn so that it faces him directly, and the camera catches on Brando's face the same sly private smile that was the final image left lingering in our minds after his funeral oration. Brando's smile here is more than just one of relishing the irony of his triumph. It is a smile that acknowledges that he is the force through which Caesar's demonic power will be released.

The last great scene in the film is the quarrel between Cassius and Brutus. Gielgud's Cassius, always tightly wound, has now become emotionally unstrung and there is real yearning in his "Do you confess so much?" after Brutus has diffused the tension by admitting his own ill-temper. Mason has made his Brutus the most patient and long-suffering of men, and that patience is here stretched almost to the breaking point. The playing of the scene precisely captures the centrality of Caesar to both men's identities. Mankiewicz's film gives us four impressive performances while also providing us with a cool modernist reading of the ambiguous stance the play presents on the interrelationship between power, politics, and personality.

Almost twenty years later the play would be revisited on film in a very different historical moment. Stuart Burge's film appeared at the end of the decade dominated by the assassination of John Kennedy, the war in Vietnam, and the student revolt in Europe and America. The film's look and tone and feel reflect its historical moment. The opening shot catches an eagle soaring over a battlefield in Spain littered with fallen bodies. The camera then cuts to a ravaged skull still wearing its helmet and as it closes in on the skull's gruesome expression we hear the shouts of "Caesar . . . Caesar . . . Caesar" on the soundtrack as we segue to Caesar's triumphant procession into Rome.

The film seems intentionally ugly; nothing quite matches, from the satin sheen and gaudy colors of the costumes to the graffiti carelessly carved on the wall in an antechamber of the Forum, to the seedy look of Casca's untrimmed beard, to the ridiculously mannered spit curls that deck Brutus's forehead, to the embarrassing way in which the four central performances—once again evenly divided between British and American actors—fail to quicken our interest. For example, Gielgud's performance as Caesar is—along with Diana Rigg's Portia—the most interesting in the film, but it bears no resemblance to the opening image of military carnage. In fact it is impossible to imagine Gielgud's sweet, gentle, kindly— if a bit vain—Caesar as a great general or even a decadent dispenser of military might. The opening sequence—including narration from Plutarch about Caesar's campaign in Spain and his desire to be a dictator—just doesn't square with the genial, jovial, even slightly daft, Caesar Gielgud creates.

Heston's Antony is far less complex than Brando's. It is hard to imagine what Gielgud's clever, witty Caesar ever saw in Heston's earnest bore. The funeral oration displays none of the ironic modulation that distinguished Brando's performance, but is delivered with a deadly grimace. Brando's eyes flashed fire, here the only gleam comes from Heston's teeth— tempting the viewer to reflect that, alas, some of the fault is in our stars.

Richard Johnson creates a solid, workmanlike portrait of Cassius even when he is required to perform such tacky gestures as scratching out Caesar's name on a graffiti-covered wall and carving Brutus's next to it. Unfortunately he is paired with Jason Robards's Brutus, who delivers all his lines in a monotone with no understanding of the inflected rhythm of Shakespeare's iambic pentameter line. Robards comes alive only in the quarrel scene in 4.3, where Shakespeare's material most resembles Eugene O'Neill's. Here Robards is at home; the exchange between Brutus and Cassius about money and corruption, loyalty and betrayal is an early version of the famous late-night bouts of family incriminations played out by James and Jamie Tyrone in *Long Day's Journey into Night*. The little smile he provides on "O Cassius, you are yoked with a lamb" is a small glimmer of the deft touches that distinguish the great Robards film performances in *All the President's Men, Melvin and Howard,* and *Julia.*

Robards and Heston labor through their performances without ever capturing the sheer joy for the actor provided by Shakespeare's language. Robards—except in the quarrel scene— wants to underplay every moment, while Heston overplays most of his. He delivers the entire funeral oration by first scolding, then sneering at the crowd; every posture he strikes and gesture he makes is meant to underline his own rectitude. And this from an Antony who has smeared his face with Caesar's blood as a prelude to "Cry 'Havoc' and let slip the dogs of war."

When Burge later shoots Antony's and Octavius's exchange in 4.1 in a Roman bath while each is getting a rub, or when we come upon Antony at Phillipi stretched out on the ground eating grapes and squirting his mouth full of wine from a wineskin, we witness other examples of moments in the film which just don't square with the performers. Heston's strengths as an actor are not those capable of capturing this quick-spirited, gamesome, calculating character.

Burge's film, in contrast to Mankiewicz's, reveals a postmodern, rather than modern, aesthetic. Its details jangle and jar with one another in an attempt to make the play speak to a time clearly out of joint. By reducing all of the play's central characters to stereotypes— Gielgud's effete Caesar, Heston's crass Antony, Johnson's radical Cassius, and Robards's dim, mumbling Brutus—the film sees in Shakespeare's Rome a cynical reflection of politics and politicians spawned by Vietnam and Watergate.

Dennis Kennedy (1993), in writing about stage productions of Shakespeare in our century, has wisely observed that "there is a clear relationship between what a production looks like and what its spectators accept as its statement and value. . . . the visual signs the performance generates are not only the guide to its social and cultural meaning but often constitute the meaning itself."[11] Kennedy's remark has even greater significance for film, where image generally predominates over word. These two Caesar films are vivid examples of the way Shakespeare's text continues to inspire production images which spring and speak out of the cultural and historical moment of their generation.[12]

Notes

1. *Reinventing Shakespeare* (Oxford: Oxford University Press, 1990), 204; "Shakespeare Then, Shakespeare Now: What They Read in High School," *New York Times,* 20 May 1992.

2. John Ripley concludes his thorough history, *Julius Caesar on Stage in England and*

America, 1599–1973 (Cambridge: Cambridge University Press, 1980), by remarking *"Julius Caesar's* stage history . . . is a tale of unrealized potential" (275).

3. *Unfinished Business: Memoirs: 1902–1988* (New York: Applause Theatre Books, 1989), 324.

4. *Shakespeare on Film* (Bloomington: Indiana University Press, 1977), 101.

5. *Still in Movement: Shakespeare on Screen* (Oxford: Oxford University Press, 1991), 12.

6. *The Whole Journey: Shakespeare's Power of Development* (Berkeley: University of California Press, 1986), 36

7. *The Whole Journey,* 36.

8. *Method Actors: Three Generations of an American Acting Style* (New York: Schirmer Books, 1991), 160.

9. *"Julius Caesar"* in *Modern Shakespearean Criticism,* ed. Alvin B. Kernan (New York: Harcourt, Brace and World, 1970), 297.

10. *Shakespeare on Film,* 100.

11. *Looking at Shakespeare* (Cambridge: Cambridge University Press, 1993), 5.

12. For a fuller treatment of Shakespeare's Roman plays on film, see my "A World Elsewhere: The Roman Plays on Film and Television," included in *Shakespeare and the Moving Image* (Cambridge: Cambridge University Press, 1994), edited by Anthony Davies and Stanley Wells. Some of this material (about eight paragraphs) first appeared there.

CHAPTER 28

Shakespeare Festivals
Materials for the Classroom

Eva B. McManus
Ohio Northern University
Ada, Ohio

McManus acknowledges the increasing availability of films and other videos, but in this chapter she explores another resource that can help teachers make the study of Shakespeare more dynamic for their classes: the educational programs at festivals and theaters. She believes that such theaters and festivals offer "wonderful learning opportunities," and that distance will not be an impediment if teachers take advantage of the companies' educational outreach programs, traveling troupes, and so forth. McManus has conducted a two-year study of these programs and has high praise for the quality of their work. She offers a wealth of suggestions about accessibility and urges teachers to take of advantage of these resources.

To teach and to delight—this classic dictum leaps to mind when we prepare to teach Shakespeare. Although the ideal is that all teachers anticipate this task with joy and the expectation of creating memorable classroom moments, many teachers find guiding their students through one of Shakespeare's plays leaves them nervous, even depressed. This reaction is not too surprising when one considers that teachers go through such varied training, much of which emphasizes literature other than Shakespeare's works. To these people as well as to those who have the training but lack the confidence, teaching Shakespeare looms large, compounded further by the undeniable burden of "doing it well" since the Bard is such a major literary figure. How to approach Shakespeare, then, is an important question, a question whose significance to English courses at all academic levels is exemplified by this book on teaching Shakespeare, the second by these two editors. The recent increase in teaching workshops across the country and the advent of a journal such as *Shakespeare and the Classroom,* devoted to issues for all Shakespeare teachers, attest to the interest as well as the need many of us have to improve our work with students studying Shakespeare.

One of the chief prohibitions to a smooth, relatively easy approach to the playwright lies in his language. Credited as the single greatest force in shaping the English language, Shakespeare's extensive vocabulary stretches to include standard words, new words, and archaic usages. Logically, that makes him hard to follow, for teachers and students. For some instructors, this barrier leads to a sense of failure, to a belief that they are inadequate to reveal the subtle nuances of language and expose buried themes. One "cure" for this dismay has emerged only recently. Sweeping the country over the last several years, performance theory has led to more interactive classes that help the students grasp the language more fully. As they perform scenes themselves, they learn to speak the lines, understand those subtleties, and recognize the dramatic nature of the works. Even on the elementary level, such aids as Albert Cullum's *Shake Hands with Shakespeare* allow students to appropriate Shakespeare's language and to claim ownership of a scene or a full production. Additionally, educators frequently use the growing number of films and videos available to show classes how the plays work and why they continue to be so popular. Although these options enhance Shakespeare studies, some teachers wish they could make the Shakespeare experience still more dynamic for their classes. In order to do that, I recommend another resource — the educational programs at Shakespeare festivals and theaters throughout North America.[1]

Obviously, many teachers already take their pupils to performances at a nearby Shakespeare festival. For the students, the learning situation is ideal; they are able to study a play first and then see a full-length, well-staged production of it. Their experience also enhances subsequent classroom discussions. A particular feature of the festivals and theaters that has an immediate impact on the students is the facility in which the performances are staged. Plays occur in venues such as large circus tents, outside amphitheaters, tiny studio theaters, and large, formal stages. The costuming and sets can also differ markedly, reaching from such elaborate productions as those at Alabama, Ashland, Utah, and Stratford with their complex sets and period costumes to the Hudson Valley's use of "vintage" clothing from second-hand shops and their minimal sets that merely suggest location. Most festivals offer "get-to-know-the-theater" tours — backstage, to the costume warehouse, and to the green room to meet the actors. Some even offer pre- and post-performance speakers and miniature Renaissance festivals preceding the performances. Visiting any of these theaters clearly offers wonderful learning opportunities. Unfortunately, many schools are not close enough for even a day trip to a Shakespeare production, but that is cause for little concern because of the educational outreach programs.

Most of these companies offer educational programs, both on- and off-site, and employ staff education liaisons to work with teachers on building strong Shakespeare experiences for the students. The programs differ, as do the materials each group offers. The range is impressive, providing a cache of wonderfully rich resources for all of us. Just a glance at the list of programs reveals marvelous options: a week or longer residencies in which members of the company work with students in the schools towards the class's production of a scene; teacher workshops; traveling troupes who perform entire plays, shortened plays to fit into a class period, and/or scenes from various plays along with lab sessions with the actors; summer camps and internships for students on various related performance topics — acting, swordplay, speaking, set design; week- to month-long summer institutes for teachers taking certification credits. Most companies publish teacher resources that also range widely from short synopses of the plays to in-class exercises, detailed study questions and innovative classroom activities. Some festivals even publish extensive teacher's workbooks, and Colorado has the ultimate form of help, a teacher hot-line for those who are really stuck. Some others offer kits on staging a Shakespeare festival, requiring the students to involve the entire school and community.[2] Besides the more traditional programs, these companies provide unique opportunities in many untraditional areas as well. For instance, senior citizens groups seeking a challenging program can try the Utah Festival's Camp Shakespeare for Seniors. If teachers have non-traditional students such as those at a correctional facility and can't figure how to work in the junior or senior Shakespeare requirement with such disenfranchised, even hostile, students, they might want to contact Shakespeare & Co. at the Mount (Mass.). This company has its own correctional institute program in which members work with students (inmates) in the facility and then bring them out (in chains) to perform their play (unshackled but under tight security) at a local community college play contest. Those working to keep juveniles out of detention centers and off the mean city streets might contact the San Francisco Festival about its Midnight Shakespeare, a program built on the concepts behind Midnight Basketball. This quick glance at a few programs clearly indicates that the materials and opportunities to enhance the classroom study of Shakespeare abound. They fit almost any educational situation one can envision, offering challenging ways to meet the needs of each student group.

In my two-year study of these education programs, I have found that some of the best teaching of Shakespeare and some of the most creative work with students is being done by these festival and theater groups. They take their mission seriously; linking it to their strong emphasis on performance, they build lively, engaging classroom opportunities that can enrich a class's experience with Shakespeare while also transforming the burden of teaching Shakespeare into a joyfully anticipated part of the curriculum.

Additionally, I want to emphasize that not being close to a regional festival does not preclude any classes from participating. Many of these companies travel for much of the off-season. They will visit schools in any part of the state (some even cross state lines). Others may not bring an entire company but will send small groups of actors to run their in-school residencies. For a listing of main companies, check the spring *Shakespeare News-letter*, available in most college libraries or directly from the Department of English, Iona College, New Rochelle, NY 10801. It provides addresses, phone numbers and the upcoming season's playlist for many of the companies. Since some groups also offer special educational materials for a small cost, teachers might want to check this list to see which companies are offering what plays and send away for their materials to evaluate them, particularly as they usually write their materials keyed to their own specific productions (rather than as generic studies of the plays). The study guides with the rationales for the interpretive choices each company makes in staging a play offer another bountiful resource for class discussions on performance.

While I have contacted about thirty companies, I have not covered all of the companies in the United States.[3] Therefore, the information that follows is a compilation based on these contacts and is not comprehensive. The failure to mention a festival's or theater's programs does not automatically imply that they do not have them. Also, I have not attempted to rank them in any way or to value one company over another. My goal is simply to start teachers thinking of these companies as resources; to do so I will present an overview of programs and materials rather than a festival-by-festival listing. Since many festivals are building their educational programs, their offerings change from year to year due to fluctuations in funding as well as shifting priorities and available staff; therefore, educators should check with them from time to time. I found that many are open to suggestions and clearly share ideas with each other. Their commitment to educating the public about Shakespeare has led them to develop these programs that help teachers work with their classes in exciting ways. To enhance their classes, I urge teachers to contact whatever festival or theater groups are in the region. Due to these educational outreach programs, rewarding relationships have blossomed between teachers and festival/theater staffs all over North America.

Traveling Companies

Besides their on-site stage productions, many Shakespeare festivals and theaters have touring companies. These groups can mount full-scale productions of a play in a large school auditorium/gym or in a civic center, usually making advance contact with the local high schools to allow as many as possible to attend. Shakespeare on Wheels, unique among Shakespeare companies in the U.S., presents a full-length play on a flatbed wagon that converts from a tractor-trailer to an Elizabethan stage. Limited only by the requirement of power hook-ups and room for the audience to sit or stand, they can perform in a variety of settings—in school parking lots, at hospitals, and on the premises of other institutions. Because of space and time limitations of the school groups, though, some companies tailor their productions to meet the needs of their student audiences more particularly by offering a shortened version of a play, running from fifty to ninety minutes, which allows the show to be viewed during a class period. Another option is to present selected scenes from a variety of plays centering on a specific theme. For instance, the Kentucky Festival offers a choice of programs—"Boy Meets Girl Meets Shakespeare" with scenes from *Romeo and Juliet, Macbeth, Hamlet, A Midsummer Night's Dream, Twelfth Night, The Taming of the Shrew, As You Like It,* and *Much Ado,* or "Shakespeare's Clowns: A Fool's Guide to Shakespeare," which includes monologues and songs from *Twelfth Night, Hamlet, A Midsummer Night's Dream, The Winter's Tale, Henry IV, The Tempest,* and *Two Gentleman of Verona.* Some companies will send study guides for the students and various teachers' guides prior to arriving. A number of companies arrange for time either before or after the production to have actors in costume come into the audience, answer questions and generally lead a discussion of a particular scene or of the entire play. The rationale is that the students will talk frankly to the actors about what it is like to play these scenes or to handle whatever stage business is required in a specific scene. These encounters frequently generate a discussion about performance choices and indirectly about the play's language. I was pleased to learn how many companies stress the importance of language and have found interesting ways to help students do so. Most troupes build programs around the idea of moving the kids from the page to the stage. For instance, Shakespeare and Company at the Mount follows up their ninety-minute performance of a play such as *Julius Caesar* with the actors (as themselves, not in character) asking students questions about their understanding of the play. They will then replay a scene and ask the kids what they would have done differently in terms of reactions between characters. Replaying the scene one more time, they incorporate the students' suggestions to show the effects of different interpretations. This process allows the young people to act as directors who are sensitive to the language in a particular scene.

A few companies travel with other types of shows besides a play or specific scenes from plays. For example, the Utah Festival offers its "Costume Cavalcade," a wonderfully detailed, entertaining fashion show of costumes used in their productions, which are based on actual clothing of the times they depict. The narrator provides astonishing details about the various periods and the rationale for the clothing styles. Utah has made this traveling show available on video (last year's price was $19.95 per tape plus $2.55 shipping and handling). When I showed it in my class last quarter, the students howled over the women's dresses lined with small pockets to hold rodents that helped keep the ladies warm during the winter. I had a few thoughts of my own on the pregnancy look women once thought was high fashion. In a like manner, Stratford (Ontario) sends out its "Theatre Trunk" to introduce costuming to local students. Meanwhile, San Francisco reaches the younger set with its "Tell the Tales of Shakespeare," a show in which the main character, a puppet, tries to find out who Shakespeare is. Four children from the audience are picked in advance, rehearse briefly with the company, and then perform with the group. All these programs enhance the classroom experience for students.

While most companies limit their travels to in-state locations, some groups are more far-ranging. For instance, the San Francisco actors visited about 350 schools last year alone. The Ashland (Oregon) troupe visits eight western states, Shakespeare and Company at the Mount covers all New England, while the North Carolina touring group travels widely throughout the south, and the Three Rivers Festival (Pittsburgh) covers a tri-state region. Bill Brown's Shakespeare on Wheels (University of Maryland at Baltimore) visits three east coast states, and the Shenandoah Shakespeare Express crisscrosses the entire U.S. Obviously, such productions have a price. The Festival at the Mount charges $1,700 for a performance and a forty-five-minute program while *Globeworks,* the touring company for the North Carolina Festival, runs close to $1,000 for its forty-five-minute collage of scenes from several plays. Since many school budgets barely stretch to cover the basics, those seeking special theater productions may want to band together to find outside funding through humanities or arts endowment grants, either on the national or state levels. However, because some theater companies also receive grants or subsidies that allow them to make these trips and thereby cut costs to the schools, teachers shouldn't be daunted if they are interested in bringing a company to their region or school. Last year the Shenandoah Shakespeare Express secured an NEA grant that enabled them to keep their rates low while visiting a hundred schools throughout the country. Sometimes the theater festivals will also make suggestions based on their past experience. For example, they may recommend coordinating budgets with several schools to combine resources or working with a local civic center. Educators should remember, too, that some civic groups and corporations are willing to help pay for certain types of educational ventures. For instance, Fred Adams, founder of the Utah Shakespeare Festival, credits the Cedar City Lion's Club with helping them survive their first year by a substantial contribution (Chidester 1995, 14). Coca-Cola pays for the distribution of teachers' guides for the Alabama season's plays to all the high school teachers in the state and helps to fund some of their outreach programs as well, much as Shell Canada does for the Stratford, Ontario Festival. So teachers shouldn't be shy about asking for information or funding.

In-School Residencies

As an offshoot of the traveling companies, many festivals and theaters send ensembles of actors into the schools to run special workshops with the students. Most take an interactive approach, encouraging the students to participate, and usually culminate the residency with a performance by the class. These programs again vary in length and topic. Some hold single-class sessions while other companies extend their programs from one to two weeks. Shakespeare and Company at the Mount has the longest residencies—ten weeks—during which they help the students prepare production of a complete play. As representatives from the Great Lakes Theatre Festival told me, when they go into a school, they often work with several classes and grade levels, maybe on three or four different plays. They will work all day with different groups, usually for a week at a time. The demands on the actors during these residencies are heavy, yet all I canvassed raved about the results.

Although the festival companies have differing concepts of their goals, all work to bring the students closer to the plays. David White, director of Outreach Programs for the Three Rivers Festival, said their goal is to make the plays accessible. His troupe concentrates on making the students' responses "more visceral" by helping them understand the characters' emotions. He explains that "even if the kids can't get real plot details, they can understand emotions." Amy Atwell of the Georgia Festival says that her actors discuss obstacles characters have to overcome. The students puzzle over the characters' methods of achieving their goals and analyze the emotions they experience while doing so. Shakespeare and Company at the Mount encourages the students to understand the physical work of the actors as well as the language in the plays. The Ashland Festival refers to their workshops as "on-your-feet" explorations of the different aspects of acting. The Hudson Valley company makes the students "shareholders" in a production. Bill Rudman of the Great Lakes Festival sees the company's role as supplementing the academic teacher's preparation. He says the actors do not envision themselves as visiting artists; instead, they regard themselves as people who come to work with the students. They aim to "help provide an entry point that only serves to deepen the students' understanding." The actors then are "facilitators." He adds that their goal is to help the student-actors "find the character in themselves and in so doing to find themselves." Most companies insist that their actors be teachers as well; they train them well before sending them into the schools. These companies also view their mission as two-fold: to educate their audiences and to deliver Shakespeare to the informed audience.

Most residencies or workshops provide a series of warm-up exercises to free the students mentally and physically before their first acting instruction. From there, they progress through lessons on such topics as staging, history, speech, sword-fighting, and set design. Watching last fall as the Great Lakes Theatre Group presented its program to eight teachers in northwest Ohio, I was able to see first-hand how such sessions develop. A detailed syllabus for each day outlines certain goals, tasks, and related discussion topics. At our workshop, the Ohio teachers expressed interest in the perceptiveness and depth of the actor-teacher's questions used to start the students thinking and responding to the scene. When I asked director Bill Rudman about this, he mentioned that, a teacher himself for years, he had worked with other teachers to design questions to lower the natural barriers students feel towards involvement. He assured us that by the end of the week, the students, each claiming ownership of a character, are ready to perform a unified scene. These workshops provide teachers with wonderful ways to break down the barriers they see in their students, replacing boredom with excited enthusiasm.

To receive an idea of the diversity available in these workshops, one need only look at a short list of programs. Orlando offers "Shakespeare: In the Mind's Eye," a multimedia education supplement to be used in conjunction with their performances. Kentucky adds to their traveling programs the following: "Sonnets from Shakespeare," which covers a range of the bard's poetry; "Staging a Scene," which isolates one scene from one play for focused study; "Favorite Tales from Shakespeare," a series that keys in on the playwright as a storyteller in a program for kindergarten through third grade students. Colorado creates "Living Shakespeare," a program in which three actors (one of whom looks like the Bard himself) come into the classroom to perform a variety of activities. They provide a "historical, cultural and literary presentation of the man and his work." This is followed by a demonstration/performance session by the actors that addresses "performance as textual interpretation." As CSF's publication notes, the final third of this program is a session in which students participate in performance-based activities. The Mount's program includes two workshops in addition to the post-performance one already mentioned. In one workshop on performance the students are divided into smaller groups to work on bits of text that they then combine into a scene together. In the other, entitled "Shakespeare and the Language that Shaped the World," actors give students information about Shakespeare, the history of the times, and the language. The goal is to connect the human aspects of the author to the plays, thereby making the language more accessible. Usually five to seven actors in the group make the points, which are divided by snippets of scenes, in this lively and information-packed event. As this short list indicates, a broad range of programs exists.

To facilitate the workshops, many of the festivals offer additional teacher assistance. Some send advance materials to the teachers that include study questions, analyses of particular scenes, and in-class activities to start the students thinking along performance lines. Mrs. Sarah Bennett, a high school teacher from Cleveland who accompanied the Great Lakes group to the workshop at Ohio Northern University, spoke of their help in preparing her classes, pointing out that they give her specific tasks to initiate the approach they will follow and that she can tailor to her own teaching methods. They do not replace her; instead, they augment her work. Other festival/theater groups provide workshops for teachers prior to beginning the study of a play or during the in-school residency. For instance, Nebraska holds after-school sessions for the teachers during the actors' stay in the schools. They also schedule a weekend program to get the teachers involved in production ideas as well. Alabama and the Shakespeare Repertory Theatre (Chicago) both offer day-long workshops for teachers at the festival/theater facilities. At Alabama the teachers work with directors, designers, actors, and scholars on teaching strategies. The day tops off with the group viewing the production. Chicago's Shakespeare Repertory's approach is similar but includes dinner and post-performance discussion.

Taking a different approach, the Idaho Festival has devised a means to build up anticipation before their in-schools programs. They have the schools they will visit set up their own Shakespeare festivals before they arrive. These involve such activities as hosting a dinner, having students write papers, and holding poetry competitions. Sometimes the teachers tap into resources at the local college to add to their festival. Shakespeare and Company at the Mount does this in reverse by having the in-school residencies culminate with a large Shakespeare Festival at which the school groups present the plays they worked on. Strictly not a competition, it is a celebration of Shakespeare studies among the school groups. All schools use the same sets; they take turns doing tech work for each other's performances. The event is held at the local community college and draws a large audience. As these examples reveal, the opportunities for in-class assistance vary widely to meet the teachers' and students' needs.

Teaching Institutes

Because some teachers would like more formal instruction in teaching Shakespeare, many of the festival/theater companies arrange special summer institutes. Attendance can earn continuing certification credit, depending upon the program. Again, the emphasis varies from year to year and from program to program. Dr. Judith Bock's syllabus at the Colorado Festival in Boulder states that in this intense two-week class teachers will focus their study on "developing innovative, effective, performance-based strategies for teaching Shakespeare at the secondary level." Participants "will take part in seminar sessions, performance-based workshops and curriculum development sessions." Utah's three programs, "Shakespeare for Teachers I, II, and III," suggest different teaching strategies for a set of plays in each session; additionally, Utah hosts "Current Developments: Shakespeare Performance," a clinic for high school drama coaches. Kentucky's offering in this area is "From the Page to the Stage: Teaching Shakespeare in the Classroom," which provides the teachers "an interdisciplinary, performance-based approach to teaching Shakespeare's works." Their advertised goal is to give students and teachers "a hands-on, active and meaningful experience . . . usually eliminating the boredom or confusion that may arise when students are given only reading assignments." Boise State University offers "Shakespeare for Teachers" for one week each summer, gearing it to the Idaho festival's productions.

According to Education Liaison Marilyn Halprin, the Shakespeare Repertory thinks of its four-day teacher program as a way "to find the hidden jewels" in the city, teachers who are already teaching Shakespeare well and who are willing to work with other teachers. Ashland maintains that "teachers are crucial to the connection between theatre and education." To facilitate that connection, they host two teachers' symposiums, "Shakespeare on the Stage" and "Shakespeare in the Classroom." Some of these teachers join others who return for a weekend in the fall called a "Preview Weekend for Educators," an introduction to the next season's playbill. Ashland's publicity on this event states that "Directors and designers, already deeply involved in the coming productions, talk about their understanding of the plays." Additionally, the educators meet with company members to generate ideas about teaching that season's plays.

Shakespeare and Company at the Mount also has a number of programs for teachers. Since 1988, they have hosted the National Institute on Teaching Shakespeare, at which internationally recognized directors, scholars, and actors work with the festival staff to introduce secondary school educators to the methods they use in their productions. They also discuss current literary criticism and scholarship and provide a personal component as well. The institute's mission is to "assist teachers in bringing to their classrooms a clearer, more personal and more powerful approach to the texts of William Shakespeare" (*Teacher's Guide,* 1995). Besides the Institute, the Mount Festival has the Teacher Center, a program of five-day workshops in the Berkshires each summer and a series of weekend workshops, each on a different play (these weekend programs are held at various sites). The workshops "offer teachers dynamic methods of presenting Shakespeare in the classroom through work in acting, directing, voice, movement and writing" (*Teacher's Guide*).

Stratford, Ontario holds an annual institute that draws people from all over North America. The topics vary from year to year, but the constant goal is to bring teachers to the stage, to allow them to discuss production challenges, and to link these discussions to the performances at the Stratford Festival Theatres.

All these institutes offer helpful information, strategies and encouragement. The majority, obviously, stress a performance approach. Candidates need to apply and go through a screening process for acceptance into these institutes. Rates vary widely.

Occasionally, special programs will be offered just one time. For instance, in the summer of 1995, with the funding from the National Endowment for the Humanities, James Madison University in conjunction with the Shenandoah Shakespeare Express hosted the "Center for Renaissance and Shakespearean Staging." This institute offered participants the chance to work on various staging issues with the twelve-member Shenandoah Shakespeare Express company, thus allowing the educators to stage various interpretations of scenes from *Hamlet, Twelfth Night,* and *The Tempest.* Other such opportunities exist at locations throughout the United States. Teachers must apply for acceptance to these institutes. Depending upon the grant agency, some have no costs and even include a stipend for participants.

Special Community Programs

Shakespeare is for everyone? According to many festivals and theaters across North America, that is the right idea. To broaden the audience for Shakespeare's plays, these companies create other types of programs than those just for students or for people who already attend the plays. Again, the range is broad, the offerings rich.

While many theater groups offer productions at local festivals such as Spoleto or Fort Worth's Imagination Celebration or Main Street Festival, some also provide more specifically educational options. One program offered by San Francisco's company is the aforementioned Midnight Shakespeare, a community opportunity for growth in which actors work on increasing self-esteem for young people and emphasizing the values of an education in a four- to five-week program. Actors work with these teens twice a week. Remarkably, some of these Midnight sessions end in a performance as well.

Moving beyond performance, other companies focus on the intellectual needs of their audiences. For instance, Tulane believes part of its mission is to educate the public, to create better audiences for its productions. One way it does this is to invite to their "Swan Series" critics who discuss performance standards and techniques with actors, directors, and the audience. In that same vein, Alabama presents their statewide "Theater in the Mind" program. At the Festival facilities, every Saturday from November to July, ASF offers pre-show lectures by scholars, actors, the director, and/or the dramaturg. Those living at a distance from the theater can schedule a TIM program in their town. A scholar and actor meet with each group. Additionally, participants will receive a copy of *Prologue,* a publication giving commentary by dramaturg Dr. Susan Willis on the plays in production. Along similar lines, Stratford hosts its "Talking Theatre" program, an open forum discussion moderated by Pat Quigley, education liaison for the company. Their "Celebrated Writers Series" features a select group of writers throughout the season who discuss topical issues of the theater or the current productions. These programs are extremely popular, often only available by advance ticket purchases.

Working in still a different direction, the Utah Festival's entry in the community outreach category starts with kits they send out to communities and schools that instruct them how to stage their own Shakespeare Festivals. These full-scale festivals can involve either an entire school or a community and can run a full day or a weekend. Teachers who want more formal instruction on running a festival can enroll in Utah's "Shakespearience," a summer workshop. Additionally, USF also runs a high school Shakespeare competition that creates community interest. To augment these and their other programs, they are working with Southern Utah University to establish a reference section in the school's library for resources on performance. They coordinate their efforts also with the NCTE to build better programs.

The communities all benefit from such creative programs. Certainly, the efforts of these companies make Shakespeare come alive to many people who would not ordinarily attend plays or study his works. The result is a wider audience for Shakespeare and more community support for the schools' programs.

Materials

The printed materials from the festivals and theaters are a gold mine for teachers. Talented, creative, thoughtful staff members write publications that include study guides for students, teachers' guides, newsletters for students, program notes, synopses of the plays, historical backgrounds, and overviews of performance and literary theory as they impact on individual productions. I can hardly think of a topic on which I might want information for a specific play that has not already been covered by one of the companies. These materials range from short prompts for the plays that highlight characters, themes, and plots to actual workbooks.

To provide a quick glance at what's available, I'll give an overview of a few publications. Looking at some of the more extensive materials, one should begin with the Shakespeare and Company at the Mount's thirty-two-page "Teacher's Guide for the 1995 New England Tour" of *Julius Caesar.* This "small" volume contains a list of the cast and support staff, notes from the director, a synopsis of the plot, a six-page timeline of "Important and Interesting Events" in the ancient world, profiles of the main characters, an analysis of the Roman military, a discussion of the system of government, a section on Roman philosophy, information on women of Rome, another section on Roman social life, interviews with the actors about their characters, followed by notes on the actors and directors of the company. The wealth of material in this one document is invaluable. But this is just one publication by this company; they offer others for different audiences and purposes. Another source comes from Canada, where the Stratford Festival publishes *Stratford for Students,* a publication that provides more useful materials. One edition contains a long interview with the director on that season's run of plays as well as interesting articles on details of the costuming for a particular production. Each edition rounds out its offerings with articles about the various plays running that season as well as special interest topics. Offering a wonderfully rich combination, Utah publishes a study guide for students—*Insights*—and a teacher supplement to this guide. While the student version has information about the characters, plots, themes, and language of each play, the teachers' copy contains interesting approaches to character analysis, vocabulary guides, and historical information, as well as a breakdown of each play in the season's repertoire, famous lines from each play, and other classroom activities. Without a doubt, however, two of the most comprehensive publications for teachers are Idaho's *Shakespearience: Teacher's Guide* and Colorado's *Insights: A Compendium of Good Ideas for Teaching Shakespeare,* both of which are complete workbooks chockfull of ideas. Differing strongly from each other, the workbooks contain such materials as charts, diagrams, and sketches as well as introductory activities, language activities, creative writing and composition prompts, and inter-active exercises that will get students involved with language and performance ideas, as well as useful articles and bibliographies. Colorado's shorter publication, entitled *Preview,* is an eight-page study guide that contains synopses of the four plays in production each season, an overview of production challenges, and an article on a theme within each play as well as a brief bibliography.

Using an entirely different approach, Georgia's *Folio,* a quarterly newsletter of the Shakespeare Festival published as a newspaper, provides much helpful information. The "Supplement on Education" gives a range of details on the programs the festival offers and information helpful to teachers and students. For instance, each play of the season is highlighted with a brief overview; then side articles on each play are presented to focus attention on particular problems or challenges in each production. Such topics as anti-Semitism and fascism are addressed head-on. This supplement also informs readers of what Shakespeare's theater was like and provides an actor's examination of a brief dialogue to guide us in reading the play. The section concludes with a crossword puzzle. Stratford has a similar type of publication in its *Stratford Festival,* published by *The Beacon Herald.* It gives an overview of the musicians, conductors, costumers, etc. who are involved with various parts of each production, as well as providing lengthy articles on and by the director and about the productions.

As these few examples reveal, the festivals and theaters have much to offer in materials to augment classroom study. Some publications cost (Utah's *Insights* runs about $8.00 per copy) while others are included in the price of a ticket or a workshop. Just by collecting these publications, teachers can accumulate a vast store of supplemental materials that will greatly enrich their teaching.

After reading through this overview of programs and materials available from the festivals and theaters, teachers should recognize that they are not alone in educating students about Shakespeare. Help for those who find the prospect of teaching Shakespeare daunting is only a phone call or a letter away. Once the contact is made, an abundance of materials and options for creating rewarding classroom experiences will be provided by these companies. Their eagerness to participate in the schoolroom side of their audiences makes them willing to work with educators to find the best possible programs and materials for each type of student. To facilitate these contacts, a list of the festivals/theaters I canvassed follows.

Alabama Shakespeare Festival, 1 Festival Drive, Montgomery, AL 36117-4605. (202) 271-5300

Carmel Shakespeare Festival, P. O. Box 223035, Carmel, CA 93922-2035. (408) 622-0700

Colorado Shakespeare Festival, University of Colorado, P. O. Box 261, Boulder, CO 80309-0261. (303) 492-0554

Georgia Shakespeare Festival, 4484 Peachtree Rd., N.E., Atlanta, GA 30319. (404) 264-0020

Great Lakes Theatre Festival, 1501 Euclid Avenue, Suite 423, Cleveland, OH 44115-2108. (216) 241-5490

Houston Shakespeare Festival, University of Houston School of Theatre, Houston, TX 77204-5071. (713) 743-3003

Idaho Shakespeare Festival, P. O. Box 9365, Boise, ID 83707. (208) 336-9221

Kentucky Shakespeare Festival, 1114 South Third St., Louisville, KY 40203. (502) 583-8738

Nebraska Shakespeare Festival, c/o Department of Fine and Performing Arts, Creighton University, 24th & California Streets, Omaha, NE 68178. (402) 280-2391

New Jersey Shakespeare Festival, Drew University, 36 Madison Ave., Madison, NJ 07940. (201) 408-5600

North Carolina Shakespeare Festival, P. O. Box 6066, High Point, NC 27262-6066. (910) 841-NCSF

Oregon Shakespeare Festival, P. O. Box 158, Ashland, OR 97520. (503) 482-4331

Orlando Shakespeare Festival, 30 S. Magnolia, Suite 250, Orlando, FL 32801. (407) 423-6905

San Francisco Shakespeare Festival, P. O. Box 590479, San Francisco, CA 94159-0479. (415) 666-2222

Shakespeare and Company at the Mount, Lenox, MA 01240. (413) 637-3353

Shakespeare on Wheels, Department of Theatre, University of Maryland at Baltimore County, Baltimore, MD 21228-5398. (410) 455-2917

Shakespeare Repertory, 820 North Orleans, Suite 345, Chicago, IL 60610. (312) 642-9122

Shenandoah Shakespeare Express, P. O. Box 1485, Harrisonburg, VA 22801. (703) 434-3366

Stratford Festival Theatre, Box 520, Stratford, Ontario, Canada N5A 6V2. (519) 273-1600

The Theater at Monmouth, P. O. Box 385, Monmouth, ME 04259-0385. (207) 933-9999

Three Rivers Shakespeare Festival, Stephen Foster Memorial Theatre at the University of Pittsburgh, Pittsburgh, PA 15213. (412) 624-7529

Tulane Summer Shakespeare Festival, Lupin Theater, New Orleans, LA 70118. (504) 865-5106

Utah Shakespearean Festival, Southern Utah University, Cedar City, Utah 84720 (801) 856-7880

Virginia Shakespeare Festival, College of William and Mary, P. O. Box 8795, Williamsburg, VA 23187-8795. (804) 221-2660

Wisconsin Shakespeare Festival, Center for the Arts, University of Wisconsin, Platteville, WI 53818-3099. (608) 342-1298

Notes

1. Not all theaters with focused offerings of Shakespeare's plays and related programs are considered festivals, hence the distinction I make between the two throughout the paper.

2. The Teaching Shakespeare Resource Center at the University of Wisconsin-Parkside, not a festival or theater but still a good resource, holds a sonnet contest that culminates in a banquet and an awards ceremony for the regional winners followed by publication of the finalists' entries in *Teaching Shakespeare News,* a newsletter circulated throughout the state.

3. A new book entitled *Shakespeare Companies and Festivals: An International Guide,* edited by Ron Engle, Felicia Hardison Londre, and Daniel J. Watermeier, from Greenwood Press (1995), offers a comprehensive overview of the more than 150 Shakespeare companies and festivals worldwide. This study does not deal with the education programs, focusing rather on the theaters themselves and their production philosophies. However, it provides the most comprehensive list I've seen of the festivals and theaters.

References

Chidester, Phil. 1995. "Center Stage at SUU: Fred Adams and the Utah Shakespearean Festival." *The Sanctuary: The Magazine of Southern Utah University* (Spring): 13–17.

VI

Into the Future

CHAPTER 29

Making Media Matter in the Shakespeare Classroom

SHARON A. BEEHLER

Montana State University
Bozeman, Montana

In this final section we attempt to explore what the future may hold for teachers of Shakespeare. No one can seriously doubt that technological advances, especially the computer, will touch all that we do in our teaching. Beehler discusses the strengths and weaknesses of some common audio-visual materials, describes elements of film criticism (for example, the interpretive function of the camera), provides sets of questions and exercises that would be especially useful at the secondary level, and concludes with a section on newer resources like the CD-ROM and laserdisc.

Shakespeare is facing stiff competition these days. Wherever we look, we are bombarded by televisual, cinematic, and computerized messages and entertainments. How can the works of a sixteenth-century playwright, even a great one, hope to hold their own against these media giants? The amazing fact is that Shakespeare remains in the thick of it. Major movie productions of his plays, computerized resources, and Internet communications have sent Shakespeare zooming into the twenty-first century as if he were indeed our contemporary. But how can these advanced technologies fit into our classrooms where the budgets are tight and non-traditional teaching methods are suspect? Quite frankly there is no point in spending big bucks on these resources unless we can demonstrate that they provide genuinely enhanced learning opportunities and improve students' abilities to use their minds productively. The following remarks explore ways of meeting this challenge in the Shakespeare classroom through the use of videotape and computer technology.

I have recently been disturbed by the comments of English teachers who feel frustrated by their lack of ideas for doing more with videotapes than comparing their treatment of a literary work with the work itself. At one time this strategy seemed exciting because it was new and offered advantages that the showing of films did not—in particular, the simple operation of VCRs and the remote-control ability to quickly stop, rewind, and replay a section of tape. But gradually that novelty became less important, and teachers were left wondering if there weren't something more that could be accomplished through this advanced technology. Among the most popular responses to this puzzle was to create new videotapes that placed various versions of a single scene from a Shakespeare play side-by-side so that students could identify the differing interpretations made by directors. This strategy, while full of potential for learning, ran into some strong opposition from the producers and distributors of videotapes who argued that this practice violated copyright laws, an argument that has prevailed in many cases and caused teachers to be wary about the use of videotapes at all. Moreover, for many teachers access to a variety of versions has been difficult if not impossible. This situation led teachers back to the original habit of showing a videotape production in its entirety as a means of providing students with at least a rudimentary experience of Shakespeare on stage.

Part of the difficulty for teachers arises from their lack of sophisticated consciousness about film strategy. Whereas most English teachers are well versed in the complexities of literary text composition, they fail to realize that film composition is equally complex. The result is that they and their students continue to view videotapes as pure and unmediated by the camera. Certainly teachers address questions of blocking, costume, casting, set design, and sound with their students, but the role of the camera is virtually invisible, both in the watching of the videotape and in the classroom discussion. When I bring up this feature in conversations with teachers, they usually express surprise that they hadn't thought to consider such an important aspect of filming, and they are eager to know more.

In order to make visible what is deliberately hidden, a viewer must acquire a different way of seeing and a vocabulary for identifying the masked features. Naturally, this strategy has potential for the Shakespeare class, but its advantages carry over to other areas of study as well. Helping students become intelligent viewers of cinematic media means assisting them to recognize the tricks used by producers of that media in the same way that we help them to be critical readers of written texts. The use of Shakespearean audio-visual materials to accomplish this makes a great deal of sense because of the large number of filmed productions that have been preserved on videotape. No other writer has so many versions available of any one work.

One of the first points of recognition to consider when thinking about filming strategy for a Shakespeare play is whether the production is made for stage or film. In other words, is the camera taking a prominent interpretive role or is it merely recording, often from a fixed and distant point, what happens on a stage? In the latter case the camera's involvement might be limited to a few close-up shots of speakers, but it does not interfere to any large extent with the stage interpretation of the play. On the other hand, a production that is designed primarily for the camera will draw on many other subtle devices to convey impressions and to contextualize the action. Once this distinction has been acknowledged, then a closer analysis of those devices is in order. In Figure 1 I provide a list of the terms of greatest use to teachers and students when undertaking such an analysis. While most of these terms are not entirely unfamiliar to modern movie-goers, they are infrequently thought of as an important part of the English curriculum and so, consequently, awareness of them is sporadic and unproductive.

Figure 1: Filmic Devices

Field—The image visible within any segment of film.

Camera Angle—The position from which the camera views the filmed subject.

Movement & Stasis—The camera can move with moving subjects, can rise above them or sink below them, can pan the action or move in on it.

Wide Angle vs. Close-up—The camera can take in a panoramic scene or focus tightly on a face or other object.

Color vs. Black and White—The film type creates differing effects, especially with light and shadow.

Special Effects—Through special splicing and combining of film, images can appear and disappear, can change feature, can grow or shrink, can appear to carry out supernatural acts or mix with other media [e.g., animation with live action].

Tracking—Camera follows (without necessarily moving itself) the movement of the subject(s).

Cuts—The sudden ending of one scene (might be momentary or lengthy) and beginning of another.

Pacing—The speed with which the camera records the action: influenced by slow or rapid cuts and by camera swings over the action. Also slow motion or fast motion of film.

Framing vs. Marginalizing—The camera's positioning of the subject within its view, either at the center or on the border.

Mirroring—The doubling of images *or* the use of mirrors in the camera's field of vision to show action or subjects outside that field.

Clear Shot vs. Fuzzy Shot—The degree of sharpness given to the filmed image.

Contrast—The degree of distinction established between light and dark, sharp and fuzzy.

Depth of Field—The amount of dimension established by various camera positionings and contrasting elements.

Superimposed Images—The arrangement of one image upon another through the overlapping of film segments.

Foregrounding—Placing an image as close to the viewer as possible.

Freeze Frame—The stopping of all motion on and around a single image.

To ease students into this sort of analysis, I begin with slides that depict photographs of actors who have played Othello (although any major character would do). Pictures like this are readily available and slides of them can be made quite easily and inexpensively. I begin with slides to call attention to the way in which photographers can create impressions through camera angles, shadows, and special film effects, such as showing the actor reflected in a mirror or by making the image slightly fuzzy. A famous shot of Orson Welles as Othello shows him frowning into a space just over the viewer's shoulder as the camera views him from a low, side angle, giving him a sense of stature, but that sense is undercut by the predominately dark shadows cast on the face of the figure as the light shines against his far side. The intensity of the gaze is sufficient to make the viewer suspicious and want to look around and see what holds the figure's attention. Very subtly the photographer conveys the dual nature of Othello—his heroic potential and his fatal flaw. By looking first at still shots like these, students can begin to recognize the enormous role that the camera can take in manipulating viewer response and can anticipate the even greater effect that can be achieved with a moving camera.

Once students are comfortable with this way of thinking, I show them three cinematic versions of the handkerchief scene between Othello and Desdemona, a scene whose tension is intensified in all three versions by the camera. The first scene I show is the 1982 BBC version with Anthony Hopkins as Othello and Penelope Wilton as Desdemona. In this version the camera is very active as it moves closer to the principal figures in a hopscotching of close-ups. At the same time, the camera also enables us to see Emilia in the background behind Desdemona and visible to Othello. As we close in on husband and wife, whose conversation becomes more intimate and their words more quickly spoken, the anxiety reflected in their voices becomes increasingly visible in their faces. Emilia's presence in the scene in full view of Othello allows us to understand her failure to comment on having previously found the handkerchief and given it to Iago: she cannot hear all the conversation because she is too far away, but the anxious look on her face indicates that she might overhear part of what is being said and wonder. As Othello ends the conversation by turning to the door, the camera jumps back to frame both Desdemona and Emilia, letting us feel the release of tension without negating its effect.

The second version, the Bard production of 1982, keeps the camera on Othello (played by William Marshall), emphasizing both his own spoken part in the conversation and his listening to Desdemona (played by Jenny Agutter), but in this case the camera does not serve a strong interpretive function, preferring instead to allow the viewer to form his or her own conclusion. Only in one respect does the camera insert its own implication, and that is with regard to Emilia. Emilia stands on a step slightly above the two principals and seems to oversee their argument, but the camera makes sure to keep her in the periphery of the picture where her reactions to comments she can clearly hear are only occasionally evident. Though she appears curious about the reference to the handkerchief, she does not seem to reflect any awareness at all of the connection between her own thievery and the subject of their debate. We are thus invited to assume that she is either rather slow in the uptake or that she is continuing the deception deliberately by pretending complete innocence. By keeping her on the margins of the frame, the camera encourages us to regard her as only minimally significant, an impression she herself tries to maintain despite her prominent placement with respect to Othello and Desdemona.

The third scene I use for this purpose is Orson Welles's 1952 black and white version. After viewing and analyzing the other two productions, students immediately recognize the elaborate and sophisticated filming technique characteristic of this film. Welles uses the black and white medium to effect by emphasizing light and shadow and shades of gray to create an aura of darkness and threat around Othello while placing Desdemona (played by Suzanne Cloutier) in a bright yet softened light that emphasizes purity and innocence. The two characters in this scene (Emilia is not present) sit at a table and face each other across it. The camera moves back and forth between close-ups of each speaker, but seems to look down when watching Othello and up when watching Desdemona, giving superiority to the latter. As the passion heats up, the camera (often at a tilted angle) moves more quickly between the faces, increasing the chaotic feel. Shortly after this encounter, Welles depicts Othello crouched against a wall with his gaze fixed on a crossbarred window through which light comes, casting a net-like shadow upon the suffering man. As the camera looks down on him, he seems to acquire the status of an imprisoned martyr, both noble and condemned.

By assisting students to pick out devices such as those described above, I help them begin to see others, and by referring to the list of terms, they can become extremely adept at noticing the effects created through film strategies. At the start I choose to show only short clips from the plays so that students can better focus on the film devices than they would with longer segments in which they become so engrossed in the story that they fail to maintain a critical distance. Nevertheless, even with short segments, I find that it is necessary to show each one several times so that students can check their impressions and my claims. After demonstrating the analyzing technique through the examples mentioned above, I put students into groups to generate ideas about the film strategies used in Zeffirelli's *Hamlet* (1990) during the closet scene. Among other evocative tactics, this scene uses a moving camera to create the effect of fearful confusion for Queen Gertrude. As Hamlet upbraids her, he and the camera move in on her in a relentless fashion, leaving her and us feeling rather breathless and claustrophobic. When students recognize this effect, as well as others, they get excited and begin looking even more closely at how the camera shapes the scene. Because students are part of a TV culture, they usually pick up these strategies quickly and find pleasure in being able to identify the obscured manipulations of filmmakers.

If students have trouble thinking of ways to "see" such practices, though, they can be assisted by the questions in Figure 2, most of which are my own but a few of which I have adapted from others raised by Peter Reynolds in a 1991 article on Shakespeare and film. The questions are designed to focus viewing and thinking upon various devices without being specific to a particular scene or production. By applying these questions to whichever videotaped play they are studying, students can begin to realize not only the stage director's influence on the production of the playtext but also the film maker's. Such consciousness increases awareness of the complexity of interpretation and calls attention to the myriad of ways in which we have the world interpreted for us on a daily basis through the media as well as through more localized communications.

Figure 2: Questions for Film and Videotape Versions of Shakespeare

1. Where in the scene is the camera looking from?*
2. How does that positioning affect the view of the scene?
3. When is a close-up replaced by a distance shot, or vice versa, and how is the transition achieved? What effect does the shift create?*
4. What does the camera angle prevent you from seeing? How does this affect your response?
5. How does the camera focus your attention?*
6. What difference in mood, tone, or feel is created by a moving camera?
7. Does the camera "become" one of the characters (filming as if through their eyes)? a supplemental character who looks over other people's shoulders or peers around corners or through keyholes?
8. Which characters are framed by the camera? which ones are marginalized? How does this affect your interpretation of those characters?
9. How does contrast help to create the mood of a scene?
10. Does the filmic pace correspond with or contribute to the pace of the drama? (Pay special attention to the frequency of cuts.)

11. How many cameras are used in a scene? How do their functions differ?

12. How does the depth of field help to establish a "frame of reference" for characters? In other words, are the subjects enlarged or diminished by the field?

13. Do windows, draperies, barred dividers, walls, porticoes, or other barriers intrude between the subject and the viewer? To what effect?

14. Has the filmmaker used mirrors or other mediating devices for particular effect?

15. How does the soundtrack relate to the filmed images?

16. What does the film maker want us to notice indirectly? In other words, what are we supposed to be aware of even if it is not the center of focus? How does the film maker achieve this?

17. How do facial close-ups influence your interpretation of the drama?

18. How do opening and closing shots "frame" the drama? What implications do they have?

*Adapted from Peter Reynolds.

Figure 3 provides a step-by-step procedure for using these materials in a unit of study on Shakespeare, especially at the secondary level. What many educators and parents find troubling about the use of media is that the "basic" knowledge of Shakespeare (and other subjects) is sacrificed to less intellectually rigorous and culturally essential topics that entertain students rather than educate them. I can understand this concern, but the program I outline in Figure 3 ought to indicate quite clearly that a unit of study on Shakespeare will only be enhanced through the inclusion of media studies. In particular, these productions offer such engaging nuances of interpretation that the study of meaning in Shakespeare's plays becomes rich and complex for students as they view and analyze the subtle and not-so-subtle strategies used to influence meaning. Close analysis of Zeffirelli's *Romeo and Juliet,* and Branagh's *Henry V* and *Much Ado About Nothing*, while paying close attention to the written text, can assist students in developing thinking and reading skills ("reading" in the sense of interpretation) that they will take home to their televisions, to the movie theater, and to live stage performances. When students realize that even in Shakespeare's own day, the presentation of a play meant the use of clever stage devices to influence the audience's understanding and response, they will be even more intrigued by the skill of a master technician like Shakespeare, whose own staging tricks are evident in the playtexts themselves.

Figure 3: Recommended Classroom Procedure for Using Films/Videos of Shakespeare Plays

There are two obvious objectives in using films and videotapes in a Shakespeare unit: one is to increase students' enjoyment of Shakespeare and the other is to help students become more astute readers of non-print media. By keeping both of these objectives in mind, we can make literary instruction more practical and skill instruction more aesthetically pleasing. I would recommend the following steps as a means of keeping these objectives balanced.

1. Present students with the script version of a short scene from the Shakespeare play to be studied. It doesn't have to be the opening scene, but sometimes that's a good choice. Be sure to explain the context. Here are some possibilities:

Julius Caesar—1.3.131–64 or 2.2 (Conspiracy or Portia's anxiety)

Macbeth—1.1 (Witches' incantation)

A Midsummer Night's Dream—1.2 (Mechanicals' rehearsal)

Hamlet—1.4.38–91 (Ghost's appearance)

Romeo and Juliet—1.5.93–144 (Banquet encounter)

2. In groups have students read over the scene and work out its difficulties, interpreting as they go along. Then have them think about how the scene could be staged, taking into account the usual elements of theatrical performance (e.g., casting, blocking, character interpretation, lighting, setting, costuming). Then have each group prepare to explain their performance ideas to the class and/or perform them.

3. Show students a videotape of the scene or a compilation of several performances of the scene. Ask students to compare these performances with their own.

4. Reshow the tape and ask students to think about the way the performances have been filmed. Explain that in a theater no one controls where the audience members look, but a camera's eye prevents them from seeing anything other than what the filmmaker decides to "frame."

5. Distribute the list of filmic techniques and explain them, asking for examples from movies and television programs that students have seen. [A homework assignment here would be to have students watch commercials on TV and write a description of the filmic strategies used.]

6. If students have not yet done so, ask them to consider how the filmic techniques evident on the tape influence interpretation of the scene. What ideas do students develop as a consequence of those techniques?

7. Give the students a second scene from the same play and have them decide how they would film it, using the techniques already discussed and included on their handout. What purpose would those decisions serve?

8. Let students explain their ideas to the class, or if time and equipment allow, let them make an amateur video of their scene, using as many of the techniques desired as possible. These could be shared with younger students or another class.

These suggestions are arranged in an order designed to lead the students logically and sequentially into a dialogic engagement with the text, the performance, the film, and each other. Such procedures should enable teachers to discover new ways of dealing with the intellectual substance of videotapes rather than being bogged down by a seemingly trivial treatment that begins and ends with the question, "How does this production elaborate on the playtext?"

There are, however, other even newer resources available for the teacher interested in a multimedia classroom. In the 1990s we face an explosion of new media in the form of CD-ROM and laserdisc technology that promises to open new opportunities for Shakespeare instruction. In addition to providing enormous resource potential for gathering information through the Internet and other programs, including the Shakespeare Database on CD-ROM (from Olms Neue Medien, a German manufacturer, but available in the U.S. and Canada through Norman Ross Publishing, Inc. in New York), this new technology offers the ability to download videotape and laserdisc images directly into a computer where they can be set next to actual text. The resulting compilation can then be transferred back to a videotape and shown to a class so that a scene can be frozen and students can analyze the movement of text into production without having to locate passages in their books. Moreover, the computerized text of Shakespeare's complete works includes the capability to click on a given word and have a glossary and/or commentary appear in the window. Teachers with access to a computer projection system can manipulate text and video for class discussion purposes. Another resource now available from World Microfilms is a CD-ROM entitled "Shakespeare: His Life, Times & Works" that (according to advance promotion) includes the sources of Shakespeare's plays; contemporary pamphlets, newsletters, and broadsheets; First Folio editions of the plays; personal documents and certificates; and details of the Elizabethan and Jacobean theaterhouses. The newness of these resources means that they have limited compatibility, being available only for Windows. One item currently available for the Mac is a CD-ROM on *Macbeth* that includes a new edition of the text together with an audio performance by the Royal Shakespeare Company and clips from three famous films. As more of these products become available, the potential for using them with students and the need to invent creative classroom applications will become even more pressing. What is remarkable is that Shakespeareans have managed to keep up with the speed of developing technology. There is much more to come, but The Writing Company's 1995 catalogue of Shakespeare resources for teachers devotes an entire page to computer software and in several other places indicates the availability of laserdisc versions of various productions.

In the long run, however, we need to remember that despite the attractiveness of these resources, there is no substitute for professional or even amateur live performance of Shakespeare's plays. Even films cannot adequately convey the sense so crucial to an appreciation of intimate encounters between living bodies on stage and in the audience. Of all the tricks and effects practiced by performers and producers, those undertaken beneath our very noses are the most daring and the most exciting to witness. The strategies of film are indeed magical, but Shakespeare was able to create enchantment of another sort, through words uttered by actors on a stage. Students who can appreciate this skill will have learned more about the powers of language and communication than all the computers in the world will ever convey.

Recommended Reading

Coursen, H. R. 1993. *Watching Shakespeare on Television*. Rutherford, N.J.: Fairleigh Dickinson University Press.
Davies, Anthony. 1988. *Filming Shakespeare's Plays*. Cambridge: Cambridge University Press.
Donaldson, Peter S. 1990. *Shakespearean Films/Shakespearean Directors*. Boston: Unwin Hyman.
Reynolds, Peter. 1991. "Unlocking the Box: Shakespeare on Film and Video." In *Shakespeare in the Changing Curriculum,* ed. Lesley Aers and Nigel Wheale, 189–203. New York: Routledge.

CHAPTER 30

Computers in the Secondary Shakespeare Classroom

WILLIAM J. GATHERGOOD

Reynoldsburg High School
Reynoldsburg, Ohio

Gathergood turns to some of today's new technologies as he attempts to "build bridges" between his secondary students and the world of Shakespeare. He explains the introductory exercises and activities he has designed to get his students moving toward the play, that is, building bridges; and then he describes taking his students to the computer lab, in this case to work on Hamlet *(accessed on the Internet through Electronic Bookshelf). Finally, he discusses his most futuristic project: "With an email account, a teacher can link students all over the world and communicate on a daily basis about the play they are all studying."*

Shakespeare Has Something for All Cultures in All Times

Many years ago, I was directing a production of Jean Anouilh's *Becket*. I asked a group of my students if they were coming to the play. One responded negatively by saying, "Nah, I don't like that Shakespeare stuff." I asked him why he thought it was a Shakespearean play and he told me that it was an old play about dead people and he just "doesn't like that Shakespeare stuff." For too many teenagers in America—and perhaps quite a few adults as well—that is what Shakespeare represents, old plays about dead people. And yet most of us agree that Shakespeare is alive and well. How can this dichotomy of opinions exist in the same culture?

The other negative statement I hear from students is that "I just can't understand this stuff." Fair enough on that one. After teaching a Shakespearean Seminar for twenty-one years, I still don't understand it all. How boring my job would be if I did! I'm sure other teachers have faced these same statements from students. In this paper, I plan to deal with these questions, offer a few solutions, and also show how some new technologies can be used to help build bridges between these contemporary teenagers and the world of Elizabethan England.

The Plays Are Alive with the Sound of Music

There is an important assumption that I make in studying Shakespeare. It is that I do not believe that Shakespeare ever intended to have people sitting around, silently reading his plays. His soliloquies, his intricate descriptors and his riveting dialogues were written for the ear, not for the textbook. One can no more appreciate Shakespeare's genius through silent reading than one could comprehend the mastery of Mozart by silently poring over a written score of his music. Shakespearean plays were meant to be heard and seen. Yet for centuries, students have been forced to read silently—or even worse, to struggle through a reading by fellow students who have neither the desire nor the skill to interpret the lines with any emotion. I believe students can learn much about Shakespeare by performing lines, by "tasting the words," but their main exposure to the text should be with professional actors interpreting that text. This can be accomplished in three ways:

1. **Watching Videotape Productions**
2. **Listening to Audio Recordings**
3. **Viewing Live Readings by Competent Teachers or Acting Students**

When listening to audio recordings, students should read along either in a textbook or on computers (more on this later).

The First Day of Class

I believe that it is important for students to get a sense of TIME on the first day. So when they enter my class, they hear very old music playing in the background. None of them admits to liking the music and that leads to a discussion of what "good music" is. We then have the opportunity to talk about Madison Avenue's planned obsolescence in the music industry. "Whatever happened to The New Kids on the Block?" I feel it is important for students to understand advertising's control mechanisms and the assumption that "old is bad, new is good." Unless students understand the commercial reasons for this philosophy, they will never be able to build the bridges necessary to appreciate classical literature. Students grasp the concept of planned obsolescence quickly. They are experts at it. So it is a simple step to make the point that culture, as we define it, requires the passage of knowledge, attitudes, and emotions down from one generation to the next. That passage is becoming more and more difficult when it is so easy for Madison Avenue to redefine cultural heritage based on projected sales revenues. One of the major goals in my Shakespeare Seminar is to help teens discover that there are important concepts in the plays that need to be handed down. I explain that the music playing in the background was recorded at great expense, without hope of turning a profit because it is not Top 40. But the artist felt the need to pass the music on in the permanent form of CD technology so that future generations can have it. The music may have been performed live in Shakespeare's time, but it was not from his time. The music is from the eleventh century. It is eight hundred years old. There seems to be some significance for the students to listen to music that was as old in Shakespeare's time as he is to them. This is an example of what I call a "Bridge." The music helps to connect the students as they prepare to leapfrog back in time to another period.

I Don't Understand This Stuff

Because of Shakespeare's complexity, students are often frustrated by not being able to understand everything the first time through. Remember that television, including the nightly news, is written at a fourth-grade level. They are rarely challenged by television. Most of the movies they see are even less challenging. So I try to make them comfortable with partial understanding. I use the image of a swimmer in the ocean, trying to stand in the surf and catch the energy of a wave as it swipes over him. If he caught all the energy, it would knock him over and pull him under. There is just too much. He can only capture part of the energy, which lifts him off the sand and moves him slightly. The rest of the energy passes around him. But he has a chance to catch more of it on the next wave. This is how Shakespeare works. There is just too much in it to catch it all the first time. The reader who tries to capture all the energy will be knocked over. The student should catch what he or she can and let the rest pass by. This concept helps them not to shut down in frustration, but to flow with the literature and grab what they can.

Let's Play House!

Students who have survived the first day or two, when we discussed music and Richard II and ocean waves, may now be genuinely interested in finding out what this is all about. But there ARE complexities in Shakespeare that challenge students. One of the methods I use to minimize them is "PLAYING HOUSE" before each play. When little children play house, they take on characters and they make up situations and dialogue. As I prepare my students to study *Richard II,* we play "House of Plantagenet." Because *Richard II* is a play that requires knowledge of the royal line and the Divine Right of Kings, we begin playing house with Richard's grandfather, Edward III. I like to be Edward III because he had some control over his kingdom. I then assign the role of each of my sons to a student and we get up for a family portrait. Each son has a son and I have them all go to the area of land of which they are in charge. They receive maps of England and the Duke of Gloucester goes to that area in the classroom. The Dukes of Lancaster and York must protect their land. If the Duke of Norfolk travels to Calais, he must go out into the hall. NOTE: If there is one student who refuses to listen, make him the character who has to leave the room. While out there, he'll listen very closely so he can find out what is happening to him.

In playing house, we act out the story of the play. They go through the motions. If Norfolk kills Gloucester, I let Norfolk act out the killing of Gloucester. If there is a moral decision one character must make, "Should Richard II resign the crown?" I let them consider the options. Of course I have to lead them to make the same decision so the story can remain faithful, but they understand what we are doing and do not challenge my corrections. When we finish with the play, the students know the plot. They will not struggle through the lines trying to figure out what is happening. They know what is happening and can concentrate on how Shakespeare tells the story instead of what the story is. The first time they actually see the play, it is a rerun and they can look for details they would have missed if they were watching to learn what happened.

There is a second benefit in playing house. We know that there are many different kinds of intelligences. Some people are more visual. Others are verbal or auditory or tactile. Still others are geographic. This is, I believe, a combination of visual and spatial. Watching students move around the classroom in character helps many of the students to keep those characters straight. It is not uncommon, on an objective test, to see students look around the room at another student in order to spark their memory as to who was John of Gaunt's son. They are not cheating. They are looking back at bridges they have built in their minds between twentieth-century friends and eight-hundred-year-old men. Each step in the processes I have described is designed to connect these teens with an ancient cultural heritage. I have used the example of *Richard II* because I choose to begin with that play. But I play house with all of the plays we do. Sometimes playing house only takes a day. Sometimes it takes a week. The more relevant the play, the longer it takes because we stop to build a few bridges along the way. If time allows for a review day before a test, I permit the students to play house again after the play. I take on the role of a dull student and ask them to get me ready for the test by playing house. One person volunteers as the storyteller, getting others up to play the parts. If the storyteller makes a mistake, someone quickly offers a correction and takes over as the storyteller. They can usually get through the basic plot in twenty minutes. The next day, everyone is confident going into the test.

To Read or Not to Read, That Is the Question

Many years ago, an opinionated guidance counselor chastised me for letting the students watch Shakespeare instead of reading him. She insisted that students needed a sense of the literature and that can only be discovered through looking at the text. While I disagree with her in general, she does have an important point. We take something different away from the literature when we read it than when we observe it on a stage. But until the students develop the ability to interpret the literature, it does no one good to force them to plow through it. In deference to that counselor, I try to balance their exposure. For some plays, we watch videotaped productions; for others we listen to audio recordings and read along with the text. But I have found that students have difficulty concentrating on the lines in a large book with small print. It is also frustrating for them because most productions drop some lines out. Then they feel that someone has cheated someone and they claim they cannot follow along. I found the solution in a computer room. Instead of handing out the textbooks to read along while listening to *Hamlet,* I took the students to the computer lab. I loaded *Hamlet* onto the hard drive. But first, I edited the text to be the same as the production we were going to play. In this case, it was the 1964 New York production of *Hamlet* with Richard Burton, which I think is one of the finest productions of the twentieth century. No, I did not type all of *Hamlet* into the computer. All of Shakespeare's plays can be accessed on the Internet through "Electronic Bookshelf." It is a simple matter to connect to the fileserver and download *Hamlet* to disc. Then I simply used a word-processor to edit out the lines they cut out in this particular production. The students accessed the text to their computer, I turned on the audio tape, and the students read along with the words on the screen as they listened to Richard Burton bare his soul. The most important aspect of this computerization is that, in order to keep up with the actors, the students need to relate to the text physically every fifteen seconds. They have to hit the arrow key to move on to the next screen of text. Using the huge textbook, which had an average of two hundred lines on each two-page spread, students tended to open the book to the page and then put their heads down—or look around the room. They had five minutes until they needed to turn the page.

But with the computer, they were forced to arrow down every fifteen seconds. No one objected to this. It is just what they needed to do. They tended to look at the lines constantly. They also were aware that, if they did not look at the lines, the teacher, moving behind them, could easily see that they were not in the right place. So they worked harder to stay with the text. In addition to making the reading process more effective, I also feel that the process of reading text on the computer is important training for how we will receive most of our textual information in the near future.

The computer text creates an environment which is useful for the next phase of our study of Shakespeare: Global Communications. If it is true that Shakespeare holds something for all cultures in all times, then our students should have a common ground to discuss issues with people of other cultures.

All the World's a Stage and All the Men and Women, Players

This quote, from Jacques in *As You Like It,* is well known. But that world he refers to has gotten much smaller in the last few years, thanks to a technology known as "Electronic Mail." With an email account, a teacher can link students all over the world and communicate on a daily basis about the play they are all studying. While reading *Macbeth,* a student in Chicago can coauthor a paper on a preselected theme with a student in England or Scotland. It is not necessary for students to have accounts, although they are becoming available through freenet systems in local libraries. With one teacher account, students can write letters on any word-processor, save them in ASCII text, and have the teacher upload and send them to a teacher in a different location. The process of uploading does not create a burden on the teacher. It takes only a few seconds, especially if there are several letters going to the same place. They can be merged into one document and sent to the teacher, who then separates them for printing. I can easily merge and upload twenty letters and then send them to another location in less than fifteen minutes. Let me share three typical projects that use this technology.

The Epistolary Novel

This concept was created by Dr. Brent Robinson of Cambridge University. I used it to study *Macbeth*. First, I found an interested partner in another school, in this case, Gayle Tidwell in a high school in Florida. We created a series of letters that might have been written by characters in the play. We concentrated on finding a reason for characters to write at strategic points in the play. For example, as Macbeth is writing to Lady Macbeth about the witches, Banquo might have written to Fleance about the same experiences. Later, after the murder of Duncan, Malcolm might write to the king of England to request sanctuary. Donalbain might write to Malcolm in England to find out how the counterattack is coming. Lady Macduff might write to her husband asking what time he expects to get home from England. Lady Macbeth might leave a suicide note to her husband, apologizing for having dragged him into this mess. Each letter assignment is given to a student. The person representing the character they are writing to is in the other location. So Malcolm's letter from my school is sent to the king of England in the other school. Lady Macbeth in that school writes to Macbeth in my school. The students are responsible for understanding the play to the point in the play when the letter is written. They may not use any information that comes after that point because the character doesn't know it yet. Of course, they can put words into the character's mouth, which creates foreshadowing. Once all the letters are exchanged, the students must edit the letter they received and write bridges or segues between their letter and the letters that come chronologically before and after their letter. So they end up working with two students in their own school to blend the letters together. The final product is an epistolary novel: a story told through a series of letters from different characters in the story. An example of a formal epistolary novel is Bram Stoker's *Dracula,* which unfolds through a series of diary entries and letters between characters. Our final product is a retelling of the story of *Macbeth* through characters' letters back and forth between schools in two states.

Mail Order Anya

When we spend so much time building bridges between time periods, we often find other literature which supports a concept in one of Shakespeare's plays. "Mail Order Anya" is a project which links individual students in the U.S. with students in Russia in order to study the roles of men and women in society from Shakespeare's time until the year 2020. The project involves two classical pieces of literature, two songs, several relationships, and an unborn child.

Because the Americans are initiating the project, the Russians get to select their part-ners. The Americans write to the Russians, trying to convince them that they should select them as a bride or groom, depending on the sex of the author. The Russians receive the letters and select a partner of the opposite sex, then write back, asking them to marry them for the purpose of studying male/female roles and relationships through the ages. They begin by reading *Taming of the Shrew.* Afterwards, they write to discuss Kate's speech at the end of the play. They consider how the expectations of both men and women have changed since then. They also discuss how references to "Duty owed the Prince" may have changed in societies which have no royalty. How does the loss of royalty change our opinion of man and woman's role in that world?

In studying Shakespeare, both groups discover the universality of Shakespeare and how it transcends even vast changes in attitude. It also provides an opportunity for each to discover how roles vary and stay the same between American and Russian cultures.

The next step involves studying a cultural experience unique to each country. The Americans discuss a song by Harry Chapin entitled "Mail Order Annie." It is this song which gives us the title of the project. The song is about the first meeting between a dirt farmer and his mail order bride in the mid 1800s. Mail order brides were a strictly American concept, used to pair homeless girls in the East with lonely farmers in the West. In spite of the stress of agreeing to marry without ever seeing their partner, many of these marriages led to large families that dominated their region of the country through strong basic values.

While the Russians are considering mail order brides, the Americans read a small novel by Pushkin called *Dubrovsky.* It is a story that deals with arranged marriages. The concept of parents selecting the bride or groom for their child is foreign to Americans. The Russians will explain the advantages and disadvantages of this system and what it meant to the development of male/female relationships.

Next we study the roles of men and women during the 1950s, a time when our cultures were so strongly opposed to each other politically. The Harry Chapin song, "Why Do Little Girls Grow Crooked While Little Boys Grow Tall," is used as a motivation to discuss how their parents were raised. The assignment is to write what their mother's life was like when they, the students, were five years old. For the most part, when the child is five, the mother is deciding whether to go back to work or stay home. Americans see this as the "June Cleaver" syndrome. Russians see it quite differently. Choosing the 1950s as the period to consider encourages each student to discuss with his or her parents what life was like for them as children.

Finally, after looking at all these roles and relationships, the partners have to come to some conclusion about how they will raise their own children. What former pitfalls will they avoid? What new ideas will they incorporate so that their children don't face the role model problems of previous generations? Invariably, they find themselves back in the sixteenth century, dealing with that speech by Kate. In spite of all the changes in roles over the centuries, Kate still brings us back to some very fundamental questions.

"Mail Order Anya" has been a wonderful opportunity to study Shakespeare, a foreign culture and the student's own family heritage in just a few simple letters.

Dear Will Shakespeare, I Have a Few Questions . . .

The final project idea I would like to share is called "Literary Personification." The concept springs from Dr. Brent Robinson's Epistolary Novel. It involves Shakespeare writing to students via email and then inviting them to ask questions about his work. Distance is an important factor here. I would never try to play Shakespeare with my own students. But I have played the role for students in several different countries. Ninth graders in Australia have written to ask why I had to kill off Romeo and Juliet. A fourth grader from Virginia wrote to ask if I knew that Disney stole my idea for *Hamlet* and used it in *The Lion King*. By playing the role of Shakespeare, I can bring the Bard to life and help show them how to make modern bridges to his work. Use of email helps to suspend the students' disbelief long enough to get something out of the letter. I find that the students often write back a second or third time to comment on the play afterward.

I have also used this concept with characters. There is a web of fine volunteers around the country who have agreed to respond to letters within forty-eight hours of receiving them. My students are invited to write to Hamlet, Claudius, Polonius, Gertrude, or Ophelia. Afterward, they must turn in an essay which includes a quote that is not in the play. The students never need this motivation. They enjoy writing to the characters and asking why they did a certain thing, or chastise them for not having more faith in the other characters. The result is that the characters become real, vibrant people for the students. It then becomes much easier to build a bridge between the character and people they see everyday. The literature comes alive. It is no longer an old play about dead people. It is "that Shakespeare stuff," alive and well and ready for the twenty-first century.

CHAPTER 31

Beyond the Gee Whiz Stage

Computer Technology, the World Wide Web, and Shakespeare

Roy Flannagan
Ohio University
Athens, Ohio

Flannagan focuses on the World Wide Web and discusses its capacity for surveying many of the resources on Shakespeare available today: complete screenplays, interviews with directors and actors, criticism, board games, films (new and restored), and other teaching aids. He offers valuable advice about constructing one's own home page for a class, about searching dedicated databases, and about using media not directly connected with computers. In brief, he provides a host of forward-looking suggestions about how to work with the newest technological innovations in this rapidly changing world.

When buying a computer this minute (October 16, 1996), the average family is forced by the marketplace to buy one with a modem, with a sound card, and with a fast CD-ROM drive, all built in. Each component is necessary to have access to current sources of information and entertainment. Along with the computer comes an invitation to join America Online or CompuServe, so that the purchaser can pay to access email facilities and the World Wide Web. Bill Gates of Microsoft Corporation is said to be catching up in the process of producing software that will allow him to rule the world by controlling the Internet. Is Shakespeare on-line? You bet. As I write, the movie of *Othello* directed by Oliver Parker and starring Laurence Fishburne and Kenneth Branagh has already been released on video. Before I check it out of a video store, I can search the Web not only for publicity about the movie and interviews with the director and stars, but for a complete screenplay (Shakespeare's lines are cut to the bone and modernized for American theater-goers, but still, it is a complete screenplay). Once I have dialed up from home through a SLIP connection into the Ohio University Dialnet system, I activate Netscape. There I choose one of the indexing services available through Netscape (Lycos and Excite are two good ones) and enter the keyword "Othello." Amazed at how many people are interested in the board game of that name, I search on until I find Harley Granville-Barker's comments on the play, a hypertext edition, and Verdi's *Otello* (not free but for sale through the Web). Finally, I arrive at Fishburne and Branagh and Oliver Parker, after discovering that Orson Welles's film of *Othello*, newly restored, is available from the Voyager Company on two laser discs for $99.95

and noting that someone has made a comic book version following the *Riverside Shakespeare* text. I pass through the "Shakespeare Homepage" at MIT,[1] noticing that the complete text of the recently rediscovered "Funeral Elegy for Master William Peter" (London: G. Eld for T. Thorpe, 1612), a "Normalized text, ed. Donald Foster," has been posted there. I found out recently by listening in on the SHAKSPER list that David Bevington will include the "Funeral Elegy" in his new edition of the complete works, making it canonical, although the debate over its authorship still rages.

Serendipity plays a large part in my random search. Finding odd things is part of the fun. I didn't succeed in finding the complete screenplay of *Othello*, but at the end of the notes on performers in the Castle Rock production of *Othello* I did find the address of the person who set up the page, so I could send him an email message asking if the complete screenplay will be there soon or will be posted elsewhere. I learned of the Castle Rock promotional page on the listserv I just mentioned, SHAKSPER, which began under Ken Steele at the University of Toronto and recently moved to Bowie State College in Bowie, Maryland, under the watchful eye of Hardy Cook. One of the nicer aspects of SHAKSPER is that it includes in its membership all sorts of Shakespeare nuts, buffs, and scholars, so that one may be listening to a New York director one day and a textual critic the next. I have posted nutty questions like "Why and how does the wounded deer cry, the one that Jacques describes in *As You Like It*," for which I received some fascinating answers, all of which are preserved, where they can be searched, in the available log of back files. When you subscribe to SHAKSPER, which you might be able to do semi-automatically through email software like Pine or Eudora, you will be given instructions on how to retrieve or search back files of conversations on the list. Most listserv groups now have a file of FAQs, or frequently asked questions. Such files help to prevent duplication of queries.

We have not quite lost print culture, though older scholars on the Net are now complaining that current articles don't venture back more than ten years in their review of scholarship, and computing in the humanities people argue on the Humanist[2] list whether or not it is easier to read a book on screen or on paper. But we do have almost instantly retrievable articles and abstracts through the World Wide Web. I am on the Board of Editors for one electronic journal in Shakespeare's area, *Early Modern Literary Studies*, or *EMLS*, edited by Ray Siemens at the University of British Columbia, and I can testify that, through such a journal, current information in the field gets out much more quickly and is read more thoroughly by more scholars than is material published in the average scholarly print journal. In an electronic review I help edit, the *Milton Review*, I myself finished a review of a recent book one day, and by the afternoon of the next day the review had been shipped to, and was probably read by, about sixty scholars. Because *EMLS* reaches a broader audience yet, it is an ideal medium to publish significant new articles for scholars whose work commands instant attention and respect. Because *EMLS* is juried (one of my fellow editorial board members complained to me recently "We really have to *work*!"), being published there has the same clout, in a list of publications, as does being published in a print journal.

I have shown how the constantly expanding world of the World Wide Web might be searched, by serendipity, but there are other ways Internet connections may be used by Shakespeare scholars or Shakespeare lovers, and their pupils.

Resources in Lists

The community of scholars is an enormous resource. If there are more than 1,250 subscribers to SHAKSPER (and there are as of early September 1996), from more than 20 countries, and 25–30 of them are premier editors and another 200 have written significant monographs on Shakespeare, the expertise represented by the list is profound. James Harner listens in and participates on SHAKSPER; he is the chief bibliographer of Shakespeare and sees a copy of any new article published anywhere in the world. The average listener might not want to bother Professor Harner too often—he has work to do, obviously—but, for an esoteric query, he is the person to ask. Bernice Kliman is working on a list of productions of *Hamlet*, for the Variorum edition of that play. If you were to want to know if or how often the play was produced in London after 1660, she might be the best person in the world to ask. Or, if you just published a note on one word in the play, in, say, a journal published in Singapore, Jim Harner would want to know about it.

Teaching Aids On-Line

One can surf the World Wide Web for Shakespeare games, Shakespeare movies, condensed versions of Shakespeare plays, even comparative syllabuses at major universities. Professors with local Shakespeare home pages may be including lecture notes, handouts, quizzes, or take-home examinations. If you check the home page for a large university, then branch off into English Department or even General Catalog holdings, you are apt to find course materials that you can compare with your own. How many teachers include *Richard III* or *Richard II* in a tragedies course, or, alternatively, in a histories course? You might be able to take a census of preferences by visiting the Web pages of ten or fifteen major universities.

Constructing Your Own Shakespeare Home Page, for Your Class

Through fiercely competing software manufacturers, all grappling for a piece of the World Wide Web and its advertising potential, an individual now can capture the design elements of someone else's home page and use them to construct one's own (after asking permission to do so, of course). If, for instance, a Shakespeare class were to be set up as an interactive exchange between students and professors (check the WWW home page of the University of Texas for various how-to-do-that manuals), another professor wanting to do much the same thing might borrow the look and feel of that class, using the newest versions of Netscape Navigator Gold or Hotdog (yes, it is named that). Or, if that same professor wanted a link to the Shakespeare Home Page, he or she could easily attach it to a class's home page. Students would then be able to search the complete works of Shakespeare stored at the MIT site of the Shakespeare Home Page.

Searching a Dedicated Database

A database useful to a teacher of Shakespeare might come in three or four different varieties, each of which might be stored on the server of a major university. A "full-text database" will have the complete text of any primary work or work of criticism. The full text of Shakespeare's sonnets, for instance, is available from the Bodleian Library,[3] as are the full text of the plays, back at MIT. The MIT texts are all searchable, so that one can go to the site just listed and begin to search the plays immediately. Full texts of all the Shakespeare quartos and the Folio, entered by scholars from the originals, are available from the Oxford Text Archive, which has its own home page.[4] Full texts of articles and a few scholarly books (those released by publishers or out of copyright) will be available through university library services. Scholarly journals like *ELH* are now going on-line as well: if your university or high school has access to a subscription,[5] students or professors can locate and print out the full texts of articles they might need for research. Dedicated bibliographies are beginning to emerge, some of which are provided free to universities or made available through the World Wide Web. I have placed the Relational Database of the *Milton Quarterly,* an annotated bibliography of all books received at the *Quarterly* for the last thirty years—many of which have to do with Shakespeare and Renaissance English literature—at the server of *EMLS:* that bibliographical database and its interface, in what is now a beta version, is located at http://edziza.arts.ubc.ca/english/iemls/mqlibrary/search.html. Use is free and unrestricted, though the data is copyrighted, and one can, through the software, receive the results of the search through one's email account. Since books having to do with the intellectual milieu of Milton often have to do with that of his fellow Londoner Shakespeare, searching the *Milton Quarterly* database might often help the Shakespearean scholar and teacher.

What the Internet Is Especially Good For

Since storage space at major universities is enormous already and growing to accommodate student and faculty email, and, since scholars need text files more often than image or sound files, storing documents, such as the complete works of Shakespeare, or all the Folio and quarto texts, is easy on the university servers. Searching them very quickly (or making available esoteric texts), as the software is developed, becomes easy as well. Also, maintaining and replenishing enormous bibliographies, which can be searched with powerful search engines such as PAT and LECTOR (used at the University of Waterloo to search and replenish entries in the *Oxford English Dictionary*), or WordCruncher, or Folio Views, or TACT—that also becomes easier. The second edition of the OED on CD-ROM, which cites Shakespeare more than any other author, has just had its price reduced by Oxford University Press to $395, a considerable drop from the more-than-$700 it cost when it was first released.

The Internet is also excellent for stimulating, preserving, and distributing the best in current critical opinion, through dedicated lists like SHAKSPER. For a high school or university teacher of Shakespeare, just listening in on the public discussions held, at the rate of two or three threads a day, is enough to make a "lurker" (listener only) into a critically perceptive teacher, up-to-date on the concerns of current editors and critics.

The possible uses of the Internet and the World Wide Web for storage and dissemination of information are boundless. For instance, the as-yet-unrealized ability to combine various media in one storage area, as on a CD-ROM or videodisc, should become a regular part of the World Wide Web, which now has the capacity to store and broadcast music and images as well as text—if only the cable companies, the universities, and the personal computer industry can match the capabilities of Netscape or Microsoft software.

The ability to transact scholarly searches using Internet communication one-on-one or through a consortium of scholars (as with asking someone in the Bodleian to look up something for you or posing a question on SHAKSPER such as "Who's your favorite Shakespeare teacher, and why?") will become more important as the home office becomes more of a reality for the virtual scholar and teacher. News like this may seem ominous to someone used to classroom interaction, since it appears to isolate both teacher and pupil from class; but the technology of Shakespeare studies should allow students and professors to enter high-level scholarly debates and to use primary and secondary resources they could never have had access to in the past. Shy students can be urged to respond to class through the quieter medium of email, and I already have scholarly correspondents from isolated New Zealand or the island of Malta: how could they otherwise keep up with what is going on in scholarship, without enormous travel budgets?

A high school student in Oregon, Michael Groves, has designed his own "Literature Resources for the High School and College Student" (http://www.teleport.com/~mgroves/), a home page designed to help students find texts and secondary sources for English and American Literature. What Michael has done is to collect resources for everyone from Melville to Shakespeare from all around the Web, on one site. Yes, his page is a little amateurish, and a few names are misspelled, but his labor will probably turn up sources that the sophisticated viewer will not yet have thought of.

Life will not be less complicated in the future world of teaching, which will certainly involve using cyberspace and virtual reality to enrich the lives of students by exposing them to the texts and performances of Shakespeare. Commercial publishing companies like Norton or Houghton Mifflin, multimedia publishers like Films in the Humanities, and formerly stodgy university presses like Cambridge University Press or Johns Hopkins University Press are all expanding the meaning of "publications," by including electronic versions of journals (Project Muse at Hopkins), by publishing electronic dictionaries that accompany word-processors (Houghton Mifflin), by accompanying videos on Shakespeare with CD-ROMs filled with images of archival material like Shakespeare's will (Films in the Humanities), or by CD-ROMs that use their more than 500 megabytes of storage to hold multiple versions of texts (Cambridge; Chadwyck-Healey).

Works in progress can also be announced on the WWW. And one can advertise oneself through home pages full of publications or job applications—even Shakespeareans can do that. And if one is a Shakespearean with a beloved hobbyhorse, such as painted images of productions of Shakespeare in the eighteenth and nineteenth centuries, one can create a home page devoted to the subject. Harry Rusche did just that, at Emory, focusing on painters like Blake, Fuseli, and John Singer Sargent, and considering the work of visual art as criticism. The URL for Harry's page is http://www.emory.edu/ENGLISH/classes/Shakespeare_Illustrated/Shakespeare.html. As one can see by looking at the complete address, the "Shakespeare Illustrated" project is one that began and now flourishes in the classroom.

I should not forget the media not directly connected with computers. The Films in the Humanities people at (800) 257-5126, knowing how many Shakespeare courses are out there, and knowing that popular actors like Kenneth Branagh, Laurence Fishburne, Kevin Kline, Keanu Reaves, and Mel Gibson all play Hamlet, Othello, or Iago, are besieging us academics with videotapes we are asked to buy for our students. The videotape medium, while not as effective as large-screen movies or live performances, still works well in the classroom. Presentation has gone beyond the talking head of Maynard Mack lecturing at the podium and on to performers like Patrick Stewart (never underestimate the power of *Star Trek*), David Suchet, Jane Lapotaire, Peggy Ashcroft, Ian McKellen, and Ben Kingsley, all talking about how to act and perform in Shakespeare's plays. The kicker is the price: the series *Playing Shakespeare,* in eleven parts, will cost your college or university $939. On the other hand, if you are the purchasing agent for your department and you place an order that amounts to more than $1,195, Films for the Humanities will send you an AT&T cordless phone. That means you get that prize if you order *Playing Shakespeare* plus, say, *The War of the Roses,* a collection of the history plays ($595). We academics are asked to sell our souls subtly.

The Films in the Humanities people have also issued two CD-ROMs that have to do with Shakespeare. The first is *Shakespeare: His Life, Times, Works, and Sources* (#AJH6016), advertised as having the endorsement of the late Samuel Schoenbaum, together with the scholarly help of a much lesser-known scholar, Jane Donawerth. The CD has images of original documents and claims to be "based on about 5000 pages of manuscripts and printed documents from the 16th and 17th Centuries" (promotional flyer). In fact, the printed documents are extremely hard to read or even, sometimes, to see, on a computer screen (even seventeen-inch and of a high resolution), and the text often seems peremptory. Shakespeare's will, for instance, is indecipherable, and no text is given for it. The CD might have reproduced photographic images of all the pages of the First Folio, but it doesn't. It does reproduce contemporary images of the various theaters associated with Shakespeare, and the various famous maps or views of London, but it doesn't reproduce the text and pictures of Holingshead's *Chronicles,* or Harsnett or Scot on witchcraft, or images from books about city hawkers and street criers, or madmen and beggars, or jousts and royal processions. I would uncharitably classify this CD as a toy, not a tool—something that a bright high school student would look at quickly, grow bored with, and not use again. A teacher on various levels might capture the Droeshout image from the First Folio and show it to his or her class, and perhaps show images of Elizabethan handwriting, but I can't see how the CD would be used extensively, even if a class were built around it. The cost is $99.

Another similar product, but one which I have only seen the adverts for, is *Shakespeare Interactive,* published oddly via G. K. Hall (home page http://www.mlr.com/gkhall), with the collaboration of Twayne, Macmillan Library Reference, Simon & Schuster, and Scribner. The Shakespeare CDs contain synopses of various plays, the "Cambridge Edition" text (which, I wonder?), running commentary in the left-hand margins, buttons for listening to "radio theater-style" audio, pop-up definitions of hard words, character profiles, and a gallery of more than a hundred images of actors, costumes, Shakespeare portraits, and memorabilia (many of nineteenth-century productions). Each title published so far costs $99, or four for $350.

Shakespeare's work is also included in *English Poetry Plus,* published by Films in the Humanities and described in the flyer as a "full-text multimedia database with images and sound." Five thousand poems represent the work of 275 poets, from the time of Chaucer through the end of the nineteenth century. Fifty poems can be heard read aloud, including "Jabberwocky"; and a hundred portraits, plus illustrations of styles of dress or architecture contemporary with the various poems, are included. This database is meant to compete with similar projects such as the enormous and horribly expensive Chadwyck-Healey full-text database of all the poets represented in the *Cambridge Bibliography of English Literature*. The Films for the Humanities CD-ROM, for PCs running Windows only, costs $395, and represents a collaboration with Chadwyck-Healey in that it uses some of the texts from the full-text database ("but the disk," the cynical reader will say, "costs only about $10, and the production costs can't have been all that high"). An English Department in a large to middling university ought to be able to afford that much from its yearly library budget.

Only large libraries will be able to afford the Chadwyck-Healey collections such as the Shakespeare editions and adaptations, collections that cost over $4,000 each. Chadwyck-Healey's *Editions and Adaptations of Shakespeare, CD-ROM Edition* is a much more sophisticated and dedicated product, aimed at professors and dramaturgs who want to recapture, say, a performance version of *King Lear* as it was acted in the 1850s by the great actor Charles Kean. The complete First Folio is on this CD, as is the 1599 *Romeo and Juliet* and the 1600 *Much Ado about Nothing*. This CD would also be valuable for the editor of Shakespeare, since it contains many annotated editions, such as those of Capell, published in 1767–68, and of Samuel Johnson, all eight volumes, published in 1765. The advantage of the large storage of the CD-ROM (and other similar storage devices that might soon render it obsolete), is enormous capacity—fitting the twenty-odd volumes of the OED on one little disk, or Samuel Johnson's edition of Shakespeare in a tiny corner of the CD.

A much more affordable (about $300) CD-ROM product of use for teachers, scholars, and students writing papers is *The World Shakespeare Bibliography, 1990–1993, on CD-ROM*, edited by James L. Harner. Cambridge University Press has produced a better combination of text, software, encoding, and GUI (graphic user interface, in computer talk) in this CD than any other publisher, with the possible exception of the *OED on CD-ROM*, which is, of course, the product of Oxford University Press, Cambridge's chief rival in the U.K. Even though the bibliography now ranges only for three years, it will in the near future be extended forward and backward, and it is amazingly complete, having been compiled by Jim Harner and Harrison Meserole as co-editors—Harry Meserole having been the long-time bibliographer for the Modern Language Association and *PMLA*. The bibliography is an extension of the printed bibliography published yearly in *Shakespeare Quarterly* and thus has the authority and expertise available at that premier scholarly journal. This CD has the easiest to use and most intuitive searching software, provided by DynaText corporation, that I have yet come across.

You can't actually *read* Shakespeare on a CD-ROM, in the sense that you can crinkle a paper page as you turn it, or keep one finger in the glossary as you keep reading in Act 4, scene 3 (but you can get to 4.3 quicker than you can in a book). The new electronic media aren't really reading media, exactly, but they can provide scenes from plays, music from performances, great performances by great actors. CD-ROM is a kind of onanistic medium, in that it can absorb one person and carry him or her into a virtual fantasy world with sound and light. Some have feared all along that the new technology will replace teachers and reading, but they may make teachers and reading more valuable by contrast. It could be that computers with CD-ROMs and speakers attached, the new wave in home computing, or the even newer wave of "home entertainment centers" that include computers, will eventually discourage reading and learning, since "books" or encyclopedias on CD seem to present sound bytes instead of deeper learning. People who believe that books are under fatal attack are now being described as Luddites or technophobes, but there are problems in the gee whiz land of computer and software manufacturers who try to please a mass audience with a short attention span. MTV has extended its hold even on Shakespeare, to the point where some audiences would rather see the "Moonlighting" version of *Taming of the Shrew* than the BBC production, even with John Cleese (better known for Monty Python skits or *A Fish Called Wanda*) in it.

Some CD-ROM tools for learning Shakespeare are being put together by reputable scholars with knowledge of the text as well as the video. The power of putting the printed word together with the fine acting performances is obvious: I really learned *Hamlet*, many years ago, by listening to John Gielgud perform the part, on a series of vinyl LPs. I know what I don't like in Olivier's languid Hamlet now, because I have seen the film over and over, or what I do like in Derek Jacobi's intensely bright, wired BBC Hamlet. Why not put all of them together on a CD-ROM, or at least as many moving images and texts as one could assemble on that 500+ MB worth of storage space, and why not play them back through a multimedia system that allows one to see fairly high-quality images and hear voices and music, while at the same time one can stop the action from time to time and see what the text is, or what the words mean. It might be the closest thing to having Shakespeare's talking head on a platter, or having your Shakespeare meal in an easy-to-digest form.

Of course it is better for students to read the plays first, understand the words, then see a really good performance, even if it is by Keanu Reaves. If Mel Gibson can give Shakespeare to thousands more people than would come to read him on the page, then fine, it is good for Shakespeare's public relations, and what's good for Shakespeare's PR is good for us teachers of Shakespeare who live off his industry.

Talking heads can't compare with live Shakespeare, of course, even if the talking heads are those of Maynard Mack or Harold Bloom. Talking heads are especially dull in the picture within a picture one sees on a computer screen. Even PBS or Arts and Entertainment now realize that a dialogue is better than a single lecture. And probably a play is better than any number of talking heads. I should qualify that, however, and say that some of the rehearsal videos or master classes for actors preserved by the Films for the Humanities are excellent for informing classes how lines should be spoken or action blocked off onstage.

I have a vision of the perfect teaching tool for Shakespeare, a CD-ROM or some better means of storing data invented in the future, which will allow our imagination really to roam in serendipity from text to song to dramatization to footnotes to glossary to annotated bibliography to variorum editions. You read the words to "Under the Greenwood Tree" on the page, then with the touch of a hot-button you hear the words recited by a fine actor, then you see the music for the song in the first recorded manuscript, then you hear an excellent singer, playing the lute artfully, and singing the song in context, in the play.

Notes

1. The Web site for the MIT complete and searchable texts of the plays is http://the-tech.mit.edu/Shakespeare/works.html. Note, however, that all Web sites mentioned may change address without notice or even be disconnected at any time.

2. To see what is current on, or subscribe to the list find: http://www.princeton.edu/~mccarty/humanist/ on the World Wide Web.

3. The address is http://www.bodley.ox.ac.uk/bardhtml/helpfiles/dart_shs.html.

4. The present address for the Oxford Text Archive, which has recently changed its management, is http://info.ox.ac.uk/ota. As an alternative, check the holdings of the University of Virginia Electronic Text Library, at http://etext.lib.virginia.edu/english.html, or the lists of electronic texts maintained by Christopher Fox at the Center for Electronic Texts in the Humanities at http://www.ceth.rutgers.edu/. It is also worth hunting for texts at the University of Michigan and the University of Toronto.

5. Project Muse, which publishes electronic versions of *ELH* and other Johns Hopkins Press journals, is at http:/muse.jhu.edu/.

6. Hardy Cook, of SHAKESPER, has a review of this CD-ROM in *Shakespeare Newsletter* that declares it "the best bibliographic software I have ever used" (email correspondence 10 September 1996). I would agree without reservation.

Sites Cited

Bodleian Library, Oxford University:
     http://www.bodley.ox.ac.uk/bardhtml/helpfiles/dart_shs.html
Cambridge University Press: http://www.cup.cam.ac.uk/
CETH (Center for Electronic Texts in the Humanities): http://www.ceth.rutgers.edu/
Chadwyck-Healey: http://www.chadwyck.co.uk/
G. K. Hall: http:www.mlr.com/gkhall
Humanist: http://www.princeton.edu/~mccarty/humanist/
Milton Review: http://www.urich.edu/~creamer/books.html
Oxford University Press Home Page: http://www.comlab.ox.ac.uk/archive/publishers/oup.html
Oxford Text Archive: http://info.ox.ac.uk/ota
Project Muse (John Hopkins University Press): http://muse.jhu.edu/
The Shakespeare Home Page: http://the-tech.mit.edu/Shakespeare/works.html
"Shakespeare Illustrated" home page (Harry Rusche):
     http://www.emory.edu/ENGLISH/classes/Shakespeare_Illustrated/Shakespeare.html
University of Virginia Electronic Text Center: http://info.ox.ac.uk/ota
Michael Groves's Literature Resources for the High School and College Student Home Page:
     http://www.teleport.com/~mgroves/
Address of a company cited which does not yet maintain a Web site: FILMS FOR THE HUMANITIES & SCIENCES, P. O. Box 2053, Princeton, NJ 08543-2053, Phone: (800) 257-5126; FAX: 609-275-3767

CHAPTER 32

The High-Tech Classroom
Shakespeare in the Age of Multimedia, Computer Networks, and Virtual Space

JAMES P. SAEGER
Vassar College
Poughkeepsie, New York

In our final essay, Saeger surveys some of the most futuristic technological innovations and resources available today and describes how they can "enrich the teaching process." Specifically, he explores three ways in which the newest computer technology can be used to teach Shakespeare: "a computerized system of video presentation, text-based virtual classrooms, and the World Wide Web." He offers detailed advice to teachers about how to incorporate something like the MIT Classroom Presentation System into their teaching; how to set up virtual classrooms, communities of teachers and students participating in electronic exchanges and discussion groups; and how to create a class-related Web site.

Multimedia, the Internet, email, digital video, hypertext, networked computers, the World Wide Web. Some of these tools of our high-tech culture were developed and found their first homes in our nation's colleges and universities; others are just now entering classrooms across the country. The widely heralded information revolution is upon us, and with it come predictions not only of large-scale social change but changes to our educational system as well. In courses from preschool through the college level, teachers look to new technologies for help in what many see as an increasingly difficult educational environment. Some teachers may find new technology appealing for its own sake; others quickly become suspicious of anything vaguely new. For either group (and for those who lie somewhere in between) the gauges of new teaching resources are simple: How will it enrich the teaching process? What benefits does it have over current methods and materials? Will it speed preparation time? Will it engage students in new ways or offer them new information? Will it increase contact with students? Teachers must also consider how difficult new technology is to learn and use. This essay addresses these questions and explores three ways in which new computer technology can be used to teach Shakespeare—a computerized system of video presentation, text-based virtual classrooms, and the World Wide Web.

Although this essay discusses a few specific tools, each of the technological resources described also represents a method of teaching and learning that can be achieved in a number of different ways. If the exact systems described here are not available, others will be. The computerized system of video presentation is a hardware/software combination developed by the Shakespeare Interactive Archive project at the Massachusetts Institute of Technology. It facilitates the incorporation of video into the classroom by linking searchable texts of Shakespeare's plays to versions of them on laserdisc. The other two resources are based on networked systems to which most college or university teachers (and an increasing number of secondary school teachers) have access. Virtual classrooms and forms of electronic discussion based in electronic mail or other types of networked communication provide an environment of increased teacher-student contact and student-student discussion outside of regular class meetings. The World Wide Web (often called WWW or the Web) offers a means by which students and teachers can reach the increasing amount of information available on the Internet; it also serves as a platform upon which teachers can create and present information (including text, images, sound, and even video) to their classes. Because these latter tools are both Internet-based, they also allow for the sharing of resources among a wide range of people. Teachers and classrooms across the country can talk with one another, create Web pages in common, and even conduct virtual classroom sessions.

However new and innovative they may seem on the surface, none of the technological tools discussed here *radically* alters established pedagogical methods. Rather, they build upon standard forms of interaction, presentation, and analysis and create new ways to approach traditional teaching methods. Although new technologies can offer a range of benefits to teachers, they do require time and patience to learn, prepare, and incorporate into a class. All of the computer resources described here have a largely open-ended format. They do not provide the Shakespeare teacher with pre-packaged classes but rather with the means to expand how those classes run and the shapes they take. Because each of the tools discussed is itself highly adaptable, any one of them can be molded to fit very different types of classes and teaching styles. And the teacher who uses these resources may happily discover a few new approaches to teaching made possible by the new technology.

Shakespeare and Digital Video: The MIT Classroom Presentation System

The Classroom Presentation System developed by the MIT Shakespeare Interactive Archive project provides an innovative way to use video in the Shakespeare classroom by combining a Macintosh computer, a laserdisc player, a video monitor or projector, and laserdiscs of Shakespearean films and videos.[1] The system links computerized searchable texts of Shakespeare's plays to corresponding film/video versions of them. On a practical level, this means that the user can browse through the text of a play on a computer, highlight a passage, and then, with the click of a mouse, see a performance of that passage appear on a connected television monitor. The user can also navigate through Shakespeare's plays—and thus through performances—by using the search feature to locate specific words within the text. And the software includes a note-taking feature with which the user can quickly mark and save clips from the film(s) and add notes or descriptive commentary. This note-taking feature makes it possible for a teacher to keep an outline or set of class notes with any selected clips; it also provides a way for students to write multimedia presentations and "papers" of their own.

As many teachers of Shakespeare already know (and as several of the essays in this volume have discussed), using film and video in the Shakespeare classroom can be extremely effective. Students are often proficient at seeing and reading what's actually on the page but are less skilled at trying to imagine what's not there: the nuances of performance that give breadth and depth to a line of verse. A well-acted performance can increase student understanding of the language and action of Shakespeare's plays. It can open them up to the concept of dramatic interpretation and to a new range of possible meanings contained in a text. Most importantly, of course, Shakespeare's plays are scripts for performance, and bringing performance into the classroom adds a crucial dimension to students' reading of a play. But while video does offer much potential benefit to students, the technical limitations of videotape can make realizing those benefits difficult.

The experience of using film or video in a Shakespeare classroom usually begins with a screening outside of class or during specific class periods. But if a single screening serves as the only contact students have with a particular production, any class discussion about it tends necessarily to be relatively generalized. Just as with a printed text, any close attention to detail requires bringing the object of study under direct scrutiny in class. Even when brought into class, however, a videotape—unlike a text with its act, scene, and line numbers— does not readily allow immediate access to all of its parts. Anyone who has lost precious class time trying to cue up just the right moment on a videotape knows that using video can be as frustrating as it is helpful. Examining a single scene in a class period generally poses few technical problems, but following a visual image or pattern of action through a production is virtually impossible without dubbing one's own videotapes—something few have the time, energy, or equipment to do. Even with such dubbed tapes, the class becomes limited by the moments of a film selected and this approach can thus close off directions for a class discussion even as it tries to open up new possibilities.[2]

A similar risk to using Shakespearean video—particularly films with high production values and well-known actors—is that students take a production as the only authoritative version.[3] Even though there is rarely time in a course to see more than one version of a particular play, exposure to multiple and varied performances gives students what many hours of textual explication in class can still fail to achieve, a sense that specific lines, whole scenes, and entire productions can bear significantly different approaches that can conflict but do not necessarily negate each other. Showing students multiple versions of a play is theoretically possible—many of the major plays have two or more versions available—but is difficult in practice. With the Classroom Presentation System the teacher can bring video into a class in a number of ways—from putting a few visual "quotes" into a discussion to creating an extended lecture with dozens of clips. And because the system streamlines the process of finding, reviewing, comparing, and saving a clip, teachers will find themselves adding significantly more performance analysis to a class. Despite fears that, by using such technology, video may dominate the classroom and displace the text, teachers using the system have found that the printed text gains a renewed centrality under such conditions. Students presented with multiple and varied performances become increasingly interested in textual detail to make sense of the differences and to ground their own ideas about a given play.[4]

Not just a high-tech way to show Shakespearean scenes in class, the Classroom Presentation System is in fact a powerful tool for researching and analyzing Shakespearean film and video. Since a fully outfitted workstation is capable of running two laserdisc players, each with its own television monitor, the system makes easy a form of side-by-side comparison and analysis of performance that is virtually impossible with other media.[5] Preparing a set of video segments for class thus becomes more than a rote task of marking and recording individual clips: details that might have gone unnoticed or unremarked when using videotape can suddenly take on deep significance as the user gains more control over the medium. To illustrate the possibilities, what follows is a description of the preparation and presentation of a sample class discussion on the Ghost in *Hamlet*.

Fascinating audiences and critics alike for hundreds of years, the Ghost in *Hamlet* continues to engage students and teachers of Shakespeare. Students raised on modern ghost traditions, however, sometimes have difficulty grasping the deep ambivalence in *Hamlet* of the Ghost's status and what that ambivalence might mean for an understanding of Hamlet's characterization and the play as a whole. When used to underscore more standard classroom approaches to the Ghost—such as providing cultural and theological background and examining closely specific moments in the text—a strategy of comparative performance analysis enables students to comprehend more readily the implications of variant readings. Presenting almost diametrically opposed visions of the ghost in the play, Laurence Olivier's 1948 production of *Hamlet* and Franco Zeffirelli's 1990 production (the two versions of *Hamlet* available on laserdisc and thus to the system) give form and action to the textual and thematic questions surrounding the Ghost.[6]

Using the Classroom Presentation System to prepare lectures or class discussions allows instructors to concentrate on the films themselves rather than being distracted by the technical problems usually associated with reviewing multiple versions of a play. By moving to the play's first scene in the computerized text, the user can quickly identify and view the Ghost's initial appearance. Selecting the Olivier version first, the user sees Horatio, Marcellus, and Bernardo sitting in the darkness on a high battlement. Immediately before the Ghost appears, a rhythmic noise like a heartbeat grows in intensity as the camera, tightening in on Marcellus, moves in and out of focus with the pounding. The Ghost then appears shrouded in a dense fog; it is large and menacing but its opacity suggests the insubstantiality of an unearthly spirit. This wraith-like incarnation, hovering in the mist rather than resting on the battlements, fulfills many of the modern stereotypes of ghosts as haunting figures risen from the grave.

After viewing this excerpt of Olivier's version of the ghost and forming a few initial impressions, the user now moves to the Zeffirelli version for a comparison. The user soon finds, however, that Zeffirelli cut the entire first scene and substituted a new non-textual one that takes place at the burial of Hamlet's father in the royal crypt beneath Elsinore. The dead king's body occupies the center of the frame for much of the scene as each of the major characters reacts to it and to each other. Thus, although Zeffirelli does not show his audience the ghost in the first scene, he does provide an important analogue to that missing scene— one that serves as a fruitful point of departure for class discussion. From just these two clips (which together take only a few minutes to show) the teacher can begin to explore not simply the presentation of the Ghost but, in asking why Zeffirelli might have made the substitution he did, what formal and thematic purposes the Ghost's initial appearance serves in the play.

For the user of the system, copying and saving both of these moments into the notecards takes less time than viewing them in the first place. And once the scenes have been marked, the user can return to them later, add additional commentary, and fine-tune the excerpts so that they begin and end at precisely the right moments.

Following the presentation of the Ghost through both films is as simple as finding the sequences described above. To find the Ghost's next appearance, the user can either move to Act 1, scene 4 in the computerized text or use the search feature to jump to each successive instance of the word "ghost." Either method will soon bring the viewer to the scenes in which Hamlet himself sees the Ghost for the first time. Like the initial appearance of the Ghost, the meeting of Olivier's Hamlet with the Ghost tends largely to reinforce modern notions of ghosts as dark, evil, and foreboding. The pulsating camera and the rhythmic beating sounds become more intense in this scene as they center now on Hamlet, who falls helpless into the arms of his fellows when the ghost finally appears.[7] Even after he rises from his collapse, Hamlet proceeds with a cautious fear. As he climbs the tower steps, Olivier's face holds a terrified look while the camera shows him dragging his feet on each upward step then falling to his knees when he finally confronts the Ghost. Whatever the truthfulness of the Ghost's message, Olivier's vision of the Ghost strongly emphasizes its position as a "goblin damn'd" rather than a "spirit of health." The viewer sees a skeletal figure with glowing eyes wrapped in a suit of armor, and when the Ghost speaks, its voice—a tortured and distorted whisper—seems to come from the fog rather than from the figure that floats before Hamlet. Students raised on the understated acting styles of recent decades may initially be put off by what they perceive as Olivier's overly theatrical approach. Once past their initial reactions, though, they are quick to recognize the imagery with which Olivier surrounds his ghost. They immediately understand the evil potential in this Ghost and thus Hamlet's uncertainty in the face of its murderous request.

The Zeffirelli version of the play, however, presents students with an entirely different set of dramatic possibilities and thematic options. Mel Gibson's Hamlet appears less afraid upon the Ghost's entrance, his warnings to his fellows are more powerful and decisive, and his movement through the battlements to meet the Ghost are stronger and more assured. In Olivier's version the darkness of the tower and the mist surrounding it transform the meeting site of Hamlet and the Ghost into a semi-mystical place; whereas, the meeting of Gibson's Hamlet with Paul Scofield's Ghost occurs in a much more tangible, concrete, and earthly space. While a blue light bathes the Ghost and makes the stone walls that enclose the two figures seem even colder, Zeffirelli gives to the meeting an intimacy between the two characters that is wholly absent from Olivier's version. Scofield's is a fully human ghost frightened by the position in which he finds himself and feeling the full pain of his nightly torments. A careful student may remark that this Ghost does not wear the armor that the text specifies, but when guided to ascertain why Zeffirelli might have done this, that same student will begin to understand a purposefulness behind the choices the director has made here.

Comparing these two versions of this scene brings to immediate recognition Hamlet's own questions about the Ghost and the dramatic implications of each possibility. The Ghost in Olivier's version seems one whose truthfulness is easy to doubt. But Zeffirelli strongly reinforces the Ghost's veracity: the dead body of the king in his grave first seen in the opening shots of the film is clearly the same figure that appears before Hamlet. Shown in class either the Zeffirelli or the Olivier production alone, students will assume that either one is the way that the ghost is *supposed* to be portrayed. Taken by itself, neither will necessarily generate a lively discussion. But put them side by side and students' eyes light up at the dissimilarities, and their sense of who and what the Ghost is immediately expands. They begin to become engaged with an important moment of the play that may otherwise have passed with little note.

The Classroom Presentation System allows the teacher to prepare and present comparable scenes like these with a flexibility that encourages class discussion and exploration of both the text and the related performances. Once the user has marked the desired clips and added any necessary descriptive text, running the chosen segments in class requires only a mouse-click.[8] The system also gives the teacher the ability to organize material in ways that take advantage of how students read visual information. When shown video excerpts that run for more than a minute or two, students tend to lose the ability to recognize and retain detail. To address this tendency, the system allows for easy breaking up and organizing of clips: the two versions of Hamlet's meeting with the ghost can be divided into their component parts and shown in alternating segments in order to concentrate at each stage on specific elements. The way in which the teacher initially selects and orders the clips does not need to affect the direction of the class. The teacher can move to any point of a prepared outline, skip over segments that seem unnecessary, return to certain clips and repeat them, or even stop on still frames.

If used only to lecture, the MIT system would already be significantly better than standard videotape. But it also enables teachers to respond quickly in class to student questions and ideas about other moments in the play not previously selected. Suppose, for instance, one bright student during the class on the Ghost anticipates the topic of the next day's class and asks if the tower on which Olivier's Hamlet first meets the ghost is the same as that from which he gives the "to be or not to be" speech. Wanting to capitalize on the student's interest and on the close visual and emotional resonance that Olivier gives to these moments, the teacher can quickly call up and show a brief portion of Olivier's rendition of the later speech. Within a few seconds it becomes clear that the tower is the same, and after moving back and forth between the two excerpts the class may also find the position and movement of Olivier's body to be very similar in each scene. A class now engaged with this relationship might take the next step and wonder if Zeffirelli draws any similar parallels. In another few seconds the teacher can show Mel Gibson giving his version of the speech. A class that has already seen Zeffirelli's introductory scenes will soon make the connection that the director has placed this speech in the same crypt where his father was buried in the opening sequence. Although quite different in their significances, both directors draw important visual parallels between the opening of the play, the first view of the dead king, and Hamlet's "to be or not to be" speech. Sorting out the meanings behind these connections may not be simple for a class, but it will teach them how a play generates meaning and how to explore that meaning.

Among the important discoveries I have made while using the system and the method of comparative performance analysis it enables is that it can be done, and is sometimes done to greater effect, when students have not actually seen the whole performance of a given play. While seeing entire performances is important for other reasons, students can quite readily make observations about specific dramatic moments and begin to draw conclusions about interpretations without having a comprehensive idea of the production. In fact, some students, especially those who might be new to Shakespeare, are often able to generate better ideas about a scene when limited to discrete moments from a given production. This may seem problematic to some, but without the sense of a whole production students are forced to concentrate with increased scrutiny upon the details available in whatever excerpt is presented for discussion. If they have seen the film, they will often try immediately to generalize to the whole, making their observations more bland.

By far the most valuable use for the MIT system lies not in the teacher's hands but in those of the students. Using the same means by which a teacher would create a lecture or discussion, students can write their own multimedia essays or create their own class presentations. Unlike attempting to analyze a Shakespearean text in isolation—a daunting task even for the best of students—reference to performance can help break down many of the barriers presented to students by a text. One of those barriers is a sense that a Shakespearean play has a single meaning or set of meanings. Students who carry this assumption with them are often afraid of making an "incorrect" observation about a line or passage; they are also at times paralyzed by the sheer weight of Shakespearean commentary, assuming that they cannot possibly say anything original about a given play. Seeing, reacting to, and working closely with multiple performances in the way that the Classroom Presentation System allows can minimize (though perhaps not completely erase) the effect of these assumptions.

Virtual Shakespearean Classrooms: Electronic Discussion Lists, Newsgroups, MOOs

While multimedia computers and interactive video are flashy and exciting for students and teachers alike, much simpler forms of computer-use can be highly effective as well. The use of local or worldwide networks for the exchange of text-based information remains among the most established and versatile ways of bringing computers into the classroom. Before the World Wide Web gave the Internet pictures, sound, and hypertext documents, users of the Internet turned to each other in the form of electronic discussion lists, newsgroups, chat rooms, and other types of electronic exchange that relied exclusively on text. Text-based communication, in whatever form it takes, still comprises a significant bulk of the Internet's traffic, and it largely defines the range of virtual communities, including those devoted to the discussion of Shakespeare, for which the Internet has become known. In the early days of the Internet, college and university faculty made up the majority of these virtual communities whose discussion revolved primarily around academic and professional issues. But as teachers found their own scholarly lives enriched by the virtual communities in which they participated, many began using similar types of virtual spaces for teaching as well.

On a technical level, these virtual communities exist simply as any of the different systems in place to get messages from a single user to a larger group. With an electronic discussion list (using a program like Listserv), members of the group can send electronic mail (email) to a single address, and their messages are immediately redirected to all members of the group. Members can read, respond to, or delete messages as they like. Usenet Newsgroups operate on a slightly different model in which posted messages reside in a central location rather than being distributed to each member. Unlike with a discussion list, however, messages and responses in a newsgroup are organized by topic (usually called a thread), and users can easily review all contributions to a particular discussion. With both newsgroups and mailing lists, users can follow discussions at their own pace—from occasionally glancing at postings but not contributing (called "lurking") to active daily engagement in ongoing debates. Still other types of communities allow for exchanges between users who are simultaneously connected. Described as taking place in *real-time*, these systems—which include MOOs, MUDs, and various forms of chat-rooms—give the feeling and immediacy of a spoken conversation: a message typed by one user instantly appears on the screen of everyone else who is connected.

Virtual classrooms and communities can serve the Shakespeare teacher in two important ways. One of the uses for these types of networks is for teachers to find help and support from their peers. Established electronic discussion groups like SHAKSPER, FICINO, and RENAIS-L consistently provide useful tips for inquiring teachers.[9] And while the Usenet Newsgroup currently devoted to Shakespeare (humanities.lit.authors.shakespeare) is less academically oriented, it too provides a place to ask questions, get answers, or just "listen" to discussions about Shakespeare. Although some teachers have students follow and even contribute to discussions on some of these lists, the more common approach is to adapt models of these virtual communities for their own classrooms. Most colleges and universities have some sort of campus-wide computer network, and many are using these networks to experiment with virtual classrooms. The types of networking systems and the forms of virtual spaces that are possible differ from campus to campus, but the basic principles and the uses to which they are put are easily adaptable.

Perhaps the simplest way for teachers at the college level to begin using a virtual classroom is with an electronic mail discussion list. Since many colleges and universities across the country rely heavily upon electronic mail for the conduct of daily business, new students often receive computer accounts and email addresses automatically. When such a system for communication is already in place, adopting it for class use becomes quick and easy; usually a phone call (or email) to the campus computing center and a couple of days for processing is all that is needed to initiate a list. At its most basic a class email list can be a good way to get announcements to students about the class itself: changes to assignments or due dates, distribution of study questions, or even reminders about particular deadlines. But using an email list as a means to extend and expand upon in-class discussion has many benefits as well. Students can raise questions or make comments that the direction of class discussion or time constraints would not otherwise allow. And the informality of the medium—existing somewhere between casual conversation and formal writing—allows students to write without being constrained by the often rigid ideas they hold about more formal paper-writing.

For all the benefits of electronic discussion, however, there are some things to watch out for. The same informality that frees student writing can also loosen the restraints of common courtesy. Another potential problem is that assignments posted electronically can sometimes feel less tangible to students—unreal in some way—so even if postings are required they get missed. Both of these issues can be addressed with clear policies for conduct and for the amount and frequency of posting. A base requirement of 100–200 words per week in this medium will begin the discussion and will often generate even more than the required amount. The way in which students receive discussion list postings has both its benefits and drawbacks. Receiving class postings through their regular mail accounts serves as a constant reminder to students of the class and its assignments, but receiving important class postings along with other personal mail can also be distracting. Using a newsgroup-type format combats some of the drawbacks of email-based electronic discussion, though it also creates others. With a newsgroup or other dedicated type of virtual classroom, the student must specifically connect to the group. In this type of forum, students come to the electronic discussion prepared to deal with the material. Another benefit is that discussions can be grouped (threaded) by topic so that students can follow and/or add to a specific discussion topic in order. Teachers who have used this type of system say, however, that many students— even those who usually keep up with assigned work—can fail to do the assignments.[10]

A more dynamic use of networked technology develops by using some form of simultaneous, or real-time, conversation tool. A real-time virtual classroom involves any system in which all participants must be connected to the group through their computers at the same time. Depending upon the type of network involved, these computers can be in the same room, different points on campus, or different points anywhere in the country or the world. These real-time environments go by various names, each with its own variations, but all work under the same basic principle: whatever one participant types on her/his computer is immediately relayed through the central computer to all other connected participants.

This type of real-time system recently helped one Shakespeare course taught by Rachana Sachdev at Susquehanna University and another Shakespeare course at the University of Pennsylvania taught by Peter Parolin come together for regular discussion sessions that combined both classes into one. The two classes were designed to share several plays in common, and at regular intervals throughout the semester Professors Sachdev and Parolin would alternate leading a real-time discussion in cyberspace. The class discussions took place within a virtual environment called PennMoo, a system developed and maintained by the English Department at Penn to explore the uses of virtual classrooms.[11] Although the virtual classroom was not the only facet of the interaction between the two classes—who also got together in Philadelphia to see a local production and in Selinsgrove for an undergraduate conference on Shakespeare—it was an important one. While both teachers noted that some technical problems arose when doing such a linked class for the first time, both also found that the students' responses to the virtual class meetings were quite enthusiastic and plan to do more combined classes in the future.

The Shakespeare Classroom and the World Wide Web

The World Wide Web is a loose but vast collection of Internet resources that contain text, pictures, sound, and even video. Many of the Internet resources previously accessed through simple text-based terminals (using telnet connections, gopher menus, and the like) are now also available through the Web. Not only is the Web more visually pleasing and simpler to navigate than earlier means of finding Internet resources, but publishing one's own material on the Web is also much easier. For these reasons, mainstream use of the Internet has exploded since the inception of the Web. Already the Web contains a wide range of on-line resources for the teacher of Shakespeare to draw upon (virtually all of them free and freely accessible to anyone with a computer and an Internet connection), but perhaps more importantly the Web can serve as a platform for the creation and presentation of a variety of resources for one's own classes.

The creation of a class-related Web site is a much simpler process than it might seem. Since a large percentage of the materials teachers give to students are already routinely written on a word-processor, transforming them into a Web-ready document takes only the addition of a few simple commands. Collectively these commands comprise the HyperText Markup Language (HTML) in which all World Wide Web documents are written and allow the creator of a Web site to format text, images, sound, video, and also to create links to other documents on the Web. The first step in creating a class Web site is to contact either one's campus computer center or Internet service provider. They will provide information about where on their system Web information is stored and how to create and transfer files. Each distinct document on the Web, usually called a page, exists as a separate file on the host computer. An individual Web site can be comprised of a single page of information or a linked collection of many pages. For those who do become interested in creating their own Web pages, there are many good books available, a number of on-line tutorials,[12] and an increasing number of computer programs that work like a word processor so that the user does not even need to learn HTML itself.

Just as with a class discussion list, among the most basic but helpful uses of a Web page is getting information about the class into the hands of students. A simple Web site that contains a version of the syllabus, descriptions of the course assignments, procedures for the course, along with any other relevant material can insure that students always have access to this information. If these materials are posted before the semester begins, students can easily find out whether the course interests them or not, and students enrolling in the class late can go to the Web site for any information they might have missed. Another important aspect of a class Web site is for the teacher to provide links to the available resources on the Internet World Wide Web: sites that allow searching Shakespeare's works by individual words, library card catalogs and bibliographical databases that help students conduct research, on-line journals that provide commentary and criticism of Shakespeare, and even facsimiles of original printed editions of Shakespeare's plays. As a simple and practical means of getting information to one's classes, a Web site is an extremely useful tool, but with its ability to deliver images and other multimedia formats like sound and video it also opens up new ways to present students with other materials as well.

For many Shakespeare teachers, images can be important supplements to student readings of the plays, but getting visual materials into the classroom is often difficult, particularly in large classes. Photocopies, for instance, are expensive and time-consuming to produce; and they often result in images that are only barely recognizable. And other methods of bringing visual aids into class—such as slides, transparencies, or even single copies of picture books—have drawbacks ranging from a long or expensive setup to difficulties working with them in class. For these reasons, many who might otherwise bring a range of visual materials into their classes decide that the difficulty involved precludes them from doing so with any seriousness.

With the World Wide Web as a platform, however, any image one can locate—whether printed or on-line—can potentially be made available in a class Web site.[13] To include pictures in a set of class Web pages all that is needed is a color scanner (most campuses will have a computer/media center for scanning). Depending on the scanner itself and the detail that is required from an image, scanning a picture or photograph generally takes only slightly longer to do than making a photocopy. After scanning, the image will usually need slight adjustment for quality (something accomplished with photo manipulation programs that accompany scanning software) and saving to the proper image format. This process generally takes a few minutes, depending upon the user's familiarity with the software and the complexity and quality of the image. Once the image has been scanned, adjusted, and saved, loading the image into a Web site takes only another minute or so. While the quality of images on a computer screen cannot match that of a well-printed photograph, it is far greater than a photocopy and much easier to use and prepare than other image-based media.

For many teachers, having this resource will mean sending students to computer stations outside of class to look at the images, but an increasing number of classrooms have the ability to bring the Web directly into class. Such a setup requires a networked classroom with a computer and some sort of system for projecting the images from the computer onto a wall or screen large enough for students to see. In a classroom like this, the World Wide Web becomes a high-tech slide projector able to show any image that can be scanned. While this may seem like going to a lot of trouble and expense for a relatively simple function of projecting images, classrooms designed with this capability usually serve a variety of functions for a range of disciplines. But just as the MIT Classroom Presentation System gives more flexibility for classroom uses of video, the Web makes the use of images much more able to accommodate a class discussion. With digital images on the Web and using the right software, teachers can make images larger or smaller, toggle between two or more images for comparison, or even put them side by side on the screen. With such a system, images can become an integrated part of class discussion rather than simply peripherally illustrative materials. Another benefit to presenting these materials on the Web is that they are also accessible to students outside the class.

Shakespeare and Computers

As I noted at the beginning of this essay, the real test of any new technology is the tangible effect it has upon students. For Shakespeare students this means anything that can broaden their understanding of the plays. Each of the technological resources discussed above can help Shakespeare teachers toward that goal by providing a range of new possibilities for classroom presentation, analysis, and interaction. While they do facilitate certain types of activities, none of the tools provide ready-made classes for teachers. Using each resource requires the same teacher preparation and involvement as any more traditional methods. In addition they require that both teacher and student learn and become comfortable with new pieces of technology. And, of course, when technology is involved, teachers must always assume that things will go wrong at first, perhaps even the first few times. But when used to their fullest potential, the resources here can pay back many times over the effort teachers and students spend to put them in place.

Notes

For sharing their teaching ideas and methods with me, I would like to thank Rebecca Bushnell, Peter Parolin, Rachana Sachdev, and, in particular, Pete Donaldson, who laid the important groundwork (both technical and intellectual) for the ways in which I approach Shakespeare and film. I would also like to thank Mark Seidl and Ann Imbrie for reading early versions of this essay and giving me many valuable suggestions.

1. Peter S. Donaldson, who directs the project with Janet Murray and Larry Friedlander, provides a more technical description of the system, and of the larger project of which it is a part, in "The Shakespeare Interactive Archive: New Directions in Electronic Scholarship on Text and Performance," *Contextual Media: Multimedia and Interpretation*, ed. Edward Barrett and Marie Redmond (Cambridge: MIT Press, 1995), 103-27. The Shakespeare Interactive Archive evolved from an earlier project developed at Stanford by Larry Friedlander, who describes the project and its pedagogical goals in "The Shakespeare Project," *Hypermedia and Literary Studies*, ed. Paul Delany and George P. Landow (Cambridge: MIT Press, 1991), 257-71.

2. Stephen Buhler strongly cautions against the possibility that teachers impose on students their own singular reading of films; see "Text, Eyes, and Videotape: Screening Shakespeare Scripts," *Shakespeare Quarterly* 46 (1995): 236-37.

3. Larry Friedlander identifies this as one of the primary drawbacks to using film versions of Shakespeare ("Shakespeare Project," 259); see also Buhler, "Text," 236.

4. Pete Donaldson has found that with comparative performance he can even get students interested in questions about variants in the original printed editions of the plays; see "Archive," 110-11.

5. It was this ability to analyze the details of performance that first directed Larry Friedlander toward computers and laserdiscs in developing The Shakespeare Project at Stanford. For a list of his goals when teaching performance, and thus his requirements for an interactive computer system, see "Shakespeare Project," 260-61.

6. In a multimedia essay entitled "Ghostly Texts and Virtual Performances: Old Hamlet in New Media," Pete Donaldson brilliantly analyzes the way each film presents Hamlet's initial encounter with the Ghost. See "Archive," 112-23, for a discussion; the multimedia essay was originally presented at the 1993 meeting of the Shakespeare Association of America. My own understanding of these two films owes much to the approach taken in the essay and to numerous conversations with Pete Donaldson about the films and how to present them to students.

7. See Donaldson, "Archive," 118-19 for a more thorough reading of Olivier's treatment of this scene.

8. What is actually retained by the program is not a digital video image but rather a set of markers to the laserdisc. Each frame of the laserdisc has a number accompanying it. What the software does is to mark the beginning and ending frame number of the clip, along with the information concerning the disc to which the frame numbers apply. In the notebook window

these references appear as text and numbers underlined and enclosed in angle brackets. Thus, the video link that appears as

    <Olivier Hamlet 1,333429,334158>

means that the clip is on the first side of the Olivier Hamlet disc, and runs from frame reference number 333429 to frame reference number 334158. By clicking on that reference link with the mouse, the computer immediately tells the laserdisc player exactly where to begin and end. Because the program doesn't retain any video itself, only the links, it does not require the powerful computers and high storage capacities usually associated with digital video. Additionally, since all users purchase their own laserdiscs, there are no copyright problems associated with using the films.

    9. SHAKSPER is the worldwide electronic conference devoted to discussions of Shakespeare; FICINO and RENAIS-L are devoted more generally to early modern European history, literature, and culture. Information about these discussion groups can be found, among other places, through the World Wide Web pages of the English Department at the University of Pennsylvania (http://www.english.upenn.edu/Lit-resources/index.html).

    10. A new form of discussion list/newsgroup hybrid addresses many of the separate drawbacks of either system. Called *Hypermail*, the system works with a standard email discussion group but then automatically archives all postings to the group in a World Wide Web site. Members of the group receive postings in their electronic mailboxes but can also view the material through the archive. I am currently using this system for my classes here at Vassar College.

    11. For discussions of the ways in which others have been using MOOs for teaching see David Bennahum, "Fly Me to the MOO," *Lingua Franca* 4 (May/June 1994), 1, 22–36, and Lisa Guernsay, "College 'MOOs' foster creativity and collaboration among users," *The Chronicle of Higher Education* 42 (9 Feb. 1996), A24–A25. Additional information about PennMoo can be found through their Web site (http://www.english.upenn.edu/PennMOO/index.html).

    12. One of the best introductions to HTML can be found at the Web site of the National Center for Supercomputing Applications (NCSA) at the University of Illinois Urbana-Champaign (http://www.ncsa.uius.edu/General/Internet/WWW/HTMLPrimer.html).

    13. Putting copyrighted materials on-line, even for education purposes, may be a violation of copyright law.

Editors

Ronald E. Salomone is professor of English and chair of the Division of Humanities at the Chillicothe campus of Ohio University. He has served as president of the Southeastern Ohio Council of Teachers of English and as editor of *Focus*. He was co-editor, with James E. Davis, of *Teaching Shakespeare Today* (NCTE, 1993) and has published in the areas of modern British fiction and faculty evaluation and administration. He is currently working on a study of the novels of Charles Williams.

James E. Davis, professor of English and former department chair at Ohio University in Athens, is a past president of the National Council of Teachers of English (NCTE) and of both the Ohio Council of Teachers of English Language Arts and the College English Association of Ohio. He is the author of many chapters in books and over three hundred articles on teaching English. He has edited the *Ohio English Bulletin, Focus,* and the book *Dealing with Censorship*. He co-edited the 1988 edition of *Your Reading* (NCTE) and *Presenting William Sleator* (McMillan, 1992) with his wife, Hazel Davis. With Ron Salomone he co-edited *Teaching Shakespeare Today* (NCTE, 1993).

Contributors

James R. Andreas was a Fulbright Lecturer in American Studies at the University of Paris, XII. He edits *The Upstart Crow: A Shakespeare Journal* and has published extensively on teaching Shakespeare, Shakespeare's comedies, Shakespeare and music, and Shakespeare's influence on African American literature. In 1995/96 he established the South Carolina Shakespeare Collaborative with a $180,000 grant in outright funds from the National Endowment for the Humanities.

Sharon A. Beehler, associate professor of English at Montana State University in Bozeman, is past president of the Montana Association of Teachers of English Language Arts (MATELA). She is on the editorial board for the *Shakespeare in the Classroom Newsletter* and has published articles in venues as diverse as *Shakespeare Quarterly* and *English Journal*. She was a contributor to *Teaching Shakespeare Today* and has written a book-length study entitled *Shakespearean Dialogics: The Negotiation of Character and Meaning*.

Harry Brent is professor of English and former chairman of the Department of English at Baruch College of the City University of New York. He has served on the Executive Committee of NCTE and twice has been elected chair of the NCTE College Section. He has co-edited seven books dealing with the teaching of writing, chief among them *Rhetorical Considerations*. He currently edits the *Quarterly Review of Doublespeak*.

Mary T. Christel is an English instructor at Adlai E. Stevenson High School in Lincolnshire, Illinois, where she teaches courses in world literature and media analysis. She has published articles on such diverse writers as T. S. Eliot, Dostoevsky, James Welch, and Shakespeare, as well as on the use of media as a complement to the study of literature, in the *Illinois English Bulletin, Literature and Writing, English Journal,* and *Teaching Shakespeare Today*. She also has published a teacher's guide for Robert Cormier's *The Chocolate War* for Scott Foresman.

Leila Christenbury is a former high school English teacher and is currently professor of English Education at Virginia Commonwealth University in Richmond. The editor of *English Journal* and of the 1995 *Books for You* (NCTE), she is the author of *Making the Journey: Being and Becoming a Teacher of English Language Arts* (1994, Heinemann). Christenbury has served on the Executive Committee of NCTE's Conference on English Education and as co-editor of *The ALAN Review*.

Michael J. Collins is adjunct professor of English and dean of the School for Summer and Continuing Education at Georgetown University.

Samuel Crowl is Trustee Professor of English at Ohio University. He is the author of *Shakespeare Observed* (1992) and many articles on performance aspects of Shakespeare.

H. R. Coursen teaches at the University of Maine, Augusta. His eighteenth book of poetry, *New and Collected Poems: 1966–1996,* has recently appeared from EM Press, Virginia. His *Watching Shakespeare on Television* appeared in 1994 from Fairleigh Dickinson, *Reading Shakespeare on Stage* in 1995 from Delaware, and *Shakespeare in Production: Whose History?* in 1996 from Ohio University Press. He is co-editor, with Eva McManus, of *Shakespeare and the Classroom*.

Margo A. Figgins, poet and associate professor of English Education at the University of Virginia, directs the UVA Writers Workshop and is poetry editor of *Iris: A Magazine about Women;* her work as a teaching poet is supported by the Virginia Commission for the Arts.

Michael Flachmann, professor of English at California State University, Bakersfield, has written eight books—most recently *Beware the Cat: The First English Novel, The Image of Idleness: England's First Epistolary Novel, Shakespeare's Lovers,* and *Shakespeare's Women*—and over forty articles in such journals as *Shakespeare Quarterly, Studies in English Literature, English Literary Renaissance, Medieval and Renaissance Drama in England, Studies in Philology,* and others. He has also worked for many years in professional theater, serving as dramaturg for over fifty Shakespearean productions at such prominent west-coast theaters as the Oregon Shakespeare Festival, the La Jolla Playhouse, California Institute of the Arts, and the Utah Shakespearean Festival (where he has been company dramaturg since 1986). In 1993 he was selected as Outstanding Professor for the entire twenty-campus California State University System, and last fall he received the prestigious Carnegie Foundation "U.S. Professor of the Year" award.

Roy Flannagan, professor of English at Ohio University, is best known for being longtime editor of *Milton Quarterly.* He has published approximately three hundred reviews, articles, or books, many of them about Milton. At present, he is working on an edition of the *Complete Poetry and Selected Prose of John Milton* for Macmillan; a separate *Paradise Lost* volume came out in 1992. He is also assembling the one hundred megabytes of information necessary to begin filling the memory of a CD-ROM complete reference library for Milton, including all the texts, all the best-respected commentaries and annotations, and all the best-known bibliographies.

Charles H. Frey has taught Shakespeare since 1970 in the Department of English at the University of Washington (Box 354330, Seattle WA 98115). He has published widely on Shakespeare, children's literature, and other subjects. His email address is cfrey@u.washington.edu.

William J. Gathergood is an English and Drama teacher at Reynoldsburg High School. He has also served as a clinical educator with the Ohio State University's Professional Development Site Program. As such, he is co-coordinator, along with Dr. Keith Hall, of the TIEPDS, a professional development site which explores Technology in Education. He has headed several international projects, linking over eight thousand students with partners for projects all over the world. He has taught a semester-long Shakespeare Seminar for twenty-two years.

Loreen L. Giese is assistant professor of English at Ohio University in Athens. She has published articles in *The Bodleian Library Record* and *Teaching Shakespeare Today* (NCTE, 1993). She is currently finishing a book entitled *London Consistory Court Depositions, 1590-1610: List and Indexes* for the London Record Society.

C. W. Griffin is professor of English at Virginia Commonwealth University in Richmond, Virginia. He spent a number of years directing the composition and rhetoric program at VCU, publishing on writing and writing across the curriculum. Recently he has focused on Shakespeare studies, teaching Shakespeare at the sophomore, senior, and graduate levels. He has published articles on Shakespeare in *English Journal, Shakespeare on Film Newsletter,* and *Shakespeare Bulletin;* he has an article on Shakespeare forthcoming in *Literature and Film Quarterly.*

Christine Heckel-Oliver is an English instructor at Adlai E. Stevenson High School in Lincolnshire, Illinois, where she teaches courses in creative writing and freshman accelerated English. She has with Mary T. Christel spoken at state, regional, and national NCTE conventions on the use of role-playing as a response to literature and the use of media in creative writing classes.

Frances L. Helphinstine, professor of English at Morehead State University, is past president of the Kentucky Council of Teachers of English/Language Arts and the Kentucky Philological Association, and associate editor of the *Kentucky English Bulletin*. She has received twenty-five-year service recognition from the National Council of Teachers of English. She regularly presents papers at these organizations and at the Twentieth Century Literature Conference and the Shakespeare Association of America. She has published on censorship, teaching writing, Appalachian literature, and Shakespeare.

Kathy M. Howlett, assistant professor of English and co-director of Cinema Studies at Northeastern University, Boston, is the author of articles and reviews in *Literature/Film Quarterly*, *CEA Critic*, and *Shakespeare Bulletin* and a book on Shakespeare on film forthcoming in 1998 from Ohio University Press, *Rare Visions: Framing Shakespeare on Film*. She regularly team-teaches interdisciplinary courses, as well as graduate and undergraduate courses on Shakespeare and Shakespeare on film.

Larry R. Johannessen is associate professor of English Education and coordinator of the Secondary Education program at Benedictine University in Lisle, Illinois. He taught high school English for twelve years and has directed workshops and inservice programs for teachers in writing, thinking, and literature instruction. In addition to chapters in books and textbooks, he has contributed over thirty articles to scholarly journals. He is the author of *Illumination Rounds: Teaching the Literature of the Vietnam War* (NCTE, 1992) and co-author of two popular NCTE publications: *Writing about Literature* (1984) and *Designing and Sequencing Prewriting Activities* (1982). He is a frequent speaker at NCTE conventions and affiliate conferences.

Robert Carl Johnson, professor of English at Miami University and associate provost and dean of the Graduate School, has served as president of both the College English Association of Ohio and of the national College English Association. A former chair of the Department of English at Miami, Mr. Johnson's teaching and research interests include Renaissance drama and sports literature. His publications include a book on John Heywood and an edition of *Cambises*.

Linda Kissler is a professor of English at Westmoreland County Community College in Youngwood, Pennsylvania. She received both a B.A. and an M.A. in English from California University of Pennsylvania, where she was the recipient of the English Faculty Award. She has edited textbooks on Business Communication and was named 1994 Outstanding Teacher at WCCC.

William T. Liston is professor of English at Ball State University, where he has taught since 1965. He has contributed performance and book reviews to *Shakespeare Bulletin, Shakespeare Quarterly, Theatre Journal, Cahiers Elisabethains,* and *Brock Review,* and articles to *Southern Humanities Review, College Literature, The Midwest Quarterly,* and *The University of Dayton Review.* His *Francis Quarles' Divine Fancies: A Critical Edition* was published by Garland in 1992. His essay on Shakespearean stage history since 1970 will appear in the revised edition of *The Riverside Shakespeare.*

Mary Z. Maher is professor of Theatre Arts at the University of Arizona, where she teaches undergraduate and graduate courses in Shakespeare. She has published upwards of forty articles in *Shakespeare Quarterly* and other journals, featuring her work at the BBC. Her book *Modern Hamlets and Their Soliloquies* features interview materials from Ben Kingsley, Derek Jacobi, David Warner, John Gielgud, Kevin Kline, and others. She served as visiting distinguished professor at Arizona State University in Renaissance studies.

Eva B. McManus, associate professor of English at Ohio Northern University, is editor of *Shakespeare and the Classroom,* a journal covering issues and ideas for Shakespeare teachers at all academic levels. A member of the International Globe Association's midwest regional education team, she is also editor of the Ohio Shakespeare Conference newsletter, *Ohio Shakespeare Notes.*

Robert B. Pierce is professor of English at Oberlin College. He has written *Shakespeare's History Plays: The Family and the State* and co-authored *The Design of Poetry* with Barbara Pierce. He has published articles on Shakespeare and other topics in *Shakespeare Survey, Studies in Philology,* and elsewhere.

Marie A. Plasse is associate professor of English at Merrimack College in North Andover, Massachusetts, where she teaches Shakespeare, drama, and composition courses. She has published articles on Shakespeare's *A Midsummer Night's Dream* and *Richard III* and is currently working on a book about the theatrical body in Shakespeare's plays. She also serves as an associate editor of *College Literature.*

Martha Tuck Rozett is professor of English at The University at Albany (New York). She is the author of *The Doctrine of Election and the Emergence of Elizabethan Tragedy* (Princeton University Press, 1984) and articles and reviews on Shakespeare, Renaissance drama, and historical fiction that have appeared in *Studies in Philology, Shakespeare Quarterly, Renaissance Drama, Shakespeare Bulletin, CLIO,* and various edited collections. *Talking Back to Shakespeare* (University of Delaware Press, 1994; paperback edition, NCTE, 1996) concerns the appropriation and transformation of Shakespeare's plays by playwrights, novelists, and students.

James P. Saeger is an assistant professor of English at Vassar College, where he teaches Shakespeare and Renaissance literature. He was first introduced to the Shakespeare Interactive Archive project and its classroom applications while on a visiting teaching appointment at the Massachusetts Institute of Technology. He has also taught at the University of Pennsylvania.

Michael W. Shurgot teaches literature and writing at South Puget Sound Community College in Olympia, Washington. Besides essays on Joyce and Steinbeck, he has published on medieval drama and Shakespeare in *Papers on Language & Literature, Theatre Journal, Essays in Literature, The Upstart Crow, Shakespeare Bulletin,* and in the volume *Shakespeare: Text, Subtext, and Context,* ed. Ronald Dotterer (Susquehanna University Press, 1989). He also contributes theater reviews to *Shakespeare Bulletin,* and his book *Stages of Play: Shakespeare's Theatrical Energies in Elizabethan Performance* was published in 1997 by University of Delaware Press.

Paul Skrebels, lecturer in Professional Writing and Communication at the University of South Australia, was a high school drama teacher before re-entering university as a postgraduate student in English Literature. He coordinates foundation subjects in communication for arts and technical students, and teaches in a wide range of subjects on writing and textual analysis. He is also involved in a national English Teaching Renewal program.

J. L. Styan is the Franklyn Bliss Snyder Professor of English Literature and Professor of Theatre Emeritus at Northwestern University. In England he taught at secondary school level, then in the Department of Adult Education at the University of Hull. In America he was professor, then chairman, of English at the University of Michigan, then the Andrew Mellon Professor of English at the University of Pittsburgh. He has published some one hundred articles and chapters and fifteen books on the theory and practice of drama, and Cambridge University Press published *The English Stage: A History of Drama and Performance* in 1996. In 1995 he was awarded the Robert Lewis medal for Lifetime Achievement in Theatre Research.

John Wilson Swope is an associate professor of English and English education coordinator at the University of Northern Iowa. In addition to his work in teacher education, he has spent eleven years teaching middle and high school English, speech, and drama. He is a frequent presenter at NCTE conventions and conferences, and his articles and reviews have appeared in *English Journal* as well as various journals published by NCTE's affiliate organizations. His books include the six-volume Shakespeare Teacher's Activities Library of Ready-to-Use Materials for teaching *Romeo and Juliet, Julius Caesar, Hamlet, Macbeth, A Midsummer's Night's Dream,* and *Much Ado About Nothing* published by the Center for Applied Research in Education.

Christine D. Warner taught English literature in middle and high school for ten years. Currently during the summer Christine teaches secondary literature on a Native American reservation in New Mexico. She is an instructor at The Ohio State University in Columbus, Ohio, and teaches classes for the Drama in Education Department as well as supervising student teachers in secondary high school English classes. She has published in *Literary Matters: Journal of The English Language Arts,* as well as *The British Journal of Aesthetics.*